Henri Brunschwig

Translated by
Frank Jellinek

Enlightenment
and
Romanticism

*in Eighteenth-
Century Prussia*

The University of Chicago Press

Chicago and London

The University of Chicago Press, Chicago 60637
The University of Chicago Press, Ltd., London

© 1974 by The University of Chicago
All rights reserved. Published in 1974
Printed in the United States of America

International Standard Book Number (clothbound): 0-226-07768-3
Library of Congress Catalog Card Number: 73-87299

Originally published as *La crise de l'état prussien à la
fin du XVIIIe siècle et la genèse de la mentalité
romantique.* Copyright by Presses Universitaires de
France, 1947. Licensed by Librairie Flammarion,
Paris, France.

Henri Brunschwig is *directeur* at the Ecole Pratique
des Hautes Etudes, Paris. He has published many
books and articles in scholarly journals.

Contents

Preface to the
American Edition

This book is not entirely a new one, inasmuch as it was researched in Berlin and written in Paris shortly before the Second World War. It was published in 1947 under the title *La crise de l'état prussien à la fin du XVIIIᵉ siècle et la genèse de la mentalité romantique* ("The crisis of the Prussian state at the end of the eighteenth century and the origins of the Romantic mentality").

At the time of its first appearance it did not excite any great interest among Germanists because they were interested in Romanticism solely in the perspective of the history of ideas in the abstract, without regard for the kind of persons who expressed those ideas. Historians, on the other hand, wanted more specific evidence for the contention that the young Romantics devoted themselves to literature mainly because they were unable to engage in action within a closed society. The fact was, however, that individually the Romantics could not see this clearly and proclaim it openly since that would have meant destroying the literary sanctuary they were trying to construct.

The new definition emphasized in the book, essentially a psychological approach to Romanticism as "the mentality of the miraculous," provoked no reaction among either Germanists or historians. Yet that was the essence of the whole thesis, and, indeed, it is the essential element common to Romanticism in all its forms, from its revolutionary expression described in this book to the reactionary, Catholic, and feudalistic form it assumed in the nineteenth century, which had its attractions even for Friedrich Schlegel himself after Prussia's collapse in 1807.

Disaffected and ambitious young men invariably seek for an escape from present reality, whether in the future or in the past. They watch for intimations of the miraculous, some revelation that will take them into a dream world utterly unlike the frustrating world of the present.

In the thirty years which have elapsed since this book first appeared, the author's attention has turned to other fields. In the meantime, Germanists have never ceased to be fascinated by the varied manifestations of Romanticism and have published numerous studies on the subject. It would, however, take years to assess them and, in using them, to correct a great many details of scholarship. But a thesis does not necessarily have to be brought up to date like a textbook.

One reason for the publication of an English translation of this book may well be the recent revival of interest in it and in its subject, possibly in consequence of the student movements of the sixties. Modern middle-class societies are not, it is true, as closed as that of the Prussian state, but there are certain similarities between them, such as the rapid population growth with the consequent breakdown of constraints on the younger generation, which has become too large to be compelled to follow in its elders' footsteps; the urge to adventure; the preference for geography over history and the attraction of the East; and the challenge—a deliberately aggressive challenge in many cases—to traditional beliefs and mores.

This edition, then, has not been brought up to date; but although it is not revised, it is augmented. The lengthy appendix on the Jews in the system of the Aufklärung, which was published in part in the *Annales historiques de la Révolution française* in 1935 and 1936 and was dropped from the 1947 text for use in another work, has been added to the translation. This English version is therefore a more complete book than the original.

Henri Brunschwig

Note on Citations
Footnotes in the original French edition have been replaced in this translation by parenthetical notes giving in a shortened form the source of the quoted material. For full titles and dates of publication the reader is referred to the Bibliography, which includes all major sources used by the author, whether or not these are cited in the text.

Introduction

The Prussia of Frederick II was a model state. Its army was considered the best in Europe. Its civil service, highly bureaucratized, perhaps over-meticulous, but tightly controlled, could be held up to the absolute monarchies as an example for imitation. Its inhabitants, supervised by the officials, sermonized by the clergy, and instructed by the philosophers, gradually became accustomed to practice toleration, to reason soundly, and to believe, with a robust optimism, in the progress of the human race.

For the Aufklärung is not simply a philosophy of enlightenment, a mere reflection of English and French doctrines. Though foreign influences permeate the country, they nonetheless produce a wholly original crop from this new soil. A complete system of ideas, feelings, and government has come into being in Prussia by the end of Frederick II's reign. If we compare Prussia with the neighboring countries, we must conclude that such conventional terms as "enlightened despotism" and "directed economy" cover situations which in fact differ greatly from region to region.

This system breaks down, however, during the last years of the century. Like a disease which imperceptibly undermines a healthy organism, the infection of irrationality begins to corrupt the Aufklärung. Press campaigns, sermons, decrees, and laws are issued in abundance but in vain. Like ears of corn which spring back as soon as the storm has passed over, the irrational spreads into the towns and the parts of the countryside most strongly indoctrinated by the philosophers, the clergy, and the officials. Contemporaries fail to detect the deeper cause of the disease. They cannot grasp the fact that the rapid growth of the population is cracking the frame of the state. Vagrants in the countryside, beggars in the towns, the unemployed, old soldiers, and university graduates without career prospects no longer respond to the influence of their pastors and masters.

Rationalism is a result of education. It engenders the mentality of the civilized man. In default of it, another, more primitive, mentality grows up,

1

the mentality of the untutored child. Its main characteristic is an appetite for the miraculous.

Economic crisis, therefore, finally transforms the older modes of thought and feeling. Viewed in this perspective, Romanticism, most studies of which have concentrated on the philosophical and artistic styles fostered by these conditions, emerges as a social phenomenon, standing in the same relation to intellectual and artistic developments as the soil to the plants it nourishes.

The purpose of this book is to describe the system of the Aufklärung, to break down into its component parts the crisis which undermined it at the close of the century, and to account for the change in mentality when the elite moved away from rationalism into Romanticism.

It is by no means easy to compound so broad a synthesis. Often there are no supporting case studies; but to fill the gaps would mean to renounce the synthesis; for a historian's lifetime would not suffice for the exhaustive investigation of demographic growth and the rural crisis, of the decline of the crafts and the rise of vagrancy, of the professions and the privileges of the nobility which would be needed. But the conclusions to which such investigations might lead can in some cases be deduced from samplings. Elsewhere we must confine ourselves to posing problems which cannot yet be solved. In some cases it is hard to give the factors involved their proper weight and precisely to assess the part they played. But it seems clear enough that moral causes alone cannot account for the transition from one mode of thought to another when both masses and elites are involved. It can be explained only by taking into account all aspects, the political and social no less than the moral, of the milieu in which the transition took place.

Part 1 The Aufklärung

1

The Aufklärung in Prussia at the Death of Frederick II

The Philosophical Aspect of the Aufklärung

The philosophy of Enlightenment prevails throughout Europe in the second half of the eighteenth century. Its principles are everywhere the same and their proponents everywhere understood. Locke has as many readers in Germany as in England. To the leading intellectuals the only conceivable culture is one based upon universal reason.

This consensus is found to be less universal, however, when we begin to investigate the precise degree to which rationalism has permeated the masses, the extent to which it has been adopted by the representatives of the traditional religious denominations, and the way in which it is applied by the political and administrative authorities. Profound differences come to light, and different names have to be used for the different forms which this philosophy assumes in practice. What is often called Josephinism triumphs in Austria, and the Aufklärung prevails in Prussia rather than in Germany as a whole, where the religious denominations, political constitutions, and levels of culture differ so greatly that no single term can be applied to them all. Prussia is the true fatherland of the Aufklärung. Rationalist principles are imprinted more deeply in Prussia than anywhere else; and here they transform the Protestant religion, permeate the administrative machinery, and are embodied in a human type as characteristic as the English gentleman or the French *honnête homme*. In the Prussia of Frederick the Great the Aufklärung officially becomes a philosophy, a religion, and a political system.

It is not that the ideas prevailing at the time of Frederick II's death are particularly original. They assert the preeminence of reason and place their trust in man, who has at last emerged from tutelage (Kant, "Was ist Aufklärung?"). Capable henceforth of governing himself, he makes a clean sweep of the prejudices which have long darkened his thought. He acts in conformity with his real interests, which, in fact, cannot conflict with the interests of society and the state. Contrary to all tradition, he no longer demands unity of doctrine; although he would prefer that there should be such unity, he refuses to impose it by force, for what is demonstrably true is accepted sooner or later by all men of goodwill. Whereas force is the chief resource of obscurantists, the rational man knows that enlightenment comes from discussion. Freedom of thought is, therefore, the corollary of the faith in reason. To criticize when need be becomes the first duty of man. This "toleration"—or "liberalism," as we should now call it—is well defined in an article in the *Deutsches Museum* in 1776. Tracing the boundary between toleration and indifference, "no one," it says, "should be tolerant toward himself; no one should be intolerant toward anyone else who expresses an opinion without trying to impose it on others; but he who tolerates a person who enforces his opinions at pistol point is either intolerant or a slave" (*DM* 1776, II, 810–11).

The Aufklärung's faith in man accounts for its optimism. It is proud of the progress of mankind and is preparing to assault the remaining bastions defended by the prejudices of the orthodox. It cares little for abstract philosophy. Its principles are so simple and of such general application that they cannot fail of general acceptance. It pauses without impatience before the secrets it cannot yet penetrate. It does not, for example, reject any reasonable solution suggested by religion, but contents itself with asserting that there is no mystery. Christian Garve concludes a long treatise on the existence of God with the thought that "we cannot and need not go beyond the conviction that God is a Being as intelligent, potent, and perfect as the World, and that upon him depend the structure and the government of the World. Manifestly, it is not for us to know how perfect this Being is, how he thinks, how he created the World" (Garve, *Versuche*, V, 280). Rather than construct a metaphysic of the Beyond, the Aufklärung is concerned with augmenting man's happiness during his lifetime. Logic imposes upon institutions, customs, and current practice reforms which it carries out gradually, with neither injustice nor violence. It is never a distant goal that it pursues; it is always a useful one. Everyone can discern it, and everyone appreciates the progress it represents.

What is certainly the most general and most precise statement of the theory of the movement is published by the two editors of the *Berlinisches Journal für Aufklärung*. From the first number in October 1788 Fischer is concerned with an exact definition; the Aufklärung, he thinks, must not be confused either with learning or with refinement, either with culture or with an eagerness for innovation, or even with religion, though it partakes of all of them. It is first and foremost a matter of comprehension (*Verstand*) and involves our concepts (*Begriffe*). It therefore consists in concepts correctly understood (*BJA* 1788, I, 12–46).

Not every correct concept, however, is to be attributed specifically to the Aufklärung. The Aufklärung has no effect upon the multiplication table, for instance. If we sharpen our definition of its limits, we conclude that it is concerned only with "matters relating to our needs and our happiness."

But there are needs and needs. Many of them are artificial. Others, "which are inherent in nature itself, the knowledge of which makes us happy, the ignorance of which unhappy, are essential. . . . It is the Aufklärung's task to discover our essential needs." Or, as Riem, the journal's manager, expressed it, it is "an effort of the human spirit fully to illuminate, in accordance with the principles of pure reason and with a view to the advancement of the useful, every object in the world of ideas, every human opinion and its consequences, everything which has any effect upon man" (Schwartz, *Kulturkampf*, 2).

Utilitarian and optimistic as it is, the Aufklärung becomes accessible to the masses. In the intellectual history of Prussia only the Reformation equaled it in popular appeal. Its most original trait is undoubtedly that in Prussia, unlike France, the whole machinery of church and state is designed to further it. While this greatly enhances its popular appeal, it makes political loyalty the sine qua non for its existence.

The principles of the Aufklärung are not, however, peculiar to Germany. They were enunciated in other countries long before the Germans spread them at home. Every biography of an educated and well-bred German, be he artist or writer, prince or burgher, cleric or layman, mentions a period in his youth when he discovered the English or French thinkers. Some, like Wieland, begin by imitating Bayle, Fontenelle, or Voltaire and then go on to Shaftesbury and Shakespeare. Others, like Mendelssohn and most of the intellectuals, are interested in the English writers in the first instance. Others again, like Garve, draw their inspiration from the obscure recesses of the Scottish school as illustrated by Hutcheson and Ferguson. Garve, a writer of the second order, is a good example of the cultivated middle-class burgher of the period; the other foreign authors he quotes in his essays are Montaigne, Molière, La Rochefoucauld, Cardinal de Retz, Condorcet, Hume, Adam Smith, and Pope. This enthusiasm can impel the sober Spalding to translate certain chapters of Shaftesbury, just as it leads the Berlin middle classes to speak French. All those who have an opportunity to do so visit the countries in which the new ideas and fashions originated.

No specialized studies have yet been published on the influence of the major foreign writers in Germany. The most notable and widespread influences are Locke, Shaftesbury, and Rousseau. Locke in particular is a fertile source for the theologians, desperately eager as they are for religious peace. They take from him the principle that divine revelation cannot conflict with human reason (*Essay concerning Human Understanding*, fwd., sec. 5; bk. 1, chap. 3; and especially bk. 4, chaps. 18 and 19; see also Olléon, *Philosophie*).

Shaftesbury, whose essays are read by Lessing, Mendelssohn, Wieland, and Herder, lays the foundations of a morality independent of religion. He distinguishes in man natural tendencies which concur to the common weal, selfish tendencies whose end is a particular good and which are legitimate when they can be subordinated to the foregoing, and antinatural tendencies which are essentially destructive. Man needs the first two and cannot be happy without them, so that everything which contributes to the good of mankind is moral. He who has understood this holds the secret of happiness. He can shape his life as an artist shapes his work and can enjoy the beauty of the universe, within which evil does not exist for the man who is able to contemplate the universe as a whole.

The Scots, continuing Shaftesbury, assert that a moral sense exists; everyday experience reveals it; its influence can readily be discerned in men's behavior.

Rousseau rather than Voltaire attracts the younger generation. His educational theories and his love of nature seem to be what most appeals to them. It is the spontaneous emotions of the solitary *Promeneur* and the simplicity of his approach to the manners of the common people, rather than the *Social Contract*, that wins the hearts of the Sturm und Drang writers in revolt against foreign modes. Goethe and Schiller read him avidly in their youth; he is Herder's breviary.

The importance of English and French influence on the Aufklärung cannot be exaggerated, therefore. Yet the Aufklärung is very different from other philosophies. Foreign influence seems, like reason itself, to have been universal; the major principles are held in common by thinkers in all countries; certain artistic techniques, too, are freely interchanged; social conventions and fashions clothe every society with the same irridescent elegance. Once they have impregnated the masses, however, these ideas take over from them certain shades of their own. They are still essentially reasonable, but they are directed first and foremost to local concerns. Since they have nowhere else been taken up by the masses to the same extent as in Prussia, they form the system peculiar to that country which is known as the Aufklärung.

The Theological Aspect of the Aufklärung

In Protestant Germany the main contest is between the new liberalism and religious fanaticism. Dilthey has well brought out the theological character of the movement. For thirty years the Germans had been killing each other for religion. The principle *cujus regio ejus religio* continued to apply even after the Peace of Westphalia (1648); subjects were still expelled from their native country from time to time because they did not practice their prince's religion. The refugee was a typical feature of Protestant society and the Protestant conscience in Germany long before the Revocation of the Edict of Nantes. But now liberalism is proclaiming toleration! This liberalism is not primarily an attack on social privilege, as in France, nor an appeal to the proponents of economic reform, as in England, but a demand for religious peace. "Faith," it declares, "is a matter of conscience; it cannot be forced upon people. I am willing to allow anyone to believe what he seems to be convinced of; why will you not allow me a similar freedom?" (Nicolai, *Sebaldus Nothanker* III, bk. 7, p. 30).

Success is rapid. Locke's doctrine finds in Germany a soil no less prepared than in England. Reason can bring all men to agree by demonstrating that behind the diversity of practice their faith is identical. The German who worships a personal and good God, the creator of a perfect world in which man exercises his free will, divests his religion of mysteries which are repugnant to reason; he reduces it to a morality whose precepts are as self-evident as the postulates of reason.

The sovereign cannot but approve, for religious peace is a guarantee of the state's prosperity. No one realized this more clearly than the king of Prussia. Well before the Aufklärung came to simplify his task, he had tried to secure religious peace. Two methods were open to him at the beginning of the eighteenth century, the union of confessions under the aegis of the prince or religious autonomy through the neutrality of the prince. Frederick William I dreamed of a fusion of the churches. But even if he could bring Lutherans and members of the Reformed Church to agree on a single dogma and a single liturgy, how was he to prevent the future proliferation of new sects, whose periodic emergence promoted both vitality and anarchy within Protestantism? An administrative unification might just be possible; and though he could not wholly achieve this, he did at least demonstrate that some places of worship could be shared by the various confessions and that some consistories could extend their competence to all the denominations within their jurisdiction.

Failing the union of the churches, the princes might proclaim their own neutrality. Let each man work out his own salvation as he wished, provided only that he did not disturb the king's peace. Frederick William I resorted to this method when he forbade religious controversy and the discussion of divine grace from the pulpit; he welcomed the faithful of all religious denominations with equal benevolence. Neither the union of the churches under the aegis of the state nor the neutrality of the state was possible without toleration.

Toleration conflicts with the older principle *cujus regio ejus religio*, but it is consonant with the demands of reason. The Aufklärung rightly claims its successes, but it is probable that, even without it, toleration would in any case have triumphed in Prussia. The reason why that country became the chosen land of the Aufklärung at the end of the eighteenth century, why the new principles assumed an original character, and why enlightened despotism developed there, was that the Hohenzollerns had very early subordinated their religious conduct to their political interest reather than to their faith. It was not to fulfill a moral duty but to enrich the state that they harbored fugitives. It was because their works were useful to the state that Frederick William I protected the Pietists—whom he wished well—and that Frederick II—who did not—granted them asylum. The Idea of the State existed in Prussia, and it determined the behavior of the kings and their ministers. Frederick II declared:

There are few countries in which citizens have similar ideas on religion; they often differ completely; and there are what are called sects. The question then arises whether all citizens must believe alike or whether each man may be permitted to believe as he pleases. There is a stern policy which holds that everyone should be of the same opinion so that nothing shall divide the citizens. Theology goes further and maintains that anyone who does not believe as I do is damned, and it is not fitting that my sovereign should rule over the damned; they must be roasted in this world in order that they shall prosper all the more in the next. The answer is that all members of a society will never think alike; in Christian nations the majority are anthropomorphists; among the Catholics the majority are idolatrous, for you will never persuade me that a boor can distinguish between *latria* and *hyperdulia*; he worships in good faith the image he invokes. There are many heretics, therefore, in all the Christian sects; everyone, furthermore, believes what he finds probable. A poor wretch may be forcibly coerced to pronounce a particular formulary to which he refuses his inner consent; the persecutor has gained nothing. But if we go back to the origins of society, it is quite clear that a sovereign has no right to dictate what citizens are to believe. It is manifestly absurd to imagine that men once said to a man like themselves: we are raising you above us because we want to be slaves, and we are giving you the power to direct our thoughts as you will. What in fact they said was: we need you to uphold the laws which we are willing to obey, in order to govern us wisely and to defend us; but we shall require you to respect our freedom. This was the sentence pronounced, and it is not subject to appeal; indeed, toleration is so advantageous to the societies in which it is established that it is truly the source of the state's happiness. Where all religious worship is free, everyone is tranquil; whereas persecution has given rise to the most bloody, the most lasting, and the most ruinous civil wars. The least evil consequent upon persecution is the emigration of the persecuted; France has provinces which have been depopulated and are still being depopulated because of the Revocation of the Edict of Nantes. ["Essai sur les formes de gouvernement." In *Oeuvres* IX, 207.]

This policy produced a moral balance in Prussia which is not found elsewhere. The major official churches are imbued with the whole spectrum of shades of feeling and ideas, from the extremes of atheistic rationalism to mystical pietism; their sects are incorporated into the administrative machinery and offer everyone the religion most suited to his temperament, thereby inculcating universal loyalty to the state. The transition from one extreme to the other is easily made: the Pietist father begets Enlightened children, the Rosicrucian adolescent becomes the Deist adult. The Faculty of Theology at Halle turns out mystics at some periods and rationalists at others, depending on the talents of its professors and their utility to the state.

Early in the century, the University of Halle, founded in 1694, owed its reputation to rationalism, which kept it abreast of its famous rivals, Wittenberg and Leipzig. The jurist Thomasius discarded scholasticism and lectured in German in street clothes; he maintained that the law could be interpreted in accordance with the plain and ordinary meaning of words. Stahl taught experimental medicine. Wolff, professor of mathematics and physics in 1706, gave courses in philosophy, morals, and logic from 1709 on. It was his haughty character quite as much as his rationalist opinions that earned him the hostility of the Faculty of Theology when it managed to have him expelled in 1723. Thereafter, the whole university fell under the influence of the Pietists; the king welcomed them, not because he had been harassed by religious qualms during his illnesses, but because, as innovators, they preserved the originality of the youthful university and because the philanthropic and pedagogic activity of Francke, their leader, benefitted the state.

The Pietists were not in the least revolutionary. They approved of the Augsburg Confession and condemned every schismatic position. But they formed special groups within the official church in the secret hope of reforming it so that it could fulfill its mission of converting Jews and Catholics. Their passion for organization, the strict discipline to which they subjected themselves, and their close watch on each other differentiate them from the solitary mystics. Their active piety directed to secular ends and their readiness to commend good works is in total contrast to the attitude of the Quietists, who hold that all that can be done in this vale of tears is to watch passively for signs of grace and to long for death, the soul's release.

Though Halle University becomes the stronghold of rationalism after 1740, Pietism still subsists. Count Zinzendorf carries things to extremes. Resolved from early manhood to devote his life to the Savior, he is nevertheless compelled by his parents to study law at Wittenberg and to take up the post of Legal Councillor at Dresden. His rank dispenses him from performing his duties. A visit to France, where he consorts with the Catholic and Jansenist elite, especially Cardinal de Noailles, reveals to him the value of renunciation. For Christ's sake he gives up to his friend, Count Reuss, the woman he

loved and—though without obtaining her consent—regarded as his betrothed. He devotes himself thereafter to his "philadelphian" mission. Every
Sunday he gathers at his home "those who love the Lord Jesus." He tries to
recruit soldiers for the Savior from all the churches, thus grouping together
the elite of the Church Invisible scattered among the visible churches. These
conventicles dedicated to prayer and meditation are not schismatic. The
count is no more anxious than his predecessors to separate himself from the
official church. But his rank, his pride, and the ardor of his piety urge him
perhaps to be more eager than they were for a reformation of Lutheranism.

In 1772, shortly after marrying and acquiring the estate of Berthelsdorf,
the count is visited by four refugees, whom he permits to settle at the foot of
the Hutberg hill (hence the name Herrnhut). These "Bohemian" or "Moravian" brethren are members of a sect deriving from John Hus. Persecuted at
home, they flock in increasing numbers to the count, who imposes upon
them a constitution combining their traditions with his own philadelphian-
ism. The new sect is an integral part of the Lutheran church, but leads an
independent existence under the governance of a Council of Elders or the
count himself, upon whom Frederick William I, in agreement with his High
Consistory, confers the title of bishop in 1737. In 1742 the brethren obtain
from Frederick II the right to settle in Prussia; they congregate mainly in
Silesia.

Their colonies are placed under the guidance of God, who designates by lot
the administrators, the missionaries, and the spouses who are to accompany
them. A multiplicity of offices ensures the active collaboration of the
majority of the brethren and sisters in the life of the community. Bishops,
coadjutors, deacons, nursing elders, poor visitors, controllers of work and
wages keep a constant watch on each other and on all the rest of the
brethren. For life is public; the secrecy of the confessional does not exist;
every action is criticized by a meeting of the devout. The brethren keep
innumerable days of celebration in addition to the holy days of the official
church. They do not work on Saturdays; they solemnly celebrate all their
anniversaries; they institute special holidays in honor of God the Father, the
Holy Ghost, the Savior, children, pregnant sisters, young persons, widows
and widowers, and missionaries. They sing new hymns. Religion creates
around them an atmosphere that enables them willingly to submit to the
discipline, the perpetual reciprocal supervision, the veritable inquisition to
which they are subjected. Neither their inmost lives nor their most secret
thoughts are respected. A husband, for example, being simply the representative of Christ, the Betrothed of all women, may have to yield his wife at any
time to another man. A married man may be assigned to initiate a young
bride on her wedding night. Nothing can perturb these men and women,
convinced as they are that God has chosen them out specially to carry
through the reformation of the church.

The missions of the Moravian brethren grow up chiefly after 1735. At the count's death in 1760 they have twelve communities in Prussia and Saxony, two establishments in Holland, three in England, one in Ireland, and four in North America. Their missionaries evangelize the natives of Saint Thomas and Santa Cruz, Jamaica, Surinam, and Greenland.

In its primitive form or in that of the Moravian brethren, Pietism continues to exist alongside rationalism. In the course of the century the official churches—the Lutheran, the Reformed, and the Calvinist—fall under the influence now of one, now of the other. Between the two the older orthodoxy comes under heavy attack; the Pietists reproach it for lack of faith, the philosophers for abuse of it. To his young colleague wishing to refute doubters, Nicolai's orthodox pastor replies: "I repeat once again, you must not explain or prove anything to a layman, for he must believe! In such matters it is not reason but the Bible, it is supernatural revelation that counts" (*Sebaldus Nothanker* II, bk. 4, p. 79). His religion is that of the six Symbolic Books which have established the articles of the Lutheran faith since 1580, Luther's Longer and Shorter Catechisms, the Augsburg Confession and its Apology, the Articles of Schmalkald, and the Formula Concordiae. It is unfortunate when these texts do not happen to accord with the Bible. The enlightened minister, therefore, distinguishes between the law of the prince, which can always be amended, and the unchangeable dogma of God. When theologians accept the Symbolic Books of the sixteenth century as an immutable form of the faith, he says, they are acting precisely as intelligently as tailors would if they tried to make the stiff collar, the mantlet, and the wide fur-lined doublet of that century the immutable form of dress. Experience teaches us that opinion is no less subject to change than dress (ibid., p. 90).

These Protestants, at one in detesting the Catholics—of whom there were few in Prussia before the partition of Poland—and who are guaranteed complete freedom of worship both in the Westphalian provinces and in Silesia, do not live in amity. The enlightened despise the orthodox and detest the Pietists for their eccentricities. Especially among the craftsmen and small shopkeepers they keep coming across these people, dressed in black, with the name of God perpetually on their lips, quoting extracts from the prophetic books in season and out. May not some of these elect, forever clasping both hands above their head in invocation of Almighty, these good Samaritans, charitable only when they can expect a conversion, these humble people who barely dissemble their pride at having been touched by grace, even be criminals, as Nicolai likes to assert, and may not many of them be hypocrites? If inner experience is the sole valid criterion, how is one to tell the imposter from the apostle? The honest Semler when young saw the elect arrive at Saalfeld. Welcomed kindly by the duke, they soon came to exercise intolerable pressure on the ministers and schoolteachers. They held their conventicles at the castle, and everyone hastened to appear there. As a lively faith carries more weight than knowledge does, a totally ignorant forty-year-old carpenter managed to display such piety that he was given the post of schoolmaster. Many attended the pious meetings in the hopes of making a good marriage. His income threatened, the Reverend Semler finally adopted the pietistic mode of speech too, with its familiar and childish diminutives. By sheer insistence he finally won over his reluctant son, who was expected to convert the pupils:

My good humor vanished; I became completely glum; I shunned my dear companions of yore to the point of avoiding meeting them, and when any of them managed to accost me, I spoke in a mode so solemn and so full of devout saws that some were moved to tears. But since their parents were not in a situation such as my father apparently was, the results expected from my conversion came to little. When I seemed to have been well and truly converted, the whole troop of the four or five genuinely devout pupils was summoned to the duke's own apartment at court. Certainly no such church mice had ever been admitted to it before. The duke was alone. He invited us to be seated, conversed with us on the inclinations of the heart, and at length enjoined us to kneel down one after the other and pray before him. This pious audience lasted for over an hour. [Semler, *Lebensbeschreibung* I, 60.]

The *Berlinisches Journal für Aufklärung* expounded the faith universally held by the rationalists as clearly as could be. According to Fischer, the broader a man's general culture and the clearer, the more exact and the more sensible his concepts in other spheres, the more enlightened his religion; for enlightened religion is consequent upon Aufklärung in the other sciences. "The sharper the spirit of inquiry (*Untersuchungsgeist*) he displays, the more truth and Aufklärung he may be expected to possess" (*BJA* 1789, IV, 222–49). Such a man has a natural horror of mysticism as cultivated by the Pietists. He accepts Semler's principle that human reason accords with divine revelation. He is no atheist, and he believes in the need for religious instruction. But the state should do no more than ensure that the teachers are honest and capable. It is none of its duty to impose any dogma upon them; for, though everyone should believe something, he should remain free to believe what he wishes. (*BJA* 1789, V, 104, 206 ff.; 1790, VII, 102–40, 167–220; 1790, VIII, 241–67.)

But though they do not live in amity, rationalists and Pietists do not persecute each other; for the rationalists a conversion is valid only if it is the result of free reflection. Semler strongly condemns all proselytism and is willing to accept the conversion even of Catholics or Jews only after a long trial period (Semler I, 289–95). The Pietists demand an inner experience, which cannot be produced by force. Dogmas susceptible of evidential proof do not satisfy emotional people; when it is explained to them that there must be a God to create the world, that the soul is immortal since man is endowed with a conscience not possessed by the beasts, they listen and suffer in silence. They would be only too glad to understand nothing at all and wish that the faith so ardent within them should at last move mountains. They finally join the Pietists. But it would be wrong to look on Pietism as the enemy of rationalism; it is more like a safety valve for it. The two trends balance out. Their coexistence gives the most diverse temperaments a means of self-expression; it endows the eighteenth century with its extraordinary richness and its moral stability; it ensures to its literature that variety of inspiration which makes it so completely human.

The peculiarity of the Aufklärung in Prussia is not, therefore, essentially the triumph of a rationalized religion, but rather the victory of a liberalism imposed by the prince's policy. From the beginning to the end of the century, regardless of the prevailing religious trend, consciences remain free under the indifferent tutelage of the state. If we compare these conditions with those prevailing in other countries, the judgment all too frequently passed seems surprising; national sentiment is no stronger in Prussia than in any other country, but loyalty to the state is so strong there that the dissent displayed by the young toward the end of the century is not, as elsewhere, enough to sap the foundations of the political edifice.

The Political Aspect of the Aufklärung: Enlightened Despotism

The philosophical system would not be complete without a political system. A form of government cannot, however, be deduced from its principles. The general ideas are stated by Lessing in 1777 in his remarkable *Dialogues for Freemasons*. Contemplating an anthill, Falk asks Ernst: "Can order prevail even without government?" "If each individual is able to govern himself," Ernst replies, "why not?" "Do you believe that man is created for the state or the state for man? . . ." "Some seem to assert the former, but the latter in fact appears to be the truth" (*Ernst und Falk: Gespräche über die Freimauerei*, 2d dialogue). A man capable of using his reason has no need of the state. The functions of the state should therefore be diminished, as the young Wilhelm von Humboldt urged somewhat later in his *Essay on the Limits of State Action* (1792) (*Gesammelte Schriften* I, 27–34).

Since reason is universal, the political form it conceives to be the best should prevail everywhere. All men will then be able to live in one and the same state.

But even if they are governed by much the same constitution, they may yet wrangle because of the diversity of their manners and customs—often the consequence of geographical conditions—and the conflict among different religions or social classes. Citizens can only live in full amity, then, if they always look at the individual simply "as a human being" rather than "as an individual as such." Freemasonry assembles the elite of those who already possess the ability to regard only the human element in man, the element shared by all men, which is therefore eternal and universal. This view is identified with the Aufklärung, dedicated as it is to overcoming prejudices —national prejudice, which emerges when patriotism ceases to be a virtue, religious prejudice, which prevents men from admitting that a different faith may be just as good and true as their own, and social prejudice, which warps the judgment.

The context of political thought has not changed twenty years later. In his essay *On Perpetual Peace*, published in 1795, Kant tries to define the prerequisites for international agreement. He advocates a federation of unarmed republics; but his definition of a republic is any state which observes the principle of the separation of the legislative and executive powers (Werke IV). He believes that truth ultimately prevails in politics too; its expression is the consensus of citizens, all of whom accept the laws of reason. The only prerequisite, of course, is complete freedom of thought and its expression. There is no danger that error will be propagated, because free criticism will readily unmask the sophists. But the enforcement of the dictates of reason may be inopportune. Truth itself—and it is not only Wieland who stresses this—is relative. Should its laws therefore be ignored? No, but in case of doubt it may properly be discussed; the enlightened should meet and decide what is to be done (*TM* 1788, II, 3–30; cf. 1799, I, 94–105).

Such are the political principles. They remain so vague because the theoreticians do not feel that they should be made more specific; to create a new form of state is not their task. The state exists; and the most they are called upon to do is to define its functions.

The theory of enlightened despotism is indeed the result of matching a de facto situation with new ideas. The Prussian state has evolved since the beginning of the century; the Great Elector, Frederick William I, and Frederick II have given it a solid military and bureaucratic frame. They do not exercise a slaveholder's rights over the lands they govern. Whereas Louis XIV proudly asserted, "L'état, c'est moi," Frederick II admirably sums up his conception of the state in 1781: "We have observed," he says in his *Essay on the Forms of Government and the Duties of Sovereigns*,

that citizens set up one of their fellow men over them only for what
services he may be expected to render them, namely to uphold the laws,
ensure that justice is done, oppose the corruption of manners with the utmost energy, and defend the state against its enemies. . . . Princes,
sovereigns, and kings are not therefore vested with the supreme authority
simply so that they may plunge into dissipation and luxury with impunity;

they are not raised above their follow citizens merely so that they may strut about ostentatiously and despise and insult simplicity of manners, poverty and misery; they are not at the head of the state so that they may keep a train of loafers engendering every form of vice by their idleness and dissipation. . . . The sovereign is attached by indissoluble ties to the body of the state; consequently, he is sensitive to every evil which afflicts his subjects, and similarly society suffers from any misfortunes which may afflict its sovereign. There is only one good, that of the state as a whole. If the prince loses provinces, he can no longer assist his subjects as he formerly could; if misfortune compels him to contract debts, the citizens, however poor, are bound to pay them; but if his people is sparse and if it is sunk in misery, the sovereign has no resources at all. These truths are so incontrovertible that there is no need to dwell upon them.

I repeat, then, that the sovereign represents the state; he and his people form a single body which can be happy only insofar as they are in accord. The prince is to society what the head is to the body; he must see, think, and act for the whole community in order to procure for it all the advantages to which it is entitled. If the monarchical form of government is to prevail over the republican, the sovereign's duty is plain; he must be active and upright and must do his utmost to perform the course of duties prescribed for him. This is what I conceive his duties to be.

And Frederick concludes:

These are, in general, the essential duties of a prince. To be perpetually consistent with them he must always keep in mind the fact that he, like the least of his subjects, is human; he is the first judge, the first general, the first financier, the first minister of the realm, not for what he represents, but only to perform their duties. He is merely the first servant of the state, in duty bound to act with probity, wisdom, and complete disinterest, as if he were liable at any moment to render an account of his stewardship to his fellow citizens. [*Oeuvres IX*, 198–201, 208.]

This idea of the state is as deeply engrained in the minds of the king's officials and his educated subjects as in his own. All of them distinguish between arbitrary despotism and the Prussian system. In general, they set two limitations to the royal omnipotence, that of the judiciary, which must be independent and separate from the royal power, and that of the intermediate consultative bodies through which the nation makes its wishes known.

One of the highest-ranking officials, *Ministerdirigent* Count Hertzberg, gives his own definition of this "free and tempered monarchy" which is the perfect form of enlightened despotism:

Monarchical government is that in which a single man . . . governs the state autonomously, but in accordance with the fundamental laws and with fixed and consistent rules, which he will not change without good reason; if he does so, he degenerates into a despot. . . . A hereditary monarchy, tempered by good basic laws suited to the geography of the country and the character of the nation, is, in my opinion, the form of government best calculated to secure and maintain the happiness of men, of societies, and of nations. . . . The king may, it is true, misuse his power; but then he is a despot, and he will not long rule over a generous-spirited nation; the abuse will be neither so durable nor so widespread as the evil produced by faction in a republic. . . .

Most states in Europe have corrected, or rather altered, their former type of government and have constituted themselves either as absolute or limited monarchies or as republics, most of these aristocratic. . . . In my opinion, judging from principle, from the nature of man, and from experience, the best form of government is a free government in which a single sovereign combines the executive and legislative powers in his own person, but respects, and does not change without urgent and evident need, the basic laws, or at any rate the fixed rules and maxims which are absolutely necessary to secure to his subjects their properities, whatever they may be, and to ensure the administration of prompt, exact, and impartial justice, and one where he establishes or leaves in being the intermediate bodies or provincial estates and orders (*Landstände*), which, though not participating in the legislative power, are entitled to meet at certain times in order to deliberate on the situation and needs of the state and thus to cooperate, with the monarch's permission and under his auspices, in the domestic and civil administration. [Hertzberg, "Sur la forme des gouvernements et quelle est la meilleure," in *Huit Dissertations*, 142, 144, 148, and 156.]

The minister's confidence in his country's institutions is such that he cheerfully approves of the French Constitution of 1791, for it combines the advantages of a monarchy and a republic, and it secures the balance among the European states, the main prerequisite for a lasting peace. It cannot, however, conceivably be envied by Prussia, whose government is "one of the most benign and most just" ("Mémoire sur les révolutions des états," 1791, in *Oeuvres politiques* I, 133 ff.).

Count Hertzberg's definition of despotism is not complete; to the two limitations he imposes on the royal power must be added a third, that of public opinion. Freedom of the press is the absolute prerequisite for the existence of Aufklärung. In a famous article, Kant attributes to Frederick II the sally: "Reason about everything as much as you like and whenever you like, but obey" ("Was ist Aufklärung?" *BM* 1785). The king certainly insisted on "obey"; but after his death the emphasis was to be placed increasingly upon "reason." If the philosophers' criticisms are correct, they will impose themselves on the government, because its members are reasonable men. But the freedom to express such criticisms is essential; the king decides in his sovereign discretion, but he has no right to muzzle the press.

Kant assigns a twofold duty to the subject. As an official, he is in duty bound to obey the orders of his superiors, even if he does not approve of them. But once he has obeyed, he must, as a private person or as a human being, criticize these decisions, though he will continue to execute them until he has succeeded in getting them suspended. Everyone has an interest in seeing to it that reason prevails, and the prince, recognizing sooner or later that the criticisms of a policy inherited from a past in many ways less enlightened are well founded, will make the necessary reforms.

It would be wrong to regard this as mere philosophy; Kant truly reflects the thinking of his fellow citizens. One of Frederick II's most active ministers, Baron Heinitz, who, after governing several provinces and supporting Stein in Westphalia, reformed the Department of Mines and became director of the Excise, writes when disagreeing with the king that "his duty is to obey, but his oath equally compels him to say what he would say if he were not a minister but merely a private person" (Lotz, *Geschichte*, 219).

Officials speak in this way because they have been trained to do so. Nothing reveals more strikingly the vast difference between enlightened despotism of the Prussian type and absolute monarchy in the French style than the questions asked at the examinations for the civil service. A young graduate at law (*candidatus juris*) wishing to enter the civil service has to pass written and oral tests; the War and Domains Chamber, to which he wishes to be attached as chief clerk (*Referendar*), first sends him the documents in a case involving administrative practice. He draws up his report (*Probe Relatio*) and states the reasons for his decision by reference to the existing laws and regulations. It is obviously easy to cheat, since candidates are not proctored. The oral examination before a Commission of the Chamber is therefore far more searching. Unfortunately, most of the files contain the written test but only the marks for the oral. There are, however, a few complete records. The examiners at Minden ask candidate Hash on 21 December 1801: "What is your conception of a state?" "The state is an association of citizens who have come together in order to augment the general happiness and security to the greatest possible degree." "What does a state need in order to augment the general happiness?" "A higher power which uses the state's resources wisely for the general good." "What are the various kinds of state?" "Monarchies, aristocracies, and republics." "Which should be preferred?" "Monarchy, because we ourselves are most happy in one" (Archives, Gen. Dir. *Behörden und Bestallungssachen,* Minden, Tit. VII, *Referendarien,* no. 1, pp. 13 and 25).

Candidate von Horst, examined on 7 January 1802, considers that "the state is an association (*Verbindung*) of persons for the purpose of reciprocal security and the increase of happiness; those who enter into this association waive some of their natural rights in order that this purpose may be better achieved." The upkeep of a monarchical state requires "public contributions, partly to pay the officials, but partly too for the troops and police needed for internal and external security" (ibid., p. 48).

The examination for judges in the lower courts (*Referendarien*) is mainly in law. But on 6 January 1799 junior law officers (*Auskultatoren*) von Cramer, Dellbrück, Dorguth, and Netter are questioned about natural law before they are examined in German and Brandenburg law. Natural law is taught in some secondary schools and provides essay subjects for the leaving examination (*Abitur*).

All these questions and answers are inspired by a single conception of the state, an identical faith in a social contract. Nowhere is there the least allusion to divine right. Yet the official decrees are still embellished with the traditional formula: "Frederick William, by the Grace of God, King of Prussia." An empty decorative formula, a form of words merely, to which Frederick the Great himself has declined to attribute any meaning. It would never occur to any Prussian to think of Prussia as a despotic state. The great mass of the population approve of the French Revolution without for one moment supposing that they might take it as a model. The meanest pupil at the Friedrichswerder secondary school in Berlin is quite aware that "the revolution which has happened in our time, whereby France has thrown off an intolerable yoke of despotism, is one of the most remarkable of those recorded in history." He and all his fellow pupils know all about its causes; they note, like a Magdeburg schoolboy in 1793, for example, that the kings of France since Henri IV were led astray by "imbecile confessors, mistresses, or dishonest servants" (Schwartz, *Gelehrtenschulen*, pp. 242, 249).

It is not so in Prussia. Its subjects are stoutly loyal. Peace with France is desired because in Prussia people are filled with commiseration and with sympathy for a people in pursuit of its happiness. In Prussia they are proud to be members of a model state, for, despite the temporary weaknesses of certain princes, the Hohenzollern state has truly embodied the ideal of the Aufklärung. In a speech at the Royal Joachimsthal school in Berlin on the occasion of Frederick William II's birthday on 25 September 1789, Professor Brunn admirably explained why "the Prussian state is the happiest of all states in Europe." "A happy people," he said, "is one that, in material things, enjoys not merely the essential but the superfluous; which has a good constitution; which knows that the interests of the sovereign coincide with those of the people; in which the officials are honest and the taxes moderate; which remains in possession of the most important natural rights of mankind; which is not groaning under the yoke of the hierarchy, intolerance, the coercion of consciences, . . . in which every variety of the arts and sciences flourishes and Aufklärung is not repressed." No other European nation enjoys this concatenation of circumstances. Prussia is a solitary exception, for its monarchs, obedient to the law, are not despots. The administration is rigorously organized; the finances are in order. "Freedom of thought, the press, and publishing prevail here. . . . Theology is for the most part purged of its mystical dross; and the moral doctrine of Christianity, with its more lucid utterance, is preached from the pulpit. The Aufklärung was born among us and has led to the prosperity of the entire state" (*BJA* 1789, V, 104–61).

2 The Machinery of the Aufklärung

The Officials

The three characteristic features of the Aufklärung in Prussia are, then, a rationalist philosophy, a tolerant religion, and an enlightened despotism. The Aufklärung slowly develops in the course of the century; but it can last only if the mass of the people give it their allegiance. Its champions are well aware of this. Their task is to spread its truths. *Aufklären* means "to enlighten"; so men of goodwill must spread the light; its future depends on the means by which they spread it.

The question whether their activities will or will not be effectual depends upon what resources they can summon to their aid. Whereas in France and in many of the German states the philosophers had the church and state to contend with, in Prussia both State and Church lend them their full support. What, therefore, is to prevent them from imbuing the masses with their ideas?

It may reasonably be assumed that most officials have become enlightened before the death of Frederick II. The ministers set the example. Count Hertzberg, at the close of an honorable career in diplomacy, would vigorously repudiate any accusation of obscurantism; Haugwitz, his successor, is of the same stamp; like them, Chancellor Carmer and his friend Suarez pride themselves on their success in reforming and simplifying legal procedure and bringing the law into congruity with reason. Zedlitz, after modernizing secondary schooling, tries to introduce universal education. Chancellor von Heinitz, reforming the Department of Mines, has a European reputation; and the Duke of Schulenberg-Kehnert, several times General Director of Finance, enjoyes universal esteem.

These men choose like-minded officials as collaborators. The number of officials tends to grow as the state extends its sphere of action simply because an enlightened despot who cherishes his subjects' happiness cannot look upon them solely as recruits and taxpayers; he makes it his concern to provide for, help, and instruct them. His bureaucracy has therefore to be expanded, but he cannot recruit officials haphazard, for they must be technically competent. In 1770 Frederick II sets up a High Commission to test all candidates for the civil service by written and oral examinations; successful examinees remain under supervision, and frequent reports are made on their performance. The reports do not, however, seem to have been made annually before 1800; the Prussian archives do not have full and regular *Conduiten Listen* for all branches of the administration. The boards of examiners favor "right-thinking" candidates in Prussia, as they do everywhere, in the eighteenth no less than in any other century. The senior civil service is formed in this way, but within it there is no bar to ideological discussion; and when put to the test, the officials prove extraordinarily impervious to all onslaughts of the irrational.

The clergy are undoubtedly the most valuable of all the Aufklärung's auxiliaries. The Protestant church is a dependency of the state; the consistories of all confessions are placed under the Religious Department (*Geistliches Department*). Their jurisdiction is very broad; while that of the Lutheran *Konsistorium* is confined to Brandenburg, the consistories of the French Calvinist and the Reformed Churches are competent throughout the Prussian territories. On all of them laymen sit together with the clergy. Like the provincial consistories, they are appointed by the king, and laymen, mostly lawyers, form at least half, in some cases two-thirds, of the joint membership. In provinces in which there are few members of the Reformed Church, these are represented on the Lutheran consistories, whose jurisdiction thus extends to all the Protestant churches.

The consistories act as intermediate bodies between the pastors, whose function is essentially religious, and the General Directory or the Provincial War and Domains Chambers, whose functions are essentially administrative. They transmit to the clergy the decrees to be read out and commented upon from the pulpit; they declare posts vacant, appoint and install the new incumbents, and settle disputes between them, subject to appeal. From among their members they appoint the superintendents, who serve for life and represent them between sessions, conduct visitations in their diocese, and receive the inspectors' reports. The inspectors are pastors whose special function it is to centralize the business of an ecclesiatical diocese and who are directly responsible to the consistories.

The pastor is assisted by a lay council. He has great influence within his parish, for he knows every member of his flock. He baptizes, marries, and buries them and keeps the parish registers. He supervises the school. His deacons, choirmasters, and vergers are his closest associates, and since they engage in other occupations besides their church duties and are in daily contact with the parishioners, act as channels for his opinions. The elders of the Presbyterian consistories follow the ritual form as practiced by the pastor, even if he is not a member of the council, as he is in Lutheran provinces. In short, it is the pastor rather than any agent of the king or the local lord who represents the village; as an educated, indispensable, and friendly personage, he is at once its leader and its representative; he is like a compass which both indicates the slightest changes in direction and guides the vessel on its course.

While some pastors may have studied theology at a foreign university, a pastor who has not attended one of the five Prussian universities for at least a semester is a rarity. There are more students at the Faculty of Theology at Halle University than at all the other four universities together: 795 in 1786. Semler and Nösselt are their teachers. Semler, the son of a pastor at Saalfeld, has passed through a period of Pietism. His feelings, his taste for scholarship, and the teaching of Baumgarten (his predecessor at Halle) weaned him away from it, and at the time of Frederick II's death he is training future clergymen. Nösselt, his best pupil, becomes one of the stoutest opponents of the orthodoxy which Wöllner, when minister, tries to impose on the faculty.

The principles of J. S. Semler are those of the Aufklärung. He distinguishes the essence of the Christian religion, which determines its morality, from its forms, which vary with time and place. The essence contains its natural, eternal, and universal truths. The Bible cannot contradict them; *quidquid verum est in philosophia, verum etiam est in theologia*; if there are apparent discrepancies, it must be remembered that the divine revelation was transmitted by men, and so it has to be examined by the methods of human reason. In any case, it cannot possibly conflict with reason. Some Hebrew and Greek expressions are hard to translate, and consequently philological and historical study is essential for the understanding of the sacred texts. Mystical interpretations are dangerous; the learned exegetist will battle superstition incessantly. One of Semler's best works, *De daemonicis quorum in Evangeliis fuit mentio* (1760), denounces the imposture of exorcism. Taking as his text a hysteric who claimed to be possessed by the devil at Kemberg in 1759, he demonstrates that there is nothing in the Scriptures to support the notion of the diabolical possession of a body. He of course reserves the question of diabolical influence on the mind.

Candidates for a clergyman's living must be selected by a consistory. All the lay members of the Central Lutheran Consistory were enlightened scholars and teachers when Frederick William II came to the throne: von der Hagen, its chairman, his friend von Irwing, J. F. Lamprecht, J. C. Nagel and F. Gedike. The clerical members, except the Pietist Silberschlag, were members of the rationalist elite; Buesching had earned a sound reputation as a teacher at the Graue Kloster and as a geographer; Teller was the champion of toleration for Jews and Moslems; J. J. Spalding was the author of a book, *The Use of the Preacher's Function*, explaining what the consistory expects of those elected by it. Priests are not mediators between man and God, but "men like others"; their function is "to be useful by bringing more virtue, and thereby more beneficence, into the world." In order to fulfill it, they must be learned; their knowledge of the sacred sciences must enable them to answer objections from the faithful and to convince them rather than merely invoke the authority of dogma. Furthermore, "by keeping in touch with developments in the world of letters, they will be able to procure readily and without undue expense a few good and truly instructive works calculated both to correct their views on religion and to enlighten them on the other sciences. It must be a real source of satisfaction, therefore, that our brothers are forming reading clubs in several areas; they thus gain an opportunity to become acquainted with writings which they can use; and indeed they are able to use them in practice." They are thus qualified in case of need to succor the sick, give legal advice in order to obviate costly litigation, and supply farmers with practical advice. (Spalding, *Nutzbarkeit des Predigtamtes*, 28, 36, 38, 40.)

Turning to the relations between the clergy and the state, Spalding denies the contention that he makes the clergy the servant of the state. But he grants the state the right to supervise the clergy in order to ensure that religion is consonant with the state's own ends, namely the maintenance of order and the organization of public welfare.

As Christian morality tends to such ends, and no civil society can exist without morality, "all those who help to disseminate virtue and to increase its efficacy are also useful to the state." The clergy's relation to the state may therefore be regarded as making them equivalent to "teachers assigned to impart morals." The Abbé Saint-Pierre is to be commended for his opinion that "had we not instituted the art of preaching in order to exhort to the practice of virtue, it would be good policy and good religion—good government in short—to institute it." Since they are paid by society, teachers of religion are not only to make people happy by pointing the way to Providence and immortality, but must also impart the "civic virtues" useful to society such as "industry, obedience, resignation, fidelity, and honesty." Thus, the clergy, "the true depositories of public morality," are responsible for "making the masses wiser, better, and happier, and these masses are their brothers, they are human beings, beloved of God, endowed with the faculty of reason, created for eternity, saved by Jesus Christ." (Ibid., 68, 76, 80, 100, 156.)

There is, of course, some distance between theory and practice. Not all pastors resemble Sebaldus Nothanker, whose sermons are courses in morality. When a peasant gets drunk, he preaches necessary moderation; when a quarrel breaks out in the village, he comments on the precept about loving one's neighbor. He sometimes substitutes a spiritual song by Gellert for the hymn *Wir glauben Alle an einem Gott*. He does not believe in everlasting hell; and though he devotes his spare time to trying to understand the Apocalypse, he takes very good care not to mention it to his peasants. "His irrevocable resolution is to preach nothing that is not both intelligible and useful to them" (*Sebaldus Nothanker* I, 6–7). The intellectual level of the clergy, however, is in fact very low. The consistories are limited in their choice by the starvation wages they offer; the administrative records abound in requests for financial assistance or "promotion to a better living." Schoolmasters often refuse a clergyman's living, for their new dignity will no longer allow them to take other jobs whereby they can earn their bread.

The fact remains that where the pastor is able to exert any influence, he almost always does so along the lines of the Aufklärung, and he is the main channel through which it flows out into the countryside.

The Teachers

The whole of Germany is deeply interested in education at the end of the eighteenth century. The belief in natural equality concentrates on education as both the source of and the remedy for inequality. Cranks like Basedow or outright crooks like Bahrdt gain the support of honest men and the collaboration of scrupulous schoolmasters, who try to correct and apply their systems. Fervent educators, fully aware of the difficulties of their task but prompted by a sincere love of mankind, such as Salzmann, Rochow, Gedike, and Campe, whose journal attracted contributions from many outstanding teachers, manage to interest princes in their experiments.

These teachers all subscribe to the same principles. Almost all of them endorse Locke's *Reflections on Education* (1693) and Rousseau's *Emile*. Philanthropists echo one another from country to country in an era of internationalism. All of them want to see education modernized. In place of a concentration on Latin and Greek, studied almost exclusively from the Bible, they want the young to learn modern languages, starting with their mother tongue, and to acquire a grounding in the sciences, mathematics, geography, and history. The new teaching is concrete. Its purpose is to prepare the child for life rather than to make a casuist of him.

The reformers also attack the existing teaching methods: "No more dictation and rote learning," they proclaim, "but free discussion between masters and pupils. Questions and answers to put some life into the class! No more over-long lessons which tire the children unnecessarily, but games and walks!" Basedow proposes that a half-day should be devoted to physical exercise, and he organizes a camp for his pupils at his *Philanthropinum* at Dessau. Salzmann takes his pupils on excursions. Almost all of them publish illustrated primers designed as guides for masters and pupils alike. The fullest, Basedow's famous *Elementary Primer*, is based on La Chalotais's book in French. Others, such as the *Experimental Classbook for Peasants' Children* (1772) and Rochow's *Children's Friend* (1776), are written specially for quite small children.

The utilitarianism and liberalism of these ideas and methods appeal to the Aufklärung. Christians of the various denominations are often assembled in a single class. Schoolteachers in Prussia impart a moralistic tone to religious instruction and take care to avoid stressing the differences between the denominations.

Most of these reformers try to put their principles into practice. Some, like Salzmann at Schnepfenthal, succeed brilliantly. But his school still has no more than sixty-one pupils in 1803.

It would be a mistake to overrate this movement. The investigations prompted by it disclose that education is stagnating in a wretched plight, and the remedies proposed are applied only in a few exceptional cases. In 1763, Frederick II issues a general ordinance making school compulsory for all children between the ages of five and thirteen. They must attend every day, except Wednesday and Saturday, in winter from eight to eleven in the morning and one to four in the afternoon; in summer there is morning school only; there are no holidays; even on Sundays the children repeat their catechism at the same time as the village bachelors, who practice reading and writing from the New Testament and other works of edification.

Nonattendance is punished by a fine of sixteen groschen under the royal edict; the inspector collects it from recalcitrant parents for the benefit of the school funds. The schoolmasters must have attended the Berlin teachers' training college, where they are taught "silkworm breeding and pedagogy." The inspectors are the local ministers, who examine the teachers before they are appointed. The timetable and curriculum—catechism, sacred history, psalms, reading, and writing—are rigidly fixed.

But the edict is hardly applied; parents try to evade schooling, since it is not provided free. The schoolmasters are too badly paid to be equal to their task. When Minister von Zedlitz wants to set up a training school for country schoolmasters, the king himself opposes him, stipulating that these posts should be reserved for ex-soldiers invalided out of his armies.

Zedlitz makes another attempt after Frederick II's death; he calls for a schools policy. It can be successful only if education ceases to be a poor relation of the church; but education is administered by the High Consistory.

The best schoolmasters are pastors awaiting a living, but it would never occur to them to make a career of teaching. In these circumstances pedagogy inevitably remains a dead letter. Zedlitz persuades Frederick William II to let him establish a special administrative board, the Higher Board of Education (*Oberschulkollegium*) (*BM* 1787, 97–116). The members of this council are von Hoffman, the chancellor of Halle University; von Irwing, a lawyer specializing in school administration; von Wöllner, the king's favorite minister; Steinhart, a clergyman and professor at the University of Frankfort-on-Oder; and Meierotto and Gedike, headmasters of *Gymnasia* (secondary schools). Zedlitz presides in person.

When they assemble for the first of their Tuesday morning meetings, they find themselves faced with a task well calculated to damp their enthusiasm. They decide to embark on an inquiry to determine an order of priority for the reforms.

The first reform relates to the teachers' need for better pay; schoolmasters must be properly trained, and it is essential to allay the hostility of the local authorities, who are afraid of the additional charge on their funds, and that of the incumbent schoolmasters, who block the new methods by the sheer weight of their *vis inertiae*. Nor can schooling be improved until clean and well-ventilated schoolhouses have been built. Furthermore, the dual system of private and public schools will have to be abolished, grades will have to be introduced in the schools, and the distinction between upper secondary schools and universities will have to be clearly defined, so that every student will obtain more or less the same education.

The inquiry reveals that there are too few village schoolhouses. In many cases the only classroom is the living room of the schoolmaster and his family. The pupils are packed, boys and girls together, into a single room, which is, depending on the building, too large or too small, too dark or too bright, too hot or too cold. Some schoolmasters are barely less ignorant than their pupils. "Sometimes the pupils are totally free and undisciplined," Gedike wrote. "Some of the masters are so simpleminded and ignorant that they even permit their class to play during school hours if it feels like it. Some of them are so depraved that they seduce innocent boys. The teaching method in some cases is completely wrong and senseless; some of the textbooks are bad and useless" (*BM* 1784, II, 337). Teaching means the recitation of the catechism, each mistake being corrected by a stroke of the cane, and teaching children to read and write "without spelling," and occasionally to count. The overworked schoolmaster is so badly paid that he cannot live without some other occupation. At best, he is also the verger or organist; and inspections by the pastor are not too infrequent. In the Electoral Mark there are 1,760 verger-schoolmasters; 49 have a yearly income of over 100 thalers, and 33 of 100; 250 village schoolmasters earn only 30 thalers, 301 only 20, 184 only 10, 111 only 5, and 163 are not paid at all.

The reforms at the end of the century improved the teachers' material lot hardly at all. According to an official survey in 1796, of 213 teachers at the Latin colleges (*Gelehrtenschulen*), that is, at the most privileged state establishments, 8 are paid less than 100 thalers yearly, 42 between 100 and

150, 55 between 150 and 200, 42 between 200 and 250, and 30 between 250 and 300. At that time the wage of a messenger at the Higher Board of Education is 160 thalers.

In the circumstances, the chief effect of the new theories is to incite a few outstanding educators to do what they can within their own narrow sphere. Schleiermacher, for example, when a minister at Stolpe, interests himself deeply in education.

The schoolmasters make pathetic efforts to acquire a grounding in the sciences of which they know nothing but which they are required to teach. Others try to relieve their school's poverty. For instance, Oesterreich, the headmaster of a village school, has for fifteen years given six or seven hours instruction daily to some eighty small children in winter and thirty or forty in summer. He longs for an assistant to teach elementary reading; so he founds a school fund with the meager resources at his disposal. It is customary for the headmaster and his pupils to supply the choir at marriages, for which they are paid 14 groschen, 12 groschen going to the headmaster; the children give up their share to the fund. The schoolmaster no longer cuts the pupils' quills free of charge, but makes them bring three quills already cut and keeps one; having gathered a stock, he sells four quills for 3 pfennigs. The receipts from the Michaelmas collection also go to the fund, which manages to accumulate a capital of 17 thalers 79 groschen in seven years. Oesterreich levies a fee of 6 pfennigs on each pupil entering and leaving the school. He hopes that in a century the fund will amount to a capital sum yielding an income sufficient to provide for the masters' subsistence, the poor pupils' studies, and the repair of the schoolhouse. He does not include the 200 thalers sent him by the king with a request that they be shared with the fund, nor gifts from other quarters. His efforts and the publicity they receive testify to the idealism that moves so many honest men to devote their whole lives to tasks which they are well aware can only be brought to completion in a distant future that they will never see.

The situation is no better in the other German states, in which the church has far greater control over the schools. Jung-Stilling, a schoolteacher in a village in Salm at the age of fourteen, is forced to give up his post, to the distraction of his pupils and their parents, because he lodges with a charcoal burner disliked by the pastor. He finds another post, but is unable to keep it; the peasants demand his dismissal because, in an attempt to amuse and instruct, he invents a sort of card game with the numbers of the questions in the catechism on each card, the loser having to learn by heart the passages shown on the cards he has been unable to discard. A third effort fails because of an intrigue worked up by a rival. He never manages to earn enough to buy the cloth for a coat, for he devotes his spare time to reading instead of working at his tailor's trade.

The state of affairs is not much better in the towns. True, there are some good secondary schools in Prussia, reorganized by Zedlitz in 1779. But most of the teachers are still mediocre. Alongside some educators inspired by the sacred fire at the head of the great Berlin *Gymnasia*, Gedike at the Friedrichswerder, Meierotto at the Joachimsthaler, Buesching at the Graue Kloster, there is a vast crowd of headmasters, assistant teachers, and parish schoolmasters engulfed in routine and inertia. The reminiscences of almost all former pupils of *Gymnasia* in Prussia and elsewhere reveal that the only useful work ever done there is that performed voluntarily out of class. All the promising secondary school pupils are virtually self-taught. Thus, Karl Philipp Moritz acquires an education despite the school at Hanover, where pupils stay in the same class for years on end, unflaggingly repeating the same elementary lessons (*Anton Reiser* bk. 2, pp. 151 ff.); Perthes is regarded as a dunce at Rudolfstadt, while, unknown to his masters, he devours everything in the library (*Friedrich Perthes Leben*, 5); and Tieck, after passing through the hands of a journeyman tailor who has been permitted to open a French school in Berlin simply because he once plied his trade in Paris, writes novels while at the Friedrichswerder *Gymnasium* which are published by his young teacher, (Koepke, *Ludwig Tieck*, I, 15 ff., 116–22).

Beside these institutions controlled by the state to a greater or lesser degree there are a vast number of Latin or private schools which accept children of craftsmen and shopkeepers. The Protestant church endows many of them with scholarships, but these subsidies are not large enough to pay for good teachers. "That is why no really intelligent person capable of introducing a new system ever applies for a teacher's post," a visitor to Berlin writes.

Others, however, flock in. When a craftsman is no longer able to live by his trade, when a noncommissioned officer is invalided out of the service, he at once opens a school. . . . If he cannot get scholarship pupils, he solicits the favor of shopkeepers who pay for their childrens' schooling. . . . I find it strange, all the same, that if I, as a layman, were to begin teaching horse riding, I should be fined 100 thalers and my pupil 50, whereas I am perfectly at liberty to teach morals, politics, or any other science to anyone I like and in any way I like.

These establishments have no inspectors . . . or textbooks. In not more than two of these private schools (out of at least a hundred) are the pupils divided into classes. In all the rest, boys of fifteen, who have been attending the school for ten years, sit together with small children learning their alphabet. Boys and girls are assembled in the same room. Absolutely no trouble is taken to teach boys to use their hands or to instruct girls in housework. [*Jahrb.* 1799, I, 146–56, 362–72; II, 25–48. Spazier, *Carl Pilgers Roman* I, 54.]

Competition from these private institutions merely aggravates the defects of the public schools. The teachers live partly on the schooling paid for by the parents, but when pupils are few, destitution looms. Sometimes, therefore, they detain a child in the same class for several years so as to keep their income undiminished, and sometimes they promote a dunce to a higher form because his parents have threatened to remove him from school. As there are no specific curricula, promotion cannot depend on the acquisition of specified knowledge and is, therefore, wholly arbitrary. To augment their income teachers give private evening lessons and see to it that they become indispensable; for example, French grammar is taught in class, but French literature is read only at the evening lessons. This increases attendance by children under fifteen to as much as fifty hours a week.

The first result of the work of the Higher Board of Education is the creation of the *Abitur* examination. It sets the seal of approval on secondary school courses; its aim is to reduce the number of inept students who impede the universities' work and form an intellectual proletariat which cannot be absorbed by vacancies in the civil service or the church. The examination procedure is established by the Ordinance of 23 December 1788. During a half-day at the school and without proctors, candidates compose written essays on each of the subjects taught. The themes of the essays are chosen by the headmaster and the delegate of the provincial board responsible to the Higher Board of Education. This delegate also presides at the oral examinations, which are held at the *Gymnasium*. The teachers question the examinees in classical and modern languages and the sciences, the principal scientific subject being history. The examinees are then awarded a certificate of aptitude or nonaptitude. Holders of either may go to the university, but only the former are entitled to the scholarships or other benefits on which most students will have to live. Pupils from private lower-grade secondary schools (*Bürgerschulen*) have to sit for an examination at the time when they are enrolled at a university.

The first examination boards meet at Easter 1789. The hasty reform satisfies no one. The standard is extremely low. Since there is no curriculum, the inequalities between one school and another are so great that the universities' task is made no easier. The Higher Board therefore sets out to devise curricula calculated to set a standard for the *Abitur*, but these are not issued till after the disaster at Jena. The teachers' training school and the Pietist colleges, deservedly famous when founded at the beginning of the century, have fallen to a relatively low level. It is quite understandable, therefore, that parents who are at all well-to-do should resort to tutors for their children's education.

This depressing state of affairs might well lead us to conclude that the educational movement and the enlightened philosophy underlying it have no practical results. This would be wrong, however. For, in the first place, the individual efforts, however limited, do in fact help to improve teaching methods, and, second, the spread of the belief in progress, the awakening of a real enthusiasm for every form of knowledge, and the notion that education is the best of good things do make it possible for very many of the poor to gain access to education.

Peasants learn to read at the Sunday schools and poor children obtain the backing and help needed for acquiring an education. Discovering promising poor scholars is an act of philanthropy; coming to their aid ensures commendation in the public press. No matter that the teaching at the secondary school at Hanover is mediocre and that most of the pupils learn nothing there; without the Aufklärung young Anton Reiser, a hatter's apprentice, would never have been awarded the scholarship by the Prince of Mecklenburg-Strelitz which enables the studious lad to acquire an education. The life is certainly hard; it is hard to have to depend upon bourgeois families, who, equally influenced by the spirit of the age, invite the young student to their table but do not have sufficient tact to refrain from talking about their condescension in front of him (Moritz, *Anton Reiser*, bk. 2, pp. 134 ff.). After a poor scholar has completed his courses by dint of privations, he is eager to take up a post commensurate with his abilities; and he becomes justifiably impatient with the fresh obstacles which arise at this point.

By developing education the Aufklärung simultaneously helps to reduce the number of illiterates and to increase the number of impoverished scholars; many of the latter, ill content with a social order which is changing too slowly for their liking, become tutors in noble families and sometimes infect them with revolutionary ideas. Forster, whose faith is so shrewd and whose judgments are so perspicacious despite his enthusiasms, defines his age admirably in the following passage:

The richer the culture of our age, the greater is the number of concepts we can envisage and the more discriminating can be our choice among them; the further the scope of our thinking and action is enlarged, the more relationships we establish with the world around us and the more attractive we find them. . . . It is to this weft, whose threads, selected from all the specific subjects possible, have been so happily woven, it is to this combination of the most varied forms of knowledge that we owe the rapid progress of our education; and, as a result, our youth possesses at the age of sixteen a more perfect and more stable system of useful and practical concepts than could have been acquired in thirty years in the age of Locke. . . . We shall succeed if we accustom ourselves to *finding employment for these intellectual powers* and *everywhere* promoting the development of reason, the possession of which has so long and so arbitrarily been denied to the greater part of the human race when, indeed, it has not been inhumanly withheld from it. [*Ansichten*, chap. 3, p. 23.]

The Press

Freedom of speech existed in Prussia at the end of the eighteenth century. It is true that Frederick II was sometimes rather touchy on this point; although he permitted the publication of any and all attacks upon religion, his censorship controlled the political columns of the periodicals. His agents even watched journalists who attacked him from abroad. Any political news which was not divulged by the Prussian press could, however, be disseminated in Prussia by the chief German papers and was also disclosed in innumerable pamphlets, against which the king could take no action.

Freedom of thought is in any event a dogma so widely held that the king cannot arbitrarily infringe it. His own officials oppose him, for they remain "enlightened" even when the prince ceases to be. It is in vain that Frederick William II, under the influence of the Rosicrucians, revives and strengthens the Censorship Edict (December 1789), and in vain that he convenes all his ministers to a Grand Council of State on 6 February 1792. He does indeed sign, on 21 February, a lengthy edict against bulletins and other revolutionary writings, which he bars from his realm, together with the *Gothaische Gelehrte Zeitung*; he announces that the mails will be watched, and on 27 February he appoints special commissioners to see to it. Threatening notifications are sent to the provincial governments, the consistories, and the universities. These measures are relatively ineffectual; most of the officials fail to comply; and the few publications prohibited are of little political importance (Archives Rep. IX, F, 2a, fascs. 23-24). When the newspapers and periodicals no longer dare to comment on the political news after 1795, pamphlets and booklets, which are not subject to censorship, proliferate (Tschirch, *Öffentliche Meinung* I, 7-9). How lukewarm was the administration's compliance emerges, for example, in the affair of the *Journal de Strasbourg*.

Von Wobeher, the director of the Domains Chamber at Bromberg, an official eager to display his zeal, suddenly discovers the *Journal de Strasbourg* and reports, on 27 August 1792, that this journal, which is read at Bromberg and Berlin alike, ought to be prohibited. Chancellor Carmer, one of Frederick II's old officials, remains unperturbed and asks for a more detailed report. Wobeher, in some embarrassment, regrets that he cannot send the journal; on investigation he finds that there is only one copy in all Bromberg, that belonging to the Fräulein Dietrich; and Tchepius, the postmaster, refuses to confiscate the journal without the subscriber's consent, since it is duly authorized in Prussia and even advertises in the Berlin press. He attaches a letter from the Fräulein expressing her regret that she cannot send her copies to Wobeher, "but," she adds, "as I am not the only person using the journal in question, the subscription cannot be changed.

Since, however, my interest in it has completely vanished with the resignation of Mayor Dietrich, who, as you can see from his name, is a cousin of mine, I have decided not to renew my subscription, so it is not worth making any changes" (Rep. IX, fasc. 23, p. 91). Berlin decides, on 27 September, that there are no grounds for action, since there is nothing in the report to justify banning the journal.

In the last quarter of the century there is an abrupt and very large increase in printed publications. Almost none of the leading periodicals existed before 1773. A reliable authority estimates that in 1716 the total number of periodicals published in the whole of Europe was 140; in 1790 there are 247 in Germany alone (*JD* 1789, I, 39–43). The five-and-a-half pages of the catalog of the Leipzig Fair in 1770 increases to seventeen-and-a-half in 1788. The period of peace in Germany starting in 1763 undoubtedly fosters this proliferation, but is not enough entirely to account for it. For publishing on this scale to prosper there must be both writers and readers. The emergence of a literate public avid for novelties and eager to combat prejudice is one of the larger effects of the new philosophy.

If we scrutinize these publications more closely, we find a change in their character, inasmuch as the proportion of periodicals concerned with the domestic affairs and the international relations of states becomes very much larger. While there are only 7 of them in the whole of Germany between 1770 and 1779, there are 24 between 1790 and 1799. To list them all would be tedious; but the principal periodical publications must be cited to give an idea both of their very varied origins and of their vitality, for they flourish despite the persecution to which many of their editors were subjected.

The earliest of the major reviews was Wieland's *Der teutsche Merkur*. First published at Weimar in 1773 in pamphlet form like the *Mercure français*, to which Wieland was a contributor, it gathered around it all the major writers of the time and became a champion of every form of liberalism. From 1789 to 1810 it was published as *Der neue teutsche Merkur*.

Some professors at Göttingen published their reflections on past and present, also addressed to an educated public. Schloezer, who had studied theology, oriental languages, and medicine, had been a tutor in Sweden and Russia, and had taught philosophy, history, and politics, published the *Briefwechsel meist historischen und politischen Inhalts* from 1776 to 1782 and the *Staatsanzeigen* from 1783 to 1794. He retired, however, when his review was banned in that year despite his caution. His colleagues Meiners and Spitteler were largely responsible for the contributions to the learned *Göttingisches historisches Magazin* (1787–92). Two senior Prussian officials in the diplomatic service, von Dohm and Boie, published the *Deutsches Museum* at Leipzig from 1776 to 1789 and the *Neues deutsches Museum* from 1789 to 1791.

The less academic magazines intended for a wider public had a more chequered career. Before he launched his *Deutsche Chronik* at Augsburg in March 1774, Christian Schubart, a graduate in theology and a remarkable musical virtuoso, had led an adventurous life. Owing to his unstable character, he had been compelled to resign as Director of Music and organist at Ludwigsburg, a post worth 230 florins, in 1769. He became a remarkably successful journalist. His weekly magazine was distributed throughout southern Germany, and 1,600 copies of each issue were printed in its first year. In 1775, however, he was compelled to transfer it to Ulm, an imperial city, because the Jesuits were harassing him. A joke about Franziska von Hohenheim, the mistress of Karl of Württemberg, led to his imprisonment at Hohasperg in 1777. He spent 377 days in the dungeons, four years in the cells, and five years in the fortress and was released only in May 1787, when Frederick II, to whom he had dedicated a plaintive ode, intervened to rescue him. He then resumed publication of his periodical, besides acting as Director of Music and Theater at Stuttgart, where he died in 1791 at the age of fifty-two.

Wekhrlin's irrespressible spirits got him into trouble too. In retirement at Baldingen, near Nordlingen, this cosmopolitan encyclopedist published in succession the *Chronologen* (1799), *Das graue Ungeheuer*, and the *Hyperboreische Briefe*. Though imprisoned in fortress by Prince von Oettlingen-Wallerstein, he continued to publish the *Briefe*. In 1792 he escaped to Ansbach and died there shortly after launching the *Ansbachische Blätter*, which led to his denunciation by the local population as a French spy.

The Württemberger Baron Karl von Moser served several princes. Joseph II conferred a title upon him in 1772; his forthrightness got him into trouble everywhere. In the end he devoted himself to censuring prejudice and injustice in his *Patriotisches Archiv für Deutschland* (1784-92), published at Leipzig and Frankfort, followed by the *Neues patriotisches Archiv* (1792-94). Von Goekingk, the head of the Ellerich Chancery Office, published the *Journal von und für Deutschland* along similar lines, but after an attack on him in 1785 by the Elector of Mainz, a member of the Fürstenbund, with which Prussia had to keep on good terms at the time, he had to make way for Baron Bibra, who edited the paper until 1792. It continued to appear until 1828. The *National-Zeitung der Teutschen*, edited by Zaccharias Becker from 1796 to 1805, played an important part when Germany was being threatened by Bonaparte. The most important newspaper in the strict sense was Cotta's *Allgemeine Zeitung*, published first at Tübingen on the strength of promises by the Duke of Würtemberg, who waived his censorship (1798), and then at Ulm, when the duke went back on his word in 1803; supported by an Imperial Patent of November 1803, this daily managed to remain independent till 1805, when Napoleon subjected it to French influence. It survived until 1837, and from 1798 on it had 1,400 subscribers and printed 2,000 copies.

The government often encouraged the larger counterrevolutionary papers which opposed their rivals' liberalism. The most important of these was the *Hamburger politisches Journal*, edited from 1781 to 1804 by Gottlob Benedikt von Schirach, a professor of history and statistics at Helmstadt University. He was mainly concerned to combat the influence of periodicals openly favorable to France, such as *Minerva* (1792–1808), published first at Berlin and then, when the censorship became too strict there, at Hamburg. Its editor, J. W. von Archenholz, a former Prussian officer, became so enthusiastic about the French Revolution that he went to Paris in order to witness for himself the events his journal was dealing with. Returning to Prussia on the outbreak of the war with Prussia, he left a correspondent, Oelsner, at Paris and published regular articles from him.

Reichardt's *Frankreich* was published at Altona in 1795 along similar lines; during the ten years of its existence its articles were regarded as authoritative.

The chief semiofficial Berlin periodicals, such as the *Jahrbücher der preussischen Monarchie, Berliner Monatsschriften, Berlinisches Archiv der Zeit* and the *Berlinisches Journal für Aufklärung*, published copious details on daily life in Berlin, in the larger Prussian towns and in the country.

If we look not only at these newspapers but also at the purely literary publications, the best known of which, but not the most interesting to the historian, are Nicolai's *Allgemeine deutsche Bibliothek* and Schvetz's *Jenaische allgemeine Literatur-Zeitung* (1785–1848), leaf through society journals such as the *Zeitung für die elegante Welt* (1801–05), to which Spazier welcomed the young Romantics, and glance at a few pamphlets, we can understand why most travelers brought back from Germany an impression that there was a plethora of public prints there. In Berlin, as in Paris, everyone read, and everywhere, as at Breslau, any café owner who wished to keep his elegant *Biertrinker* customers had to provide them with periodicals free of charge. The small print runs are misleading as a guide to the number of readers, for most subscribers took in a periodical on behalf of an entire community. People not only read their papers at a café or reading club, but grouped together to subscribe to them. The wife of the Reverend Sebaldus Nothanker could no more dispose of the papers she read than the Fräulein Dietrich at Bromberg, for she passed on the *Bremische Beiträge* to the schoolmasters and pastors of "the small neighboring towns" (*Sebaldus Nothanker* I, 12). The two thousand purchasers of the *Allgemeine Zeitung* represent, therefore, a far larger number of readers.

Almost all the prints, even those which are politically conservative, preach toleration along the lines of the Aufklärung. Moser's sole aim is to serve the truth; it is in order to be able to "judge the great from a human standpoint" that some of the articles he publishes have to be anonymous (*PAD* 1784, I, 1). To strengthen toleration, Goekingk publishes letters from readers denouncing the ill effects of prejudice and lists unfounded local traditions and beliefs in a column entitled "Superstitions and Vulgar Errors" (e.g., *JD* 1787, II, 340–45; 790, II, 26–30, etc.). Becker publishes a collection of anecdotes sent to him from all over the empire; Schlosser contributes his political fragments for meditation by the readers of the *Deutsches Museum*. All the periodicals comment on the reports of everyday happenings and demonstrate that error and credulity engender absurdities, suffering, and misery.

Toleration is not, however, wholly dispassionate; committed as it is to a fight to the death against prejudice, it cannot remain objective. Most liberals in Prussia harbor a real hatred of Catholicism. It is a feeling virtually innate, inasmuch as the Catholic church, firmly entrenched behind its doctrine and able to live financially on its own resources, opposes a stubborn resistance to the spirit of innovation. Protestantism finds no difficulty in accommodating itself to reason and is able to take a broad deism under its shield. The Aufklärung spreads easily enough in northern Germany, where it can win over the clergy without unfrocking them and can even appear in guise of religion. In the south it is harder to reconcile the two. Battle is engaged between the dogmas of the church and the imperatives of reason. The philosophers do not shrink from defamation in attacking the principle of the monastic life, miracles, and Jesuitry (*NTM* 1797, 142–47; *Briefwechsel* 1781, VII, 218–59; IX, 1–34; *Chronologen*, almost any issue). They accuse Catholic priests of deliberately keeping the people in poverty by unduly increasing the number of holy days and days of obligation, in ignorance by neglecting their education, and in a state of dependence by encouraging begging by an indiscriminate charity (*DM* 1777, II, 362–73; Jung-Stilling, *Lebensgeschichte* II, 18). For the most backward parts of the empire are those in which industrial and technological progress is powerless to break down tradition, the Catholic states of the Rhineland and Bavaria, where the courageous lead given by Joseph II finds no followers.

Lastly, the press displays an encyclopedic spirit consonant with the need for education and the proselytism which is an invariable characteristic of the Aufklärung. The periodicals claim to answer every question and provide information on every subject (*JD* 1784, I, 1). "Ignorance," Forster announces, "is the prime cause, the universal cause, of the voiding of all social contracts. To overthrow it by spreading the gentle and beneficent light of reason is certainly the noblest of all retaliations" (*Ansichten* II, chap. 24, p. 89). As the papers are written in German for a German public, their tone becomes increasingly nationalistic. To bring home to the German nation its own originality, they do not hesitate to contrast it with its neighbors (*NZT* Jan. 1796, pp. 1-24).

The Reading Clubs

The reading clubs supplement the effect of the press. They extend in a close-knit cultural network over the whole of Germany. The enlightened in every town meet in the club rooms where German and foreign newspapers, periodicals, and books are available. Within an official society still dominated by caste prejudices they form a society of a different type, one more in tune with the spirit of the Aufklärung. Noble rubs shoulders with burgher, Christian meets Jew, women mingle with men. The stranger enquiring for the local notabilities is sure to find them at the reading club. Through the clubs, travelers are sent on with introductions from one town to another, correspondents are put in touch, news is exchanged. Raised in the same school, all the enlightened discuss the same questions which are debated in the press. The acts of every prince are reported and judged, foreign innovations are imitated despite local hostility, injustice and error are denounced or corrected.

It will not do, of course, to overrate the members' intellectual capacities. "Sectarian fervor" causes a good many people to congregate in the clubs who would have done better to stay beside their own fireside (*GH* 1785, V, 11-13). What is regarded as conversation is often no more than idle gossip, a run of tittle-tattle, with many an ejaculation of "Terrible! Awful! You don't say!" (*JD* 1786, II, 195-202). New prejudices, no better than the old, take root in these parochial circles, in which everyone displays the breadth of his views by dressing in the latest fashion and imitating the latest eccentricity. But the very lack of a critical spirit among these small-town philosophers who take their tone from the press without demur helps to instill the new ideas into the masses. The reading clubs muster the troops of the Aufklärung, the press supplies the field officers and the philosophers the general staff. Their members man the front line, denounce backsliders to the journalists, disseminate opinions, and clear the way for reform. They are the arbiters who decide whether a person is to be honored or ridiculed through all the Germanies; and this check on the intellectuals forestalls many excesses, for every intellectual is aware that what he does and what he writes will be judged and that the verdict will be widely reported; he thinks twice before publishing stupidities which the masses would seize upon as fuel for their passions if there did not exist between them and their would-be leaders this fine net of enlightened principles, through which stupidity cannot pass.

We should not conclude that these groups were of little importance simply because little is known of them. They can hardly be distinguished from the earliest Freemasons' lodges founded in Germany in the middle of the eighteenth century. The principles set out by Lessing in his *Dialogues for Freemasons* are indistinguishable from those of the Aufklärung and the reading clubs. The Masons form a liberal, international society bringing together reasonable men, one which will ultimately embrace all mankind through the progress of enlightenment.

Basically, Lessing is simply saying in 1777 what the pseudonymous Philalethes the Younger said in his 1722 program for the London Lodge. Far from dying out, the reading clubs proliferate toward the end of the century because they remain faithful to a spirit which was being betrayed by the lodges' trend toward mysticism and alchemy.

We have, however, very little detailed information on them. Any archives that have survived are no doubt gathering dust in municipal or family collections. The clubs are congruent with the spirit of the times and so are not suspect or watched, and the police take no interest in them. They worry the government of Prussia only for a brief moment, when Minister Wöllner discovers their importance as the stoutest bastion of the opposition during his earliest onslaught on the Aufklärung. A special commission is appointed to supervise books and periodicals. "We have undertaken," the censor Hillmer writes to his colleagues in January 1797, "to propose methods for combating the damage caused by the universal malady, I might almost go so far as to say mania, of reading; it is caused by the many reading clubs and institutes, whose numbers are continually increasing."

The provincial commissions are consulted, but their replies are vague and dilatory; no doubt their members belong to the clubs, or at any rate dislike the job. The commission at Königsberg alone displays any zeal. It reports that most of the books in the clubs' catalogs are hostile to the Christian religion, to morality, and to the state; drastic action is needed, for it is not only the men who are infected, but youths and even schoolchildren.

Frederick William II's death puts an end to the investigation; the surveillance slackens just as it is becoming organized. Full information is available only from the printed material; though this is, it is true, super-abundant. Methodical research would probably reveal the pattern of a network covering all Prussia and Germany.

Several clubs exist in Berlin at the same period. Beside the Monday Club, where Nicolai, Lessing, Mendelssohn, Stammler, and Sulzer lit the first flame of the Aufklärung around 1755, there are the highly respectable Society of Friends of the Natural Sciences, meeting every week in a mansion placed at its disposal by Frederick II, the Monday Society, presided over by Ben David, the Jewish Kantian philosopher, and the Wednesday Clubs, the first of which was founded in 1783 by Suarez, councillor at the Ministry of Justice, the second by Professor Fessler in 1797. The latter has many notabilities among its fifty members, including Marcus Herz, the physician,

Zelter, the musician, Schadow, the sculptor, Berger, the educator, Friedländer, the philanthropist, Rambach, the poet, and Iffland, the actor. Men and women meet there on Wednesday afternoons from 5 to 9. "Open meetings" for conversation alternate with concerts, lectures, and plays. Iffland stages *Emilia Galotti* and *Nathan der Weise.* The success is such that a Friday Club is soon founded on the same lines, and Fessler himself founds his Society of Friends of Humanity, which meets on Saturdays at the Royal York Lodge. In 1799 it runs a competition for the best essay on the improvement of schools in Prussia.

Even the smallest towns have their club. There are two rival clubs at Wittenberg. The club at Luenenberg has over a hundred members in 1774; it buys three or four hundred books yearly for its circulating library. At Oehringen, Hildburghausen, Schweinfurth, Frieddorf, everywhere in fact, the wealthier burghers devour books. At Halberstadt, officers of the Duke of Brunswick's regiment are members of the reading club founded by the poet Gleim. They share the burghers' pacifist and Francophile sentiments. A lively correspondence is exchanged during the campaign of 1793, the officers telling the civilians everything they are doing and not concealing their distaste for the war.

The larger towns have the best clubs. The three hundred members of the club at Mainz receive 24 political newspapers, 23 other newspapers, and 41 French and German periodicals. The club at Frankfort-on-Main has been the meeting-place for foreigners visiting the Fair since 1774. At Ulm the club subscribes to all the principal newspapers and leading periodicals. At Strasbourg Goethe introduces Jung-Stilling to the Society of Fine Sciences, where "the finest books" are read; and Stilling sends the first part of his memoirs to it in 1772. Jung-Stilling, indeed, owes his career in part to support from these groups; in 1775 he lectures to the club at Schoenthal, whose members meet on Wednesdays and club together to buy books. He sends papers to the Rittersburg Academy, which earn him a reputation, and a professorship in 1778. The meetings are not always devoted wholly to serious matters. At Erlangen the membership of the reading club founded in 1788 includes some hundred university professors, nobles, and students; they meet once a week in winter and twice a month in summer in their sumptuous salons, their smoking rooms or their grand dining room, in which excellent meals are served. There is reading, card-playing, and even occasionally dancing, so that the ladies, who are usually excluded from the club, can also be entertained.

3

The Economic System
of the Aufklärung

Prussian Mercantilism

The economic system prevailing in Prussia as in all other European countries at the end of the eighteenth century was mercantilism. Theoretically, it was designed to ensure a favorable balance of trade and the enrichment of a state by the consequent increase in its stock of specie. Frederick II explained this on several occasions, notably in his *Essay on the Forms of Government and the Duties of Sovereigns.*

If a country is to remain prosperous, it is absolutely necessary for it to have a favorable balance of trade; if it pays more for imports than it earns by exports, it must necessarily grow poorer year by year. . . . It can prevent this drain by manufacturing all its own raw materials, by processing foreign materials and thereby attracting foreign workers into the country, and by keeping manufacturing costs low enough to acquire markets abroad. . . . We have now to speak of the best means of maintaining at all times an adequate store of the foodstuffs which a society must have if it is to remain prosperous. The first thing necessary is to see that the land is carefully tilled, that all potentially arable land is cleared, and that the herds are increased so as to furnish a more abundant supply of butter, cheese, and manure; the second is to keep an exact account of the number of bushels of the various sorts of grain harvested in good, middling, and bad years, to deduct the amount needed for domestic consumption, and then to calculate how much of the surplus may be allowed to be exported or how far the crop falls short of what is required for domestic consumption and must therefore be procured elsewhere.

Every sovereign who truly cares for the public weal is bound to provide himself with well-stocked granaries to supplement bad harvests and to make provision against famine. [*Oeuvres* IX, 206–7.]

In Prussia the system in reality amounts to a managed economy, and it is this that differentiates it from the systems in other countries. This is something more than increasing the revenues of the state simply by prohibiting the import of certain luxury articles or trying to produce them domestically, inasmuch as every area of the economy is brought under direct state control; private enterprise is entirely governed by directives from the state, which at times stimulates it, often supplements it, and sometimes even curbs it.

No single ruler devised this system all at once and abruptly introduced it into his states. It is quite wrong to attribute to Frederick the Great any logical and consistent organization of a system. On the contrary, the most characteristic trait of the Prussian economic system is the way in which its component elements emerged one after another between 1661 and 1786 under pressure of immediate imperatives. The major innovations were the work of Frederick's predecessors, and he had only to complete and coordinate them. They were not motivated invariably by economic considerations, but far more by the desire for an efficient army and a regular income than by any mercantile theory. When we look at this system more closely, therefore, we find a remarkable complex of political and economic institutions, and we see that the country in which economic and mercantilist regulation appears to be more rigorous than in any other is in fact the country in which that regulation is the least purely mercantile.

Immediately after the Thirty Years' War, the Great Elector sought by every means in his power to restore his devastated lands to prosperity. He attracted foreign immigrants to repopulate them. He introduced the economic institutions of the Dutch, whose wealth was proverbial. What he most needed was soldiers and money. The excise became the keystone of the Prussian system, for it brought in a regular revenue. This internal customs system affected both economic and domestic policy, since it became the main form of taxation. It was introduced in some of the towns in 1667 in imitation of the Dutch, became state-administered in 1688, and was thereafter extended to every province in the kingdom. After 1709 it was universal. Frederick II and his successor, Frederick William II, established it in the conquered territories. In a state as fragmented as Prussia it would have been hard to collect duties at the frontiers of all the dozens of enclaves; collecting the duty on raw materials at the town gates had the same effect. This meant, however, that raw materials might not be worked up in the country, for, if they were, the peasants would have had an undue advantage.

The effect of the system is therefore to separate the towns completely from the country. The guilds are reorganized and brought under governmental control between 1732 and 1735. Craftsmen are compelled to congregate in the towns, which must therefore be surrounded by some sort of enclosure, even if no more than a pale. Materials produced in rural areas may not be processed till they have passed through the excise. The few exceptions to the guild monopoly that are permitted are the craftsmen essential to the villages and estates. As late as 1787, an ordinance specifies once again that only one carpenter, one blacksmith, one wheelwright and one tailor may ply their trade in a village; and the tailor must in many cases double as verger or schoolmaster.

Though the tariffs vary from district to district, the excise everywhere acts as a filter. Its agents are stationed at the town gates and keep a record of incomings and outgoings. Frederick is thus able to keep accurate statistics. He is able to see, oversee, and foresee. His tax collectors play an important part in determining prices, since the rate of excise is one of the components of price. In addition, his tax inspectors supervise the craftsmen's output.

The excise, however, is only a partial remedy for the endemic plague which reduces the customs duties levied at the frontiers to relative insignificance; though the towns are "protected islands in an ocean of free trade" and contraband is almost unknown in them, smugglers supply the rural areas with all the prohibited articles, since, once goods have passed the frontier, they do not have to go through any further controls in the open country.

By raising or lowering the rate of excise the government simultaneously procures relatively large revenues and controls the flow of goods, fosters or restrains domestic production, and promotes or restricts the growth of large-scale trade. Every economic measure it takes has immediate repercussions on its finances. The connection between tariff policy and the budget is so close that it is not possible to reform one without reforming the other; the state cannot, for example, introduce free trading within the kingdom without setting up an entirely new fiscal system and thereby causing a social revolution. This inevitable interrelationship explains why the liberal theories generally accepted abroad reached Prussia so late, because they seemed to be much harder to put into effect there, and why all attempts by the state to relax its hold on the country invariably came to nothing, because they would have been bound to provoke a budgetary crisis.

The Great Elector encouraged manufacturing in his own territory in order to avoid importing foreign goods. It was Frederick William I, however, who was mainly responsible for creating a Prussian industry. His chief concern was for the requirements of the army. Money and men was the watchword passed down from each sovereign to his successor; we find exactly the same motive underlying the humanitarian discourses of the Philosopher King and the coarse sarcasms of the Drill Sergeant. Frederick William founded the State Depot (*Lagerhaus*) at Berlin at the very beginning of his reign; it supplied the weavers with wool, so that poor artisans who could not build up stocks when prices were low were protected when they rose. He then opened a state factory to make uniforms for his army. He imposed heavy duties on foreign cloth and went so far as to prohibit its import from all countries east of the Weser in 1718–19, though the Westphalian provinces, being scattered, were inevitably left outside the system. He also prohibited the export of wool and induced foreign weavers to settle in Prussia. He exempted domestic linen and cloth from the excise in 1722. In 1723 he instituted an export bounty in order to supply uniforms to part of the Russian army. Everyone was compelled to weave by order of the king, the peasants in their cottages, the poor in the earliest workhouses especially set up for this purpose, and young craftsmen in special schools, in which the government ensured that they were instructed in the most up-to-date methods. Frederick II tightened the ban on exports of wool and imports of cloth and intensified sheep-breeding, but it was not till 1786, shortly before his death, that he brought in merinos from Spain to replace the degenerate Prussian stock.

Iron too received attention. Frederick William imposed duties ranging from 25 percent to 100 percent on imports of nails, axes, sickles, and other tools in common use; foreign wares had to be more expensive than the domestic.

Here again Frederick II applied similar principles. He began taxing and prohibiting imports even before Prussia was self-sufficient. It was not till almost the end of his reign that the mines, managed by Heinitz on behalf of the state, produced fairly adequate supplies of ore; the Magdeburg copper deposits produced up to 250 tons a year; the abandoned lead mines at Tarnowitz were put back into production. The coal of Silesia and the Rhineland gradually replaced wood and was now used for heating barracks. The Magdeburg salt works even began to export.

An industrial policy alone cannot guarantee the army self-sufficiency. Frederick William I's major Corn Ordinances completed the policing of the economy. The import of Polish grain was prohibited as early as 1723; in 1725 prohibitive duties were imposed on grain from Saxe-Mecklenburg. The duties are relaxed only occasionally thereafter when the harvest in Prussia is bad, for Prussia can and must supply its own needs. The import of foreign wheat is forbidden in the central provinces and Silesia; a special permit is required to export part of the harvest and is granted only in good years. The western provinces, normally exporters of corn, enjoy more freedom, for they bring money into the country. Trading in corn remains free in the eastern regions, where the great estates produce large quantities of wheat, and it is here that the king makes huge purchases, especially when prices fall under pressure of Polish competition. From this source he fills the civil and military depots, a whole network of which covers his states. When the harvest is bad everywhere, the king may buy abroad, for the depots must be able to intervene to keep prices steady in the markets in the towns; when prices rise, the depot puts on the market the amount of corn required to restore the balance. In bad years the king orders a thorough search of private stocks and, when necessary, compels the owners to put them on the market before he applies to foreign sources of supply. He sometimes imposes a maximum price for corn and often fixes the price of bread.

The depots feed the army in wartime. The soldiers are paid in a currency whose value has not kept pace with the rise in the cost of living, which has continued throughout the century. They are therefore allowed to buy their corn from the depots in peacetime too at a special price based on their pay, known as the *Brotgeld*.

Prices in Prussia, then, may neither rise above the soldiers' rations allowance nor fall below the level of the tax for tenure (*Kammertaxe*) paid by the royal demesne peasants, for they raise the cash to pay it by selling their corn. The whole system ultimately rests on them, for they produce the grain and supply the army with its best recruits.

Frederick II thus finds the elements of a mercantile policy in existence when he comes to the throne; but it had been pursued by his predecessor only insofar as it related to the army and the budget. The excise, the regulation of corn prices and corn supplies, and the recruitment of peasants, together with the protection of the textile and metals industries are institutions which are no less political than economic, and their operation ensures the state both independence and stability. Frederick II gives them a new shape by carrying them further and extending them more widely. Whereas increasing freedom of trade promotes the rise of large-scale private capitalism in England and France, Prussia becomes the home of state capitalism.

State Capitalism

It may broadly be said that modern capitalism developed from large-scale trade. The profits from it enabled the merchant to set up as banker, to provide craftsmen working for him at home with raw materials supplied by him, or to set up workshops and become a manufacturer on his own account. In Prussia the state monopolizes large-scale trade. Frederick II builds canals to facilitate trading among his provinces and awards the Berlin and Magdeburg boatmen a monopoly of navigation on the Prussian rivers, thus excluding the Hamburg shippers. Freed by his conquest of Silesia from his dependence on Saxony, the great center of the textile industry, he tries to replace Saxon with Prussian textiles on foreign markets. He imposes heavy tolls on the Saxon textiles carried to Hamburg on the Elbe. Driven by fiscal necessity, he vastly increases this levy on goods in transit after 1763; in 1765 Saxon goods consigned to Poland or Hamburg pay up to 30 percent *ad valorem*. Several shipping companies are encouraged to free Prussia from dependence on the Dutch and English, but they are not generally successful. The *Seehandlungsgesellschaft*, granted the monopoly of the Baltic trade in tallow and salt in 1772, prospers, however. A marine assurance company excludes the Hamburg brokers from the Prussian market.

The profits from trade flow into the coffers of the state through the excise and the customs. It is the state, therefore, that has to create the tools of large-scale capitalism, the banks and industries, for no private persons are able to found them with their own resources. In the period after the Seven Years' War there is not a single professional banker in Prussia; the government has to found the Berlin Discount and Loans Bank (*Giro-Diskonto und Leihbank*) in 1765. It hopes thereby "to make commerce more prosperous and subsequently to expand it . . . by increasing the circulation of money." It gets no support from the merchants, for they are too poor to put up the capital; it is the government which pays in the 400,000 thalers—raised to 8,800,000 by the end of the reign—required for the operations of the Berlin house and its subsidiaries at Breslau, Königsberg, Magdeburg, Stettin, Elbing, Frankfort-on-Oder, Emden, and Cleves. They advance money to merchants and industrialists and pay depositors interest at 2 or 3 percent, in accordance with their social circumstances; orphans and the poor are granted a higher rate than the wealthy.

The creation of credit cannot in itself, however, convert merchants into manufacturers. They are not adventurous enough to make money by laying out borrowed capital to their advantage; they fear a war, which might ruin them and cause them to fail to honor their commitments through no fault of their own. They are not accustomed to look beyond the limits of the local excise barrier, the provincial fair or the frontier customs post. But the government cannot wait until they eventually pluck up courage. Being the sole capitalist, it becomes an industrialist, just as it became a banker, for it cannot permit Prussian specie to be exported. In his Political Testament of 1752, Frederick II tells his nephew:

The basic principle of trade and manufacturing is to prevent money from being exported by making at home all the goods which were formerly procured abroad; they can be identified from the extracts from the excise registers which record all goods that enter and are sold in the state. By means of these extracts it is easy to determine what factories can be enlarged and what new manufactures can be established. Furthermore, money is prevented from going abroad in such large amounts as would go otherwise if one hunts down the sources of supply of wares which the country cannot dispense with and bargains for them on the spot; for goods which cost a crown at Hamburg may cost only a florin in Spain. . . . Manufactured goods in the natural course bring a great deal of ready cash into a state, and they could earn us far more since we border on Poland and Russia, countries which lack everything and are compelled to buy from the industry of their neighbors. These are reasons which should induce sovereigns to encourage manufacturers and merchants, either by granting them all kinds of privileges and immunities or by helping them with cash to mount large enterprises. [*Political Correspondence.*]

In the tables for industrial production at the end of the century we are struck by the large number of small enterprises. The state subsidizes many of the manufacturers to enable them to help it combat foreign goods. It advances them the money for new equipment or grants them a monopoly of production for varying periods, seldom less than ten years. The concern for increased production is likewise most remarkable. But while most of the statistics, even the fullest, record the progress in production, they do not give the slightest information on the number or size of the enterprises (full details in *Magazin* . . . , pt. 1, pp. 18–26; Korff, *Goethezeit*, 114 ff.). Prussian industry as a whole is made up of many small enterprises whose operations are governed quite as much by the state in its capacity as a large banker and a heavy purchaser as by the operation of the free market.

The king compels his subjects to set up factories. By his orders, cotton mills are installed in Berlin and in Silesia and are soon prosperous enough to need no further support from the state. By awarding the Berlin refinery the monopoly of sugar, Frederick frees his states from the tribute formerly paid to Hamburg. Although, like his father, he prefers private enterprise or the system of farming out contracts, which bring in a guaranteed revenue, to the more hazardous system of state monopoly concessions, he does not hesitate to found factories himself when no private person comes forward; he establishes out of his privy purse the knife and scissors factory at Eberswalde, the paper mill at Spechtshausen, and, in 1781, the clock and watch factory at Berlin.

He does not confine himself to providing necessities, but goes further to put an end to the import of luxury articles. Mercantile policy is always in favor of trying to produce these articles locally, for they are costly and their acquisition drains the country of specie. Though Prussia is not at all suited to a silk-weaving industry, he introduces one and continues his father's efforts to acclimatize the mulberry at Potsdam. In 1777 he prohibits the import of silk textiles and ribbons. His perseverance is rewarded; silk production rises from some 50 pounds in 1751 to 13,500 in 1784. Though after his death the worldwide crisis caused by the failure of the Italian silk crop in 1787 and 1788 hits this industry very hard, the disappearance of France from the market after 1789 enables the Prussian industry to recover speedily and to become an exporter. But in 1796, Lyon resumes its place on the international market, and the Italian campaign gives France control of the raw material. The Prussian industry is ruined and cannot absorb the unemployed hands, whose numbers grow progressively till the collapse in 1806.

Frederick II also manages to deprive Saxony of the near monopoly of porcelain it had enjoyed; but he runs into an unforeseen difficulty. He soon has many imitators; the pettiest German princeling must have a porcelain factory of his own, and the Berlin factory stifles under the bulk of its own output. To remedy this the king compels some of his subjects to load themselves up with articles for which they have no slightest use and of which they can rid themselves, even at a loss, only beyond the frontiers.

Frederick induces clockmakers from Neuchâtel to come to Berlin in 1765.

But the factory managed by A.L. Huguenin is not a success. The twenty-two workers he has managed to recruit—after promising to bring in a hundred—rebel; some lack work, others desert their jobs. The magnificent clocks find no purchasers, for they are too expensive, as, too, are the watches, the movements for which still have to be imported. Truitte and Dan of Geneva resume the business in 1770 on a smaller scale. The king grants them subsidies and privileges, but the Berlin clock merchants obtain a reduction in the duties on imported clocks! Truitte then proposes to create in Prussia a rural labor force to make the movements as cheaply as in Switzerland. The project seems promising, and the king accordingly settles twenty-one families of watchmakers at Friedrichsthal, near Oranienburg; they are to teach Prussian peasants the craft and to supply the Berlin factory with parts. But this is a lengthy undertaking. The Prussian clocks, having to absorb the high price of foreign labor, will obviously cost more than their competitors' for several years. The king fails to secure them the local market, and such small articles as watches are very easy to smuggle. Huguenot Hovelac, succeeding Truitte, who died in 1783, tries in vain. He registers defeat in 1793; neither can Prussia furnish the kind of customers he needs for his magnificent clocks, nor can he make them cheaply enough for export. The undertaking does not survive the crisis of 1806.

At the time of the king's death the duties on all articles manufactured abroad are so heavy that it is practically impossible to import them except as contraband. Financially the results are excellent, for whereas the trade balance in 1740 showed a deficit of 500,000 thalers, in 1786 there is a surplus of 3 millions. Agriculture, however, has been sacrificed to industry. To enable industry to keep its prices down and to compete abroad, the king prohibits raising the price of raw materials. Producers of flax, tobacco, and leather complain to no avail. The export of wool is prohibited, while the import of foreign wool is permitted because the Prussian cloth manufacturers must have ample raw material; there is no objection, therefore, to a rise in its price, but how can the peasants buy the manufactured goods?

The extreme case of porcelain fully illustrates the artificiality of setting up a completely new industry. Where essential goods are concerned, the king can regulate successfully, but how can the peasants, who are not permitted to charge more for their produce, the craftsmen, whose wages are kept low so that costs are not overburdened by them, and the burghers, who are excluded from large-scale international trade by the export and import prohibitions, buy the costly brocades, chiming clocks, and fine porcelains produced by the new factories? By retarding the formation of private capital, the government's policy of a managed economy is bound to prove wholly self-defeating. The correct course would be to adjust production to consumption, influence all the components of price formation, and achieve genuine autarky. The king, however, has no notion of doing this, and the budget is too tight to allow of reforms likely to cause a deficit during the transitional period. In reality, there never is any such thing as an "economic policy" in Prussia; there is no economic policy, but simply military and budgetary imperatives met by blind application of mercantile expedients as ineffectual and outdated as tax-farming and the venality of offices in France. If revenue falls off or the state's needs increase, the only recourse is to tighten the screw slightly; toward the end of the reign a monopoly of sugar, coffee and tobacco is set up, extremely lucrative articles because they weigh light in carriage and are in great demand—yet another source of profit from which private merchants are excluded. As it is, the merchants have been complaining since 1766 about the reform whereby the administration of the excise and customs has been withdrawn from the General Directory and entrusted to a Frenchman, de Launay, and several hundred French officials, with whom it is impossible to make deals.

This system is continued under Frederick the Great's successors. Criticisms by philanthropists always come up against the same objection, the unity of the economic and the political systems. To satisfy the lower classes an attempt is made to abolish the unpopular ban on the import of certain foodstuffs (beers, wines, fruit, semolina) and the excise on some articles which the kingdom does not produce in large enough quantities, but these petty reforms upset the balance of the budget. After the abolition of the coffee, tobacco, and sugar monopoly in 1786, Frederick William II is compelled to tax them and to collect a fresh excise duty on flour. The abolition of the duties on silk, cotton, and hides is likewise followed by the creation of a special tax to be paid by manufacturers using these raw materials, for any revenue lost must always be replaced. Prices do not fall, therefore, and smuggling becomes increasingly lucrative. Not only tobacco and coffee now, but, around Halberstadt and Magdeburg, stockings and caps are smuggled in as contraband in such large quantities that the domestic industry is threatened with extinction. Mercantilism is a two-edged tool; while it prevents domestic specie from escaping over the frontiers, it incites foreign countries to raise, by way of imitation or reprisal, barriers which hamper the inflow of gold and silver.

Economic policy perhaps needs changing, but the official system in Prussia is too closely bound up with the basic institutions of the state. To substitute freedom for regulation would entail finding a new basis of taxation and a new method of recruiting for the army. Free trade would require a positive revolution, so that clear-sighted ministers such as Stein, who abolishes the internal customs in 1804, dare not propose more than reforms of detail.

The industrial policy causes a real crisis of overproduction at the end of the century. Looking at it, one is sometimes tempted to conclude that the system broke down completely; yet it is undeniable that governmental intervention gave Prussia a large-scale industry several decades before it would have been brought into being by private enterprise.

It is not intervention as such that is responsible for the setback, but rather the way in which it is practiced. If kings had concerned themselves with the needs of all their subjects and had not concentrated solely on the needs of the army, on the imperatives of a budget which paid no heed to social realities, and on the movements of specie, they would have subsidized few luxury industries and would have reduced the price of prime necessities. The only industries to prosper are linen- and cloth-weaving and the small metallurgical enterprises. If the rulers had adjusted production to consumption, influenced the components of price formation and taken population movement into consideration, they would have achieved something more intelligent and more durable. They would have rationalized the methods of producing prime necessities instead of ruining themselves by making articles which nobody needed. The table published by Count Hertzberg in 1785 shows this disproportion between the number of craftsmen working for a limited local market and the subsidized industry with a far larger output, but no demand corresponding in any degree to the supply. There were at that time 80,000 makers of linen textiles, each of them producing the equivalent of some 138 thalers yearly, as against 6,000 silk weavers producing 500 thalers and 700 porcelain and china makers producing more than 2,850 thalers!

The alternative between intervention and freedom did not necessarily arise; the real question in Prussia should rather have been between intervention well directed and intervention ill directed. The enlightened despots could have created an autarky rather than a mercantile system. They would thus have spared their economy the paradoxical situation in which a crisis of overproduction in large-scale industry existed side by side with a great increase in population and in the demand for goods for current consumption.

The Traditional Society

Prussian society is divided into three quite separate orders, living such entirely different lives that they hardly ever mingle. They live side by side, each of them cherishing its own conventions, just as each of them dresses, eats, drinks, and speaks in its own way.

There is perhaps no country in Europe in which it is so difficult as in our Germany to obtain in intercourse with people the general approbation of all classes in all regions and of all ranks, to feel at home in every circle without effort, without falsity, without becoming suspect and without suffering the consequences, and to make the effect one wishes on prince, noble and burgher alike, on merchant and cleric, without arousing their displeasure, for undoubtedly nowhere else does there prevail so great a diversity in the tone of intercourse, in the manner of bringing up children, and in opinions, religious or other; nowhere else is there such a vast variety of subjects with which every class of people in every province concerns itself. The reason is the interest which each German state takes in so many diverse aspects of other German states and foreign countries, the variety of the bonds between them and each particular foreign state, and the very marked distinction between class and class; for inveterate conventions, education, and, to some extent too, the political constitution have drawn between them boundaries sharper than those in many other countries. Is there any other country in which the notion of quarterings of nobility has such a fundamental political and moral influence on ideas and culture as in Germany? Any other country in which the merchants have less influence on the life of the other classes? (I should perhaps make an exception for the imperial cities.) In what other country do the courtiers as a body form a completely separate class, within which only persons of particular birth and rank can make their career, as is the case in the entourage of most of our princes? [Knigge, *Umgang*, 29-30.]

Fifteen years later Madame de Staël similarly notes:

The relations between the classes in France were such as to promote a certain savoir-vivre, a self-control, and the conventions of social inter-course. There was no sharp cleavage between rank and rank, and social pretention was incessantly busy in the undefined interval between them, in which everyone might either gain or lose ground. Nothing was finally and irrevocably settled, neither the rights of the Third Estate nor those of the Parlements, the aristocracy, nor even the power of the monarch himself. . . .

In Germany everyone is in his appointed place, with his rank and post, and there is no call for the ingenious turn of phrase, the aside, the hint in order to give expression to any advantages of birth or title which one man believes he may assert against his neighbor. High society in Germany is simply the court; in France it was all those who could stand on an equal footing with the court, and anyone could hope to do that, just as anyone had to dread that he would never be able to. The result was that everyone tried to acquire the manners of the court. In Germany an academic degree earned one the entrée; in France a lapse of good taste earned one the congé, and everyone was far more anxious to adopt the manners and tone of high society than to recommend himself by his merits once he had entered it. [Staël, *De l'Allemagne* pt. 1, chap. 11.]

These observations apply to Prussia no less than to the other German states, even though the Aufklärung in Prussia tried to base a new society on personal merit rather than birth. "I cannot but add a few words in commendation of the nobility," Frederick II writes in 1768.

I have always distinguished it and treated it with consideration because it provides officers for the army and suitable persons for all the great offices of state. I have helped it to retain the ownership of its estates, and I have done my utmost to prevent commoners from buying up the properties of nobles. My reason for doing so has been that once commoners become landowners, they have a prescriptive right to office. Most of them have a vulgar outlook and make bad officers; they are not fit for any employment. [*Political Correspondence*, 129–36.]

The General Code issued in 1794 confirms the nobility in all its privileges, such as the sole right to own manorial estates, to be liable solely to the jurisdiction of the highest court in their province, and to be exempt from the "contribution" in the country, from the excise in the towns, and from billeting. Since the nobles may not derogate from their rank by becoming manufacturers or merchants and may not contract misalliances, they either farm their estates or enter the king's service.

Their estates are very large. It is estimated that they farm one-quarter of the arable land directly and two-thirds indirectly through tenant farmers with holdings on precarious tenure. They are sole masters of their manorial estates. They are vested with and exercise patrimonial jurisdiction on them, collect their feudal dues and services, and have plenary rights over church and school. The state interferes only in exceptional cases where depopulation might impair recruiting for the army.

There are too few adequate studies on the nobility and the feudal system in the eighteenth century to give a really detailed notion how the system works in practice, but we can get some idea of the institution itself. In the Rhineland and throughout southern and western Germany the nobles are in much the same position as they are in France. The poor quality of the land they farm themselves, the fact that feudal dues paid in cash have remained at the same level, as well as the general growth of the population, have impoverished the nobles, who become absentees early in the century, many of them seeking careers at the court of the local prince or in the service of the king of Prussia, the emperor, or the tsar. East of the Elbe, however, the nobles keep their prestige and traditional status.

Here they are still great landowners. In the Electoral Mark they own one half of the land outright and extract feudal dues in cash, kind, or services from one-seventh more. Until 1799 a noble was exempt from all taxes; but after that date the government collects duties on the import of luxury articles and sugar and coffee and on the export of crops. A noble can obtain loans at the very low rate of 4 percent plus one-quarter of one percent for the costs from an institute set up especially to help him operate his estates (the *Pfandbriefinstitut*). He is the overlord of the whole countryside, for the authority of the Prussian state stops with the rural commissioner (*Landrat*); the royal administration is organized and centralized only as far as the *Kreis*, or circle, a subdivision of the province. Over the Provincial War and Domains Chamber and the local court of law (*Regierung*) there is no agent of the state in the country other than the *Landrat*, who is invariably a noble.

Nominated by the king from a panel of three candidates selected by the provincial diets, which are assemblies of nobles, he is wholly devoted to the interests of his fellow nobles. He keeps the registry of mortgages, and from the height of his authority he supervises the activities of the many local dignitaries, such as the irrigation officers, the directors of public welfare, and the organizers of the fire brigades, all of whom are also nobles.

The objection raised by the Aufklärung that the nobles' titles and privileges have long ceased to correspond to any useful function is far less pertinent as regards the country than as regards the towns. Indeed, their privileges too are far more remunerative in the country. Both their influence and their income are enhanced by their powers of patrimonial jurisdiction, criminal as well as civil, their patronage of church livings, and their control over the village schools. They enjoy the virtually unfettered disposal of the chapters' very lucrative prebends and benefices. In the Electoral Mark the cathedral prebends, which are shared equally between the king and the chapters, are worth 2,000 thalers a year, the equivalent of the emoluments of a very high official or a minister of state. The least-endowed canonry is worth 700 thalers.

These appreciable perquisites provide a very decent living for many younger sons, so that there is no question of any crisis in the Prussian nobility such as that which occurs in the French aristocracy at about the same date. Of all the orders of society the nobility seems to be the most stable and the most faithful to its traditions. It suffers, however, from a dual malaise, social and moral. The Aufklärung, with its universalism and rationalism, tends to detach the noble from his country estate and bring him into the town, where he no longer enjoys most of these advantages. With larger expenses and less scope for command, he guards his privileges jealously, stands on his rank, and asserts his right to preempt offices for which his upbringing has by no means fitted him. The increase in the population, on the other hand, makes life more difficult for large families which are no longer decimated by epidemics or wars. The right of primogeniture does not exist in these regions; the ancient family bonds remain, by virtue of which all the descendants of a common male ancestor, the agnates, must live on the same estate, which must therefore be large enough to satisfy their needs.

They farm it in usufruct only and must take in all those who return to the fold after failing to make a career in distant parts, in the army, in the civil service, or abroad. This community, the *Lehnverband*, imposes very strict rules on all its members. They may not mortgage or sell a property without the consent of all the agnates, and any loans they contract must be recorded in a special register (the *Ritterschaftliches Registrarbuch*) supervised by the suzerain.

Owing to the increase in the population, however, they must almost inevitably run into debt. The members of the family who do not reside on the estate, and would find it hard to subsist on it because it has become too small for them, demand their portion of the inheritance in cash, as do the daughters when they marry. To satisfy them the owner goes into debt, which is easier for him now that the suzerain has waived his right of supervision. In 1777 the king offers to release his vassals from most of their feudal obligations in return for a fairly moderate fee, the *Lehnpferdgeld*. The other feudal overlords follow suit, and the chain of feudal obligations is snapped. The manorial estates thus become freehold properties and so are more easily encumbered. The customary form of inheritance, however, continues. Frederick II's efforts to induce his vassals to create entails and turn their estates into trusts to be inherited by only one son, the others receiving only a small cash indemnity, fail to make headway against principles of equity which are too deeply entrenched to be overcome. Estates are still subdivided or pledged, but those who lend the money on them are still uneasy. Even when they have taken every precaution, even though the king's permission is no longer required owing to the conversion to freehold, and even though the agnates' consent has been duly recorded, it may well happen that one of the agnates may not have signed the register either because of bad faith or because he was overlooked, and he may suddenly come forward, bring an action, and seize the pledged property. It is stipulated in a royal edict of 1723 that the agnates' consent shall not be required where encumbrance is conducive to the improvement of the estate; but this leaves ample room for litigation.

Finckenstein, a contemporary writer, estimates that in 1799 the manorial estates are encumbered up to one-half of their value. The lenders press for redemption of the pledge, and the rise in land values and the attractions of urban life impel the owners in the same direction. But the legal provisions forbidding the sale of a manorial estate to a burgher are extremely strict, whereas it is precisely the burghers who make the best offers; under the ordinance of 1750, royal permission is required for such transfers; that of 1762 prohibits a burgher who has purchased a manorial estate from selling it to another burgher; and the ordinance of 1775 states that a burgher may not succeed to a manorial estate owned by a commoner if there is any other claimant to the succession who is a noble; it also refuses burghers the hunting rights, marks of distinction, and seat on the provincial diet appertaining to manorial estates. Frederick William II and Frederick William III, however, readily give permission to sell. Even when they refuse it, it is easy to circumvent the law; it is possible to "rent" on very long lease, with the stipulation that the rent shall be paid in a single instalment, or an estate can be sold to a nominee who is a noble. This accounts for the fact that 13 percent of the manorial estates in the Electoral Mark are held by burghers in 1800.

The absentee nobles seek to enter the royal service. Around 1800 only 27 percent of the landowners in the Mark have not at one time served in the army or the civil service; but increasingly the nobles try to remain in the service rather than merely spend some time in it. They insist on retaining their nobiliary title. They no longer discard it when, exceptionally, they derogate from their rank to enter a profession, and they renew it if an ancestor renounced it to engage in a burgher occupation. As they usually have some private means, many of them are content with quite minor offices, virtual sinecures but barely remunerated; in the *Addressbücher* a vast number of aristocratic names are to be found in minor posts in the civil service. If the nobles try to earn a living, however, they run up against either Polish nobles or French refugees or else burghers with a better education than theirs. Greater attention is therefore paid to their education.

In the great families the young nobles often have good tutors, who open their minds and accompany them on long tours through Germany or abroad. Schleiermacher, for example, tutors the Counts Dohna. Count Schoen's instructor is that remarkable person, Berger, whose influence on the young Romantics at Jena is so impressive; Schoen's father consults Kant about his son's studies when attending his courses in philosophy and Kraus's courses in economics at Königsberg. Young Schoen, as a student of sixteen, makes friends with able men such as Woeysch, the future clergyman, and Fichte. After passing the "greater" examination which admits him to the civil service at the age of twenty-three in 1796 he travels through the Prussian provinces and pays a lengthy visit to England. Prepared by three and a half years of well-spent vacations, he makes an excellent official in the War and Domains Chamber and later collaborates with Stein and Hardenberg in the reforms they bring in after 1807. (Schoen, *Aus den Papieren. . .* , I, 3–28.)

But such cases are the exception—successful careers that are made possible only by the possession of ample means and useful contacts. Alongside a few individuals such as Marwitz, Schoen, and Humboldt, countless nobles spend their lives in the army, at court, or on civil service boards without leaving the slightest trace of what they thought or did. We know as little about them as we know about their brothers who remained in the country. A noble residing at court can hope for the prince's favor in the form of pensions, sinecures, or embassies, but court life at Berlin is by no means as brilliant, as luxurious, and as filled with intrigue as it is at Weimar or Dresden. It is often extremely boring, and the atmosphere of the capital sometimes drives noble lords, wearying of etiquette and official hauteur, to cross the gap between them and the enlightened burghers who lead a more interesting life. If a noble enters the army, he is certain of promotion to the higher ranks, since commoners are almost wholly excluded from them. If he is educated well enough to pass the entrance examination and then enters the civil service or even the law, he will likewise rise to the highest posts, for there are often more of these than there are nobles capable of filling them. This, however, is the utmost he can do; for a noble may not now renounce his rank to become a manufacturer or merchant.

Conscious of his superiority, he jealously cherishes his precedence and enforces it. He is meticulous about his titles—Lord Chesterfield mentions that a letter was returned to him unopened because one title out of twenty had been omitted in the address—and would regard it an insult to his honor if he had to eat at the same table or enter the same drawing room as a burgher.

The nobility, however, remains the first order in the kingdom. It does not compete with the church, as in France. It takes in little new blood, for in Prussia the holding of office does not ennoble. Frederick II confers titles only in exceptional cases. His successor, it is true, sells patents of nobility for 400 thalers plus a fee of 53 thalers and distributes five times as many as his uncle; but these titles are little esteemed in society; the older nobles who are also great landowners easily obtain the coveted titles of *Graf* (count) and *Freiherr* (baron). Class distinction in Prussia remains more marked than in the western countries.

The burgher, however, observes that after the conquest of Poland there are still only nine thousand manorial estates in the Prussian state, with its population of some ten million. He lives shut up in his town, in which several different societies rub shoulders without mingling, hardly less exclusive with respect to each other than the nobility with respect to the middle classes. Workmen drearily toiling at home, craftsmen bound by their guilds' financial regulations, shopkeepers extracting meager profits from the jaws of the royal excise and the municipal taxes, whose teeth threaten at any time to grind them to pieces, intellectuals distraught by the competition of their too numerous fellow intellectuals, wholesalers and town councillors proud of their armorial bearings, officials ranged by rank and relatively well salaried —all of them move and have their being within the narrow plot within which the excise pens their class.

The most wretched condition is that of the peasants, who grow the grain and supply the army with its best recruits. As their circumstances vary from province to province, the great Rural Code of 1794 requires each province to draft a provincial code to govern relations between landlord and peasant. The East Prussian Code was promulgated in 1802, but the others had not been prepared by the time of the disaster at Jena. The inquiry conducted by the War and Domains Chamber, however, supplies reasonably accurate information. The main features, more important than the vast number of local divergences, are those which distinguish the eastern areas from the lands west of the Elbe and from Silesia. West of the Elbe, as throughout western Germany, many of the landlords are absentees living on their revenues; they have little capital; they do not themselves farm their estates and they seldom exercise their rights of justice and police. Their peasants are usually freeholders. As owners of their land or tenant farmers they perform their feudal services, pay their feudal dues and personally are completely free. The few "subjects" (*Eigenbehörige*) may acquire holdings and bequeath half of them to their wives and children. The landlord takes only half, and any of the children who wish to settle away from the estate are thus able to buy themselves out.

The nearer the Elbe, the harsher the peasant's lot. In the provinces of Magdeburg and Halberstadt the lord collects his right of mortmain on a cow or a horse. In the Old Mark a peasant must obtain the lord's permission before he may marry.

East of the Elbe the lord is suzerain of his estate and exercises his rights of police and justice. Freeholders are rare. The peasant "protected" by the lord (the *Einlieger* or *Schutzuntertan*) owes him feudal services, but may leave the estate, as distinct from the serf who is bound to the soil. Peasants who own their land, for which they pay a rent (*Erbpacht*), may bequeath it to anyone they wish. If they do not own their land, they pay a quit-rent (*Erbzins*) over and above the ordinary rent and must let their landlord decide which of their children is to inherit. The country nobleman is only bound to ensure his peasants a livelihood, but may evict any tenant who does not own his land; he can even evict him if his work is not satisfactory. The farm laborers (*Insleute*) are a class intermediate between freeholders and "subjects," and their lot is particulary wretched. Employed and paid a wage by the noble, they are given a cottage and a few acres of land, which can be taken away from them at any time; but they may move away when they wish. At the end of the century they constitute the greater part of the population of East Prussia. The increase in their numbers is undoubtedly the most important social phenomemon in the countryside. The statistics for the rural population of Pomerania give a total of 356,765 in 1795 and 361,616 in 1797. The *Insleute* account for 17,191 and 18,392 as against 16,257 and 16,303 peasants and 4,691 and 4,747 shepherds or cowherds. Farm laborers form, therefore, by far the majority and their numbers have risen by 7 percent in two years, whereas the number of freeholders has barely increased. But Pomerania is not entirely rural; besides the craftsmen working in the country there are more than 150,000 glass and metal workers.

It is something of a paradox that there should be so many underemployed laborers living side by side with settled "subjects" bound to the soil by rigorous legislation, as though labor were still scarce. The landlords, however, do not realize how paradoxical this situation is, for they are interested only in a feudal peasantry which will enable them to farm their estates more intensively. From early in the century they tend to make the feudal services more onerous and to enforce their feudal rights more strictly. The *Erbuntertanen*, hereditarily subject peasants, may not move away without permission; the lord may pursue them, and it is a criminal offence for a neighbor to shelter them. They may not marry without permission; their children may learn a trade or craft only with their lord's consent. At the age of twenty-four they have to settle at the place on the estate assigned to them. If there is no room and they wish to settle elsewhere, they must obtain the lord's permission, and he is entitled to take them into his household service instead. All children owe him domestic service, except for one boy and one girl in each family who may remain with their parents. Domestic service lasts for five years in East Prussia and is paid at a standard rate. In Lower Silesia service is for an indefinite period, and for the first three years domestic servants are paid almost nothing. Domestic service ends when the boys are settled and the girls are married.

Feudal services vary a great deal. Frederick II is unable to limit the feudal corvées, six days a week in the East and in Silesia, two to four days in the West. This does not mean that the peasant works continuously for his lord, but he must always be available. He farms the estate, clears the forests, and erects the necessary buildings. He drives the lord's carriage, carts his harvests, and runs his errands.

In the new Polish provinces the peasant is to all intents and purposes a slave. His feudal services are subject to no regulation; a contract, where there is one, is binding on the peasant alone. His master may sell him separately from his land.

The peasant's position in Silesia is rather better defined. The king is anxious for popularity in his newly won province, and he can act as he likes there without fear of collective opposition, since the diets of nobles (*Stände*) have never met and the peasants in Silesia seem to be more intelligent and better aware of their rights than elsewhere.

The king therefore gives orders in 1784 that the rights and duties of both lord and peasant shall be precisely stipulated in a definitive document, the *urbarium*, for each estate, thereby putting an end to litigation and enabling the two orders to live in peace. But only 342 of 6,600 manorial estates receive their constitution between 1799 and 1805. In the first place, the local subcommissions responsible to the main commissions at Breslau and Glogau are wholly in the hands of the nobility, which places every sort of obstruction in their way, and, in the second, once Frederick II is dead, the central administration at Berlin ceases to support Governor von Hoym's efforts to carry out the project. In 1799, Chancellor von Goldbeck adopts the principle that the *urbaria* shall be prepared only if the peasants demand them.

The documents collected by the commissions furnish a great deal of information on the contemporary management of estates. Since the end of the seventeenth century the lords have suffered losses because, as the fixed quit-rent has brought in practically nothing in cash owing to the rise in prices, they have been trying to impose feudal services of man and beast on the peasants and to restrict their freedom of movement. The *urbaria* oblige the peasants to work for the lord for an average of two or three days a week. Domestic service is also due.

Farming is traditional and intensive with compulsory rotation to fallow and the right of pasturage and estovers one day a week in the lord's forest.

The villages are constituted under the mayor (*Schulze*), an official often appointed by the lord, sometimes on a hereditary basis and always salaried, and contains a church, a school, a herdsman's shelter, and a poorhouse. Besides the mayor there are usually two sworn assistants, a schoolmaster who acts as a public letter writer, a watchman, and a messenger (*Bote*).

The ancient feudal services are everywhere maintained, therefore. There is no trace of an agrarian reform such as is taking place at the time in the west.

Besides the feudal dues he owes the lord, the peasant has to pay tithes to the church; and to the king, in addition to the "contribution"—the main direct tax, which brings in some 2 million thalers a year—he owes military service, a period not taken into account in reckoning his feudal service. In many cases, these dues and taxes devour more than half his earnings.

The king is concerned with the peasant solely as taxpayer and recruit; he is very reluctant to dry up the main source of his military power, but he has also to accommodate the nobility, from whom he draws his officers and officials. Frederick II manages to institutionalize the traditional relations between peasant and landlord. He forbids feudal landlords to settle any more peasants on their estates, so that holdings can be kept at their existing size; he forbids them to annex holdings to the estate reserves, and to commute peasants' obligations, so that there will be no reduction in the number of recruits needed for regiments whose muster rolls are filled from a local quota; but his attempts to limit the duration of feudal services can be enforced only on the royal demesnes.

His successors make no changes in his regulations. Excesses on the part of the feudal nobility provoke frequent revolts, especially in the Polish provinces. The Edict for South Prussia of 28 March 1794, reenacted and extended to East Prussia on 30 April 1797, indeed reminds the peasant that he has recourse to the royal justice against the nobles' exactions; but the very form of the edicts, the listing of abuses—arbitrary increase of feudal dues, hiring out to third persons of services performed under feudal obligations, corporal punishments—show that these practices are still customary.

The liberation of the peasants is a generous notion. But by granting the peasants freedom of movement it hampers recruiting for the army, deprives the lords of their household servants, and eliminates the supply of cheap labor. At long last, between 1799 and 1805, Frederick William III decides, at the insistent demand of Cabinet Councillor Beyme, to free the serfs on the royal demesnes, thereby creating more than fifty thousand smallholders. But he dares not require his vassals to carry out a similar reform, any more than he dares levy a tax on their land. All that they are prepared to accept is the abolition of their customs privileges.

Slow-moving traditionalists as they are, the nobles fail to see where their refusal to move with the times is leading them. Frederick II's Reglement was based on the assumption of a sparse population, and its aim was to curb the depopulation of the countryside. But now the rural areas have been fully settled; the rise in the birth rate has led to an actual superfluity of manpower. Since the landowners cannot find employment for the sons of the settled peasants, they permit them to establish themselves elsewhere; the number of day laborers increases, much to the satisfaction of those who use them. They move frequently from place to place, learn a trade to enable them to live through the winter, or take to the road. An agrarian reform designed to abolish the fallows system might possibly feed these laborers, but no one in Prussia pays any attention to this problem until early in the nineteenth century.

The government does very little. Though Frederick II vigorously drains marshes and clears forests, he fails to make any determined attack on the problem of fallow land. It is true that he compels the peasants in 1770 to grow fodder crops, but his main incentive is purely mercantilist, to be free of further imports of cattle feed. Growing fodder crops does not, in any event, entail the abolition of the fallows ipso facto, and there does not seem to have been any very active campaign in favor of abolishing them. Thaer and his novel methods of farming do not become influential until he publishes his *Principles of Rational Agriculture* in 1809. It takes the famine of 1770 to move the potato from garden to field. The beet is still merely a curiosity in 1799. When Achard claims to be able to extract sugar from it, Frederick William III instructs Professor Klaproth to conduct an experiment, and its success holds out great hopes from both a mercantile and a humanitarian standpoint, for sugar cane will no longer have to be imported and the slaves in the Americas can be freed. This new kind of sugar, however, arouses considerable distrust, for it readily absorbs moisture and melts when exposed to the air. In any case, it is still scarce and costly; in Berlin, strollers buy lumps of it on the street as a curiosity. Its success becomes assured only after a better selection of the tuber, an improvement in the manufacturing process, and the crisis caused by the Continental Blockade.

The peasants are no more receptive to the ideas of consolidating holdings and the big landlords are almost equally recalcitrant. Wheat is selling well, so why propose all these reforms?

Prussia is not the leader of the movement for agrarian reform in Germany, for several princes award bounties to peasants for raising fodder crops and potatoes, and Holstein is more actively concerned with consolidating scattered holdings.

The various groups are therefore distributed, as it were, through the rooms of an edifice erected by the mercantilist state. For nearly fifty years they manage in them more or less comfortably; the edifice would fall into ruin if they were unable to live in it. But we must beware of the idea that it was erected for their sake. The principle is that the people exist for the state, not the state for the people. No one class can be said to be sacrificed to the rest; but each class is protected only insofar as it is necessary to the state. The nobles, privileged in Prussia as they are elsewhere, are not at liberty, as they are in England, to depopulate the countryside by enclosure. The peasants are protected only because the budget and the army require it; the reforms carried out on the royal demesnes show that there is a genuine wish to free the serfs, but as their freedom is of no direct benefit to the capitalist state, the state makes no attempt to impose it on the nobles, whose interests would be damaged by it. The only feature common to all these groups is that none of them can grow rich rapidly, for the state stands at the door of each room and takes its share of the profits of each of them.

It does seem occasionally to have occurred to Frederick the Great that this fiscal system was calculated to hamper the harmonious development of his country. "Here again," he writes in 1768, "a large question arises, whether, as regards taxation, the good of the state is to be preferred to the good of the individual, and what its attitude is to be." But he speedily allays any remorse he may have felt by the false assertion that taxation is very light. "My answer is that the state is made up of individuals and that the prince's weal is the subject's weal. Shepherds shear their flocks, they do not flay them. It is just that every individual should contribute to the expenses of the state, but it is not at all just that he should share half his yearly income with the sovereign. In a well-administered state the farmer, the burgher, and the gentleman should enjoy the bulk of their income and only give the government some share of it" (*Political Correspondence*, 129).

The state prospers, then, and no one complains of the regime, provided that the balance is not disturbed. The judicious ratio of the sum of what is produced to the number of consumers must be maintained if the edifice is to remain stable.

Berlin, the Capital of the Aufklärung

It is in Berlin that the Aufklärung reaches its full flowering at the end of the eighteenth century. The Hohenzollerns' capital begins to acquire a European reputation; high officials and ambassadors maintain their residences there; the intellectuals are attracted by the schools, academies, and publishing houses; the growth of trade and industry swells the burghers' wealth. A new society thus comes into being beside that of the nobles and pensioners, whose resources have not increased. "Le monde où on s'amuse" grows up beside "le monde où on s'ennuie." It is a curious situation, seldom found else where, in which the past and the future exist side by side in the present without ever mingling with it.

No spectacle [Madame de Staël writes in 1803] equalled that of Berlin. This city, situate in the center of northern Germany, may be regarded as the source of its enlightenment. The sciences and letters are cultivated there, and at male dinners at the houses of ministers and others there is no attempt to maintain the distinction between ranks that is so prejudicial to Germany; men of talent from all classes assemble together. This welcome mingling of the classes does not yet extend, however, to female society; there are a few women whose talents and charm draw every person of distinction around them; but in general in Berlin, as elsewhere in Germany, female society is not really amalgamated with male society. . . .
There were only a very few men in society in Berlin, a circumstance which almost always spoils them by making it unnecessary for them to take pains to preserve their position and to please. The officers who had obtained leave to spend some months in the city looked only for dancing and gaming. The use of two languages at once hampered conversation; and large parties were no more interesting in Berlin than in Vienna. . . . Nevertheless, the freedom of the press, the assemblage of men of talent, the knowledge of literature and the German language, which has become widespread in the past few years, made Berlin the true capital of the new, the enlightened Germany. [*De l'Allemagne* pt. 1, chap. 17.]

The population of Berlin was 50,000 in 1712, 108,000 in mid-century and nearly 140,000 in 1799, in addition to a garrison of some 45,000. Its growth and rebuilding were vigorously stimulated by Frederick II. To the east of the older districts of Coeln and Werder, on the other bank of the Spree, whose dusky waters enclose the monumental and somber mass of the old castle, a new town has grown up, with broad streets intersecting at right angles and bright and regular uniform facades, some of them simply fronts for older buildings; the king has sometimes been too impatient to build for eternity, but his object has been attained. The city's appearance is imposing and it is brilliant in the sunlight. Broad arteries channel the traffic in parallel lines from the gardens cultivated by French refugees at Moabit in the north to the military exercise grounds at the Halle Tor far in the south.
The Leipzigerstrasse runs into the octagon at the Potsdamer Tor, where the "daily" at six every evening puts down at the customs barrier passengers who have left Potsdam at noon. People stroll down Unter den Linden to the Quarré, whence carriages leave for Charlottenburg, the royal family's summer residence; aged, grim-faced hags, very different from the neat *soubrettes* who sell refreshments in Paris, proffer sausages and rolls.
In their new houses the wealthy are not plagued with boredom as the people at court are. They leave the manners of yesteryear to the elderly, the officers, and the royal pensioners. It is they who give travelers the impression that the progress of luxury is slower than it is elsewhere. They remain

immured in their homes, emerging only to take a dish of tea on Sundays at Richard's in the Tiergarten, not far from the gay and busy crowd thronging the *Zelten*. The ladies knit, the men smoke their pipe. In winter they take a turn around the Christmas Fair at noon. Toward evening the market held in the Old Town opposite the City Hall is invaded by the lower classes. The confectioners display masterpieces of sugar and puff paste, miniature reproductions of the fountain at Freyenwalde or the Pichelsdorferbucht. Once a year, in January, during the carnival season, the boldest spirits venture to organize a *Redoute*, a masked ball at which the merry-making goes on as late as midnight. They hardly ever venture to the theater, though seats at the Opera, wholly subsidized by the state, are free. Performances begin at three in the afternoon and end at eight; the pit is reserved for the garrison. Berlin audiences like only "plays filled with adventures, quarrels, swoons, Sturm und Drang, complications and dramatic surprises, or else sentimental comedies, their whole plot apparently floated on floods of tears" (*JLM* 1791, 365).

For these unfortunates, receptions are heavy chores. The ceremonial hardly varies, no matter whether it is only an invitation to coffee or a "party" to which invitations are issued long in advance.

About 7 in the evening the ladies begin to arrive, one after another. Those who are already seated in a semicircle at either end of the sofa rise, and the newcomer ceremoniously drops a curtsey to the whole company, all of whom respond in kind. Then the hostess comes forward, takes the guest by the hand, and the introductions begin. . . . There is much ado about the newcomer's place on the sofa; then everyone sits down. The gentlemen appear only in the doorway and present their homage to the ladies with a graceful bow. The ladies drink coffee, knit socks for their helpless spouse, speak to their neighbor on the left with an air of hauteur or (assuming a—somewhat comical—tone of vast amiability) to their neighbor on the right, with whom they are already well acquainted. The subjects of conversation are usually the gossip of the town, dress, and housekeeping; they display at all times a vast interest in those not present, in whom no one has the slightest interest, etc., etc. Seldom is there any mention of the theater or literature. Any guest who ventured on such a course would be a solitary voice, and a disdainful hush would remind her that such talk is misplaced. [*JLM* 1792, 111; *Jahrb.* 1798, II, 17–33; *BM* 1784, 147–48; *BM* 1791, 633–45.]

Card playing is the sole distraction of these people, who are always the same at every reception: "Ombre and whist, like quadrille, assemble players in sets, a prey to impatience or boredom, for there is always a third or fourth who commits fault upon fault." They long for the servant to enter at length to announce that supper is served. But supper drags on, dreary and dull, for the neighbors at table have nothing to say to each other. And when one finally takes one's leave at ten, one quits the party with the sole satisfaction of having done one's duty.

As against this society there is the society of the people who dine at two in the afternoon, drink tea instead of coffee, and spend their Sundays in excursions to Pichelsdorf or elsewhere; who organize picnics and surprise parties; who go away for the summer, and even maintain that they are in the world to enjoy themselves.

These new rich parade their wealth too ostentatiously. They display the most extravagant dresses on Unter den Linden between six and eight on summer evenings. They greet each other with delirious delight, embrace and loudly admire each other solely to attract the attention of the strollers, the gentlemen on horseback, or the lords driving in their resplendent carriages on the four side-alleys. Have these "enlightened" women nothing else to do but parade before the dowagers sitting on the benches of the "Circle" in the Tiergarten in the morning, and show off their curls and laces on Unter den Linden in the evening?

They frequent drawing rooms very different from those of official society. These salons are open to all. The nobles are welcomed there with open arms, the intellectuals are accepted without distrust, actors are treated as if they had not for centuries been the pariahs of mankind. Jews are honored guests, foreigners are adulated by polyglots eager to exercise their linguistic talents. Women mingle with men in groups that form and dissolve in tune with the conversation. Young men come and go from room to room, anxious that everyone should find them "charming"; they prance about, talk for the sake of talking, make their impression on all the company, and at length plump down nonchalantly on a divan, "tangling up the knitting of one lady, playing with another's fan, dropping an epigram, and quoting their Wieland at every pretext" (Varnhagen von Ense, *Denkwürdigkeiten* VII, 565–66). The mistress of the house makes the tea herself in the drawing room, as she discourses amiably with her guests. In Henrietta Herz's salon Friedrich Schlegel chats freely with Dorothea Veit, with whom he is in love. No one is at all shocked, though she is married and has left her legitimate husband, to the great scandal of the bourgeoisie of conventional morals.

Luxury, however, is demoralizing a people which has not acquired sufficient intellectual culture to resist its excesses. The ravages of ostentation affect every grade in the social hierarchy. Minor officials run into debt or live miserably in order to make a greater display. They sell off their old family silverware and buy silverplate, which makes a better impression. Their wives demand rare and costly flowers for their hair and richly decorated drawing rooms for their receptions, but they neglect their children. They have no hesitation about deceiving their husbands in order to procure the luxury with which they cannot dispense. Middle-class women wear plumed hats instead of the older lace bonnet and style themselves *Madame* or *Mamselle* instead of *Frau* or *Jungfer*. Servants doff their livery as soon as their service is finished and dress fashionably, with silk underwear. It is impossible to tell them from persons of quality on the street on Sundays, for they too greet each other with embraces, invite each other to picnics, or wander the city in quest of adventure.

License makes rapid inroads. The proportion of illegitimate births is 11 percent at Berlin, 14 percent at Leipzig and Jena, 16 percent at Göttingen, and 25 percent at Munich. At Dresden, where stiffer morals prevail,

everyone, from the meanest drummerboy to the bachelor chamberlain, has to have a little friend of his own, for there are no public brothels. The Saxon girls have soft and philanthropical hearts; they do not leave their swains to languish for long. Thus, the two sexes find what they are seeking in strict privacy; . . . there are, therefore, very few houses of ill fame relative to the size of the town, and they are frequented only by persons of the lowest order, soldiers, journeymen, craftsmen, and the like. [*TM* 1785, III, 53.]

In Berlin in 1798 there are 658 sellers of beer, 53 coffeehouses keepers, and 140 innkeepers—one purveyor for every 164 inhabitants. Many establishments "offer their clients music, dancing, and girls for a few groschen." The girls often live two or three together in lodgings. Others are to be visited in all sorts of small houses, almost as picturesque as those of Amsterdam and almost as luxurious as those of Paris. Madame Schulitz's house is one of the most elegant in the city; the furniture is in the best of taste and the tableware is silver. The loveliest girls in the world make up a company more agreeable than that at Madame Gourdan's, the most famous house in Paris.

Such facilities for dissolute living are naturally irresistible. The city is full of servants seeking employment, idling soldiers, and dressmakers who have the entrée to the best families. These seamstresses pass love letters and presents from the suitors to the lady of the house. They are supposed to be buying lace from the middle-class women who make it at home; the husband knows therefore that his wife is earning money and is not surprised to see her wearing new jewels. They let out rooms for assignations, whispering the address in the ear of the fair one, who, when the time comes, will simply be going out "to visit a female friend" (*Berlin* I, 17).

The older conventions are certainly no longer fashionable in Berlin. "Since licentiousness cannot be prevented in a great city" one observer remarks, "it would be tolerable if it went no further. Unfortunately, the Italian taste has also met with much favor. If, as Herr von Archenholz says, the fact that men in England never embrace is to be taken as proof of the aversion of the English to pederasty, what a sign of evil omen this must be to Berlin! At no other time or place, alas! has this custom been so generally practiced" (*TM* 1787, IV, 75).

Despite its vices, Berlin is certainly not a world capital like Paris or

London; but in Prussia and in Germany it certainly has the air of a capital city. Its influence spreads to all the countries of the Aufklärung; but only to them. Victims of prejudice like Fichte, Fessler, and the company of martyrs take refuge there. It is the center of fashion and social events, and Germans turn to it rather than to distant Paris. But however much the philosophers feel at home there, they are forcibly reminded at every step, even as they are working out their social reforms, that Berlin has been created by the Hohenzollerns and for the Hohenzollerns.

4

The System in Operation

The Campaign against Prejudice

One of the best ways to see how the Aufklärung operates as a system is to study the principal journals, whose campaigns do in fact lead to reforms. In order to instill in their readers the habit of reasoning, the journalists cull and comment on miscellaneous news items, denounce the superstitions and customs which blind so many honest folk, and good-naturedly mock at their misadventures.

A journeyman barber at Wesel, for example, plunges into debauch with such ardor that he runs fourteen thalers into debt. The only way of getting the money that he can think of is to sell his soul to the devil; so he writes a letter to Satan and leaves it in his room for him to sign. But it is his father who reads the contract, and the poor lad has to undergo both a good thrashing and the absolution he has to beg from his confessor (*JD* 1784, II, 47).

A blacksmith's apprentice is in despair because his new bellows will not work. There can be no doubt that some neighbor has cast a spell on them. The apprentice applies to the minister, but he will not listen to him. He then appeals to the Franciscans: "One of them comes at once, with bell, book, and candle and all the apparatus for exorcism. He goes through his mumbo jumbo and raises the wind with his holy art, but not in the bellows, for they remain obstinately without the least breath of air." The master blacksmith turns up and finds a hole in them (*JD* 1789, II, 46).

Or again, a man summons a Jesuit to exorcise the greenfly from his garden. A woman is so terrified by a prophecy of an imminent earthquake that she is invalided for life; but the earth does not budge (*JD* 1786, II, 339–42). Example after example is given of the evils caused by stupid superstition; everyone reading them applies them to his own case and so becomes a champion of rational philosophy.

Pleas are made for the reform of the criminal law and for milder punishments. A fact to be welcomed is that actors are at last received in society and by the reading clubs, for there is no reason whatever why the "players" who stage brilliant performances of reasonable dramas and whose traveling companies propagate the new ideas should be ostracized and despised. Everyone agrees with what Forster writes to his fiancée, Theresa Heyne: "I hate every obstacle placed in the path of freedom, everything that prevents a bud from blossoming or a seed from sprouting and producing flowers and fruit. I do not see why a girl should not read, say, and think whatever she wishes if it sorts with her feelings and her conscience" (Forster, *Briefwechsel* I, 502). Woman's place in society is everwhere discussed; in compliance with the law of nature which has made a distinction between the sexes, should woman be forbidden masculine occupations, should she be relegated once more to her kitchen and children? Unlike her sisters in Mediterranean countries, is the northern woman really incapable of politics? Or should it be recognized that she has the same rights as men in society, politics, and even in love? (*BAZ* 1799, I, 403-12, 502-10; II, 56-66. Hippel, *Versuch*. Krug, *Philosophie*. Brandes, *Weiber* II, 352. *JLM* 1800, XV, 557-63.)

Protests are raised against the cruelty displayed by mobs to the corpses of suicides. Because the churches regard these unfortunates as damned, no one is willing to touch them. In many parts the custom survives of bringing their remains to trial. Their burial almost always causes trouble. At Düsseldorf in 1784 the crowd tries to prevent the burial in the graveyard of the body of an honest official of the Department of Mines who has hanged himself; the authorities are compelled to call out the troops. In Saxony it is necessary to suppress a riot instigated by those who wish to dig up and cart out of the graveyard the corpse of an unfortunate who has committed suicide in an access of delirious fever. In Prussia it is ordered by special edict that these outcasts shall be buried secretly; it is the only way in which they can be assured of a decent burial. But what a victory for the enlightened when they see prejudice overcome even in this sphere and are able to follow the funerals of two suicides, one at Goslar, the other at Schauen, in broad daylight!

The Aufklärung counts upon the support of the churches in its battle against superstition. Even though the religion of many of the faithful itself is only superstition, it can be purged and freed from its irrational elements, and the rival churches which fought each other in the past can now be brought to coexist in concord.

Now they are to deprecate all persecution and rival each other only in toleration. The clergy are allies, whose services should be used more effectively. Why not increase their influence and help them to combat the onslaughts of religious indifference? They should be given a useful role in local life. It would be wiser not to replace them with schoolteachers and policemen, as some propose, but to turn them into schoolteachers, and then there would be no need for policemen. They could be put in charge of the children's moral education, if only for two hours daily. They really would not find it as repugnant as is sometimes believed; there is, of course, a terrible stench in the classrooms, for the pupils congregate in them and often spend the night there with the teacher and his family; but the pastor will be able to smoke and thus fumigate the room, or even have the windows opened when the weather is not too cold. Besides, the atmosphere is not really so unhealthy, for some very aged persons live and flourish in it.

Theological students might also be obliged to assimilate the rudiments of law. They will then be able to act as local magistrates and thus both benefit their flock and help out the overworked courts. They might also acquire some notion of medicine. Clergymen would then be able to prescribe a regime, carry out a cupping, and even act as midwives to the peasant women. They could curb the abuse of universal remedies, which is so lethal in the countryside, and substitute to advantage for the rustic bonesetter; and theology would once more be what it should—the mother of all the sciences.

Many clergymen hold ideas of this kind. Forster's father botanizes and also consistently sides with the peasants in his small parish near Danzig. Schelling's father trains to teach oriental languages while conscientiously carrying out his duties as a country clergyman.

But is the average intellectual level of the clergy high enough for these reforms? To alter the clergyman's role would not in itself suffice, for the ritual, in many cases out-of-date, would have to be adapted to the requirements of modern life as well. The enlightened Jews set an example in rejecting prescriptions of the Mosaic law. Why then should Catholics hesitate to give up midnight Mass, which causes so many chills, and Communion taken fasting in winter, when the cold almost deprives churchgoers of their senses on the way there; why not hold the afternoon services, which interfere with the digestion, somewhat later in the day? Might they not cancel services in sultry weather, when the bells may well attract lightning to strike the flock? Since Jews remain covered in the synagogue, might not Catholics too allow those whose health requires it to keep their hat on in church? Protestant and Catholic places of worship ought to be better ventilated. They are full of lethal draughts; one breathes in the exhalations of a crowd singing at the top of its lungs and the effluences from corpses buried under the flagstones.

The Catholics should reduce the number of their holy days and days of obligation in the fine season, for this would enable the peasant, who in any case is overburdened with feudal servitudes to get in his harvest. He would not then continue to heed the recruiting sergeant's fallacious promises and would no longer emigrate to the plains of Romania or Hungary, where the land needs hands and he can work whenever he likes.

The critical spirit leads many a deist into atheism. He does not proclaim it from the housetops, but in Prussia he need not hide it. Fessler takes refuge there after the death of Joseph II, who in 1782 was protecting him in Austria, and reforms the Royal York Lodge. Fichte receives permission to live in Berlin after being forced to leave Jena under accusation of atheism.

Wekhrlin's opinion is generally approved at Berlin:

Let us tolerate doubters! The main difficulty between the deists and the atheits rests on this question: With what degree of probability can it be asserted that an order reigns in the world, an order which reveals an intelligent cause? This is solely a matter of speculation. It is, therefore, purely a matter for each man to decide by reason, in accordance with his own point of view, or else to doubt. . . . Recognize, then, young man, how senseless it is and how vain to argue about the origin and finality of things and to seek for order where obscurity prevails. And learn to tolerate doubters. [*HB* 1788, III, 40–43; cf. for similar arguments ibid. 101–6 and 1789, IV, 47–52.]

The Spread of Luxury: The Sumptuary Laws

The philosophers are disturbed by the rapid spread of luxury after the end of the Seven Years' War. They would have preferred the aristocracy of birth to be replaced by an aristocracy of intellect rather than a crude plutocracy, but the newly rich burghers insist on making an ostentatious parade of their wealth. The *Journal of Luxury and Fashion* supplies their wives with patterns of dresses, fans, and the latest furnishings; it even gives the current price of diamonds, which are to be had cheap because of sales by French emigrés; and it publishes long articles on the most fashionable perfumes—musk and amber (*JLM* 1794, IX, 65–72, 201–5, 309–13, etc.).

The younger generation of the middle classes takes to study, learns foreign languages, and reads Kant. Travel is no longer a necessity but a pleasure; the summer vacation in the country is felt to be essential; people would lose face if they did not feel this. Spas proliferate, and all the journals vaunt their charms.

Any attempt to counter the decay of morality by sumptuary laws argues great faith in the power of the law. The princes display greater skepticism on this head than the journalists. They do not lay down by decree the limits between decency and indecency in toilets and ladies' hair styles. They do not impose on the Germans the simple and practical national costume that several out-and-out reformers prefer to French fashions, which do not respect the lovely natural line of the female body but sophisticate it, imposing, first, the "Paris derrière" and, later, false bosoms, padded shoulders, and even false bellies! Everyone agrees that French taste is bad, but it is harder to agree on what the new style of dress should be.

When it comes, however, to restricting sumptuary expenditure, which ruins so many families of small means, the lawmakers are not so simple-minded: "Five or six years ago," the *Deutsches Museum* writes in 1786, some reasonable people at Bielefeld began of their own accord to give up wearing mourning. They were pioneers. You can imagine what they had to face; people gazed at them open-mouthed, they were severely criticized, they were mocked and deplored. Two years ago a group at Osnabrück followed their example. Last year the Rottwitt family at Mainz became the first family in that city to dare to discard mourning; they were followed by the Tosetti family in the same town; the Remi of Bendorf and a large group at Hamelin followed their example. What we are waiting for now is a paternalist edict which will limit this senseless prodigality throughout Hesse-Cassel. Reasonable people will anticipate its promulgation and act in accordance with reason. [*DM* 1786, II, 312.]

The movement is actually not so recent in date. The reading clubs, or other groups drawn from similar sources, support individual initiatives. The authorities approve of these campaigns, for reasons disclosed in their decrees; the newly rich burghers have begun to be remarked for the ostentation of their ceremonies, and the nobles, especially in the smaller towns, feeling compelled to outshine them, are ruining themselves by this petty competition just as badly as the peasants and craftsmen, who are carried along by the same current. By making the display of luxury proportionate to social rank rather than wealth, the edicts dry up a source of unnecessary expenditure but fail to destroy an outworn convention, as the journalists would like to think.

The earliest restrictions on the "unnatural" luxury of christenings, marriages, and funerals seem to have been those imposed at Frankfort-on-Main in 1774. The *Deutsche Chronik* hailed the end of these immoral "orgies" (1774, 198–99, 237, 490–91).

Such edicts become very frequent after 1778. Joseph II prohibits funeral feasts and wedding banquets in 1784, for it is better to buy household furniture than spend all the money on wedding guests. But the most tenacious convention is mourning garb; this is the principal target of the enlightened and the main abuse attacked in the edicts; henceforth it is not to be worn for children under fourteen years of age. Deep mourning for the first six weeks, with the obligatory special wig, shoe buckles, and black sword, is abolished. The nobles retain the right to wear mourning, but for six months only, and only for close relatives. Others must confine themselves to a black armband or a black ribbon in the woman's hair. As an expression of grief, burghers are only permitted to wear their Sunday best—which they usually wear to go to church—every day. All alike are forbidden to dress their servants in mourning, to hire professional mourners for funerals, and to shroud the dead "in silk or other costly materials."

Oaken and hardwood coffins and wrought-iron or silver coffin ornaments are also prohibited. Wekhrlin, with his extreme propensity to the utilitarian, even proposes the total abolition of coffins: "Wood," he says in essence, is scarce in Württemberg. The population is dense and is increasing regularly. It used up about 240,000 coffin planks in 1786, or 2,800,000 planks, to the value of 700,000 florins, for one generation over twenty years. What a waste of money which could be so useful to the state! Would it not be better to equip each church with a bier and a set of coffins of different sizes. The undertakers' mutes would fetch the body early in the morning, so as not to waste working hours; there would be few followers; it would be too early for a funeral luncheon. The body wrapped in its shroud would be placed in the coffin and carried to the graveyard, where it would be taken out of the bier and buried. Everyone would profit. [GU 1786, VI, 94 ff.]

It is not at all certain how far these reforms were actually enforced. The enlightened support them; at Erlangen the schoolmaster forces all "intelligent patriots" to give a written undertaking to wear only an armlet or hat ribbon on the death of close relatives and to waive all other ceremonies. Elsewhere, "associations" on the lines of the reading clubs set a good example.

But the mockery of unbelievers who want death to be considered solely from the standpoint of the interest of the state does not carry universal conviction. A species of two-way argument arises.

The most reasonable method of clearing our corpses from the face of the earth, [Wekhrlin explains] is certainly to bury ourselves in the earth, which introduces us into the assembly of our half-brothers, the worms and slugs. We thus meet all the requirements that we may be called upon to fulfill: we fertilize the earth.

But a damnable prejudice has blocked this source of blessings. All of us have to be preserved in walled enclosures, as in an ancient arsenal. This strange usage deprives the state of a large plot of its best soil, which might feed many families; and what makes the damage irreparable is that the emanations from these corpses, abruptly dissolved and spread through the aid by a gust of wind, infect the atmosphere; travelers incur the great danger of becoming, like the Mecca pilgrim on the burning slopes of the sands of Araby, a prey to this lethal wind . . . .

Our philosophic age has already wiped out the charters of libertines and idlers; it has abolished saints' days. . . . But that is a very small gain in comparison with the gigantic task still to be accomplished. . . . Perhaps the next age may see the reform of our burials.

They lead to idling. In a town with a population of 18,000, for example, some 530 inhabitants die yearly; at the rate of six persons per family, this means a quarter of the population idle.

Thus, innocent death is responsible for the fact that 530 families in this town are granted a license to remain idle for some considerable time. . . . It should be borne in mind, too, that death is not like the traveling intellectual; it is not willing to be relegated to the antechamber and cherish the hope of a more favorable opportunity. A ceremony as disadvantageous as it is absurd may often compound the damage; for a merchant or manufacturer may well be obliged to sit beside his mother's urn, like some hermit before his modest crucifix, at the very moment when he would have had the finest opportunity, for the first and last time, of disposing of his goods to the greatest profit. . . . But even so, they alone do not suffer this calamity. When this phantasmogoria is staged on the public highway, all near and collateral relatives, neighbors and friends, Tom, Dick, and Harry, congregate and lose half a day taking part in this masquerade. This 'mummery' is imposed on all those who have ever spoken to the deceased, be it only once in their lives. . . .

If, to the great delight of the locals, it is the governor of a province or the lord of a village who has died, the knell tolls throughout the region; and on such an occasion a general license to waste time is issued. The last act of this tragedy is the worst. . . . Hardly has the deceased been borne to his last home when the glasses are filled and tears are dried in brandy. Oxen are slaughtered, pigs are boiled, calves are roasted; to help out there is brought in many a capon, fowl, pheasant, and grouse; the plenty obstructs the pineal gland. The howls of drunkards now resound in the house where silent grief reigned only an hour before. The black hangings that cover the lighter walls are covered in turn by the superfluity of the belly. [GU 1785, IV, 221-40.]

Good German folk, however, vigorously shake their head. Certainly it may be a mark of vanity to drape and decorate rooms in black, and of a pride hateful to God to dress everyone as dark as night because of the loss of a member of the family. Doubtless purchased funeral orations, panegyrics, elegies, and all such things are low and shameful. But are we to make a clean sweep? Are we to discard as well what alone can still rouse us from our sensual sloth? If we do, the funeral cortege will no longer pass before us, slow and stately; the death knell will no longer toll, the funeral hymn no longer resound outside our homes; the dull rattle from the sexton's spade will no longer terrify us, and the skull's eyeless sockets and the skeletons and the rotting planks of coffins on the fields of death no longer remind us that it is man's destiny to die and that thereafter comes the Judgment. [VC 1787, 387-88.]

In many ordinances an interval of two or three days is fixed between death and burial. In the country, and among the poor, who have little living space, it is not customary to keep the corpse in the single room in which the whole family lives. But the only way to be certain that death has really taken place is thought to be to await the first signs of decomposition. Hufeland, professor of medicine at Jena, reiterates this at length in the *Neue teutsche Merkur* (1790, 11-39). Others repeat it after him. So many cases can be cited of persons buried alive! Loss of consciousness may last a very long time, especially with children suffering from convulsions, alcoholics, and opium addicts. This danger threatens the Jews, too, for they bury their dead a few hours after death. The first edict of this nature concerns them in particular. In 1772 the Duke of Mecklenburg-Schwerin orders them to observe a three-day period. This starts a debate which divides the Jews of the empire into two camps for twenty years and gives rise to many difficulties (see Appendix). In most of the decrees issued subsequently, however, no distinction is made between Jews and Christians.

In Prussia the Instruction of the Higher Medical and Health Boards to the Clergy, of 31 October 1794, goes into vast detail, worthy of the learned men who drew it up. It advises that, after observing the usual signs of death—absence of pulse, breath, and exhalation, cold, pallor, blue marks on the parts on which the weight of the body rests, dropped jaw, open anus—further special verifications should be made: "Peppered or salted water should be induced into the corpse's mouth and a clyster of cooking salt or a decoction of tobacco should be administered. . . . The sexual parts should be bathed in cold water or the whole body should be bathed in heated wine, beer, water, and vinegar or salted lye water and chafed with it." This method is specially recommended for small children. With adults it is better to pour cold or boiling water drop by drop from as high as possible on the heart, the lower belly, the upper arm or the ribs, or to introduce ammonia into the nostrils.

But as even these tests are not decisive, it is necessary to await the sign of decomposition for two or three days in summer and three to five days in winter. In the country corpses may be placed under a tent or in a stall, depending on the season; in the towns special buildings must be erected.

The application of these measures gives rise in practice to almost insoluble problems. The living cannot be forced into a promiscuity likely to injure their health; so morgues will have to be built. The prince, however, though always prepared to issue philanthropic edicts, does not have the money to put them into effect. So it is private groups once again which erect the death houses in the cemeteries, in which corpses are watched for the first signs of decay. The model is at Weimar; eight bodies are laid out in a large room heated by a system of pipes under the floor. Cords attached to their wrists and ankles are connected with a bell in an adjoining room with a glass door, in which the corpse watcher resides; warned by the slightest movement on the part of guests, he has a small kitchen and bathroom available to give immediate succor to any corpse who awakes. He receives a special bounty for each resuscitation. (*TM* 1790, II, 11–30; 1791, III, 125–38.)

Most of the members of the groups for erecting these death houses are rich enough to be able to keep the corpse at their homes; the poor have no means to contribute. In the country a very large number of morgues will be needed, and they would be empty most of the time. So the enlightened look for other methods; they propose that a room in the village hall or a herdsman's hut be set aside for such use; in order to induce the peasants to take an interest, they counsel that they should be intimidated by reminders that they are liable to be buried alive some day (*JD* 1790, II, 44–48).

It is for this reason that the journals abound in macabre descriptions, and the scientists soon join in with some curious observations. If the three-day period is observed, one of them notes, a dead body almost never revives; but when bodies are exhumed, they are fairly often found to have moved. Should it not be concluded, therefore, that the coffin or the earth itself exercises a beneficent influence? The odor of the wood probably acts the more efficaciously, since evaporation is no longer possible below ground. Everyone knows that newly plowed earth strengthens the lungs and nerves of summer guests; it likewise cures aphasia and certain kinds of headache; some dry soils, such as those found in Hungary, prevent decay. Bodies should therefore be buried in coffins of various woods under a thin layer of earth; the season, the kind of illness, the quality and color of the wood and the nature of the soil should be noted in each case; and graves should be closely watched so that help can immediately be administered to anyone who moves. After a large number of experiments it would be possible to formulate the laws of resuscitation, to the great benefit of mankind. (*TM* 1786, III, 276–86.)

The Campaign against Coffee and Tea

The campaign against coffee and tea resembles the story of the sumptuary laws. It is waged by the Aufklärung in the name of health, but the princes approve of it because it serves their political interests.

Coffee seems to have been introduced into Germany by Frenchmen toward the end of the seventeenth century. The first coffee shop was opened in 1696 at Nuremberg behind the Town Hall. Italians brought it to Wittenberg in 1710. Ten years later it was found throughout Saxony, and shortly thereafter throughout the empire.

Its effects are well known by the end of the century; it promotes the digestion, stimulates the organic functions, transpiration, and urination, and sharpens the wits. It is not unhealthy provided that it is not used to excess; it has been consumed everywhere for three generations, and everyone has been the better for it.

But at the close of the century a number of pamphlets and articles do their utmost to prove that this is not so; coffee is deleterious, like all hot drinks. It causes vomiting, palpitations, and the shakes. It overcharges the blood with essential oils and overheats it so that the dilated blood vessels are ruptured at such critical points as the heart and lungs, resulting in apoplexy and tuberculosis. Or else it softens the arteries, and this engenders general debility, swellings, dropsy, gout, paralysis, and a whole range of horrible ailments. In the case of persons inclined to be unduly skinny it often dehydrates the body by causing excessive urination to the point where they become mere skeletons (*Nachricht*).

The real reason for this campaign lies elsewhere. Coffee is an import and so drains Prussian gold from the country. Mercantilism is the prevailing trend in political economy throughout the empire. The princes, therefore, take the lead in this crusade from the beginning of the century onward. Frederick II makes the coffee trade a state monopoly in 1766, and this leads to widespread smuggling by frontier dwellers. His successor's abolition of the unpopular monopoly does not improve the situation, for the customs duties are made prohibitive in 1787 and once again promote a lucrative contraband trade. It is the same everywhere. The older edicts depriving the burghers and peasants of Saxony of this indispensable aid to digestion are certainly never complied with. The Hanoverian peasants resolutely ignore the decree permitting coffee to be sold only to travelers at post stations on the main highways. The burghers of Hildesheim never pay the fine inflicted on those who choose to refresh themselves in the same way as any foreigner, who can in theory be served with coffee only by an approved restaurant keeper.

The intellectuals and journals of the Aufklärung support the princes. "Assuming that only 5 million of the 28 million Germans use this costly beverage daily," one pamphleteer writes, "this amounts to more than nineteen million thalers that go to enrich foreigners" (Rumpf, *Goldgrube*, 23). And Schloezer complains that workmen spend much time refreshing themselves, only to sweat even more heavily afterward, so that their work grows worse and worse. Brewing stagnates, for no one drinks anything but coffee. Idleness increases on every hand, for the workmen take time out to savor their coffee (*Briefwechsel* VIII, 120–23). Craftsmen, servants, and farm hands demand higher wages to pay for their coffee. This reasoning makes little impression even on the enlightened. They undoubtedly agree with Goethe that everyone is free to decide whether he will or will not use the beverage, depending on the effects he experiences in his own person (*Wilhelm Meister*, bk. 6).

The cause, then, seems lost; but the philanthropists discover a new weapon. Coffee has supplanted the tried and true national drinks, the beers, wines, ciders, and perries tested by centuries of use; why not replace it with a new drink owing nothing to foreign produce? Chicory, barley, acorn, beetroot, lupin, and innumerable other decoctions make delicious infusions. Rye, properly selected, washed, scalded, dried, roasted, ground, and mixed with almonds is a sovereign cure for head- and bellyaches. It can be offered to guests just as well as coffee, which is only a convention anyhow.

There is, however, another substitute which is likely to prevail. The Aufklärung realizes this and starts to combat it without awaiting the edicts which the governments, skeptical of results, no longer issue. Tea, introduced into Europe by the Dutch at the beginning of the seventeenth century, conquered England in the eighteenth. In other countries it was regarded mainly as a drug. Physicians prescribed it as their favorite remedy against the thickening of humors. Boutekoe, the famous Dutch physician, did a great deal to spread its use by prescribing his patients as many as 200 cups a day. There was a good deal of support for his method till he was found to be subsidized by the Dutch East Indies Company: "He would just as readily have prescribed rat poison as a universal remedy if the East Indies Company had happened to trade in it and had not found any other outlet for it but the stomachs of the sick—and of the healthy too" (*TM* 1784, III, 56–59).

All doctors agree, however, toward the end of the century that tea is harmful: "Brewed strong it acts on the nerves as a narcotic, blunts their edge, and weakens them. Brewed weaker, it operates in the same way as hot water and undermines the digestion. In both cases, therefore, it causes debility and its ensuing ill effects, such as nervous ailments, spasms, migraines, morbid sensitivity of the skin to changes in temperature and cold, cachexia, and, in ladies, many other ailments peculiar to their sex" (*JLM* 1788, III, 337).

If tea is taken only at irregular intervals and in small quantities, it does no great harm. But tea is the fashion; good society cannot do without it. The English are taken as an example; but this is to overlook the fact that their food is highly spiced and tea soothes the irritation, that they take a great deal of exercise, and that they do not drink coffee. German women hardly ever take exercise, gulp all sorts of liquids, and still claim that they absolutely cannot do without their tea between six and eight o'clock in the evening. Actually, they are not so much concerned with tea itself as with the ostentation of luxury for which it is the pretext; they can show off their fine china, gather round the tea table, and gossip. Why not, then, replace tea—which is often rendered even more noxious by the many falsifications introduced by unscrupulous planters and merchants, who mix other leaves with those of the precious shrub—with herb teas, which have so often been proved to have an excellent effect on health? Mint, balm, woodruff, strawberry leaves, and many other plants from German forests and gardens would restore constitutions ravaged by tea. In recommending them the Aufklärung hopes to be of service to the national health and the national economy alike. But this advice meets with little response; if tea does in fact remain the drink exclusively of society gatherings in Germany, it is no thanks to the Aufklärung.

The Students

German universities at the beginning of the eighteenth century were more renowned for dissipation than for work. Gottsched's disciples seek in vain to remedy this state of affairs. They are unable to make any impression on public opinion until near the end of the century, with the development of the larger journals. Then, however, the situation rapidly improves. The governments intervene successfully and enforce the regulations issued in the past and reissued in vain. This success is due to the new composition of the student body. The statistics provide no information on the point, but it is certain that the number of students grows rapidly and that the proportion of middle-class and poor students who cannot lead the expensive life of the university students' corporations progressively increases. The poor students are not despised by the corporations so much as those who can and should become "Brothers." The poorer students attend the smaller institutions such as the recently established universities of Erlangen (1743) and Tübingen. The enlightened despots try to attract to their faculties the wealthier students who are willing to work for the advancement of enlightenment instead of following the deleterious traditions of Jena.

Even in that citadel of dissipation they succeed in forming small groups, societies of thinkers such as the "League of Free Men," who mock the prejudices of etiquette: "It's not done, it's not proper, what would people say, such turns of speech resound like thunderclaps in the ears of slaves and keep them in the most humiliating obedience!" The Free Men and their families liberate themselves from such prejudices. Encouraged by Fichte and Wieland, who hope to reform the students' morals by the Free Men's example, they meet once a week to discuss philosophical or political topics and to cultivate friendship. "The truth is our sole, our highest aim," the statutes declare. "We love each other as brothers and honor each other as men, and our union does not separate us from anyone whose countenance is human and whose heart is noble" (Flitner, *Hülsen*, 10).

A declaration very alien to Jena as a whole. It is true, of course, that the time is past when the student knew more about fencing and drinking than disputation and when he was identifiable by his long rapier, the twenty drams he could toss off without taking breath, and when all Germany sang:

> He who returns from Leipzig unwed,
> From Wittenberg in good health,
> From Jena unbruised,
> Can call himself a lucky man.
>
> [Nicolai, *Beschreibung* I, 53–54.]

But dissipation, heavy drinking, and swashbuckling continued until the French came in 1806. Steffens met some corporation Brothers in 1798, eight- or nine-bottle men. During a banquet several of them challenged him to drink toasts with them. Much to his surprise, he found that he had become a candidate for admission to a brotherhood. Next day, "some wild Westphalians burst into his rooms, dressed in stiff leather trousers, short waistcoats, and the boots called 'canons,' with handkerchief stuck in the left boot and pipe in the right and tobacco pouch pinned to the lapel. They stuff their pipes with a stinking tobacco, fling themselves down on the sofa and order beer," and stay on for hours. Steffens was compelled to flee the town to get away from them. (Steffens, *Was ich erlebte* IV, 25-28, 65-80; Raich, *Dorothea* I, 10.)

Public opinion is rightly alarmed, therefore, at the tyranny of the Constantinists, Amicists, and Black Brothers, who barely conceal their brutality under fine titles like Honor, Solidarity, and Courage. Suppose some simple fellow thinks of working at Jena; suppose he takes the great Loder's anatomy classes, for instance, without ostentatiously displaying the idle Brothers' contempt for "theory"; suppose he wants to take the examination, which consists of noting on a piece of paper the names of the organs corresponding to the small numbered cards placed on the corpse; or suppose he tries to understand how Hufeland makes his diagnoses: his fellow students invite him to drink. If he refuses, they challenge him to a duel. To evade it means becoming liable to such persecution, bullying, and ridicule that the best course is to decamp at once, bag and baggage. Yet to accept may well mean getting one's throat cut. There was an instance as late as 1798. The killer fled with the aid of his accomplices; the honor of the corporation was intact, but the family mourned the death of a promising young man (*NZT* 1799, 11-16). Many students therefore prefer to yield and so become members of an order, obliged to obey the "senior," who commands them to fight despite the regulations. They have to attend the meetings, drink, and pay their scot, though they may not have enough to feed themselves.

There seems to be no remedy. The burghers of the small towns are most indulgent to the students, for they bring in a great deal of money. Should the universities then be transferred to the larger cities? The teaching staff themselves abet these young men, who pay them not in order to attend the courses but to become entitled to take the examinations. What use is it, then, to decree severe penalties for dueling, since the risk merely incites them to fight all the more? How can fencing masters be expected to help with measures which would deprive dueling of the fascination of danger? They will certainly be the first to take the button off the foil and to overlook the relatively bloodless hits that should suffice as reparation for slighted honor.

Though less lethal than at Jena, these disorders periodically affect all the universities. At Marburg in 1794 the students accuse Jung-Stilling of getting a Kantian professor dismissed and prepare to smash his windows in a monster demonstration. His son only manages to divert them by promising to enter their corporation! They then consent merely to parade in front of the pro-rector's house and spit on his doorstep (Jung-Stilling II, 122-23).

A form of regulation does, however, begin to grow up and gradually extends to most of the universities. It appears either in towns where the traditions are not of long standing or in states like Prussia which have an administration capable of making itself obeyed. At Leipzig the students' manners and morals at the end of the century are good. At Tübingen half the students enrolled are scholarship holders. In Hesse a series of edicts make duels between students at Marburg punishable by imprisonment without the option of a fine and restrict the rights of the corporations. At Göttingen, where the students behave well and dress in their Sunday best to visit their professors, they have to be protected against Jewish moneylenders. To prevent them from running into debt, a list is issued of nonlicensed sumptuary expenditures for which creditors cannot sue in the courts for recovery.

Taste at Halle is refined, even overrefined, for dissipation and veneral disease are ruinous to the health of these Don Juans. Zedlitz's wise administration makes this university the center of the Aufklärung. The Wolffians dominate the Faculty of Theology, which in 1786 has 800 out of a total of 1,156 students, their discipline contrasting with decadent Jena. The Prussian government has taken an interest in Halle since 1774. After the dissolution of all the corporations by the Reichstag at Ratisbon in 1793, Wöllner codifies and reinforces the measure already decreed against student indiscipline (23 February 1796). He is severe upon "brawls, debauch, slovenly dress, bathing and swimming at places not authorized by the police, unlawful entry, invasion of private gatherings, especially weddings, organized rowdyism at examinations, carrying weapons, speeding on horseback or by carriage, excesses in musketry, tobacco, fireworks, the entertainments and dinners demanded of newcomers, games of chance, etc." (Schwartz, *Kulturkampf*, 332).

These measures are part of a body of legislation directed mainly against the spirit of the Aufklärung, to which Wöllner is violently opposed. They remain in force even after his disgrace. The corporal punishments with which he threatened the students are never administered, but the system so highly reputed at the small University of Erlangen, which Prussia inherited in 1792 together with the principality of Ansbach-Beyreuth, henceforth protects the students at Halle as well; a supervisory committee, to which parents may send their sons' fees, is set up. It assigns teachers to assist the young men with their advice, to watch over their expenditure, and to report on their conduct every three months. The costs do not exceed 4 percent of the moneys deposited; the parents are reassured, the students are protected, and the teachers' authority is strengthened.

At Frankfort-on-Oder, too, the perpetual disturbances between the students and the officers of the garrison, each of them claiming precedence over the other, are allayed following the General Ordinance of 1798 abolishing the students' legal privileges and threatening them with imprisonment and flogging.

The disturbances provoked by the student corporations are thus less frequent at the end of the century, duels fewer, and dissipation less a matter of course. Excess has everywhere been curbed successfully. Even at Jena the students' corporations no longer lay down the law. As late as 10 June 1792 they demonstrated against Pro-Rector Ulbrich, guilty of renewing the edict prohibiting the corporations; they broke his windows and looted a foreign student's lodgings. But their great days were over. The Duke of Saxe-Weimar called out the troops. On 19 July, after considerable altercation, 267 students solemnly declared that academic freedom had been violated and threatened to leave town as a reprisal. No one stopped them. So they went off to Weimar, but the duke refused to receive them. Very much annoyed and somewhat ridiculous, they settled in the small village of Rohra in the territory of Erfurt. They were glad enough to be able to return to Jena on the 23d, defeated and deserted by their leaders, some sixty of whom had abandoned them rather than submit to police investigation. The duke had not yielded, and the corporations were no longer sovereign. Fichte was able to negotiate for their dissolution two years later, but failed because the Unicists went back on their decision at the last moment and preferred to disrupt their professor's courses.

The corporations grow progressively more anemic, along with the university, which owes its reputation to them. The new German universities keep the students in their own states, and foreigners are increasingly prevented by their governments from going off to spend their money in Germany. Whereas the Theological Faculty alone at Jena had 4,000 students in 1735, the entire student body amounted to only 800 in the winter of 1791, 726 in 1798, 536 in 1800, and 240 in 1805.

The Military

The Prussian army is the king's own particular concern; the civil service was created purely for the purposes of army recruiting. The General Domains and War Directory at Berlin and the provincial Chambers responsible to it see that each regiment is brought up to full strength in the canton to which it is assigned. Although the Reglement of 1792 lays down the principle of compulsory service for all, the burghers are in fact exempt. It is only the peasants and the poor who, supervised by the nobles, pay the blood tax. But the kings, anxious to keep on good terms with the nation as a whole, do not scruple to resort to mercenaries, who account for half the strength of the army at the end of Frederick II's reign. They are gradually reduced to three-sevenths by 1802. They sign on for ten years in the infantry and twelve years in the cavalry. Prussian nationals, liable to serve between the ages of sixteen and forty-five, remain in the service for twenty years; but there are only 139,324 of them in 1804, whereas more than 2 million are liable to the draft; only the tallest and fittest are actually enlisted. The average annual number of recruits actually enlisted is about one to every thirteen veterans. In 1802 a total of 9,287 are raised; their active service lasts only six weeks in any year owing to long furloughs.

Few of the burghers exempted from active service in the ranks are admitted to the officers' corps. Though Frederick II has to accept them during the Seven Years' War, he systematically relegates them to the cavalry regiments, garrison duty or the artillery, where they are still in a majority in 1806. At that date they account for about 9 percent of an officers' corps of 7,000. They are exceptions, there being only 29 of them among the 1,106 senior officers carried on the army list for 1806.

The proponents of the Aufklärung have no reason, therefore to take any particular interest in the army. They do, however, deal with it in their journals because the essential problem connected with it at the end of the eighteenth century is educational. The ranker's lot is a wretched one indeed. A musketeer under Frederick William II is still paid the same as in 1740, two thalers every five days. He gets his bread cheap, it is true, but all prices have risen in the past fifty years. Since the soldiers have to have some secondary occupation, the barracks are crowded with handlooms. Many of the men are married, 59,061 of the Prussian nationals in 1802, fathers of 40,693 boys and 38,812 girls, and 36,700 of the mercenaries, with 25,757 boys and 24,794 girls. They live in barracks with their wives and children. The unmarried men have separate quarters, with one bed for every two men.

Despite allowances for fathers of families, both the married and the unmarried have to apply frequently for leave. The captain grants it generously, since he does not have to pay them while they are on leave. The garrison towns are full of soldiers seeking odd jobs; some of them act as guides to strangers, hire themselves out as servants, or sell at a high price lumps of sugar, which they claim to have extracted from beet by Achard's recently invented method. Others deal in every kind of junk. Though they have to get permission from their officers to acquire a concession and have to produce evidence that they have a capital of fifty thalers, they compete ferociously with the second hand dealers in Berlin, Magdeburg, and Halle.

Discipline is the stricter inasmuch as poverty brutalizes the men. Corporal punishment is the order of the day; and it is often fatal. Conditions are so harsh that many men are driven to suicide or desertion. Four times as many soldiers as civilians attempt suicide; the suicide rate rises regularly each year during the army maneuvers in April and May. A special watch is kept on the mercenaries, since they cannot be recovered if they manage to escape abroad. The more suspect are quartered with married noncommissioned officers, who are held responsible if they desert. In garrison towns a special gun is fired whenever a soldier is absent from roll call. The local inhabitants thus alerted watch the bridges, crossings, and highroads; there is a reward for returning the deserter, dead or alive.

If these evils are to be remedied, rations must be improved and discipline become less harsh; the soldier must acquire a taste for his profession through encouragement of his sense of honor; conscription must replace impressment abroad. The army will then once again be the school of the nation, and all citizens, serving together indiscriminately, will share in a common cult of the fatherland. Reforms of this sort do not seem to be immediately feasible; but the outrage of persistent misconduct by the licentious soldiery amid the mansions and gardens of every prince's seat arouses the irony of travelers and causes the philosophers deep concern. "The friend of the people is moved to tears," writes Bertuch, the editor of the *Journal of Luxury and Fashion*,

at the spectacle of these little lads abandoned to wander half-savage and deprived of the restraints that are so necessary to our future upbringing, of all instruction, of all enlightenment as to their own dignity and destiny. These children are of course destined for the army. But does not the soldier need education as much, or even more, than the civilian? The author therefore suggests that a school be established in each regiment, at which the verger and a professional schoolteacher will impart instruction. The soldiers' children will be taught cleanliness, discipline, and religion. Instead of gathering in savage and destructive gangs in the towns, they will play games or perform drill out of school hours under the supervision of a soldier. They will learn to read, write, cipher, and card hemp, and this will not be any great burden on regimental funds. [Bertuch, *Erziehung*.]

Bertuch's suggestion is accepted. Several corps commanders organize compulsory schools for their men's children. General von Pfuhl, for example, in 1784 grants Moerschel, the regimental chaplain, the ten thalers monthly to be paid to a schoolmaster and the two thalers to be paid to a woman to teach sewing, knitting, and weaving. The school has three rooms in which the teacher lives and teaches, a small library and school equipment provided by gifts. The children's reports are read out in public by the chaplain every month and are submitted to the general, who rewards satisfactory pupils. The end-of-year examination is a regular ceremony attended by the general. The best pupil according to the conduct lists is rewarded in 1790 with a hat, presented by the major; two other pupils are awarded shoes and stockings.

But it is not only the common soldiers who lack education; their officers are in hardly better plight. The elite officers' corps trained in the military academies is very small. The total number of officers to graduate from the military academies under Frederick II between 1740 and 1786 is 3,258, an average of slightly more than eighty yearly. After several reforms and various increments, the Berlin cadet corps, composed mainly of former cadets from the provincial military academies, consists of 325 cadet officers distributed among five companies.

The young men who do not attend these academies receive only an elementary education. The country gentlemen are so eager for their sons' promotion that they send them to the regiment as early as possible to acquire seniority. By a cabinet order of 8 March 1804, Frederick William III prohibits their enlistment before the age of fourteen. Exhausted by plying an adult trade, the lads serving as *Junkers* or *Gefreite Corporale* give little heed to acquiring an education. Marwitz, enrolled at thirteen, rises at three every morning to curry the horses, drills outside the Halle Gate from five to ten, and returns to dress for the afternoon parade at the Brandenburg Gate. In the evening he is too tired to want anything but bed. What had he learned before he went to Berlin? Reading, writing, and arithmetic; but he is ignorant of the rule of three. He is incapable of translating Latin unseen because his tutor was never able to master deponent verbs or the use of the accusative infinitive. He has by heart the *Universal History for Children* by Professor J. M. Schroeckh of Wittenberg (Leipzig, 1779, 6 vols.) and knows the location of every geographical name mentioned in the six volumes. (Meusel, *Marwitz* I, 32–36.)

Military life is in any case very demoralizing. The young nobles associate only with noncommissioned officers, who corrupt them before they reach the rank of *Aspirant*. Very few feel, with Marwitz, that they need acquire an education. It is not until December 1799 that a cabinet order makes provision for military chaplains to teach German country gentlemen geography, history, the moral sciences, and the principles of mathematics.

The remedy suggested by the enlightened applies to officers and men alike; the age of enlistment should be raised to sixteen; an examination in general education should be required, in which the arithmetic test should even include fractions; and the conditions of service for recruits should be properly organized. Instead of being left among the noncommissioned officers, they might perhaps be grouped in each regiment under the supervision of two teachers, who would be in charge of both their military training and their general education. Junker schools are organized by some corps commanders after 1800, but they do not function very actively. Despite the efforts of Lieutenant-Colonel Scharnhorst, who transferred from the Hanoverian to the Prussian service in 1797, and despite the opening of a special officers' academy in 1802, their average level remains low in the extreme. The Prussian army of 1806 is no longer the precision instrument which Frederick II constructed, maintained, and led with such perfection;

and it is not yet the living bulwark which an elite of citizens, free and equal among themselves, is to raise against the oppressor.

The Jews

The Jews are subject to laws devised specially for them. With local variations, the main provisions of the Prussian General Patent of 1750 are in force in all the states of the empire. The Jews are only "tolerated" and pay dearly for the right to reside in the country of their birth. Their activities are restricted by law to peddling, to the few trades which are not organized by the guilds and to banking and manufacturing. They have to purchase permission to transmit their status and property to their children, to own landed property, and to travel from one town to another. They are liable to special taxes, humiliating when collected in the form of a toll at the town gate, like the excise on animals; and they are jointly liable for the payment of these imposts and for any offence committed by any one of them. Lacking civil and political rights, they are often regarded in the countryside as inferior beings; to kill them is no murder.

The doctrine of the natural equality of man and the faith in the progress of mankind cannot square with systems of legal disability. The press and the reading clubs accordingly demand the civil and political equality of the Jews with other citizens. They disseminate the ideas contained in a book, *On Political Reform concerning the Jews*, published in 1781 by Christian Wilhelm von Dohm, Military Councillor and Keeper of the Royal Archives, refuting the arguments of the opponents of equality, proving that any justified complaints against the Jews are due to their special status, and calling upon the authorities to repeal archaic laws which conflict with reason and are prejudicial to the interests of the state.

The movement for emancipation is both encouraged and hindered by the division within the Jewish community. A minority of bankers, manufacturers, and intellectuals, grown wealthy during the Seven Years' War and actuated by the prevailing philosophy, adopts the mode of living of the enlightened middle class, sacrifices the old customs on the altar of reason, and shows that the Jew can assimilate with the people among whom he has settled. No distinction is made between Jew and Christian either in the reading clubs or in the drawing rooms where they mingle. Treated as equals, eagerly listened to, and flattered, Jews forget that for centuries they have been the outcasts of mankind. When Henrietta Herz, the leading beauty of Berlin, greets visitors who are proud to be accepted among the elite of the Aufklärung with an inclination of the head which tosses her thick black curls and shows off to advantage the graceful curve of her neck; when Rahel Levin, so simple, frail, pale and delicate, lets her unforgettable gaze fall on the guests flocking to her attic in the Jägerstrasse and they include Prince

Ludwig Ferdinand of Prussia, Prince Radziwill, Countess Einsiedel, Brinck-mann, an attaché at the Swedish embassy, and the writers, artists, and actors who are the talk of Berlin, all of them personal friends of hers, it is quite understandable that they should view their future with optimism. They have only to recall their own childhood in the dreary ghetto, their strictly orthodox upbringing, even though their father may have been a wealthy man, like Dr. Lemos, who brought up Henrietta, to realize the distance they have come and to contemplate the future with confidence; and it is precisely this confidence, this cheerful and sturdy optimism, and this verve which the despairing young men seek in drawing rooms in which etiquette and society manners are ignored. Tact replaces etiquette. Their triumph would be secure but for the fact that the enemy finds allies among the Jews themselves.

For equality of rights presupposes equality of obligations. But can the orthodox Jew, bound as he is by traditions which impose religious forms on his every act, fulfill these obligations? Can he serve in the army or the civil service and risk having to renounce his special diet and the observance of his holy days? Can he be bound by an oath in court taken in a form other than that dictated by his religion? Can he, in order to work with his fellow citizens, readily submit to laws which, however reasonable they are, may not be consistent with his rites?

Alongside the enlightened minority, prepared to repudiate all ritual, the mass of the orthodox reject the equality offered by the Aufklärung.

Their obstinacy provides the opponents of assimilation with their most valuable argument. Nothing is more characteristic in this context than the long wrangle about the decrees ordering a three-day interval for burying the dead—humanitarian decrees, for there are instances of persons being buried alive; yet it takes the enlightened Jews, with the support of their friends, twenty years of fierce argument to induce the orthodox to comply with them.

The opposition to the Aufklärung is displayed with particular violence in the case of the Jews because so many vested interests are involved. Many people who pride themselves on their broad-mindedness are not in favor of the emancipation of those whose competition they fear in trades still closed to them; so that the principles seem more vulnerable and less self-evident as soon as any attempt is made to apply them to social problems. Success, though tardy, comes at last, however. The Austrian Edict of 1782 favors assimilation; partial reforms abolish the poll tax, joint liability, and some of the imposts throughout the empire. The Reglements granted by the Prussian government in 1797 are a great advance on the Edict of 1750. The French conquests in Germany and the reforms of 1812 in Prussia at last bring the Jews full civil and political equality.

(For a greatly expanded treatment of the Jews in Prussia during the eighteenth century the reader is referred to the Appendix.)

5

Aufklärung and Sturm und Drang: The Two Generations

The Generation of 1750

It is possible to date the reign of the Aufklärung in Prussia. Its beginning coincided with that of the reign of Frederick the Great in 1740. The new king did not confine himself, like his father, merely to authorizing the various churches and sects; he systematically encouraged the enlightened principles with which he cemented the institutions of his state. The year he came to the throne was also that in which Wolff returned to the University of Halle, where the Faculty of Theology later became, with Semler and Nösselt, one of the bulwarks of religious toleration. The new spirit brought three young men together in Berlin: Lessing and Mendelssohn, born in 1729, and Nicolai, born in 1733.

Lessing had graduated from Leipzig University and was publishing miscellaneous critical essays. He edited the theatrical column of the *Berlin Journal* in 1751 and again from 1752 to 1755. His first book of importance, the *Vademecum an Herrn Samuel Gotthold Lange*, was published in 1752 and his first major play, *Miss Sara Simpson*, in 1755.

Mendelssohn had left the Dessau ghetto quite young and had acquired an education in secret in Berlin. Despite the hostility of the rabbis, he had learned German and Latin, had acquired a Western culture, and had assimilated the principles of philosophy. His independence was assured, since he had been acting as bookkeeper and secretary to "silky" Bernhard, whose partner he later became; his friendship with Lessing encouraged him to publish his essays, which made him the foremost philosopher of the Enlightenment in Berlin.

Christoph Nicolai had just completed his apprenticeship at Frankfort-on-Oder and was working as a clerk in the bookshop managed by his father till 1752 and, after his father's death, by his elder brother. His education at the Pietist orphanage at Halle had given him a thorough distaste for mysticism. At Frankfort he read all the philosophers. Until 1758, when his brother died, he had enough leisure to attempt criticism. He had a clear and exact, if not a profound, mind. His *Travels in Germany* and his satirical novel, *Sebaldus Nothanker*, show a talent for observation and a sense of humor. Nothing is more characteristic, for instance, of the philosopher's positive frame of mind, as contrasted with the poetry of the unexpected so fervently cultivated by the Romantics, than the care with which Nicolai prepares his journeys. He carefully examines every type of carriage in order to select the best, decides on his itinerary and the length of time he will stay at each place, and writes to all his acquaintances telling them what he wishes to see. He collects the plans of all the towns he will be passing through and consults the statistics, the civil registers, and the lists of taxes, duties, and fees everywhere. He equips himself with a meter to measure the distances traversed by carriage and another for those traveled on foot. He carries a diary-journal and uses the fountain pen invented by Professor Funke of Leipzig. He describes this device at length and devotes a separate plate to an illustration of it: a metal capsule filled with ink is screwed on to a goose quill, and a very narrow feeder closed by a metal bar, which is withdrawn when the pen is to be used, carries the flow of ink. Nicolai's information is not always of the best, but the contemporary Prussian learned his geography from this account. To these three may be added their friend Thomas Abbt, Swabian by birth and Prussian by adoption, professor at Frankfort-on-Oder, who published his enthusiastic treatise *On Death for the Fatherland* in 1761 and died in 1766 at Bückeburg in Schaumburg, a town where Herder succeeded him as church superintendent. And lastly, Kant too, born in 1724, may be said to be one of them, though his fame did not spread until later. These men and a number of their contemporaries belong to a generation which reached maturity around 1750. Most of them evidence for the first time in Prussia a rationalist spirit which they are eager to develop and hand on to their successors.

Date of birth alone is not enough to define a generation. What is needed is for contemporaries to have a feeling of kinship; they need regular intellectual intercourse with each other. The reading clubs were the work of this first enlightened generation, and they stocked the periodicals published by Nicolai, who found no great difficulty in preparing his journeys because he had correspondents everywhere.

Indeed, Nicolai is as responsible as Frederick II for Prussia's becoming the center of rationalism. The most distinguished minds of the age only stay briefly in Berlin. Lessing is at Wolffenbüttel, Wieland at Weimar, Kant at Königsberg. The capital of Prussia can boast only Mendelssohn and talents of the second order such as Sulzer and Nicolai. But Nicolai has a genius for publicity. He popularizes the Aufklärung. In 1756 he launches a magazine, *The Library of the Fine Sciences and the Free Arts*; though he gives up the literary editorship in 1758, it continues to appear till 1806 under the management of Weisse. Then, after succeeding his deceased brother as manager of the bookshop, he publishes Lessing's *Letters concerning Literature*, in collaboration with Mendelssohn and Abbt. When Lessing withdraws from the *Letters* in 1763, Nicolai publishes his famous *General German Library* (*Allgemeine Deutsche Bibliothek*), which "reviews every book published in German" (*Beschreibung* I, 23). Every volume bears his personal imprint, for he personally selects his contributors and sometimes even rewrites their copy. But there is not a single writer of importance—Goethe alone excepted—who does not furnish him with an article. He is impartial enough to entrust to Merck, a friend of Goethe's, the reviews of the master's works, which he even dares to parody. For fifty years this magazine is to all intents and purposes the official gazette of the Aufklärung. The state in fact recognizes it as such, announcing by royal edict in 1775 that "the *Library* is a work of public utility" (Hettner, *Literaturgeschichte* IV, 203). After 1783, Nicolai is once more an editor—this time of the *Berliner Monatsschrift*, one of the most effective militants in the campaign against prejudice.

Whatever Nicolai's defects—he was vain, touchy, often superficial—he played a very considerable part in the formation of a rationalist mode of thought. Without him the state's own efforts would have been far less effective. Though his merits may well be open to dispute socially, politically, and philosophically, they simply cannot be underrated. The constant stream of his publications made him the backbone of the Aufklärung.

While the Aufklärung appears essentially Prussian because it was officially adopted by the Prussian state and popularized everywhere by Prussian publications, this does not of course mean that every subject of Frederick the Great was a rationalist. Here again, a further explanation is necessary. Combating the mystical, irrational, and sentimental trends that had prevailed in the past, the Aufklärung relegated them to the background, but by no means eradicated them. It could never have destroyed them, because all men are not alike. While some are endowed with a logical frame of mind and are capable of controlling themselves to the point of subordinating their feelings to their common sense, there are others who by nature need passion and have an instinctive propensity toward everything calculated to appeal to and excite their emotions. A good critical education sometimes makes them fully aware of their error; but that is no bar. The Aufklärung was impotent against those who deliberately acted in a way of which it disapproved.

Education really means the effort to instill a logical temperament into children until it becomes second nature. Very few are endowed with it at birth, for the primitive mentality is not logical. "Teaching children to think" means revealing the existence of reason to them, accustoming them to its use and compelling them to submit to it. A chosen few, with a predisposition to accept these principles, fulfill the ideal of the Aufklärung. Most of them do learn to recognize error and in many cases take care to avoid falling into it for fear of consequences which they are able to foresee. Their masters have, in fact, wisely kept some spheres, such as art and religion, open to the expression of expelled nature returning in force, but the most resolute characters reject any form of domination and deliberately choose the irrational. What the Aufklärung achieved was not the transformation of man, but an alteration in the range of values, placing reason at the summit. Those who disregarded it—and there were hardly fewer of them than before—no longer actually prided themselves on doing so. This is as much as the Aufklärung could do or indeed wished to do.

Theory also restrained it from extending its domination, for the very principle of toleration requires that there should be people toward whom it can be exercised; toleration would be unnecessary if everyone thought alike. The feature peculiar to the Aufklärung is that it accepts faith alongside reason; that is why most basically intelligent minds prefer it to any of the other philosophies. It creates an ideal of humanity which everyone is able to and ought to attain. This presupposes at the outset an incessant intellectual and critical activity leading to greater self-knowledge and to the acquisition of a certain experience of life; and this furnishes a sounder basis for judgment than a passing mood; it develops the sense of the relative; and this involves displaying greater understanding of others and greater indulgence toward them; and this effort to know oneself and to understand others leads to a generally optimistic attitude, to the acceptance and love of life, intenser and richer the greater its diversity.

The mystical current, therefore, flows parallel with the Aufklärung, which makes no serious effort to stem it. Reason no more bars feeling than it reproves passion; it only tries to control them and to subordinate them to itself. If hot-headed young men like Goethe and Schiller rise to self-mastery, it will welcome them gladly and will be all the richer for their experience of feeling.

One more trait emerges from our examination of the way in which this rationalism operates, and it assumes various forms. It borrows from Locke around 1750 and from Kant around 1790 the formulations which it makes intellectually respectable; it is invariably the ideas of the best minds that it popularizes. A mode of thought always comes into being only among a minority capable of self-expression. It may, however, either draw its inspiration from the masses below, in which case it becomes representative of the popular mass from which it has issued, or it may look for its watchwords from above, from the thinkers who generate new modes of thought; but in that case it necessarily has to present these ideas in a simpler, more concrete, and more superficial form in order to make them accessible. In the case of the Aufklärung, culture in fact comes from above and moves downward, for the elite minds at the upper levels are often barely intelligible. The Aufklärung requires its supporters to make a real intellectual effort; the burgher really toils to become a philosopher; the peasant really sweats to reach the burgher's level. The enlightened minority is conscious of its merit; it has "raised itself" above the crowd, but in doing so it has parted company with the masses. Its ideal is to radiate above the masses and gradually to penetrate them, not to reflect them. It is not this minority which expresses the community, but the community which painfully spells out a new alphabet of ideas which are alien to it. The Aufklärung becomes detached from its roots. It is perfectly natural, therefore, that the masses should become disheartened by the effort and should strive to defend their own traditions. But at least the Prussian state together with its schools and its church, stands firm against Reaction as such.

The first generation of the Aufklärung in Prussia, then, defines the new principles, organizes their popularization, allies itself closely with the state, and prevails from 1750 to 1770.

The Sturm und Drang

In May 1773 three articles of an entirely new tone were published together in an anonymous pamphlet entitled *On German Character and Art* (*Von deutscher Art und Kunst*). The author of one of them was an experienced civil servant, Justus Möser, a *Referendar* at Osnabrück. He was fifty-three years old and since 1768 had been publishing a history of Osnabrück remarkable for its feeling for the past, its comprehension of the violence and injustice of earlier periods, and its horror of all reforms and leveling tendencies. The preface to this history was his contribution to the pamphlet; he stands up for the old Germanic ideal and German traditions against foreign influences. In his early youth Möser had written a treatise, *The Value of Reciprocated Inclinations and Passions* (*Wert wohlgelungener Neigungen und Leidenschaften*), in praise of the passions as beneficent tempests which fill the sails of the inclinations and drive them on their course faster than the most unbridled ambitions. The second article was a panegyric of folk song and Shakespeare. Herder, its author, born in East Prussia in 1744, son of a schoolmaster, had studied under Kant and Hamann at Königsberg, and had left his native province in 1764, never to return. Tutor to the young Prince von Eutin, he had traveled with him, had met Goethe at Strasbourg in 1771, and had then become church superintendent at Bückeburg in the domains of the Duke of Schaumburg-Lippe. He had first made his name in 1767 with his fragments "On Recent German Literature," written at Riga after he had graduated from the university. In his *Critical Forests* (*Kritische Wälder*) (1769) he had already discovered folk song and had contrasted it favorably with French literature, had waxed enthusiastic about primitive poetry and had claimed to find in it, as in Shakespeare, a source of inspiration quite different from that of the Aufklärung. He had recently summarized, in 1771, his ideas in a monograph on the origin of language, which had been awarded a prize by the Berlin Academy. Language, he says, is the spontaneous product of all the human faculties, and the primitive language of mankind is poetry (Bossert, *Herder*, 67).

The third author was Goethe, a twenty-five-year old Frankfort lawyer, who had just completed his national and revolutionary play, *Götz von Berlichingen*. His contribution to the anonymous pamphlet was a eulogy of Strasbourg cathedral and Gothic art as essentially Germanic. In 1774 *The Sorrows of Werther* was to make him the most popular writer in all the Germanies.

The movement spreads and everyone tries his had at a romance of chivalry or a drama of passion. The authors are more fervent and well-intentioned than talented. The term *Sturm und Drang* itself comes from a play by Klinger produced in 1776. Klinger, with Lenz and Wagner, are some of Goethe's earliest followers. The only first-rate work which might perhaps be claimed by the new school is Schiller's *Die Räuber* (1781).

If we take literary history as our criterion, the Sturm und Drang is a reaction against the Aufklärung. It lays stress on feeling rather than on reason. It revives and glorifies the Middle Ages as against Classical Antiquity and is hostile to foreign influences, especially the French.

When we try to define the movement more precisely, we run into great difficulties. In the first place there are few specialized studies of it, whereas there are almost too many on the Aufklärung and on Romanticism. In the second place, we find that the literary histories and biographies do not agree on the classification of many of the writers. Jung-Stilling, Karl Philipp Moritz, and Jacobi could equally well be placed in a chapter on mysticism and Pietism as in one on the Sturm und Drang or Romanticism. In any case, the movement is not really as novel as it seems. Herder invented nothing; the ideas of the Sturm und Drang were represented at Königsberg itself by J. G. Hamann, who was born in 1730, was raised in a Pietist environment and really belongs to the mystical trend which, from throughout the century, under various names and either through organized sects such as Pietism or through isolated individuals such as Böhme and Franz von Baader, relieves souls oppressed by the tutelage of reason. Hamann, "the Magus of the North," opposes his "philosophy of feeling" to the Aufklärung. He does so confusedly, in fragments, many of them "Sibylline" in style and religious in inspiration. His principle is that man must involve the whole of his faculties in any action. The Aufklärung as such could have no objection to this; but Hamann does not believe in the need for reason to direct and coordinate these faculties. He despises analysis; he stands for faith against reason, inspiration against craftsmanship, man as an entity against the Aufklärung. Natural spontaneity, the only spontaneity which is worthy of esteem, is manifested in the feelings and the passions, and they are expressed in images. That is why poetry is the mother tongue of the human race. Herder develops this idea in his memorabilia of 1771, as he develops all the master's ideas. But he had attended Kant's courses and so was capable of composing completed works, whereas Hamann prefers "the exception to the rule, imagination to reason, poetry to prose, and the particular to the general" (Scherer, *Geschichte*, 521), and only published fragments, the *Socratic Memorabilia Collected for Public Ennui by an Amateur of Ennui*, published in 1759, the same year as the *Letters on Literature* by Lessing, Mendelssohn, and Nicolai. He followed this up with *The Clouds, The Crusades of a Philosopher*, and *Aesthetics in a Nutshell*.

Nor should the rediscovery of the Middle Ages be exaggerated. It appears in literature at about the same time as Classical Antiquity. While the enlightened writers had no great liking for "gothic" subjects, the reverse is not true of the Sturm und Drang. It is not that there was one era inspired by the Middle Ages and another by Classical Antiquity, but simply that there were various different ways of treating the same subjects during the same era.

Greece was quite as much of an inspiration to the Romantics as it was to the Classics; but the Greece of Winckelmann and Heinse, Goethe and Hölderlin, Schiller and Friedrich Schlegel was not common ground. In short, even if it is agreed that the Sturm und Drang, like Romanticism after it, displays a preference for certain subjects, this is not criterion enough to define a school; and even less so the campaign against French influences, which is in fact common to all the German writers of the period and in which Lessing was quite as prominent as Herder.

If the generation of the Sturm und Drang cannot be identified by any particular novelty in its productions, can it be defined by chronology? No, for Möser was born in 1720, Goethe in 1749, Klinger in 1752, and Jean-Paul in 1763. Möser, too, has few points of contact with his fellow writers. Goethe does seem to be something like the leader of a school, inasmuch as he invited his followers to Weimar; but they did not stay long, and the master rather tended in after years to disown those who claimed him as such.

It is not possible, therefore, specifically to identify a generation of the Sturm und Drang, whereas this is quite feasible in the case of the Aufklärung and Romanticism. We do have to account, however, for the fact that contemporaries certainly spoke of a "Sturm und Drang period." The main reason is that some very great writers did for a time collaborate with the mystical trend. The Sturm und Drang was not a new school; its place is within a continuous stream from Pietism to Romanticism, in which the chief names are Hamann, Möser, Herder, Jacobi, and Jung-Stilling. The writers of genius who cooperated with it for a time strengthened this stream, which later kept the name Sturm und Drang alive until it merged with Romanticism. For this stream becomes important again toward the end of the century. Psychologically there is not very much difference between the youthful champions of the Sturm und Drang and their Romantic emulators; and the ideas attributed to the Sturm und Drang in literary history are equally the property of Romanticism. The best way of looking at the movement is in relation to the history of ideas, wherein the Sturm und Drang may be seen as part of the irrationalist trend in the eighteenth century; from this point of view, the movement is in fact susceptible of ideological definition.

There are, however, two essential traits in the Sturm und Drang which differentiate it from Romanticism, even if it is a species of dress rehearsal for it. First, it makes scarcely any headway in Prussia. Herder was of course read in Prussia as much as anywhere else. But Prussia happened to be in the full flower of the Aufklärung at precisely the time when Herder's works were being published. The Prussian schools, press, and salons were propagating rationalism, and the reaction against the Aufklärung was weaker in Prussia than elsewhere because the state stood out openly and officially against such reaction. The main proponents of the Sturm und Drang settle all round the domains of the Philosopher King, at Leipzig, Weimar, Göttingen, Bückeburg, Frankfort, and Zurich and in Holstein. None of them settle in Prussia, where Nicolai publishes a parody of *Werther* and reason continues to reign unchallenged. The social malaise reflected in the criticisms in *Werther* and its imitators is, moreover, quite recent. It disturbs the wealthy and over-populated countries of the west and south, but hardly troubles Prussia and bears no resemblance at all to the profound crisis it reflected in the age of Romanticism. In point of fact, all the young men who revolt against rationalism and oppose foreign influences manage to obtain decent jobs fairly easily. Goethe becomes a minister of state, Herder a church super-intendent, and Schiller a professor; Klinger makes a brilliant career in Russia, Müller becomes content with his lot as cicerone to eminent foreigners at Rome, Heinse becomes a librarian at Mainz. It rather seems that the drive of the Sturm und Drang writers relaxes in proportion as they obtain the places and favors they merit. The leaders of the movement, at any rate, become false to it one after another. Herder, the most faithful, follows a course peculiar to himself, to which he immolates many of the idols he worshiped in the past. Goethe escapes to Italy and returns wholly converted to a classical ideal, a rationalism enriched by a refinement of the senses and the cultivation of feeling, an Aufklärung more perfected and more human-ized than that of Mendelssohn. Schiller, though his earlier writings had been imbued with revolutionary ideology and social criticism, might well be considered to be closer to the Aufklärung than to the Sturm und Drang; he sets to studying Classical Antiquity and allies himself with Goethe in 1794 in defense of classical culture. These masters, in any case, were never at odds with the Aufklärung; Goethe was influenced by Lessing, Herder by Kant, and Jacobi by Wieland. Wieland at Weimar stands at the confluence of the two streams; after 1773 he tries to gather around his *Teutscher Merkur* all talents of any merit. The leaders' desertion does not indeed hamper the development of the "philosophy of feeling," *Werther's* influence is considerable, and Goethe deplores it, for his readers do not embark on a course similar to his own; and on the whole his book certainly does more to dislocate than to enrich the Aufklärung. In his *Conversations with Eckermann* (10 February 1829) he recalls "the difficulty in the Sturm und Drang period of escaping from it to attain to a higher culture."

6

The Aufklärung:
Conclusions

The Aufklärung, then, liberal but combative, antimystical but religious, utilitarian but idealistic, encyclopedic but German, was not imported from abroad. It asserts the primacy of reason, like the English and French philosophies, but whereas in France the critique is directed mainly to the political system and in England to the economic system, in Germany, where the wars of religion lasted a very long time, its prime object is to establish freedom of belief. Its success in doing so dictates its subsequent direction. Not that it disregards social reform. Baron Karl von Moser, who launched his *Patriotic Archive* in 1784 to serve the truth and to judge the mighty (*PAD* 16 July 1784), can take the measure of his progress; he quotes a cabinet order by Duke Ernst-August of Saxe-Weimar in 1736 in which the duke complains that his rents are not coming in properly; he declares that "he does not want reasoners for subjects," and anyone who ventures to utter any criticism will be punished with six months' imprisonment. At the end of the century it can be said that the advisers to princes owe them the truth. It can be claimed that "it is hard, but not impossible, to serve loyally where the service is salaried and the nobility no longer performs its functions in the state" (*DM* 1777, 101–4). The Aufklärung has some successes to its credit; it has polished manners appreciably. Though the restictions on the consumption of coffee are not complied with, the Aufklärung can boast that it has put an end to a great many barbaric usages and customs. It has mitigated the students' excesses, improved the conditions of the Jews, and extended education to a point where the people, not merely the elite, can participate in the national life. It has transferred many beliefs, such as those in devils, omens, and ghosts, from the category of faith to that of superstition; many acts, such as student dueling and anti-semitic violence, from the category of honor to that of crime; and many usages, such as precedence, titles and fashions, from the category of privilege to that of prejudice.

But it remains first and foremost an intellectual movement.

Its most zealous supporters still regard the social question as a problem of education. Faced with a swift development of the forms of social life at the very moment when the Revolution is triumphant in France, Forster, for example, is troubled by the coarse and impure element in the popular movement and distrusts the semi-intellectuals who are propagating erroneous ideas:

True love of country can never be anything but the preserve of a few of the elect. In our time, when a blind attachment to ancient traditions is coupled with a profound corruption of manners and a rash mania for innovation, it would not be surprising if this sublime virtue had become totally extinct. When irrational prejudice, swollen with pseudoscience, leads the battle array, more harm than good to the true education of the nation must always come of it, and mankind is still far from its true end, its striving for perfection. When they lack extreme delicacy of moral feeling, it may be as dangerous to promote the other spiritual forces as it was to neglect them in the past. [Forster, *Ansichten* II, 89.]

Naïvely optimistic, the Aufklärung was never revolutionary. Its intention was not to brutalize the body but to enlighten the mind. For a long time the facts seem to justify its methods. In the drawing rooms of Berlin, in the cafés of Breslau, in the reading clubs throughout the Germanies, burgher and noble, poor and rich, devout and atheist form a society without ranks, without classes, without conventions, contrasting with the official society. True, this is still mainly the rallying center for dissidents. But tomorrow perhaps these groups will become the majority. Society will be transformed without violent revolution, by the sole effect of enlightenment. Why despair of the future? At Mainz as at Weimar, at Königsberg as at Berlin, prejudice is visibly retreating step by step. Why then doubt that philosophy will, by gradually encroaching upon the traditional society, at length assimilate it completely?

Toward the close of the century, however, symptoms of crisis appear. The Aufklärung observes them unperturbed. With the species of division of labor which has occurred in Prussia it is for the state to concern itself with material contingencies. The Aufklärung cuts new paths through the underbrush of blind superstition and absurd prejudices, but so far as everything to do with the material is concerned, the Enlightened Despot is there, and for two generations now he has succeeded in satisfying his needs without exhausting his subjects. The Aufklärung feels at ease in the Prussian state. The state does not restrict its freedom and on occasion pays heed to its criticisms. It is not, like Catholic doctrine, a system opposed to reason, an obscurantism hostile to enlightenment, a dogma raised against the evident truth. It is manifested rather in a body of skills, which are taught in the law faculties or the civil service and have nothing secret about them, since anyone can learn them, but which are of no concern to the philosopher. In a mercantile system economic affairs are a branch of statecraft, a matter for the civil service. If the economy atrophies or falls sick, it is for the state to apply the remedy, as it would in the case of the army or the courts.

The philosophers' disdain for economic affairs accounts in part for the growth of the crisis in Prussia. Everyone is affected by it at the end of the century, but no one clearly perceives its causes. The framework of the state gradually erected by the Hohenzollerns is too rigid. The officials, honest but little accustomed to take the initiative, are sunk in routine. The malaise grows, because between philosphic speculation and administrative routine there does not exist an intermediate body of citizens trained to analyze economic affairs, capable of individual initiative, and adept at suggesting novel methods such as is formed by the physiocrats in France and the economists in England.

Part 2 The Social and
Political Crisis

7

The Social Crisis

The Growth in Population

The Aufklärung holds that population is the chief source of a state's prosperity. Like Frederick William I, Frederick II stated on several occasions that the strength of a state does not lie in the extent of its lands and the possession of vast empty territories but in the numbers and wealth of its population. In his Political Testament of 1768 he said:

The first and truest principle which holds good everywhere is that the strength of a state consists in the number of its subjects. To verify this you have only to compare Holland, which is some 40 leagues long and 15 leagues wide at most, with Siberia, which is probably 300 leagues long and perhaps 100 or more leagues wide. You will find that Holland has 3 million industrious inhabitants who pay the republic 15 to 16 million crowns and once assumed the whole weight of the war against its tyrant, Philip II of Spain, wholly on its own. In the vast stretches of Siberia there are only 600,000 inhabitants, and Russia draws barely 300,000 crowns from it; any invader would easily be able to subjugate those empty spaces, for they lack hands to farm and defend them. You can see, therefore, that the decisive factor is the number of industrious inhabitants, not the extent of territory. [*Political Correspondence*, 125–26.]

The king leaves it at that, for the demonstration is self-evident.

Count Hertzberg stated in one of his *Dissertations*, in 1785:

It is now pretty generally agreed that it is a large population that chiefly makes for the well-being and especially the power of a state when a wise government knows how to derive the greatest profit by providing its subjects with the employment and necessaries they require. This being so, it is impossible nowadays to find any example of a state's being too populated and having to try to curb or reduce its population, as the Greeks and Romans once did by acquiring colonies and by infant exposure. . . . The more people there are who work in well-ordered concert to acquire prosperity for the society in which they live, and the more populous a nation is in proportion to the area it occupies, the more means it has of augmenting the sum of the common weal and especially of defending itself against its neighbors' threats or use of force.

Professor Süssmilch, whose voluminous book went through four editions in fourteen years and was regarded as the authority on the subject, does not even have Hertzberg's reservations. Should a state omit to make provision for citizens' needs, God will provide. It is an indisputable fact that the general wealth depends upon the density of population. History teaches us that periods of decadence have always been periods of depopulation. This was the sole cause of the fall of the Roman Empire, for example. God himself proclaims the principle which ought in all circumstances to guide governments: "Increase and multiply, He commands; He will see to the rest" (Süssmilch, *Göttliche Ordnung*).

The amount of land lying waste in the early part of the century certainly provides justification for these axioms. Prussia first derived its power from its internal colonization policy. To increase production and revenue from taxes at the same time as the numbers of their subjects and to build up reserves of recruits for the army in the depths of the empty countryside were the aims of the Great Elector and Frederick William I. Frederick II followed in their footsteps; he drained nearly 500,000 acres of land at the mouths of the Oder, Netze, and Warthe and in the Droemling marshes east of Stendal. He divided up the large peasant properties to make more smallholdings. He attracted foreign colonists, preferably German-speaking, by paying for their travel and offering the neediest of them farms and the stock to run them. He established in his states the workers from Thuringia and the Voigtland who migrated into the province of Magdeburg to bring in the harvest. Expenditure on this alone amounted to some 50 million thalers in the course of his long reign, not including subsidies to the foreign craftsmen who settled in Prussia and disclosed their trade secrets. At least 285,000 immigrants entered Prussia between 1740 and 1786. Their loyalty contributed to the consolidation of the conquests which enlarged the area of the kingdom from 118,926 square kilometers to 194,891 square kilometers in this period and its population from 2,240,000 to 5,430,000.

Conquests and colonization alone, however, did not account for this increase. The birth rate rose very rapidly everywhere at the end of the eighteenth century. Even such disasters as war, the famine of 1771–72, and the disastrous winter of 1783–84 failed to check the increase. After losing 66,000 inhabitants during the famine, Silesia regained 77,000 between 1773 and 1777. All the local population counts, reproduced very fully in the press, show the same upward trend. The empire had about 30 million inhabitants in 1790. In Prussia the mean surplus of births over deaths was as high as 30 percent for the whole country between 1757 and 1805. Between 1785 and 1805 the total population rose from five and a quarter to six and a quarter million. In the eastern provinces (East and West Prussia, Pomerania, New Mark), where the increase seems to be particularly marked, and in Silesia, it rose by 50 percent between 1766 and 1805; in the western provinces (Electoral Mark, Magdeburg, Mansfeld, Halberstadt, Hohenstein, Wernige-rode, Minden, Ravensburg, Tecklenburg-Lingen) by about 30 percent. In the Rhineland (Cleves, Mark-Moers, Guelder) and in Friesland, where the growth was less rapid, it rose by 20 to 25 percent.

While this fertility can only be welcome in the empty regions, is this equally true of the areas where the population has always been dense and the foreign recruiting sergeant and the colonization company have always exploited the inhabitants' poverty? The theoreticians of the Aufklärung do not doubt it. But even if the land can feed many more people, the distribution of the population and especially the distribution of the available goods among them surely raise formidable problems.

One fact which does not strike contemporaries, because it conflicts with the received idea that the land can hold many more people yet, is that the increase in population is reflected chiefly in the enlargement of the towns. Nowhere has the countryside been notably depopulated to swell the towns; all that happens is a concentration of rapid population growth in the towns.

The official doctrine has obtained such a hold on general thinking that it occurs to no one to relate the increase in population to the economic crisis, the effects of which are everywhere making themselves felt. Only a few isolated writers express any doubts, and everyone construes them as para-doxes. Wekhrlin, for example, argues in 1788 against the principle that "a state's well-being resides in its population." According to him, it depends on the region concerned. "In some of the smaller lands," he says, "everyone should marry and have children. It is for Providence, which provides for the rats, mice, and caterpillars, to discover whence they will earn the pittance they need. But since Providence no longer performs miracles, in some districts which are overpopulated and cannot possibly hold out much longer there is an abundance of beggars and thieves" (*HB* 1788, III, 137–44).

Only after the publication of Malthus's book in 1798, the German translation of which causes a sensation, and after its slow propagation, do ideas begin to change. There are attempts to restrict the birth rate. Professor Weinhold of the Faculty of Medicine at Halle adjures the princes to follow his advice: they must decree the infibulation of all young persons of fourteen years of age and up, beggars, servants, workmen and unmarried soldiers who are not rich enough to bring up a child. The state will conduct periodic inspections and punish by flogging, imprisonment, or penal servitude those who have broken the seal with which they will be marked (Weinhold, *Übervölkerung*, and Wahrhold's indignant reply).

Emigration, which is regarded as a disaster, is rampant, especially in the western and southern parts of the empire. As population is growing faster than available resources, the only thing to be done is to try one's luck elsewhere. Crimping for soldiers and colonists reaps a splendid harvest. The journals blame the princes. Poverty is driving citizens out of their own country. Citizens? If they were truly citizens, they would have no reason to emigrate. But the burgher is good for nothing but paying taxes, and the peasant, powerless to meet the growing demands of lords corrupted by luxury, is nothing but a beast of burden. Emigration might be effectually combated by reducing the number of holidays, encouraging new crops and clearings, lowering taxes, and abolishing lotteries. The peasants might be protected against foreign press gangs instead of being sold to them to pay for falcons, actors, banquets, and courtiers. "You write," Wekhrlin tells the learned, "about human rights, freedom, love of country. Has the humble dweller in a place where the prince is a brigand, the official an extortioner, and the pastor a knave any recourse but to quit?" (*GU* 1784, III, 59-63).

A taste for adventure with its prospects of sudden wealth and happiness induces the boldest to leave before they are completely ruined. The princes' prohibitions cannot deter them, despite the threatened penalties. Threats are vain against those who have nothing to lose. They leave Württemberg, the most densely populated land in the empire, for Hungary in 1779 and East Prussia in 1782. Hungary is the chief attraction to the long trains of emigrants deserting their homes in the provinces of Mainz, Coblenz, Mannheim, and Kreuznach. They are of all ages and all trades. Men and women leave with their scanty savings; when questioned, they say that there are too many people in the Palatinate, the Westerwald, Switzerland, and Lorraine. Many of them are well dressed and of decent and honest appearance. It is estimated that at least 15,000 began to emigrate before 1783 and in 1784. The movement continues in subsequent years. Joseph II tried to divert them to Galicia; in 1783 he offered colonists houses, barns, and fields there. Catherine II populated northern Russian and even the Crimea with Germans. The highroads of the empire are thronged with thousands of honest people in search of means of subsistence because they have been disinherited by the growth of the population and nothing has been done for them by way of social reform.

Hence, the crisis in Prussia is both economic and social. Since early in the century a self-serving economic policy has gradually produced a system of regulation calculated to enrich the prince. But the mercantile system may be likened to a coat of mail closely fitting the body of the state; when the body grows, the mail hampers its breathing. The fault lies not in regulation as such, however, but in the way it is applied. A less rigid and less stringent system of laws and regulations, one which allowed for the growth of supply and demand, limited the manufacture of luxuries for a shrinking market instead of compelling reluctant customers to buy them to their own detriment, and kept watch on the fluctuations in its subjects' living standards instead of blindly trying to increase their numbers might have produced an autarky benefitting enlightened despotism and the Aufklärung. By the end of the century it is too late. Mere amendments to the regulations can no longer suffice to give direction to a revolution which has already become irreversible. Industry is in crisis owing to overpopulation and the progressive deterioration in the workers' and peasants' standards of living. To convert them into consumers would be the remedy, but this would entail giving them the means to enrich themselves. No matter whether the state renounced state capitalism and turned to free trade, and in consequence required the possessing classes to submit to direct taxation to replace the revenue from the "contribution" and the excise or whether it presided over a new and more equitable distribution of goods, the outcome would be the same—a change in class relations and a reduction in the income of the wealthier classes to enable the poor to live better.

Even those who meant best and were the most intelligent dared not undertake so radical a reform. Neither Stein nor Struensee dreamed of making this sort of revolution; even those who should have impelled them in this direction would probably have failed to follow them; for public opinion in Prussia was untutored in economic affairs.

In this overregulated state, economics are the affair of government, for it is the state that has colonized the waste lands, created the industries, and built up trade. Nowhere else, indeed, is the economic system so closely welded to the political system; the two systems have grown up together like the branches of a single tree. The same officials administer both of them; graduates of the national universities, they have studied law and scientific finance (*Cameralwissenschaften*), that is to say, the political and economic institutions of Prussia; they have trained for the examination for *Referendar*, which takes in general administration, police (in the broad contemporary sense), the excise and the army. How can they criticize a system which is unified to such a degree? Almost a century's experience would give them pause at the outset; and the government's zeal in acclimatizing all innovations strengthens their faith in the future. It encourages the growing of fodder crops and potatoes; it increases the yield from the mines. It is true that critics abroad deplore the fact that it is the government rather than private enterprise which has taken this in hand, but insofar as the theories of the French physiocrats and the English liberals reach Prussia at all, it is not thought that they are in any way applicable in that country. Very typical is the story of the only liberal economist who taught at a Prussian university, at the very end of the century. Professor Kraus was first and foremost a philosopher. Born in 1753, he attended courses by Kant and Hamann; he became a professor of empirical philosophy at Göttingen in 1790. He first took an interest in economics in 1786, but did not begin to specialize in the subject at Königsberg University until 1793, at the age of forty; he popularized Adam Smith's ideas, and died at the age of fifty-four.

Two of the seven volumes of his complete works are devoted to economics, no more than are devoted to the *Encyclopedic Considerations*, which treat of philology, aesthetics, history, and geography. Kraus enjoyed a great reputation at the beginning of the neneteenth century, but he had very few pupils. His influence was negligible right up to his death in 1807.

"Prussia" connotes "enlightened despotism and a directed economy." If the direction is removed, there is no longer any justification for the despotism; the pillars upholding the development of the Aufklärung crumble. Both its strength and its weakness lie in the fact that it has adapted itself to the state. The young men it breeds are not trained for the work of destruction which has become necessary if the Aufklärung is to expand. They do not even grasp the causes of the economic crisis they are undergoing. Equipped as they are to ensure that a "world view" prevails, they rely on ideology to remedy their afflictions. Incapable of imbuing the Aufklärung with the revolutionary force which actuates the foreign philosophies, they gradually, almost without realizing it, turn away from those philosophies. Reason reels before the onset of new modes of thought, and disillusioned intelligence yields to feeling.

Vagrancy in the Countryside

Despite all the decrees, poverty impels the peasants to desert their homes. Day laborers leave to seek employment. Craftsmen go in search of the work they cannot find at home. Honest folk fall in with others aimlessly roaming the countryside. Poachers, itinerant knife grinders, "who often harbor projects which they should not," students forced to flee the consequences of a duel or to put distance between them and their creditors, puppeteers, conjurers, companies of strolling players, whose adventurous life captures the college boys' imagination, guild craftsmen, Jewish peddlers, and shepherds, idle during the off-season, tramp cross-country. In summer they sleep out, in winter, in herdsmen's huts, peasants' stalls, or low inns. Men, women, and children gather, couple, and separate as the fancy takes them, engendering unfortunates who will never know any life but the vagrant's. Boys smoke at the age of eight, girls become mothers at fifteen; all die young. In Thuringia they form gangs of ten to twenty and "burn the peasants' fences to cook the vegetables they have stolen from the fields and the meat they have extorted rather than begged." They will not work. "Only occasionally one of them polishes a gnarled stick during a halt or makes a bird cage and catches a singing bird; a very few of the women weave thin cotton stockings as they walk."

Most of them live on public charity; and when this is too meager, they can supplement it by other means, for they are sturdy. They disdainfully refuse the offer of a pfennig, will not take less than a groschen. Woe to the peasant who refuses to give alms or opposes the devastation of his vegetable plot, the looting of his orchard, or the destruction of his fences! He is rewarded by a volley of oaths and may well have his farm set alight and be set upon himself if he ventures out of his village.

In January 1799, peasants stop carriages in broad daylight on the highroad from Erfurt to Gotha and demand a toll, to which they are in no way entitled. The smaller principalities like Ansbach are literally invaded by beggars.

The gentlemen in the capital have no notion of it, for begging was abolished there, as in other towns, some time ago, by efficient institutions for the poor. The officials in the country take little notice, for most of them do not give alms to beggars and the beggars are seldom bold enough to go near them. The clergy are not affected, for they are almost always able . . . to satisfy any marauders who knock at their door out of the proceeds of the collections taken up at the service. The village mayors [*Schulzen*] have no interest in arresting these people simply to turn them over to the magistrate [*ins Amt*], so they do nothing. The special provosts assigned to some districts . . . are quite unable to cope with their duties; many of them become the accomplices of the worst vagabonds and share their booty with them. Even if they were willing to take their duties seriously, their ancient and starveling carcasses would merely be an object of derision to these youthful, vigorous, and well-nourished freebooters; in any case, it is years since their muskets have fired a shot. [However,] one cannot without anger watch these sturdy young men and strong, red-cheeked women, with their swarms of children, tramping from house to house and village to village. . . . Few of them cannot produce some certificate (none of them, of course, issued by Ansbach) to show that they have had a long illness, broken a leg or an arm, or lost their home by fire, flood, or earthquake. Many of them take up a collection for whole communities; their certificates and seals are so crudely counterfeited that they would not deceive a child.

The peasant, already overburdened with taxes, puts up with the vagrants because he values "his arms, legs, and cottage." But he has nothing left over for helping the village day laborers, whose children finally have to tie up their bundle and go off to beg—and later, no doubt, to steal.

No region in Germany is spared. Similar complaints echo from north to south, from Holstein and Göttingen to Chemnitz and Salzburg and throughout Württemberg.

Bavaria is infested with robbers. Jochum terrorizes the district of Eichstätt with his gang of seventy bandits. He is broken on the wheel on 17 February 1781 after committing eighty-three robberies with violence. A real unfortunate is Jochum, dead at thirty. A vagrant from childhood, he at first weaves baskets for sale and begs "honestly," like his parents. Then he falls in with the gang of the formidable brigand Zencken-Mandl, who teaches him to steal his first loaf through an open cottage window. Then come assaults by night on country folk who have refused to pay up. Schiller had no need to imagine his *Robbers*; all he had to do was take a stroll in the country. It is perfectly possible that some of the robber chieftains were noble characters like Karl Moor. Anton Reiser meets a journeyman binder between Gotha and Erfurt who has been roaming all over Electoral Saxony for years; who knows whether he has never robbed as well? Schubart gets to know students from Erlangen who have run up debts or fought duels and fled, not daring to face their parents, and have become soldiers, strolling players, or vagrants. In 1776 he meets a former servant of his at Augsburg, "a fellow practically falling to pieces from his excesses in debauchery." He had been a tailor, soldier, courier, trickster, thief, parasite, and a gross swaggerer. "He practically stripped me bare at Munich, stealing my boots, linen, and everything. This wastrel had the audacity to offer to become my servant again, but I refused. . . . He was even prepared to serve for board and lodging alone. He flew off like a bird of prey. And, believe it or not, he afterward made a fortune at gaming, won thousands and thousands, bought an estate, and is now living like a lord on his spoils!" In the Palatinate beggars account for one-nineteenth of the population, and domestics, grooms, and other servants for one-tenth.

The evil is irremediable. Edict after edict is issued in vain; ancient penal laws are revived decreeing capital punishment for robbery and poaching. But it is no use threatening the guilty with the rack and the scaffold and promising impunity if they peach on their accomplices. The decrees are not enforced; the military carry out the searches, because the local officials are impotent, but are seldom able to arrest the marauders. The terrorized peasants hide the vagrants in their barns. Protection by the patrols means nothing. In Erfurt and Weimar the hussars can visit each village in their manor no more than once a fortnight. As they fail to work in concert with the dragoons from Gotha, the vagrants have an easy time; they slip across the frontier whenever a patrol arrives and return as soon as its back is turned. The soldiers "are somtimes gallant enough to tell some sprightly girl among the vagrants when they are likely to be back, in return for a pair of fine stockings or some other favor" (*JD* 1787, I, 243–44). The same sort of thing goes on in Fulda, Saxe-Coburg, Hanover—everywhere.

In any case, what could be done with these people if they were all arrested? In the district of Sonderhausen they deface the posters threatening them with imprisonment and jest that "the jails would have to be pretty big. Let them jail us! They'll at least have to give us some bread! Things can't go on like this for ever!" (*GHM* 1789, V, 516–23.)

The disorder is compounded by the division of the Germanies into scores of small states; each government thinks only of expelling the marauders from its own territory. The peasant, forced to house and feed the beggars threatening him as well as the soldiers protecting him, can barely curb his exasperation and his instinct to revolt against the tax collecter, the lord who cares for nothing except his privileges, the requisitions of the soldiery, and the effrontery of the beggars—indeed against the whole of mankind, which seems leagued together to take advantage of his weakness and ignorance.

In Prussia the press carries little news of vagrancy; but this does not mean that it does not exist there. The police, however, better organized there than elsewhere, and the administration somehow manage to keep it within bounds. But toward the end of the century they too begin to be overwhelmed. The archives of the General Directory contain a huge mass of documents concerning "bohemians" arrested and jailed. They are always the same sort of people. In the course of the "inquisitions" or *Generalvisitationen* ordered from time to time by way of combating vagrancy, in East Prussia in 1804, for example, a widow is arrested who had become a beggar because she was unable to feed her two children out of her earnings as a weaver; another who has been roaming the countryside with her daughter playing the zither; two sons of schoolmasters and two fugitive domestics, one of whom had held his place for eighteen years, who have been driven by daily bad treatment to desert their masters; a sixty-year-old saddler who left Insterburg because he had not been able to find work there; he manages to earn a living in the country, but he is compelled to return to the town; and a cobbler and a tailor who have been on the tramp for several years. In Lithuania a Berlin journeyman, who has made his tour of Prussia via Breslau, Warsaw, Königsberg, Insterburg, Gumbinnen, and Stallupönen but has been unable to find work anywhere, is jailed along with three tailors and several beggars. There are a great many soldiers on furlough; the Magdeburg Chamber lodges a complaint and obtains the recall of soldiers on leave who are wandering the countryside; they may not in future quit their regiment. From one district to another and one year to the next it is always the same sort of case.

When acting in concert, the gangs invariably perpetrate much the same sorts of acts of violence—cattle thieving, breaking and entering, and arson. The Magdeburg Chamber complains in 1786 of "the great increase in vagrant gangs of bohemians in association with other robbers" and obtains permission for the authorities to call out the troops to keep order. The disturbances continue, however.

Two points are worthy of note. First, the increase in vagrancy after the death of "der alte Fritz" occurs chiefly in the provinces in which the growth in population is largest. Hardly any complaints are recorded from Friesland or the western regions. In Pomerania, however, the breakdown of order elicits complaints from officials themselves. "I cannot but inform your Majesty," Justizrat Zimmermann writes in 1786, "of the anxiety and terror to which we are prey here in the countryside, where so many robberies and burglaries are being perpetrated and so many villains are roaming all over the province. . . . Only this spring, robbers broke into my stables, emptied the grooms' trunks, and stole beds. . . . It is not possible to obtain help in the country, as it is in the towns; there are no prisons here, and the peasants are so terrorized that they let the tramps pass (instead of keeping a watch on them)." The customs collector says that on several occasions groups of as many as fifty-six bohemians, men, women and children, have passed his office, many of them in uniform. There were so many of them that he dared not demand to see their passports (Archives, Gen. Dir. West. Prussia and Netzebezirk, Tit. CXXIX, no. 3).

Secondly, the unrest is greatest in the regions adjacent to the frontiers. It is very easy to take refuge abroad after perpetrating some villainy. In the Bromberg district in 1779 there is a wave of murders, robberies, and ambushes of grooms guarding horses near villages. The authorities at Marienwerder report in 1790 that cattle and sheep stealing increase in autumn under cover of the long nights. Practically no young men hardy enough for military service are still to be found in the frontier villages. The local recruits desert, and farming suffers; the authorities dare not send recruits on furlough because they would not return.

It is not customary to desert empty-handed. There is a ferry at Drewentz, near Marienwerder; the fugitives concert with Polish peasants to help them smuggle cattle to the other bank of the Vistula. "During the night of 24 to 25 August," a squire writes in 1778, "one of my peasants named Paul Piatrowski decided to flee into Poland. He crossed over some days beforehand and came to an agreement with some people who promised to help him. They came to the estate of Dembova Lonka on the agreed night, armed with hatchets and pitchforks, with seven horses, harnessed them to one of my carriages, and loaded up Piatrowski's effects. One of them named Josef Muzin, who also had once been one of my peasants, but had run away, apparently intended to steal several more of my horses, according to Piatrowski's statement; they broke into my barn, seized sacks of corn, ropes, winnowing pans—indeed, everything they could lay hands on—and went off to the ferry with their booty" (ibid.). They were trapped by guards and not all of them got away.

The government decides to send regular patrols along the river; they are not always victorious in regular pitched battles with deserters and fugitive recruits.

The annexation of Poland hampers the traffic in stolen cattle. But vagrancy continues on the same scale. The town prisons are not capacious enough; special rural jails are built and are offered to the smaller towns, but these usually shelter behind the municipal institutions for the town and claim that they are satisfied with provincial prisons for vagrants. The prison in the Electoral Mark is completed in 1798. The regulations issued on 31 October provide that the "Rural Workhouse" at Straussberg shall shelter and reclaim beggars and vagrants from the districts of Ober and Niederbarmin, Teltow, Lebus, Bees, and Storkow. Their possessions are confiscated on their arrival, and they are given a bath and a medical examination before they are interrogated. They are then divided into two groups. The first group contains those who have been begging only for a short time because of unemployment or illness; they enjoy the privilege of taking exercise on the square in front of the workhouse during the recreation period. The second comprises those who have long been unwilling to work. Their treatment seems tolerable enough; they are given a change of linen every Saturday and of bedding every six weeks; they receive decent clothing, and beer at noon and in the evening. But the regime is strict: rise at 4 in the morning, work in the shop from 5 to 7; breakfast and recreation from 7 to 8; work from 8 to 12; then again one hour free for the meal and back to the workshop, where they again weave from 1 to 7; then dinner and two hours free. The work is tasked, but anyone who weaves more than two pieces of flannel a day receives a reward varying from three to nine pfennigs, depending how long his zeal lasts. Discipline is strict; those who behave well may be promoted to a higher group or earn their discharge; those who misbehave are beaten or put on bread and water. The children are taught by a schoolmaster; but after the age of six the boys are put out with peasants to learn farming; the girls have to learn gardening and to tend animals; both are taught weaving. Jews are confined together in a separate room, where they can keep the Sabbath and do their own cooking.

These regulations are adopted by the other workhouses built over the years in the eastern provinces. The workhouse in the New Mark is under constuction in 1795. Similar institutions have long been known in the towns; for the poverty reported by the governor of Graudenz prison in 1794 is widespread and fearful: "The clothes of the vagrants sent us by the province (of East Prussia) are in such bad shape that some of these people do not even have a scrap of shirt—hardly a rag to cover their nakedness" (ibid., no. 10, vol. 1). He asks for permission to clothe them and states that they cannot be left at liberty because they would only take to begging again, to the detriment of the poor peasants. The East Prussian Chamber assents and orders that these unfortunates are to be committed to the fortress at Graudenz.

Poverty in the Towns

Owing to the political and customs frontiers, the economic crisis enters every town in the empire. What is the use of lending money to honest burghers in distress if there is no hope that things will be better in the future? There are too many craftsmen. The village craftsmen take trade away from the craftsmen in the towns just at the time when progress in manufacturing is threatening them from another quarter. At Strahlau, a suburb of Berlin, the small weavers vainly hope to make a profit on the wool or silk they have woven. They cannot sell their cloth because the merchants, being indebted to the big manufacturers, dare not procure their supplies from any other source. The big manufacturers, however, will only pay 10 percent below their own cost prices. The small weavers are defenseless against the big manufacturers' indemnifying themselves in this way for the high price of the raw materials. But the wives and children of the poor are hungry. "The greater part of the population of the Berlin suburbs is made up of these kinds of beasts of burden." (*GU* 1785, V, 93–117.) Statistics for Berlin in 1797 give 6,622 silk weavers, with 3,588 looms. The working-class population of Berlin is therefore between 70,000 and 80,000, nearly two-thirds of the total population.

It is hard to say how the poor live. There is a dearth of studies on price movements in the eighteenth century and few documents on wages. Most of the lists of local market prices kept in the archives were destroyed after Frederick II's death. It can, however, be stated with some assurance that prices rose during the century. At Berlin one mark of fine silver was equivalent to 7.42 bushels (*Scheffel*) of wheat or about 18.5 bushels of oats between 1766 and 1775; between 1776 and 1785 the figures were 9.57 and 21. They declined regularly thereafter to 7.69 and 17.09 between 1786 and 1795 and 5.13 and 12.22 between 1796 and and 1805. A bushel of wheat was equivalent to 45 kg and of oats to 25.5 kg.

It is probable that wages did not rise at a similar rate; labor was too abundant not to be depreciated, and the state did not intervene to fix its value. The scanty information that exists shows that wages varied a very great deal according to time and place. At Zehlendorf near Berlin a day laborer earned 5 groschen a day; at Stolp, 2.

The cost of living rose while wages remained steady, so that the average level of subsistence fell and misery increased. A day laborer's budget can be reconstructed from the amount needed by a poor student to live at Halle in 1804. The student has to reckon 10 thalers a year for his lodging, 30 for his midday meals, 12 for the tailor, 8 for the cobbler, 12 for heating, and 50 for other expenses, food, and miscellaneous purchases. A workman can do his own household chores and wash his own linen, if he wears any, and need not be so well dressed as a student. He should be able to get by on 122 thalers instead of 220. At 5 groschen a day, and with about 300 working days a year, he would earn 62 thalers 12 groschen. He must, therefore, eat half as much as the poor student and be housed half as well. His wages, even allowing for the fact that prices are probably higher at Halle than at Zehlendorf, just enable him to stay alive. The day laborer at Stolp, earning 2 groschen a day, probably can only subsist by begging or stealing to make up the difference.

This random information is too scanty to enable us to draw any final conclusions on prices and wages. But pending the publication of the indispensable monographs, it may be accepted because it does accord with the abundant information on the crisis in the trades and on the increase in poverty.

The laws on the guilds are revised to prevent new masters setting themselves up. Too many young men are getting a dispensation from the rules and taking over from their fathers without completing their apprenticeship. The Domains Chambers oppose the military administration's proposal to abolish the institution in Prussia in 1790. Would it in fact mean a falling off in the quality of the work? The Patent of 1732 reducing the time to be spent in distant garrisons from seven years to three concedes that two years' military service is the equivalent of one year's journeyman service. It can therefore be seen that the technical value of journeyman travel is arguable. The journeymen's travels are helped by the brotherhoods, which have their inns in every town, where a journeyman on his travels can find quarters and help. Discipline in them is strict. The door porter sees to it that everyone is in bed by ten o'clock. As no master is allowed to employ more than two journeymen and one apprentice, a journeyman cannot always find work. For the guild regulations, too, date from before the growth in the population. An imperial law of 1731 authorizes giving alms to unemployed journeymen. They receive in cash or kind what they need for their subsistence and to go and try their luck elsewhere. At the town gate they are directed to their inn, where, on producing their papers, they receive a scanty aid to enable them to continue their travels. The police watches them until they leave town, for the numbers of the indigent have to be kept down.

Very often they cease to look further after several rebuffs. They dare not appear before their masters in their ragged clothes and broken shoes. They are corrupted by bad company and by consorting with thieves; the gawky youths are often drawn into amours that leave them gasping and sick, so that they too are finally forced to take to the road. The authorities ought to make this grave problem their business and send these lads to wherever they would have most chance of finding some work, after warning them of the dangers to which they are exposed.

There are special regulations, identical throughout Prussia, for the indigent; they are forbidden to beg, on pain of imprisonment; and, "in order that what physical strength the destitute still possess shall not remain unused," workhouses are to be built with funds derived from taxes on the burghers (Winkler, *Frey*, report by Königsberg chief of police Frey). In them are housed the "dishonest poor," who commit themselves voluntarily and receive what remains from the proceeds of their labor after deduction of the costs of their maintenance. In them are also confined the beggars sentenced to hard labor. Whether they are all confined in the same building or in separate ones, there are enough of them to make it worthwhile to serve them the economical and nourishing soup for which Rumford, the philanthropist, gives the recipe: for seventy persons boil in 20 gallons of water 24 lbs. potatoes, 7 lbs. dried peas, 7 lbs. bread, 2 lbs. meat, 5 parts vinegar and 1¼ parts salt. Fuel included, the whole comes to 1.5 or 2 pfennigs a head; or if it is seasoned with gelatine, as it is at Hamburg, slightly more than 2 pfennigs.

The Berlin workhouse is one of the largest. Founded by Frederick II and enlarged by his successors, it can house over a thousand inmates. The edict of 1774 sets aside the first floor for voluntary inmates; they weave wool in separate shops and are better fed than the journeymen, soldiers on leave, and burghers on the second floor. Sentenced first to three months' hard labor and then, if they repeat the offense, to a year, several years, or even life, these beggars are harshly treated. But the ex-convicts on the third floor and the debauchees cured of their venereal diseases at the Charité hospital and confined in order to wean them from their vices are even more wretched. The children are taught in the workhouse. In 1785 there are 1,250 inmates, 641 on the first floor and 609 on the second, including 46 small boys and 71 small girls.

There are similar institutions at Halle, Augsburg, Cassel, Hanau, Erlangen, Würzburg, Fürth, Göttingen and Erfurt; in short, in most towns in the empire.

"The number of poor is abnormally large in proportion to the total population" at Friedberg in 1790 (*JD* 1790, I, 27–30). At Cologne the beggars account for one-third of a population of 40,000. Whole boatloads of them disembark at a town like Aix-la Chapelle where their profession is specially favored by Catholicism, the rivalries of political factions, and a deplorable economic structure. At Cassel the beggars are "inordinately numerous" (*DM* 1784, I, 87). At Magdeburg it is impossible to conceive where they come from. In Berlin relief is distributed to 7,300 persons in 1784, but this figure is deceptive. From every quarter the beggars throng to the towns. The small towns are invaded on market days. The watch at the gates has to be reinforced and passports strictly inspected; and at Bremen, Hildesheim, and Mülhausen, where Anton Reiser has to use cunning to get into the town, he mingles with the Sunday strollers returning home in the evening; he is lucky enough to be well dressed and to be wearing stockings of such good quality that he cannot be taken for a marauder (Moritz, *Anton Reiser*, pt. 3 passim).

The increasing luxury has its counterpart in this poverty. If even the New Town in Berlin is not above criticism, with its uneven sidewalks and badly-paved streets, so that people have to leap over the puddles from stone to stone after rain, where strollers are choked by dust on Unter den Linden, and instead of sewers there are mere ditches running beside the house fronts giving off a stench "as bad as that at Paris" in summer and overflowing on to the roadway in winter, these are petty discomforts compared with the Old Town. There the inhabitants are crammed in low houses along narrow streets, which are not lighted at night and in which garbage lies stagnant.

You stumble over dogs or dead cats. At Strahlau "half-naked men live in one-story wooden huts" (*Berlin* I, 46). The town is full of hooligans, showmen with performing dogs, and soldiers soliciting strangers with offers of service. One insists on doing all your errands for you, another forces you to buy dainties from him. They all crowd round the wooden stalls which obstruct the bridges and cumber up the avenues and squares, where old clothes dealers sell or raffle the rags cast off by these wretched men.

The statistics, impersonal as they are, make the picture even darker. In Berlin, a town with a population of some 140,000, including a garrison of 35,000 in 1798, there are 658 beer houses, 53 cafés, and 140 inns. In 1796 the principal causes of death are consumption, with 1,114 cases out of a total of 5,396, including 264 stillbirths, and "misery" (*Jammer*), with 707 cases. Old age comes seventh, with 288 deaths.

The inhabitants' boorish manners are the result of this misery. Behind the old facades at Potsdam there are barrack-rooms, where the soldiers hang their drawers out of windows delicately ornamented with cherubs and dress without troubling about the passersby. The incautious traveler admiring the palace's splendid architecture at dusk is abruptly shocked out of his rapt contemplation by the hiss of one of these sons of Mars relieving himself into the street from the third floor. The educated note despairingly "the bad habit prevalent in Germany of mutilating the works of art entrusted to the public." "Everywhere the German people incur reproach for destroying everything that has any semblance of art, breaking statues, soiling paintings, in short, settling firmly down at the antipodes of art. There is no denying this state of affairs. Whenever the lower class has any chance of displaying its malice, it destroys, and rejoices in the destruction." (Pilat, *Arme*, 37-47.)

In Berlin, as in Potsdam, every statue on every building is mutilated. In Unter den Linden the wooden barriers separating the central walk from the side avenues are replaced not with splendidly wrought chains—that would make things too easy for the vandals!—but with thick iron bars sunk into heavy blocks of stone; bars and stones are torn up the very night after their inauguration. The only way to preserve noses, hands, "all projecting parts on the new statues, is to place them under constant police guard until the people have had time to get used to them" (*Berlin* II, 213-18).

The economic crisis accounts for the abundance of domestic servants. The time is long past when *Gesindeordnungen* made it compulsory for young people to go into service because labor was scarce. Large numbers of peasants and craftsmen apply. The mania for ostentation induces middle class and nobility alike to hire more servants than they need. In a population of 142,000 (including the garrison) in 1798 there are 4,492 lackeys and 11,443 female domestics. They wander the streets in their spare time, swagger in fine clothes, play the lottery, and prostitute themselves. All attempts to enforce the strict police regulations on hiring and time off, certificates given by masters and declarations to be made at the time of employment on rates of wages, are vain. The law rests on a moral axiom: like master, like man.

Can anything be done about the poverty in town and country? Is there anything more that can be tried beyond prohibiting lotteries and encouraging philanthropy? A few publicists here and there will have it that there can. But the remedies they propose once again imply social revolution. Abolish serfdom and relieve the peasant of his burden of taxes? Fine! He and his large family will be able to live on his holding. Allocate state subsidies as equitably as possible, reform the budget, establish an institution for mortgage loans? Fine, fine! But who is to make a start?

The Troubles

Since no reform is made and since the poor have the example of the French in bettering their lot before their eyes, troubles break out continually. Hardly have they died down in one place when they burst out in another. Though French influence was not as direct as has sometimes been claimed, it nevertheless inspired the peasants and workers to demand rights which it enabled them to define.

In Electoral Saxony the peasants in the Meissen district refuse to pay their feudal dues in 1790. They assemble and protest against the lords' game rights, for the birds destroy their crops. From time to time they go to the castle and demand a waiver of feudal dues in writing. In August, during the gap between one harvest and the next, the movement spreads to the districts of Torgau and Pirna. It is suppressed by the troops. The prince-elector is wise enough to slaughter his game himself. Another "conspiracy against feudal dues" is discovered in 1792 between Zeis and Alterburg.

In Prussia the countryside begins to stir late in 1792. The army is fully occupied with the French wars; and its failure in them encourages the malcontents. The troubles occur mainly in the smuggling districts. In February government circulars order that the peasants in the district of Magdeburg are to be disarmed and that any revolutionary literature found in house searches is to be confiscated. Disturbances seem to have occurred, despite official denials.

Revolt is more serious in Silesia, where the drafting of the *urbaria* angers the peasants on the estates. In the districts of Löwenberg and Goldberg, between Liegnitz and Torgau near the Bohemian frontier, troops protect the lords against peasants refusing to pay their dues and threatening them with massacre. In January 1793 all Silesia is astir; the peasants of the Ohlau district refuse to perform their feudal services, and the districts of Nimptsch, Neumarkt, Grottkau, and Oels-Berstadt follow suit. Von Hoym, the governor of the province, tries vainly to resist. The investigations show that all too often the lords have been demanding more than their due. Quiet is restored by the needs of the harvest. Then, during the winter, the countryside in the principality of Ratibor is on the move. In the Old Mark in 1794 the serfs on the vast Schulenberg and Alvensleben family estates demand reforms.

These movements are everywhere spontaneous. The foreign ringleaders, whose agitation is supposed to account for the sudden outbursts by loyal subjects, are never found. But the investigations show that the peasants are often compelled to perform unjust corvées. No one, however, dares to make the necessary reforms; the sole outcome is the publication of the Edict of 15 February 1797 advising the peasants to appeal to the royal justice instead of revolting, and warning the lords that they must behave more justly. The discontent continues, since its causes have not been removed.

The craftsmen suffer from the war and from the mercantilist system; supplies to the army cause a rise in the price of corn and yarn. But the shopkeepers pay less for the cloth supplied them. Destitution drives the weavers to revolt. On 30 March 1793 they throw the merchants' stocks of yarn into the mud and shut up in a convent the platoon of soldiers trying to restore order. The weavers devise a password; as a recognition sign they tie a sack over their left shoulder. They assemble at the markets at Schweidnitz and Striegau on 6 and 8 April to compel the merchants to sell them yarn below the market price and the shopkeepers to pay more than cost for cloth. They threaten the millers, bakers and butchers. Von Hoym is well aware that they are not in the wrong; but he dares not resort to force, and finally compels the merchants to sell their yarn at a price fixed by himself.

His magnanimity encourages the craftsmen of the towns; throughout the empire the disturbances occur for no deeper reason than the economic turmoil. At Schmiedeberg the journeymen carpenters and masons seize the town hall and manhandle the burghers because a carpenter has been arrested for smoking at work in breach of the police regulations. At Breslau the jailing of a journeyman tailor by order of an unpopular mayor provokes a regular municipal revolution (28 April–2 May 1793), with thirty-seven killed.

In Berlin, journeymen and burghers come to blows in May 1795. Brawls break out everywhere: at Aix-la-Chapelle, where the town hall is pillaged in 1786 during the struggle between the two parties disputing the election for mayor; at Brunswick, where the journeymen wheelwrights on strike against their masters are backed by the other guilds, while the peasants in the surrounding countryside refuse to billet troops; near the Bremen frontier reinforcements have to be sent to compel them to do so. At Hamburg the locksmiths go on strike in August 1791. At Mainz all the guilds rise following a brawl between students and journeymen millers. These "patriots" force their reforms on the governor till the prince elector's soldiers bring them into subjection again. The peaceful town of Göttingen experiences days no less disturbed. The journeymen cobblers, who boast a great reputation for turbulence, are feared throughout the land.

It is very fortunate for the governments that these troubles break out sporadically. If the peasants and craftsmen had revolted everywhere in Prussia at the same time, the old regime would certainly not have been able to resist their drive. Everyone is aware that the crisis is approaching; but it does not actually break out until the foreign invasion diverts this slow-growing movement into other channels; and then the most eager reformers seek only a personal solution to their problems.

8

The Crisis
of the Middle Classes

The Problem of the Middle Classes

The effects of the economic and social crisis on the middle classes are harder to determine. By and large, we can designate as middle class, or burghers, all those who are not "well-born" and who live in towns. The class of burghers has a well-defined upper boundary, the nobility, but is not so sharply delimited at its lower end by those other commoners, the peasants. The peasant can obtain scholarships to send his sons to the university and thus enable them to rise into the middle class. Dr. Jung-Stilling, for example, came from a poor woodcutter's family. In some respects schoolmastering is a sort of intermediate stage in the ascent into the middle class. The two classes, peasants and burghers, are not, therefore, completely separate, though the division is more marked in Prussia than in France because the excise regulations prohibit craftsmen from plying their trade outside the towns and the burghers are not permitted to acquire property from the nobility and seldom live in the country; any appetite they have for landed property went no further, as a rule, than gardens in the suburbs. The modes of living do not, therefore, overlap from one caste to another and from castle to town house and town house to cottage.

There is, however, an infinite range of varieties within the burgher class itself. Most urban statistics give only the number of inhabitants or a list of the corporations and principal industries, but some directories are more complete and show in detail that the main component of the middle-class townsmen are the small craftsmen and small shopkeepers. The small masters work alone or with one or two journeymen; many of them are dependent on an entrepreneur, who advances them money to buy their raw materials, or on a large employer, who nevertheless does not have a large number of hands working for him under the same roof. The shopkeepers' wealth varies with the goods they deal in. By way of illustration, the population of Magdeburg in 1816 is around 30,000. In the occupations employing more than fifty families each, the directory lists 331 cobblers, 222 tailors (8 of them women), 118 carpenters, 63 fishmongers, 58 butchers, 54 linen weavers, and roughly similar numbers of coopers, bakers, and *musici*. The occupations in which less than 50 persons are engaged embrace all the other small trades essential to urban life: a fair number of locksmiths, distillers, coachmen, and cart drivers; only a single person is engaged in some trades: sculptor, sweep, salt merchant, tar seller, pigeon dealer. The complete list classifies 2,382 persons under 106 different headings. If we reckon five persons to a family, the total would be about 12,000, two-fifths of the total population. The directory also lists the wealthy; there are 53 wholesalers, brokers, and shippers; 13 bankers and money changers; and 15 wine merchants. There are not many "factories," and it does not appear that they represent any considerable fortunes as understood by contemporaries; the largest are the 15 silk, cotton, wool, and linen factories and the 9 stocking factories. Next come the 10 chicory grinders; 6 vinegar distillers and 6 makers of leather gloves; 4 purveyors of yarn, tobacco, porcelain, sealing-wax, or liqueurs; and one seller each of sugar, stoves, pipes, ribbons, lace, hides, gold- and silverware, and feathers. There are 146 wealthy families in all, besides 16 doctors, 13 surgeons, 2 veterinary surgeons, one dentist, and 5 apothecaries. The well-to-do burghers, therefore, total some 720 persons and their families. The 104 "private persons and individuals in receipt of pensions" (*Particuliers, einzelne gratuirte Personen*) and the 147 widows and "unmarried persons of distinction" (11 of them nobles) are probably also to be counted among the better-class citizens. Thus there are 971 persons in the higher ranks of the middle class, less than one-thirtieth of the total population. There remains out of the total 30,000 the mass of 17,000, no trace of whom appears in the directory, which lists only persons of independent means, persons engaged in a trade, and titled persons. There may not be very many factory hands, and even assuming that the directory listing is not complete and that some persons in the liberal professions, such as clergymen, professors, and artists, may be included in "individuals in receipt of pensions," the fact remains that there is an enormous proportion of unskilled workers and beggars doomed to utter poverty.

The conclusion to be drawn from the picture given by the directory for Halle in 1804, though less complete, is somewhat similar. The population is 25,000. The wealthy own the 12 stocking factories, the 7 large textile stores and the 55 fair-sized groceries, tobacco stores, and caterers. It is undoubtedly for them that the 183 stocking weavers work, employing 306 journeymen on 484 looms, and the 60 cloth weavers with their 60 journeymen. Then come the 162 tailors, the 156 cobblers and the mass of petty trades, only some of which belong to the six organized corporations (grocers, cobblers, bakers, butchers, blacksmiths, and catering). The high proportion of doctors and grogshops is accounted for by the large military and university population. There are 12 doctors, 17 surgeons, 4 apothecaries and 20 midwives in the one group and 140 grogshops, 33 distillers, and 34 inns in the other.

In none of these towns is there any mention of the illiterate and poverty-stricken masses. Most of them, being a charge on the municipal or provincial authorities, usually do not have the citizenship which would give them at least a semblance of sharing in the town's administration. In the broadest sense of the term, they are part of the burgher class, since they live in a "burgh," or town. In the narrow sense, that of more general acceptation at the time—as the directories show—they are excluded from citizenship because they are not engaged in a skilled trade. If we disregard them and consider the group of economically active and independent persons who account for nearly half the town population, two characteristics emerge, common to all members of the burgher class and both typical of the class and the cause of the diversity within it: the burghers have cash in reserve and at least a smattering of intellectual culture. Their cash in hand seldom amounts to any very large sum in a country where private capitalism hardly exists as yet; but even if it amounts to no more than the scanty savings of a clergyman or craftsman, it nevertheless enables them to send their sons to the secondary school and to dispense with their sons' earnings when they are somewhat older and hold scholarships to the university.

Their culture may be superficial and recent; but it could not, at all events, be more so than that of the nobles. Owing, however, to their intimate connections with the clergy, who are members of the same class, the burghers have gained a species of monopoly of moral judgments. This characteristic peculiar to Protestant countries needs stressing. Most burghers are the fathers, sons, or brothers of clergymen. Though they envy the nobles, they are distinguished from them less by their mode of life than by their scruples and their consciousness of virtue. The nobles are accustomed to authority; from birth they move in an ambit of their own within which they exercise their privileges as simply and naturally as if they were obeying a reflex. The burghers pass judgment; their universe is essentially a moral one. With their ability to express their opinions and feelings, it is chiefly the burghers who take to writing. They impose their modes of thought upon all those who claim to be thinking people. Since an individual seldom creates his own means of expression, a nobleman who wants to think can only do so in bourgeois terms; and so public opinion under the Prussian monarchy is the opinion of the middle classes. Reason is, of course, universal; it may seem an over-simplification, therefore, to try to tie the laws of reason down to a single social class. But reason alone does not produce a mode of thinking. The way it tackles one or other of the problems posed by circumstances, by social conditions, or by professional writers depends on time and place. The near-monopoly of culture acquired by the middle classes in Prussia is precisely the reason why almost all the great questions canvassed at the end of the eighteenth century are ones with which those classes were ,mainly concerned. The impact of the economic crisis on their members is beyond their grasp; and all the nuances and all the infinite variety of this one fact shapes the course of the history of Prussia in the eighteenth century.

The middle-class birth rate cannot be established from the incomplete contemporary statistics, but there is no reason to suppose that it was lower than that of the other classes. Almost all the contemporary memoirs mention large families. The reader even has some difficulty in following the thread when he finds his heroes associating yet another scion with each of their joys or griefs and scattering their children broadcast all over the country, so that on all their travels they keep running into one or other of them and introducing brother to sister, taking advantage of a brief stopover to inculcate some worthy principle into their progeny. In any event, even if the burghers are not really so prolific, the fact remains that the population of the towns is becoming larger and larger. No matter whether this is due to the birth rate or immigration, the urban population is increasing; and this is the important fact socially, for it brings up the problem of openings for careers—the most disturbing, the most constant of all problems, and the most intractable. Yet the most general implication of this problem is not even perceived. Little notice is taken of the inarticulate. Vagrants and beggars are relieved or sent to the devil, as the case may be, pending the great wars which will furnish them with abundant alternatives of living or dying. There remains, however, the great problem of the sons of the well-to-do middle class and of the civil servants and clergymen.

Some of the sons of the prosperous burghers succeed their fathers in their trade or business; others go to the universities, to which they are attracted by the prestige attaching to culture and are also constrained by the lack of openings for a career of their own elsewhere. At that time, as today, the sudden rise in the numbers of students makes for a form of unemployment; they study in order to mark time and to improve their abilities by way of bettering their chances of finding a job.

There is no doubt about the proliferation of students, but it is hard to estimate it quantitatively. The enrolment lists were not published, except those for Frankfort-on-Oder. Such figures as are known, moreover, are not conclusive, because the Wöllner regime deterred students from attending the Prussian universities and appreciably reduced the numbers of theological students, while it increased those of law students. We shall therefore have to confine ourselves to comparing the figures for before 1790 with those for after 1797 and dispense with the five-year or ten-year averages which alone would furnish conclusive data. But even if we had all the information we could wish, we should still have to use it with the greatest caution. Despite the decrees ordering future officials to attend one of the monarchy's five universities, many Prussian subjects went elsewhere to enrol and many foreigners came to Prussia for their education; several of the most eminent officials at the end of the century, such as Stein and Struensee, were not educated in Prussia. The university population increased, diminished, and moved from place to place from one semester to the next; and it was not possible to determine what proportion of it was native Prussian. With these reservations, the known figures support the contemporary opinion. They establish the fact that the number of students continued to increase and that, even after Wöllner's disgrace, the law faculties continued to grow at the expense of the theological, for it was becoming harder and harder to find posts in the overstaffed clerical profession.

At Halle, by far the largest university, there were 54 students in the Faculty of Theology in the winter of 1789–99, and 90 the following summer. At the same periods there were 30, 53, and 78 students in the Faculty of Law, totals of 242 students in 1789–90, and of 296 in 1798–99. At Königsberg there were 10 theological students in the winter of 1790–91, 12 in the summer of 1791, 3 in the summer of 1799, and 8 the following winter. The law students at the same times were 20, 15, 44, and 23, totals of 57 students for the year 1790–91 and 78 for the summer of 1799 and the winter of 1800. At Frankfort the annual statistics give 16 theological students and 35 law students in 1788 and 15 theological students and 94 law students in 1800. The annual totals between 1788 and 1800 were 48, 55, 47, 53, 62, 46, 60, 70, 71, 84, 97, 49, and 99. With variations less marked than at the larger universities, which were more exposed to political factors, they give a picture of a regular average increase; and much the same was probably the case at Königsberg, Duisburg, and Erlangen.

Thus, some of the young burghers succeed their fathers; as craftsmen, shopkeepers, and bankers they carry on the old traditions and find no problems in making a living. Some, on the other hand, sink into poverty and become *déclassés*. Adventurers, soldiers, vagabonds, or beggars, they live on the margin of the state and society, which takes cognizance of them only to assist or prosecute them, as the case may be. Lastly, some of them study. Having acquired the ability to grasp ideas to which their fathers had no access, these represent the intellectual elite, not merely of the middle classes but of Prussia and Germany as a whole. The problem with the middle classes, nationally and even internationally, is to ensure them a future. The main openings presented to their youthful ambitions are the civil service, the clerical career, and the liberal professions.

The Civil Service

Many branches of the civil service have to be excluded because they are not exalted enough. Enlightened young men who have spent years at secondary school and the university cannot without demeaning themselves accept petty jobs in the executive class with no future to them. Even if the posts were better paid, they would not want them, because of their estimation of their own worth and dignity. They consider the insecure life of the adventurer with all its hazards more enviable than that of the village schoolmaster or the innumerable scriveners thronging the chanceries with such titles as secretary, registrar, protonotary, or copyist. Similarly, only very small fry are found in the excise, particularly ex-soldiers. Between 21 June and 21 July 1776, for example, for 18 appointees, all of them of commoners, we find ten army pensioners, two corporals, and one sergeant. In the following month, for 38 appointees, fifteen are army pensioners, one is a cavalry sergeant, and two are lieutenants. Between 21 December 1776 and 31 January 1777, 25 persons are engaged, including four nobles and nine army pensioners. Between 1 January and 30 January 1784, of 34 appointees four are nobles, two have served in the army as lieutenants, and one has served as a cavalry corporal. The very small proportion both of nobles and of soldiers becomes even smaller after the death of Frederick II. The 18 persons appointed in January 1790, the 15 in October 1791, the 17 in October 1794, the 29 in February 1796, and the 36 in December 1796 are commoners exclusively. The nobles, being aristocrats, do not want these petty jobs and the educated middle classes leave them to the poor.

Besides the careers which the middle classes do not want there are some which they cannot have. In the civil service for example, the sensitive job of rural commissioner (*Landrat*), responsible to the Provincial War and Domains Chamber for administering districts for the most part composed of large feudal estates, would be well worth having; and the state too would find it advantageous to entrust it to a burgher, inasmuch as he would be an independent person little disposed to shut his eyes to the illegalities of the territorial nobility. To try to place the country squires directly under a commoner would, however, be to risk stirring up a revolution. The nobles assembled in their provincial diets (*Landtage*), already deprived of all real power by the Royal War and Domains Chambers, would have simply refused the king their obedience. Appointing nobles from outside the province they are to administer is as far as the government dares go. The burghers themselves do not enjoy a similar monopoly of the office of local commissary (*Steuerrat*) representing the royal power in the administration of the towns. We find two nobles, for instance, among the seven local commissaries responsible to the War and Domains Chamber of the Electoral Mark in 1806.

While the rule excluding burghers from the higher ranks of the army is less strictly observed, they are not overeager to expose themselves to the snubs of their aristocratic fellow officers, whose promotion has been retarded by a long period of peacetime, nor to the sneers of the intellectuals, with their scant respect for military prestige.

Burghers intending to enter the civil service have two main careers to choose between, the civil service and the law. Almost all of them begin their career in one or the other; they acquire their training in them and sometimes go on to more specialized branches. There are many more candidates than posts to be filled. "The number of young men applying for posts in the civil service," a chronicler writes in 1788, "is so great that all the administrative services are overwhelmed. If you compare their number with the number of posts which, even if there were to be an epidemic of deaths, are likely to fall vacant, you can see that there is now no hope whatever of placing all, or even most, of them in any way that bears the slightest relation to the many sacrifices which their training has required of them" (*BM* 1788, II, 251-67).

The extent of the problem may be seen from a few samplings of the files of the administrative service. Students leaving the law faculty after about six semesters usually serve a probationary period of practical work as junior law officer (*Auskultator*) to a court. The less talented or less ambitious apply to one of the many municipal courts (*Stadtgerichte*). Most of them prefer the higher courts, a form of appellate court known as *Regierung, Obergericht*, or in some cases, *Hofgericht*; there is at least one of them in each province, often several, owing to the gradual coalescence of the territories which eventually came to form the province. The most gifted enrol with the High Courts of Appeal at Königsberg and Berlin. The latter, known as the *Cammergericht*, is by far the more important. Its jurisdiction embraces the old provinces of the Electoral Mark and the New Mark; its judgments make case law; its staff is larger and choicer than that of the *Oberappellationsgericht* at Königsberg having jurisdiction over the remaining provinces.

After serving for eighteen months or two years working up cases or acting as assistants to the judges, the *Auskultatoren* pass an examination, usually a fairly easy one, which permits them to use the style *Referendar* and gives them the right to sit as judges in the lower courts and the municipal and manorial courts. If they are aiming at higher posts, they stay on as *Referendarien* at a court of appeal. The Berlin *Cammergericht* has a lower section, the *Hausvogtei*, distinct from its Court of Appeal, the *Obergericht*. This section hears and passes on minor local cases; two *Referendarien* sit on it, assisted by clerks of the court selected by the *Auskultatoren*. The Court of Appeal comprises two chambers, or *Senaten*, the *Instruktionssenat* for appeals from the lower courts and the *Oberappellationssenat*, which hands down advisory opinions to the provincial appellate courts. Owing to this institution there are a great many *Referendarien* at Berlin, where they can prepare themselves for the "major" examination better than elsewhere. They are often selected from the experienced staff of the lower municipal courts. In October 1783, for instance, the chief judge of the Berlin *Stadtgericht* sends his colleague at the Court of Appeal the reports on his sixteen *Auskultatoren* and twelve *Refendarien*, all of them commoners, ten of whom are to be selected for posts with the *Cammergericht*. The "major" examination comprises both written and oral tests and demands a profound knowledge of the theory and practice of law. Candidates sit this examination only after several years—five on an average—of service as *Referendar*. Passing it entitles a jurist to become an *Assessor*, or junior judge, and opens the way to appointment as councillor in a high court or to entry to other branches of the civil service. The diplomatic service, for example, recruits part of its staff from the *Assessoren*, who constitute what may be regarded as a species of nursery for senior officials.

The career is governed by strict regulations, and the various grades in it are too sharply marked to leave room for favoritism. It is true that the sons of important personages can take short cuts and sit the "major" examination after three, or even two, years instead of five. It is true, too, that the written part of the examination may not be strictly honest, since candidates work at home getting up a brief. But there is the fact that the oral examination is lengthy and thorough; several detailed records of them have been preserved in the officials' files. At Minden in 1800, for example, the *Referendar* von Bessel is asked thirty-four questions on procedure and public law (What is a writ of summons? What is a surety? What is *jus reformandi*? What is the Treaty of Westphalia? What is the difference between the papal system and the episcopal system?) and seventy-five questions in Roman law (What are adoption and adrogation and what is the *patria potestas*? What is personalty and what is real property? What is a composition? and so on).

A *Referendar* who has spent three years at the university and two as *Auskultator* is about twenty-two when appointed. An *Assessor* is therefore twenty-seven when he first gains access to the higher posts he is aiming at. We can safely say, even though we lack accurate data on officials' salaries, that he cannot earn his keep before he passes the "major" examination, if we also take into consideration the official expenses which a young man entering the administrative or legal service must inevitably incur.

We need to know how many appointments were made yearly if we are to estimate the outlets furnished by a career in the legal service. The registers of the provincial departments record appointments; the yearly totals differ by only a few units from those given in the files themselves; and as the variations do not in all cases go in the same direction, they may be ignored, and we can use the tables compiled from the registers.

The real difficulties are of another kind. It is surprising, when we analyse the catalogue of *Cammergericht* documents, to begin with, to find no appointments subsequent to 1800. Research in the provincial archives of the Mark Brandenburg is equally fruitless. It is hardly likely, however, that no *Referendar* was appointed after the turn of the century. As a matter of fact, the directory for Berlin and Potsdam continues to give the names and addresses of the *Referendarien* at the *Cammergericht* after 1800, and they are not the same as those before that date. We might therefore go no further than to observe that the archives are at present catalogued in such a way that we should have to hope that some lucky chance may reveal the registers or items under which these names were entered, did not the appearance of similar facts compel us to raise the same question afresh elsewhere. All the tables of appointments of legal posts compiled for the various provinces by means of the registers stop at 1800. The items, however, are still recorded; they sometimes mention a promotion, more often superannuations (*venia aetatis*), never an appointment. When we look at the files themselves, often catalogued as continuing until 1806, we find no appointment after 1800 either. It is not possible to cross-check by means of the directories, because they were published in the provinces only at irregular intervals; neither the university nor the municipal libraries at the towns where the high courts sat now possess directories relating to either one of the last years in the eighteenth century or one of the first in the nineteenth.

Does this mean that the practice of appointing *Auskultatoren* and *Referendarien* in the provinces ceased after 1800? No decision of such great importance could have been taken without leaving some trace somewhere in the many surviving registers or even in the press. But a scrutiny of the minutes of the cabinet reveals no trace of anything of this sort. Moreover, if the overburdened courts had all simultaneously ceased to recruit new staff without taking any decision on the principle and without concerting their action, the files should be crammed with applicaions for employment and complaints by candidates; and these would undoubtedly have been echoed in the literature. But references to the courts' being overburdened are the exception. Three commoners were not allowed to sit the "major" examination for the *Cammergericht* in 1799, though three nobles and three commoners had already been admitted. The only reason given for the refusal is saturation (*Überfüllung*).

Cases of this kind are, however, commoner in the administrative service, where a similar problem does not arise, since appointments to it were made regularly up to 1806. On 28 January 1802, for example, the Magdeburg War and Domains Chamber ruled that candidate Friedrich Wilhelm von Madai of Halle could not become a *Referendar* "because His Majesty has on several occasions informed the said War and Domains Chamber that, owing to the excessive number of serving *Referendarien* and *Assessoren*, it would be wholly inopportune to admit still more of them." (Archives, Gen. Dir. Magdeburg, Tit. VIII, no. 5, pp. 27–32.) Which, incidentally, did not prevent von Madai from getting his way on 28 March!

The most probable explanation is that the administrative services were embarrassed by the sudden upsurge of candidates for the posts of *Auskultator* and *Referendar*. Their numbers did not fall, and indeed even tended to rise, under the pressure of newcomers who became so insistent that it was felt that some sort of barrier must be raised. After 1800 a tentative move was initiated to make access to the administrative career more difficult. On 7 April 1804 a cabinet order was issued containing a reminder that all candidates for senior posts must have spent at least three years at a Prussian university; in exceptional cases, however, the period might be reduced for those who presented a university leaving certificate (*Abiturienten Prüfungs-attest*) certifying that they have acquired the necessary knowledge in less than the specified period. Not much notice seems to have been taken of this decree, however. The first thing the authorities did was to omit to send it to any of the universities except Halle. Candidate Lehmann was obliged to lodge a complaint in October, asking that Frankfort be notified of the decree, since he wished to appear before the board of examiners there; at his request, it did at last assemble.

The lists of law officers compiled for the period 1786–1800 and the administrative service for the period 1786–1806 are not, therefore, wholly exhaustive; in many cases there are slight differences between the entries in the registers and the figures in the files. But these gaps are spread almost evenly over the years and the provinces. Though not absolutely accurate in detail, then, the lists are accurate enough to enable us to study the course of recruitment.

On the whole they disclose, in the first place, that of careers in the civil service those in the law provide by far the most openings. In the fifteen years from 1786 to 1800, 841 *Auskultatoren* and 705 *Referendarien* were appointed to the higher courts in the provinces, and 20 and 189 respectively were admitted to the *Cammergericht*, a total of 1,755 appointments, or an average of 117 yearly. If we take only one of the two figures to obtain the number of newcomers, since the legal officer almost always has to serve a probationary period as *Auskultator* before becoming a *Referendar*, we find that the average is 57.4 for *Auskultatoren* and 59.6 for *Referendarien*. These figures are far higher than those in the lists for the administrative career compiled by the same method for a period of twenty-one years, which record the appointment of only 278 *Referendarien*, an average of 13.2 yearly. Not all the Chambers have *Auskultatoren*—of whom there are far fewer in any case—attached to them; and *Auskultatoren* from the legal branch may transfer to the administrative service as *Referendarien*.

In the second place, these tables show that the proportion of commoners in the legal branch is extremely high; of the 1,755 officials mentioned above, only 178 are nobles, or 10.15 percent—9.76 percent in the provinces, rising to 13.39 percent in the *Cammergericht*; the nobles seem to make for the choice jobs, with some success. A comparison between provinces shows that there is a fairly high proportion of nobles in the older provinces and at places like Berlin, where a considerable middle class has grown up. At Magdeburg the nobility holds 20.17 percent of the posts of *Auskultator* and *Referendar*, at

Cleves-Ravensburg 15.53 percent, in Pomerania 10.85 percent, at Minden 10.75 percent, and 10.71 percent in the Electoral Mark. In East Prussia, on the other hand, and in the recently conquered province of West Prussia the proportion falls to 5.05 percent and 5.34 percent. The nobles are therefore more numerous in the middle-class areas, while the middle classes enjoy a near-monopoly in the regions with large manorial estates. This seeming paradox is accounted for by the fact that the resident landowners work their estates or go into the army and tend to despise the *Auskultatoren* and *Referendarien*, from whom they select the "justiciaries" for their manorial courts in the capacity of humble servants. The absentee landlords, on the other hand, are ambitious for high office and compete with the middle classes for the grades in the hierarchy leading to them.

A first glance at the yearly distribution of appointments suggests that a species of compensatory balance was maintained between the *Auskultatoren* and the *Referendarien*; when the numbers of the latter rise, those of the former fall or remain stationary. But added together they rise from 87 in 1786 to 129 in 1799, and, despite some yearly variations, the trend runs steadily upward. The five-year totals certainly reflect this movement, with their figures of 470, 540, and 551. The main increase occurs between 1790 and 1795. The proportion of nobles also tends to rise, though not a great deal: from 9.8 percent to 10.75 percent, falling back to 10 percent between 1785 and 1800. This increase is to be attributed to the fact that toward the end of the century the bulk of it is furnished by the Electoral Mark. Between 1792 and 1795 the largest number of appointments is made in the two Prussian provinces; and this obviously bears some relation to the two partitions of Poland.

Lastly, the higher the grade, the higher is the proportion of nobles; whereas they constitute no more than 10.14 percent of the *Auskultatoren* and *Referendarien* appointed between 1788 and 1800, they account for 11.65 percent of the *Assessoren*, who are likely to be promoted to the higher levels. According to the *Conduiten Listen* of officials of the legal service in 1800, 115 out 315 councillors are nobles; in 1801 we find 322 councillors, 112 of whom are nobles. The proportion of nobles, therefore, rises from 10 percent to 33 percent.

The administrative career is just as strictly regulated as the legal branch. An edict of Frederick II of 1770 sets up a "Standing Committee for the examination of all future councillors of the Finance and Domains Chambers (*Landräte, Steuerräte*, and Directors of Public Works)." It sits at Berlin under the chairmanship of the minister concerned. A candidate must be a *Referendar* and must have served a probationary period for several years with a Provincial Chamber or Chamber delegation or else be a regimental quartermaster or a prosecutor attached to a court-martial. He must produce a certificate of good conduct issued by his superior with his application to the general director. "Lacking such a certificate a candidate is absolutely debarred from sitting the examination, for anyone who is of a bad moral character will never make a good civil servant, however great his abilities."

The examination in the theory and practice of administration is compulsory. A candidate cannot be excused from taking it on the plea, for example, that he is of noble origin: "Indeed," the edict states, "if anyone asks to be excused it, we shall regard this as an evident sign of his lack of confidence in his own abilities and of his unfitness for the office to which he aspires."

However, "with regard to appointments of *Landräte*, we shall continue to consider that the orders which are entitled to elect them shall still do so. But no *Landrat* may be installed in his office without prior examination by the committee in the subjects with which a *Landrat* should be acquainted and without making two reports in accordance with the relevant provisions of the law; he must pass the examination in the same way as all the others."

The candidates pay twenty thalers, to be distributed among the members of the committee, regardless of the result of the examination.

Junior officials who wish to become *Referendarien* to the Chambers or directors of the municipal police (*Policey-Bürgermeister*) or even secretaries-in-ordinary must be examined by the board which appoints them. The king reserves the right to see that they are reexamined by the Higher Board (*Oberexaminationscommission*), if need be.

The committee's records have been preserved. Between 1770 and 1806 it examined 795 candidates, 348 of them nobles. The proportion of nobles is thus 43.86 percent, whereas it does not exceed 11.65 percent of the legal *Assessoren* who have passed the "major" examination, and it may therefore be compared with them. At the stage below, the difference is equally striking. The archives of the General Directory disclose the proportion of nobles among the ordinary *Referendarien* to the provincial Chambers. A rapid sampling shows that 96 of 374 appointments, or 34.53 percent, almost all of them between 1786 and 1806, are nobles; in the legal branch the nobles hold only 11.77 percent of the *Referendar* posts.

The high proportion of nobles shows absolutely no sign of diminishing; on the contrary, indeed, if we take, first, the period 1770–86, the last years of Frederick II, and, second, the period 1786–1806, the reigns of Frederick William I and Frederick William II up to the disaster at Jena, we find that the proportion of nobles rises from 37.8 percent to 45.23 percent. This looks like a species of small-scale reaction by the nobility, gradually eliminating commoners from the administrative service just as they have been eliminated from the army. This impression is strengthened by an analysis of the proportion of councillors. Of 171 appointments between 1786, or the years immediately preceding, and 1806 there are 45 nobles; the proportion, 32 percent, is comparatively low; but the figures are very much lower than those for examination candidates. Of 795 young men examined by the Higher Board since 1770, probably not more than 250 to 300 were placed in the provincial Chambers. These were the less attractive posts and in them the commoners were most numerous. The situation is likely to be different in the more restricted bodies to which the more talented candidates aspired. The *Conduiten Listen* for 1800, for example, show 12 nobles and 21 commoners (or 36 percent nobles) in the Forestry Department, in the central forestry administrative service, and among the provincial forestry superintendents (*Oberforstmeister* and *Forstmeister*). The proportion is certainly even higher in the diplomatic service.

There remain the municipal offices set aside for the burghers; they have long been as lucrative as they are honorific. In the German Free Towns such as Worms, members of the town council even at the end of the eighteenth century receive emoluments ranging from 200 to 500 florins a year; they are barely distinguishable from the nobles in their mode of living and enjoy great prestige.

Admittedly, these advantages were the prerogative of a few patrician families; but if the most eminent burghers in all the Prussian towns had been similarly advantaged, it would have been that much easier for plebeians to rise socially within the civil service. The Hohenzollerns had, however, brought the Prussian towns into submission to themselves. The municipal administration had been subordinated in practice to the state early in the century. The commander of the garrison took whatever police measures he saw fit and supervised the markets in the interest of the soldiers and the lower classes. The municipal finances were controlled by the *Steuerrat*, who saw to the collection of the excise, which had replaced the older taxes; his jurisdiction soon extended over the entire town administration; he intervened in the town council's decisions, and the War and Domains Chamber settled finally any disputes arising from his decisions. The State is the master, therefore. The following example will show how this came about. In nearly all cases it was the need to clear up the town's financial affairs that led to state intervention; and it took advantage of this to amend the town's statutes. Königsberg had a very complicated charter, with its three independent districts each administered by a mayor and a councillor. On pretext of economy, the government simplified and unified its institutions. The membership of the town council was reduced to three burgomasters and sixteen regular senators, together with six supernumeraries. All were elected for life by cooptation, subject to confirmation by the state. Drawing municipal stipends, they became to all intents and purposes minor officials. Municipal administration also provided the burghers with a wide range of honorific and unpaid offices, such as trusteeships, widow and orphan relief, the fire brigade, and similar empty trifles; this certainly enabled them to make a useful contribution to municipal life, but it hardly enriched them.

Most of the towns suffered a similar fate. Though we do not as yet have case studies describing the process whereby the kings alienated the old freedoms, we have only to glance over the contemporary directories to appreciate its results. At Halle, though the Stadtpräsident performs the apparent functions of burgomaster, he is simultaneously councillor to the War and Domains Chamber, and the membership of the Standing Council is reduced to fourteen.

The royal government has therefore reduced both the numbers of paid municipal officials and their emoluments and prestige. To aspire to the posts they hold is to run into a dead end. Many of them are appointed for life and can expect no promotion. The sons of the upper middle class, wealthy and well connected as they are, cannot satisfy their ambitions by vegetating in places lacking all prospects. If they wish to make a career for themselves, they enter the service of the state, the only path to a higher status in the social scale.

These random samplings plainly show, first, that the middle classes have virtually monopolized the legal posts; but the proportion of nobles in them remains higher than their numbers in proportion to the population as a whole; it tends to rise with the grade in the hierarchy.

Secondly, there are always more candidates than posts vacant, despite the openings for the middle classes especially in the new provinces. Many young men are unable, therefore, to make a career for themselves.

Their attempts to thrust their way into the other official corps run into stronger resistance from the nobility. In the War and Domains Chambers and other and more specialized administrative branches the nobles always constitute one-third of the establishment.

Lastly, those commoners who pay the Higher Examination Board the twenty thalers to sit the examination which may pass them through the narrow gate are obviously members of the upper middle class, whose wealth and mode of living enable them to cut a figure on the few boards on which they are willing to serve. The less wealthy, following an ancient tradition, turn to the church.

The Clerical Career

Literature has propagated the notion that the Protestant church provided the German middle classes with the largest number of career prospects in the eighteenth century. By and large, this is a fact; and its notoriety is due to the further fact that the members of the clergy were drawn almost exclusively from commoners. If, by way of exception, one of them is of noble origin, the first proof he offers of his conviction that his vocation is a genuine one is to renounce the *von* before his name. Owing to this humility the historian is unable to estimate the size of the aristocratic component. In his study of the biographies of 250 clergymen selected at random, Georges Pariset found fourteen who retained their title under Frederick William I (Pariset, *L'état et les églises*). Among the 584 appointments made between 1786 and 1806 we do not find a single minister whose noble origin can be definitely shown. Throughout the century the Protestant church in Prussia remains a stronghold of the middle classes; it is not surprising, therefore, that it is a bulwark of the Aufklärung. It would be well worth investigating whether the antirationalist trends which grew up in the church in the second half of the century were not promoted mainly by ministers or devout laymen of noble extraction, like Count Zinzendorf, or of foreign origin, like the French and Dutch sponsors of Pietism and Quietism.

However that may be, the young man from the middle classes intending to join the clergy finds obstacles in his path even despite the absence of nobles. Obliged to take the full course of education at the secondary school in his native town, to attend a faculty of theology, and to pass a minor test of his abilities before the members of the consistory to which he is applying for a post, he must necessarily spend a very long time in the depressing state of "candidate." This designation and enrolment on the consistory registers entitles him to act as curate to a minister but not to administer the sacraments, and is of no real use to him; he can only acquire the material independence to which he aspires through a call to the ministry, which may well be several years coming.

It is sometimes hard to distinguish the novice from the most senior pastor because of the variety of titles, which may not be equivalent from one province to another. The registers, it is true, always distinguish between appointment and promotion, but a particular appointment may relate to a pastor who has already held a living abroad, and some favored applicant may be given a place usually reserved for a more experienced candidate. Nor is it possible to take only the appointments of curates, for their situation pending promotion, in many cases worse paid than any other, is not necessarily the first step in a career.

If, however, we keep to general conclusions, mistakes about particular individuals become negligible; since in all probability not all of them run in the same direction, they cancel out. We can, then, compile a table comparable to that for the civil service by excluding first the lower grades such as verger or beadle, where no theological education is required, and second such higher preferments as archpriest and provost (*Probst*), which are not usually conferred on novices.

We then find that 584 pastors were appointed between 1786 and 1806 in all of the Prussian provinces combined, except Silesia. Pastors beneficed or unbeneficed, curates, and military chaplains are distributed almost equally over the Protestant provinces, though rather more densely in the older provinces such as the Electoral Mark, Magdeburg, and Minden than in the larger towns. Pariset notes something of the same sort in the period 1713–40. But, in contrast to his observation, there are at the end of the century almost as many appointments in the small, rural and sparsely populated province of East Prussia as in the Mark. We may suppose that the conquest of Catholic Poland impelled the Protestant church to strengthen its numbers in this border province.

There are far fewer of these appointments, an average of 27.80 yearly, than in the legal and administrative services. To take only the commoners who became *Auskultatoren* in the higher courts, their average is 56.60 yearly; and there are in addition most of the *Referendarien* in the administrative service and a large part of the establishment of the lower courts. It can therefore be stated with some certainty that the church takes one-quarter at least and one-third at most of the young commoners making a career as paid officials. We can now see why the law faculties were so well attended at the end of the century, and we begin to doubt whether the Religious Edict and Wöllner's regime were really the efficient cause of the phenomenon, the more so because if the system had lasted, it would soon have threatened rationalist laymen no less than the clergy.

The church, therefore, is no longer the main opening for commoners in search of a career in Prussia in the late eighteenth century. It now tends to take in only those drawn to it by a religious vocation and those of scanty means. University fees are lower in the faculties of theology, since they have a great many scholarships in their gift; the examinations by the consistory are free; a young clergyman's official expenses are incomparably lower than those of lay officials.

The number of appointments tends to rise regularly in the church, as in the civil service. The five-year totals from 1786 to 1805 are 124, 126, 155, and 141. There is, therefore, no narrowing of the outlet; if posts appear to be scarce, it is because of the growing crowd of candidates.

The increase in the number of places is not, however, calculated to satisfy the candidates. A comparison of the table for the last years of the century with Pariset's analysis—though it is true that his embraces only 250 clergymen—shows that the proportion of curates has risen greatly. Whereas 16.8 percent of the pastors appointed between 1713 and 1740 had begun as curates or tutors, curates alone account for 34.2 percent of places between 1786 and 1806.

Despite the miserable situation of these curates, who often have the utmost difficulty in making ends meet, their places are envied by the crowd of unplaced candidates. We cannot estimate how many of these there were, but their complaints moved all their contemporaries. One cannot open a contemporary novel, journal, or exchange of correspondence without encountering them, haggard and humble, in the black and shiny frock coat that admits them into good bourgeois or noble houses, where they are employed and despised.

Usually they become tutors; almost all the clergymen and most of the writers and professors have given lessons during some part of their adolescence. This applies throughout Germany. At Dresden one-fifth of the people one meets in the street are theological candidates, designated *magistri*, who have been obliged to take to tutoring: "They hasten from house to house all day and barely earn enough from their lessons to eke out a miserable existence. All of them are withered, pallid, and sickly and reach the age of forty before the consistory takes pity on them and endows them with a living" (*TM* 1785, II, 44). Their feelings toward those who employ them are all the more bitter because they cannot express them.

The Liberal Professions

While competition from the nobles in many cases restricts the admission of the middle classes to the civil service, it is hard to see who there is to dispute their monopoly of the liberal professions. The nobles shun them for fear of losing caste, and the other commoners for lack of education. They are ideal occupations for the enlightened, for they ensure them a freedom greater than that possessed by an official, supervised as he is by his superiors, or by a craftsman controlled by his guild. We should therefore expect to see all the dissatisfied become lawyers, doctors, or professors instead of vegetating in a state of stagnation. Yet they contine to complain, as though this were not the right solution; and when, yielding to their querulous appeals, we examine it more closely, we find that it is indeed inadequate. The liberal professions are still only an embryo of what they were to become later in a capitalist society. Under the state-directed and mercantilist regime of enlightened despotism there are few professions, because the government does not permit them to be practiced freely, or else they are not much sought after because there are as yet too few clients to make them lucrative.

Early in the century lawyers were free to set up practice in the courts. Frederick William I, indignant at the abuses to which this freedom led, abolished it. To protect his subjects he limited the numbers of lawyers; he seems to have contemplated turning them into officials. Frederick II confined himself to placing them under governmental control so as not to incur the expense of creating a new administrative class.

Although at the end of the century they are not paid by the government, they are nevertheless appointed by it and are styled commissioners of justice. Most of them are both attorneys and notaries. The most prominent may be styled councillors of justice (*Justizrat*). The Order of Advocates under this regulation fails to increase and multiply to any great extent. We find

232 appointments of councillors of justice between 1786 and 1800. All are commoners. Like the officials, they increase in number toward the end of the century; but this increase, disclosed by the five-year totals of 71, 78, and 83, is remarkably slow and regular. Most advocates are former *Referendarien* who have not prepared for the "major" examination.

The only professors' posts which are truly enviable are chairs in faculties. The major secondary schools, however, also give teachers who have distinguished themselves there some scope for acquiring a reputation for themselves. In 1775 the four Prussian universities employ 80 professors, and the secondary schools with more than five classes, 490. In 1804 the ancient universities of Königsberg, Frankfort-on-Oder, Halle, and Duisburg, recently joined by Erlangen, have 135 professors. The increase is appreciable, but it is not comparable with the expansion of Prussian territory or the rise in the birth rate. There are 130 arts and mathematics students in 1804. The number of vacancies yearly, even including the secondary schools, was probably not as much as half that of the candidates.

As for the doctors, their art is still despised. Only recently separated from the surgeon's craft, which is practiced only by barbers, it remains accessible even to Jews, who, indeed, shed luster on it. It bestows some sort of prestige only on professors, and there are not many of them; for in 1804 there are only 164 medical students in the entire kingdom. It is almost always these professors who benefit from a lucrative pluralism. For medicine too is regulated; a Higher Medical Board (*Ober-Collegium Medicum*) established in 1685, recruited by cooptation from the best-known doctors and approved by the king, exercises a general supervision over everything connected with medicine and pharmacy. It possesses a right of jurisdiction over court actions relating to medicine and cases involving doctors. It grants permission to young medical graduates who have deposited with it twelve copies of their thesis to sit the examination which will qualify them to practice in Prussia. The examination before the Board of Physicians and Surgeons comprises a course of oral lessons, one of which is given in public, and a commentary on six anatomical demonstrations; furthermore, the candidate has to write a report in Latin on a practical case in four weeks. These are formalities which can, in default of personal knowledge, be prepared by someone else beforehand. The formalities were not very strict until 1789, and even after that date the country was still infested with quacks who had never been duly authorized to perpetrate their miraculous cures. The surgeons too are supervised by the Higher Board and must have been apprenticed to their craft for three years, have practiced it as assistants for seven, and have acquired a barber's shop. Their test comprises only two anatomical commentaries and six surgical operations. There is a Medical Board subordinate to the Higher Board in each province.

The Board of Physicians and Surgeons serves both as a medical school and a permanent board of examiners. Its members—seven professors, including two anatomists, one botanist, one chemist, one surgeon, and two therapeutic and pathological physiologists—have been salaried by the king since 1724. They teach at the Berlin Anatomical Theater, built by order of the king in 1713. This institution enjoys an immense reputation because the hospitals and workhouses supply it with corpses in abundance. The students dissect an average of 200 yearly; such lavishness is rare at the period.

There is also a Higher Board of Health (*Ober-Collegium Sanitatis*), established in 1719 at the time of the plague epidemic in Hungary. Its three members, one War Councillor, one municipal health offict , and one member of the Berlin town council, supervise public health.

It is evident that all the members of the boards are persons already settled in life and ensured of ample means by their position as professor or their reputation as practitioner. Their functions, even if paid at all, are mainly honorific. This is no opening for the young men.

They may, it is true, fall back on posts as town or district doctors (*physici*). These officials see to the application of the Higher Board's decrees. They treat the poor free of charge. They sit an examination largely concerned with forensic medicine. They are, in short, health officers, with little status socially. There are 131 of them in 1786, Silesia excepted. Fourteen towns or provinces remunerate instructors to midwives.

The official services, therefore, do not hold out any enviable prospects to ambitious young men. There remains private practice. Doctors become increasingly numerous toward the end of the century, so much so that the government intervenes to prevent an overabundance of them. The unduly easy examination is abolished. The cabinet orders of 15 December 1789 and 4 February 1791 require the candidate to follow up his set lessons with a public oral examination given in German. The candidate is interrogated by two members of the Board of Physicians and Surgeons. This is not all; a further edict, that of 1 February 1798, aggravates the difficulties. Henceforth no more than three candidates will be taken at each session. Each of them will first give his anatomical and clinical course and then a standing board of examiners will question him at length. The board will make sure that he has spent a probationary period of not less than three months in university clinics and that he has done his due share of practical work.

Thus the opening begins to be obstructed at the very moment that it is most sought after. But worse is to come. At about the same period patients begin to turn away from the doctors. Following a general trend in modes of thought, the vogue passes to quacks who perform miraculous cures. The authorities make vain efforts to stem a current to which many of their own representatives abandon themselves in private life. It is obviously not possible to say precisely to what extent the craze for the miraculous deprives doctors of regular patients undergoing lucrative treatments; but the fact is certainly not negligible. A doctor who does not make a deep impression on his patient at his first visit is often not summoned again; and single visits will not earn him a living.

The official and compulsory tariff of 1802 is perhaps not always scrupulously observed, but, in view of the competition, doctors certainly tended to charge less than it rather than more. However that may be, it does give some idea of the practitioner's income. The charge for "the first visit to an ordinary patient in town or in the suburbs" is 1 thaler 8 groschen; for subsequent visits, "including prescriptions," 12 groschen. In cases of "infectious hectic fever" the fee rises to 2 thalers 16 groschen. Within the radius of a quarter of a league outside town the charge for a first visit is 2 thalers. "Performing an autopsy on specific instructions" is a windfall, bringing in 6 thalers.

Surgeons are paid 8 to 12 groschen for administering an enema, 6 to 8 thalers for operating on a harelip, 8 to 10 for tapping a bladder, 15 to 20 for a castration, 20 to 30 for amputating an arm, and 30 to 50 for operating for stone.

A midwife may charge 3 to 5 thalers for an easy and natural birth. The fee for a caesarian survived by both mother and child is 15 to 30 thalers.

Dentists are paid 8 to 12 groschen for each extraction. The charge for filling several teeth or cleaning them all is 2 to 5 thalers; for making and inserting a false tooth 2 to 4 thalers.

The liberal professions, then, do provide an appreciable range of career openings; they employ a number of young men, and would employ more if they could have their way. On the whole, their course parallels that of the civil service and the clergy; they proliferate and are then subjected to increasingly restrictive regulation. In contrast to careers in the civil service, the liberal professions are almost exclusively the preserve of commoners; and in contrast to the clerical career, they are almost entirely practiced in the towns. These features give them perhaps their most original characteristic. No one in the eighteenth century believed that they had any future; many looked upon them as a second-best solution, for entering them very often meant renouncing a more promising career and resigning oneself to an occupation of a somewhat inferior kind.

The medical students become the colleagues of barbers, though with a slightly higher status, and the competitors of quacks, though often at a disadvantage. There are 164 of them in 1804, as compared with 864 law students and 625 theological students. The well-paid university chairs of medicine are reserved for a select few.

The Writers

The students thronging the universities are well aware of the difficulties ahead of them. This makes them the more eager to attract attention to themselves. To become famous is a short cut to the heights of a career in politics or the civil service. It means gaining an embassy or a university chair without the heat of the fray; it means invitations from princes aspiring to become Maecenases. Manifestly, the elect will be few, and at the best of times no German can hope to become a Voltaire, a Maupertuis, or some similar correspondent of the Berlin Academy. But the emoluments of a Wieland or a Goethe at Weimar, the stipend of a Forster as librarian at Mainz or of a Lessing at Wolffenbüttel do rather more than keep body and soul together. Even if not very well paid, situations of this sort are preferable to a slow rise through a hierarchy, for they represent the culmination of a very special kind of career, one which is subject to no regulation and where the summits are not kept for a privileged few, as they are in the civil service. These elect are not the best born, nor do they owe their glory merely to blind chance. They are the most gifted, and they feel their responsibility to nurture a talent which might equally well have been left hidden under a bushel. By their own efforts they have risen when still young to the leadership of the Aufklärung; they are making a more honored moral career endowed with more prestige than any other. Rather than flatter a petty prince swollen with self-complacency, who would not prefer admission to this small group of oracles who are the leaders of public opinion, who hand down the dictates of reason to a multitude of less gifted intermediaries, to the chroniclers of the lesser journals and the lecturers in the reading clubs? As universal lawgivers, the great writers partake of the intellectual life of all nations; their travels through Germany or abroad are events which are on every tongue and everywhere ensure them the most flattering reception at every level of society. The young graduates are not accustomed to doubt their own genius. The press, indeed, eagerly welcomes the most gifted of them, and by opening its columns to them gives scope to their dreams.

Almost all of them are commoners; birth excuses the rest from such toil. Only seldom do "the rich and powerful" write during their spare time, "out of dilettantism or to promote the progress of the sciences." "Do we have many Ducs, Grafen, or Lords among our country's writers?" asks a correspondent of the *Teutsche Merkur*. "The writers among us who treat of the interests of the state, of trade, and of industry are theological candidates. Students have the audacity to paint a picture of our manners when they do not yet have the entrée to any good house, when they have not met a single man of distinction or a single lady of merit. We deplore our lack of a Sterne, a Richardson, or a Shakespeare . . . but many a noble would be embarassed if it was learned that he had drawn out a chair for some scribbler or other" (*TM* 1779, I, 32).

Those doomed to tutoring virtually swoop on literature, which sometimes, so to speak, signs their reprieve, and transforms a miserable debt-ridden fellow despised by all into the great Jung-Stilling; but it brings many a disappointment. Genius is rare and talent does not always gain recognition in eighteenth-century Germany. Of all the openings available to young men of the middle class, literature is certainly the most hazardous. Brilliant success is the exception; most of those who devote themselves to literature are doomed to indigence; and even when they acquire a genuine reputation, they are still only too well aware of the wolf lurking near the door. "The horde of famished poets," Wieland notes gloomily, "is growing daily." It is all very well for them to form a mutual admiration society, but "for all that, the outcome . . . is still starvation. They grow sour and write satires against princes who have not aspired to imitate Augustus and act as wealthy patrons to them or poets who have a regular meal waiting for them on the table at home" (*TM* 1776, II, 248).

According to the catalogues of the book fairs, there are 3,000 authors writing in German in 1773 and 6,000 in 1787; and these figures include only recognized writers.

The largest number are in Saxony, with one in 2,714 inhabitants in 1790; in Prussia there is only one in 5,382. Berlin is a large publishing center, with 222 writers in a population of 150,000, but does not rank first in Germany; the first place is held by Göttingen, with 79 writers in a population of 8,000.

The public to which these writers appeal is very small; it is drawn mainly from the middle-class members of the reading clubs, most of whom are too poor to build up a library of their own. The nobles only read French and subsidize foreigners instead of encouraging their fellow countrymen. Like Forster before him, Friedrich Schlegel complains that truly German culture is to be found only in the middle class, "the soundest part of the nation" (*Jugendschriften* II, 120 ff.).

There appears to be no way of accounting for this paradoxical situation; at all events, no one ever answers the questions perpetually raised in the press:

Why do so many German princes write the most flattering and obsequious letters to Paris intellectuals, who look down disdainfully from the lofty eminence of their pride on them and the institutions they have founded? Why do they send them valuable presents in the hopes of thereby gaining some sort of fame, whereas they will not pay the young scholars of their own country so much as the interest on the capital they spend on study and travel? What must an impartial traveler think who is shown these letters and presents at Paris and is also familiar with the plight of this prince's own schools and colleges? [*DM* 1778, I, 147–48.]

It would be a mistake to attribute the Sturm und Drang writers' campaign against foreign influences to disinterested patriotism; those great-hearted and talented men are campaigning to win a public, *their public*. They passionately resent the injustice done to them; whereas there are too few literate readers at home to buy their books, the French, with twelve times as many readers as Germany, still come in and wrest their scanty customers from them! The French, of all people, those "hermaphroditic minds," incapable of grandeur or invention! (*DC* 1775, 707–10.)

"In what German state can a German scholar earn a living as a scholar?" Nicolai too asks. "The best German writers have sometimes had to earn by the sweat of their brow, chiefly by hack translation, the leisure they have spent on their admirable productions. There is no other means, alas, whereby a scholar who has no official post and is not able to obtain one can keep from starving" (*Sebaldus Nothanker*, bk. 2, 108).

The writers themselves may perhaps be somewhat to blame, owing to their inability to meet the public on its own level. In England and France "the class of writers matches the class of readers." In Germany they write only for each other or for the learned; and the learned are seldom "men of letters" but "the theologian, jurist, doctor, philosopher, professor, schoolmaster, director, rector, co-rector, subrector, graduate, *collega infimus*" and write only for those who attend their lectures and their subordinates. "This tiny educated public of pedagogues and their pupils consists of about 200,000 at most, yet they so heartily despise the other 20 million human beings who also speak German that they will not trouble to write for them." Why do they not learn to "popularize," for that would be to everyone's benefit; and when will the catalogues of the Leipzig Book Fair list any but works by narrow specialists?

Authors persist in their complaints till the end of the century. Wilhelm Schlegel writes in the *Athenaeum* in 1799: "Duclos notes that there are few noteworthy books which are not produced by professional writers. This Estate has long been treated with respect in France. Here a writer used to count for less than nothing if he was a writer and nothing else. Even today this prejudice still crops up here and there. . . . The writer's trade is, depending on how it is plied, a stigma, self-indulgence, pure donkey work, a craftsman's job, an art or a virtue." Friedrich Schlegel observes: "There is a perpetual complaint that German authors have always written for a very small circle or even purely for themselves and among themselves. But this is really an advantage. It will always heighten the spirit and character of German literature, and it is quite possible that a public for it will emerge in the meantime" (*Jugendschriften* II, 1275).

As late as 1802, Vermehren writes to Schleiermacher: "Have you heard that the King of Prussia has presented Kotzebue with a fat prebend in the Magdeburg district? The purpose is to keep him available to Berlin. Most assuredly, this is a unique instance of a *German* writer making a brilliant fortune from his writing. He's now on the payroll of three great powers; he seems to me to be, with luck like this, a most remarkable *lusus naturae*" (Meisner, *Briefe*, 43).

Commercial bookselling does expand, however, because of the reading clubs. It is still rudimentary when Perthes is serving his apprenticeship at Leipzig. In the smaller towns a bookseller must combine bookselling with other more lucrative occupations if he is to grow rich. He goes in for barter, exchanging, for example, the twelve folio volumes of the *Juridical Oracles* for an ox (Nicolai, *Sebaldus Nothanker* II, bk. 4, 25).

Publishers and booksellers meet at the yearly book fairs. Reluctant to tie up their capital, they do not buy the latest publications, but exchange them for stock of their own. Booksellers are thus compelled to become publishers as well. At Leipzig and Frankfort, however, the *Kommissionäre*, or wholesale booksellers, manipulate large stocks and send retailers the books they want. The apprentice spends his time combing the bookstores for the book required, keeping the stocklists up to date and serving customers in the store, which remains open from seven in the morning to eight at night. For information on the value of manuscripts Perthes's employer has for years been consulting an aged secondhand dealer who keeps a stall and is reputed to know all about science. It is not until the very end of the century that the trade becomes more enterprising; publishers gradually cease to demand cash down and accept copies on sale or return. The bookseller is not obliged to stock books for exchange; he no longer publishes as well as sells; a sound intellectual culture is now of more use to him than the expensive equipment and large investment required for publishing.

But the progress in bookselling does not benefit the writers accordingly. Almost all of them feel they are exploited by their publisher. "The poet," they repeat over and over again, "sows and plants; the publisher reaps and gathers" (Kapp and Goldfriedrich, *Geschichte* III, 125).

A closer look shows that payments are nevertheless rising regularly. Well-known authors become more exigent. Klopstock received 3 thalers a folio in 1740 for the earlier poems in his *Messiah*; he gets 12 thalers in 1773 for the later poems. Wieland, getting 8½ thalers a folio for his *Socrates* in 1769, admits that this is a vast sum for Germany; but it would look small enough in London. The less famous writers generally regard 6 to 7 thalers as low; but translations are paid far worse, an average of only 2 thalers. On the whole, therefore, the course of literature somewhat resembles that of the civil service and the clergy. Writers complain in the same way as candidates for the civil service. Like them, while their treatment is improving, their numbers are constantly increasing and, with their numbers, the proportion of those who are not getting what they regard as their deserts.

Writers devise various means of eluding the publsihers' domination; they try to launch works themselves. Wieland collects the subscriptions for his *Agathon* in 1771, but when he tries to get it printed, he runs into difficulties and finally has to make a deal with the publisher Reich. Klopstock works up a public subscription for his *Gelehrtenrepublik* in 1774, but when the work appears, it disappoints readers so badly that they swear they will never again commit themselves to buying a book sight unseen. Plans for a cooperative to print and sell books come to naught.

The publishers are not in fact as favorably situated as they are reputed to be. Their profits are certainly higher than those of their successors in the nineteenth century, but they run greater risks, for copyright is not recognized. If a book is a success, all and sundry can reprint it. The original publisher has to bear the expenses of putting the book into circulation, he alone assumes the consequences if it is not successful, and he has to produce a well-printed book if he is to attract custom. The pirates easily sell any famous work, ill printed but cheap. For over thirty years, ever since the birth of the popular press, writers and publishers have been wrangling without result.

The writers claim that they are entitled to make a living in the same way as any other skilled craftsmen and have no patience with the notion that refuses them this right on the pretext that a work of art is something of a finer essence; the possession of genius is no good reason why its possessor should starve to death.

It is not so much to the public's advantage as it thinks to permit this piracy to continue; on the one hand, it deters publishers from printing a large number of copies of the original edition, and this raises the price; on the other, since the reprints are very faulty, the author protects himself by publishing new revised and enlarged editions; readers are obliged in the end to buy several defective reprints and spend more than they would for a satisfactory original.

The printers remind authors that a poet in antiquity would never have sought to sell his thoughts; anyone might copy anything.

There is not much that can be done to combat piracy. The fighting fund canvassed by some publishers to enable them to undercut the reprinters by selling their editions below cost never comes to anything. Though the publishers are usually wholesalers with special lines, selling for cash and dominating the market in Germany, they have no mind to risk their capital in an enterprise of this sort. They would greatly prefer a system whereby as soon as a book showed promise of becoming popular, they would themselves reprint their original edition on cheaper paper and without the illustrations. But the public is outraged when it discovers them offering the same works at quite different prices; and the pirates in South Germany, most of whom are bookseller-publishers and reset the original type, have an excellent pretext for reproaching their competitors with trying to establish a monopoly.

In the first issue of his journal in 1786, Goekingk threatens to suspend publication if he is pirated; this confession of impotence shows that governmental intervention, though often requested, is ineffectual.

The governments can indeed have some say in the matter when they confer a "privilege" prohibiting unauthorized publication in the form of reprints, digests, or even commentaries. But, in the first place, to apply for a privilege is to give the authorities a supervisory right, which infringes the principle of the freedom of the press and undermines the very foundations of the Aufklärung; for the state refuses its privilege to books it considers bad. On the other hand, the protection is valid only in the territory of the state conferring it. The only means to make it valid generally is either to apply to all the governments, which is a very costly business, or else to obtain an imperial privilege, which is of no real value, since litigation in the imperial court is a very long-drawn-out affair, and the court has no means of its own to compel a government to enforce its decisions. As a matter of hard fact, a privilege is valid beyond the borders of the country conferring it only to the extent that that country is feared. The more powerful rebut the protests. Prussia itself cannot protect its own subjets.

In 1784 twelve privileged booksellers address a lengthy petition to the king:

Your Majesty has often deigned in the past to protect our property against many vile pirates. A gang of thieves of this breed has once again set up in the Rhineland; it has hatched a plot to reprint in various collections all good and useful writings, many of which will be the property of Your Royal Majesty's subjects. This anonymous society was started in the Palatinate. One Bender, of Mannheim, and the publisher Wiese, of Heidelberg, lent their names. The publisher Goegel, of Frankenthal, joined them; this invisible society then spread to Darmstadt, where the bookseller Krämer is to print some of these unauthorized reprints. At Hanau and at Frankfort-on-Main several grasping dealers are seeking to promote the exploitation of these noxious piracies by means of advertising reduced prices and the like.

There follows a list of the publications advertised in a number of journals and a summary of the arguments which Prussia might adduce. The prince elector of the Palatinate should be reminded that some years ago Prussia prohibited the pirating of Palatine editions of Shakespeare and the Latin classics. The Landgraf of Darmstadt obtained a similar favor in 1783. The crown prince of Hesse-Cassel, the Landgraf of Hanau, and the town council of Frankfort are bound by promises made in 1776 and 1777.

To the representations made by the royal government, Hanau replies that none of the books advertised has yet appeared, and Darmstadt states that it has no powers, since the place of reprint is Mannheim. There the prince elector feels strong enough to scorn the Prussians. He refuses them satisfaction on 10 December 1784:

Whereas *imprimis* there are still grave doubts whether the reprinting of books which do not enjoy privileges explicitly binding the reprinter is to be classed among acts permitted or acts illegal, the more so in that one of the complainants, the publisher of the *Allgemeine Deutsche Bibliothek*, himself argues in favor of the reprinting against which he is now protesting (Nicolai in volume XXXX, at page 205); whereas *secundo* booksellers in all parts of Germany and in the neighboring countries engage in reprinting; now therefore if His Excellency the Prince Elector wished to impose such prohibition on his subjects, He and his subjects would be liable for damages for restraint of trade.

Another complaint, lodged on 29 November 1784, against a bookseller at Hamburg who is selling reprints of Klopstock, Kleist, Lessing, Hamler, Jacobi, Klaudius, and Mendelssohn from door to door, is no more successful. The senate summons the accused the accused before it. The bookseller states that he is not the publisher of the books he is selling but bought them himself at Carlsruhe. Though reprinting is prohibited, the sale of reprints is not. He himself is only a poor bookseller, injured by the piracy of works stocked by him by his fellow merchant, Stahlbaum of Berlin. (Archives, Dahlem, Rep. 9F, 2a, fasc. 18.)

The publishers, convinced that some general regulation similar to that existing in England is needed, finally obtain the famous Saxon Mandate of 18 December 1773. Under this decree all books printed in Saxony are protected, and any persons publishing unauthorized reprints will be prosecuted and, on conviction, sentenced to the payment of damages. Works published outside the country shall enjoy similar advantages, subject to reciprocity by other governments or the purchase of a Saxon privilege. The privilege prohibits even the setting of reprints, so that in consequence they may not be sold, exchanged, or accepted in payment, on pain of seizure by the police and a fine of fifty thalers, half of which is to go to the aggrieved publisher.

The law is strictly enforced at the Leipzig Book Fair at Easter 1774. But at this period reprinting forms such a large part of the book trade that the only result of suppressing it is to damage the great book fairs. Leipzig as well as Frankfort, from which illegal reprints are also excluded by imperial privileges, gradually lose their former importance, though the pirates fail in their attempt to organize a special reprints fair at Hanau. Door-to-door selling flourishes at the expense of the former fairs, using the abundant labor of vagabonds as hawkers. The publishers protest vigorously and vainly demand that a bookseller should at least be able to read. The regulation of the trade they wish for seems to be totally impracticable.

The example of Saxony is followed by Prussia, however. The provisions of the *Landrecht* concerning bookselling come into force in 1771. Works of literature are declared to be the property of the author. He may give a publisher the right to print or sell, but he must be consulted about any republication with a different text or in a different format. The protection, with penalization for breach of it in the form of seizure and an action for damages, is valid in Prussia, irrespective of the place of publication. All complaints are legally admissable, except of course those from states in which reprints are officially permitted.

Negotiations between Electoral Saxony and Prussia are initiated in 1776 and lead in 1782 to full reciprocal protection for works published in either of the two states.

The result is a species of cleavage between North Germany, where reprints are prohibited, and South Germany, where they have found a promised land. Protection remains generally inadequate and the market for books limited.

Thus, wherever he turns, the middle-class young man graduating from the university cannot find what he is seeking. He cannot always make a career in the civil service; and the state of society is not such as to enable him to earn a living purely as an intellectual. The consequence is that the ranks of the dissatisfied swell; petty officials, theological candidates, tutors, briefless barristers, doctors with no practice, and writers with no readers come to the bitter conclusion that society has not furnished them with a place worthy of their deserts.

9

The Crisis of the Young

The Frustration of the Young Intellectuals

When we look at the biographies of young men who were later to win distinction in literature, the first thing that strikes us about them is a species of brash careerism, a juvenile but unfocused ambition without regard to the means or the objective. These young men acknowledge no attachment to any particular country; the maxim *ubi bene, ibi patria* they find self-evident; owing to their painful memories of adolescence, many of them detest their place of birth. Nor have they any very definite notion of the sort of occupation likely to suit them; official, soldier, merchant, it is all one to them; they will do anything whatever to satisfy their hunger for fame; the sole exception is that they will have nothing whatever to do with the occupation to which they seemed destined from birth. Wackenroder has a horror of law and legal procedure, Schleiermacher will not hear of trade, Kleist resigns from the army. In so doing, they abandon the paths of the Aufklärung and launch out into adventure.

They lack neither courage nor, many of them, ability. Novalis, long regarded as the very type of the romantic dreamer, goes about making a career for himself with admirable efficiency. After a parade of dilettantism at Jena and Leipzig, he sets himself to study law in earnest at Wittenberg. Through his contacts he obtains a post as actuary at Tennstedt and cherishes the notion of a successful career in the Prussian civil service. When he meets Sophie von Kuhn, he decides to follow in the footsteps of his father, the Director of Salt Mines in Electoral Saxony, so as not to be too far away from her. This dreamer becomes a demon for work; he is spurred by ambition; he devotes three-quarters of his time to his profession. He comes to regard all the rest—poetry, philosophy, religion—as a minor matter. Even Sophie's death does not deter him for long. He goes on courses, transfers to Freiberg to study mining engineering, fills notebooks as bulky as those he keeps for his verses with notes on his technical work. His reports are highly regarded. On 7 December 1799 he receives a regular appointment at a salary of four hundred thalers. This small success augments his zeal. He spends the last months of his life making applications for a second post to double with the first. "Literature," he writes to Just, his chief and friend, "is a secondary affair; it will not improve one's judgment as practical experience does; and what I am aiming at is precisely that. . . . I regard my writing simply as a way of training my mind" (Novalis, *Schriften* IV, 329). He obtains his second post on 6 December 1800, and dies on 27 March 1801. The picture of him preserved by most of his contemporaries is not that of a dreamer creating a world of his own divorced from reality, but of a young and active official in the Department of Mines.

The second feature common to most of these young men is that, despite their best efforts, they are frustrated. The cause—whether tactlessness, lack of perseverance or overweening ambition—is irrelevant. The point is that at the very time when they are publishing their first efforts, they can already look upon themselves as "failures." They have fallen very far short of the aim they had assigned themselves. If some of them became great, it was only later, often from their writing and always in a fashion quite different from what they had dreamt. Glancing back over their past when they meet in Berlin, all of them recount more setbacks than successes. Schleiermacher loses his faith in 1786; he declares that he is prepared to study any subject whatever; but medical training is expensive and the law appears hazardous, "for a middle-class law student seldom obtains a post" (Dilthey, *Leben* I, 44). Nevertheless, he enrolls in the Faculty of Theology at Halle. His father, an impoverished clergyman, advises him in 1789 to learn French, English, and mathematics so that he will soon be able to stand on his own feet. After completing his theological training he has no idea what to become. He does not fancy the idea of applying for a post, which would in any case be very hard to obtain. A job as tutor to the Dohna family, one of the greatest in the Prussian nobility, brings him a temporary respite.

Kleist, a nobleman, is predestined to the army; he enters it at fifteen, in June 1792. He takes part in the siege of Mainz under Kalckreuth and in the Palatinate campaign. Promoted to the rank of *Aspirant* after the treaty of Basel of 14 May 1795, he leads an agreeable garrison life at Potsdam in company with distinguished young officers. He goes in for music, takes an interest in literature and philosophy . . . and, exactly like Schleiermacher, loses his vocation. The monotonous career stretching before him cannot bring him happiness. In 1799, after seven years of military life, he expresses his contempt for the army. He is enamored only of science. He resigns, enrols at the University of Frankfort-on-Oder, and becomes betrothed to a general's daughter. In 1801 he takes a disgust, to science this time. He toys with the idea of becoming a peasant, begins to write, but makes no success of it, falls seriously ill for a time, and returns to the service, this time as an official at Königsberg. "It is hell that has given me my demi-talents," he writes after burning the manuscript of *Robert Guiskard*, with which he had hoped to win fame (Ayrault, *Kleist*, pt. 1, 54). He has one great advantage over other young men of his age in that he is a noble and so can always obtain a place. But he shares with them their restlessness, their timidity with women, and the dissatisfaction that leads to a twofold setback, military and civilian, till literature in turn disgusts him and drives him to suicide.

Gries refuses to devote himself to trade after three years' apprenticeship. He goes to study at the University of Jena in 1795, and thereafter, as he has large private means, is able to devote himself to literature. Hülsen, son of a clergyman, refuses to apply for a post. The poor fellow exists as best he can, writing, lecturing, and giving lessons. He even opens a private school, and ends by tranquilly cultivating his garden, thanks to the generosity of friends who buy him a property in Holstein in 1806. Wilhelm Schlegel, after dreaming of high rank in the diplomatic service, is glad enough to obtain a job as tutor with an Amsterdam banker. As for Friedrich, contrary to what Schleiermacher believed, he dreams all his life of becoming a civil servant. The articles on Ancient Greece he writes at Dresden in 1794 and 1795 give him hopes of a professorship. He migrates to Jena and is well received there, but makes a fearful blunder and thereby jeopardizes his future. Being very hard up, he consents to write for Reichardt, who is competing with Schiller's magazines, and publishes in *Deutschland* a biting criticism of *The Muses' Almanac for 1796* and the *Horen*. Schiller takes umbrage and replies maliciously in the *Xenien*, written in collaboration with Goethe. In vain Friedrich later tries to assure Goethe of the purity of his intentions; there is no job for him at the university (Koerner, *Briefe* 7 and 11). His only possible recourse is to return to the Moderns and become a critic and journalist. But no more than hastily written books will journalism keep body and soul together. It can only be a wayside station. At Berlin he meets the woman who was to love and support him till death. But Dorothea harbors no illusions about her husband's literary merits, and hopes that he will eventually get some steady official job. After the collapse of the *Athenaeum* in 1799, she notes in her diary: "I am always dreaming that Friedrich may some day make a career other than his present one. If Fate were to give us a state, he could surely still become a citizen of it. Soon, soon, my God, before it is too late! The whole world is talking of Buonaparte. Can one not put one's trust in the fortunes of a truly great man?"

Schelling is a son of the manse; a prodigal son, he is compelled to become tutor to the sons of Baron Riedessel. At Stuttgart he learns to speak French fluently and to live in good society. He then accompanies his charges on a tour of the principal German courts and on to the University of Leipzig. During the journey he is made to feel that he is of inferior station. He is distrusted. At Heilbronn the Countess Degenfeld, the young men's aunt, "expressed her belief that tutors of noble pupils are dangerous people. Seduced by French propaganda, they defend the attractions of the French

Revolution and have undertaken to make democrats and revolutionaries of their noble young charges" (Plitt, *Leben* I, 96–97). Schelling is not happy. He might be able to get a somewhat precarious post as assistant professor at Tübingen, but "there can be no happiness for me save in a state I have chosen myself," he writes to his father.

I want nothing and ask nothing but to be able to study. If you wish me to renounce my native land for that, I am perfectly willing to do so. Anyone who has had some experience of the extent of the enlightenment and literary activity in other places, Saxony, for example, can no longer have any great desire to live in Württemberg. However, for your sake and that of my brothers and sisters, I am quite prepared to go there. Theology does not attract me in the slightest. [Ibid., 205–8.]

The Isolation of the Young Intellectuals

These young men, incapable of shaping a life for themselves, are distressed to find a world which differs so greatly from their ideal. The reason they do not resolve to engage in the struggle is not the seeming bankruptcy of the philosophy of Enlightenment. That is not reason enough to make them despair; indeed, it should rather inspire them with sufficient energy to confute those who jeer at their candor. But while their mentors instilled noble principles into them, they neglected to teach them the usages of polite society. Their main obstacle when they first begin to move in high society is that they do not know how to write to a patroness, enter a drawing room, or dance a quadrille. Not all of them are lucky enough to marry a society woman, as Professor Jung-Stilling did.

Thanks to his wife, the former tailor is at last in easy circumstances. "Of his origin and his education there remained many traces. In his mode of living and acting, in his walk and stance, in his manner of eating and drinking, in his dress, and especially in his intercourse with the well-bred, he comported himself so that his low birth was immediately apparent; he invariably underacted or overacted" (Jung-Stilling, *Lebensgeschichte* II, 92–93). His wife gradually gave him the veneer he lacked.

Most of the young intellectuals at the end of the century no longer dared venture into the unknown world of society, in which an academic degree meant nothing. The new mentality directed them into other paths. Because no one has troubled to inculcate in them the set of reflexes known as good form or polite behavior, their minds, trained to correct thinking, turn to erroneous dreaming. Psychological causes and social causes combine to isolate these young intellectuals in the midst of a society that is being transformed by economic difficulties and the appetite for the miraculous.

From this point of view the evolution from Aufklärung to Romanticism can be observed very plainly. The enlightened, too, suffer from this isolation, but they are aware that it signifies a setback. They do not attempt to vaunt its charms; they never dream of construing it to their advantage by proclaiming that it singles them out from the herd and proves their genius. The new mentality has not yet transformed them. Thus Garve, so typical of the Aufklärung from every point of view, including its pedantry, superficiality, and garrulity, does not conceal his jealousy of the privileged classes. "The lower one descends in the classes of burgher society," he notes, "the more frequently one hears disparagement of the taste for life in high society and commendation of the love of solitude. For the morality of the burgher is not the morality of the noble, and no one lacking wealth and leisure can enter 'good society.' But in the society of peasants, mechanics, journeymen, apprentices, shopkeepers, or students he will find that manners are coarse or loose and that their speech is incomprehensible" (Garve, *Versuche* III, 192–200). Better, therefore, to remain solitary.

This was the solution he finally adopted himself, poor fellow. "From my earliest youth," he says in the introduction to his works,

a passionate love of the worldly always governed and often troubled my spirits. The wish to please in society and to be sought after by it has at all times weighed more with me than the desire for literary fame. I did not wish, like Montaigne, merely to be appreciated for myself rather than for my books; I also realized that it was one thing to be received in society for some special talent that I was acknowledged to possess and another to be welcomed for some ill-defined but general amiability. And only the latter was the object of my desires. Like Pascal, I thought that he who is announced on entering a social gathering as an excellent clavichord player, an amusing raconteur, or even a celebrated poet or writer enjoys as yet only a borrowed and insecure credit; if he is to be able to regard himself as a member of society fully entitled to participate in its pleasures, he must not be commended for one particular quality but must be liked for all that he is, as a "man of honor and a gentleman." [An ideal most hard to attain.] I managed from time to time to gain the esteem of a few people, the most respectable in each class, but I never succeeded in becoming popular with the greater part of any class. Neither my talents nor my outward charms were able to overcome the hauteur of great personages or the coolness of gay sparks toward a person sober and unknown, distinguished neither by family connection nor by interest. Ill-health and infirmities drove me still further into a solitude which I would only too gladly have exchanged for the bustle of the great world. [Ibid., I, chap. 6, p. 11.]

Almost all those who were to resign themselves to solitude first make an effort to cut a dash in the drawing rooms. The fact that they found it very hard to live in high society is one of the most important features of their "apprentice years."

A number of writers were on hand to help smooth their path, the most important being Knigge. This *Reichsritter*, born at Biederbeck, near Hanover, in 1752, student at Göttingen, courtier and *directeur des plaisirs* at Hanau, living on his private means on his estates, a great traveler, a freemason, and an artist, had frequented the society of his age before publishing his book *On Intercourse with the Great*, so vast a popular success that it ran through three editions in less than two years (1788-90). Generations of Germans learned etiquette and deportment from this book, which became a minor classic. The advice is given without any hint of preaching. In these paragraphs, written and numbered like maxims, divided into three sections and interspersed with anecdotes and reminiscences, they found matter to awaken their faculty of observation, acquire a taste for life in society, and avoid social blunders.

Knigge explains his purpose in the introduction:

There is perhaps no country in Europe in which it is so difficult as in our Germany to garner in intercourse with people the general approbation of all classes in all regions and of all ranks, to feel at home in every circle without effort, without falsity, without becoming suspect, and without suffering the consequences, and to make the effect one wishes on prince, noble, and burgher alike, on merchant and cleric; for undoubtedly nowhere else does there prevail so great a diversity in the tone of intercourse, in the manner of bringing up children, and in opinions, religious or other; nowhere else is there such a vast variety of subjects with which every class of people in every province concerns itself. The reason is... the very marked distinction between class and class in Germany; for inveterate conventions, education, and, to some extent too, the political constitution have drawn between them boundaries sharper than those in many other countries. . . .

Nothing, certainly, is grosser and more contrary to the conception of a polite conduct of life than the way in which a number of young men who understand each other tolerably well take all the pleasure out of intercourse with the well-disposed stranger who has come to visit them in order to participate in the pleasures of a social gathering; they perpetually divert the conversation to topics of which he knows nothing. . . . He should surely be shown greater consideration. But closed societies are seldom so obliging as to suit their conduct to the convenience of a few individuals; and this cannot always be expected of them. It is therefore important for those who wish to move in good society to study the art of suiting themselves to the manners, tone and disposition of others. [Knigge, *Umgang.*]

The first section, dealing with general topics, is full of useful hints on how to succeed. The guiding principle is always to take people for what they profess to be.

A little "sense of appropriate behavior" is therefore enough to create the desired appearance. It prompts one never to show a lack of interest, always to appear lighthearted, to eschew idle gossip, never to ask questions, and to refrain from ill-natured witticisms. Though a word out of season in conversation may soon be forgotten, one should be very cautious about what one puts on paper, for letters remain and can still do damage even after the writer is no longer there. People should be judged by their deeds rather than their words. In society one should keep the most distinguished persons on one's right, match one's stride with the ladies', follow behind them when mounting a steep staircase, precede them when descending; at table one does not place the spoon one has used beside one's plate, one sits up straight, one does not whisper into one's neighbor's ear. In salutation in the street one doffs one's hat on the side opposite the person one is greeting; and so on. (Ibid., pt. 1, chap. 1.)

The behavior to be followed varies with the temperament of one's interlocutors, the choleric, the sanguine, the melancholic, the ambitious, the vain, the sentimental, the rancorous, the lazy, the mistrustful, the quack, the adventurer, the flatterer, the clumsy, the distrait, the imbecile, the drunkard and rake, the enthusiast, the superstitious, the hypocrite, the mystic or the tolerant, the innumerable crowd of individuals of all shapes and kinds, each wishing to be treated after his own fashion. (Ibid., chap. 3.)

The second section deals with intimate intercourse, in the family, among friends, with ladies (about whom the author is caustic, but concludes that it is best to humor them), with servants, neighbors, guests and all sorts and conditions of men. Almost every conceivable type and occurrence is considered.

The third section is devoted to the various social classes. The great have been badly brought up; they are accustomed to flattery. Anyone who counts on their gratitude is making a fool's bargain; it is best not to lend them money. Their inveterate mistrust and their fickleness makes "the shining misfortune of being a favorite of theirs" an unenviable situation. (Ibid., pt. 3, chap. 1.)

No matter what fix one is in, one can consult Knigge. This accounts for his popularity. But he is not the only writer to meet this general demand for instruction. The reviews and journals abound in good advice. The *Journal of Luxury and Fashion*, for example, gives young people pertinent warnings in three installments: when invited to a nobleman's house, they must not let their host precede them; they must avoid laughing too loudly at table, passing too many compliments, and asking questions; and in conversation prudence demands that they do not tell stories or talk politics. On the other hand, it is as well to display a lively interest in the "small change" of social life and to conceal one's claims on attention. And, above all, one must not make a muddle in the use of titles. (*JLM* 1802, 423–29, 487–501, 657–71.)

This flow of sententious maxims may perhaps suit the rationalist resolved on methodical success. But the Romantic is not seduced by rules which conspire to turn him into the current type of "gentleman." His advisers never tire of telling him what to do to escape notice. But he, conscious as he is of his intellectual merits, is repelled by the efforts required to please fine society. He is discouraged by the need to overcome his timidity, to humble his pride, and by the slow progress he makes. He prefers to renounce society and proudly to choose the solitude from which he has been incapable of emerging. "The very sight of a man," Wackenroder announces, "so oppresses me that it prevents me from breathing freely" (*Werke* II, 129–65). He drafts a theory of the way to behave in society, advising his correspondent to speak as little as possible, to retire into himself, and to suppress the urge to "unburden himself of his thoughts and feelings."

A man in any way superior to the average, he explains to Tieck, cannot live in this jejune, arid, and pitiful world. He is obliged to create an ideal world for himself, of a sort that may make him happy; only then can he lower his gaze, coolly, to the so-called happiness of the petty beings who just live.

Friedrich Schlegel has no better success in society:

I am indeed compelled to admit that I am not amiable. My inability to be at peace with myself and with others disqualifies me from possessing the sweetness and grace that attract love. . . . I should like to have the sort of effect on people that would make them always speak with esteem of my honesty . . . and with warmth of my amiability.

Everything would be all right if everyone said that I was a fine fellow, if people became animated whenever I entered the room, if each after his fashion attached himself to me, and if those who think well of themselves smiled on me affably. But I have long remarked the impression I almost always produce. People find me interesting, yet they avoid me. Everywhere, high spirits evaporate when I enter; my presence acts as a damper. They prefer to look at me from a distance, as if I were some sort of dangerous freak. . . . If I were loved, I should become lovable. [Walzel, *Schlegel*, 60 ff.]

Considering the flood of words with which he complains of his inability to talk, one wonders how long he would go on if he were not afflicted with this defect. What he really means is his timidity. As soon as he enters a room, high spirits evaporate. Whose? Those of others? Perhaps, if there are only a few present and they are infected with his own gaucherie. But most assuredly his own. A pitiable sight he is as he comes into a drawing room, a short, slender young man with fluttering gestures. His handsome, astute, and expressive countenance puckers; his motions lose all ease. He stiffens, casts an uneasy eye over the company and imagines that he intercepts a smile here, a sign of derision there. "Nothing is more pitiable at the time and more agonizing afterwards," he writes, "than the fear of making oneself ridiculous" (*Jugendschriften* II, 198). He resents others because he behaves awkwardly himself, though he is more intelligent than they are; he tries to appear natural by assuming a disagreeable tone and wounds by his witty and sarcastic observations. Women especially disquiet him; they quizz so, and they are so intimidating, yet so desirable! "The women," he confides to Wilhelm in 1791, "are even more trivial than the men. . . . I have little taste for consorting with the women of the town. . . . I am too proud to flirt with a woman I do not love. Sensual I am in the extreme, too much so to consort with young women. I have therefore determined not to follow my inclination to sensuality, for it seems to me to be incompatible with the dignity of the feelings to make oneself so common with the creatures" (Walzel, 10).

Similarly, Schleiermacher, after leaving the University of Halle at twenty-one, confesses to his friend Brinckmann, a Don Juan, that he is totally ignorant of women. As for Hülsen, his shyness drives him towards the group organized at Jena by young men like himself, away from the student corporations and bourgeois society. Women are excluded from the League of Free Men, whose members—Rist, Gries, and others—are strongly influenced by that curious character, Erich von Berger, about whom too little is known. The aim of all of them is to seek the truth, to cultivate friendship, and to found other groups all over the country in order to liberate society and the state from the prejudices which are stifling them. The group does not survive Berger's departure. The friendship lavished upon him by all the members seems to have been peculiarly exalted. Gries writes on his birthday, 7 February 1797:

Today is a good time to speak of my relations with women. I am now twenty-two and I should really have something to say on the subject. . . . But I have never yet loved. Never has any of the sex made such an impression on me as to cause my heart to beat faster. I do not know if it is their fault or mine. I have always regarded women as something alien to my nature.
I have always willingly sacrificed any women who interested me to intercourse with men, more in conformity with my being.

Kleist, on becoming engaged to be married, makes a mysterious trip to southern Germany to consult the doctors, who cure him, at twenty-four, both of the consequences of youthful indiscretions and of "the physical incommodity which had led to them" (Ayrault, *Kleist*, 23–28).

Thus, the young intellectuals, *déclassés* by a university education, rendered timid by their lack of instruction in the ways of the world and by their ill-health, impelled toward dreams by the spirit of the age, are doomed to isolation. They seldom have an opportunity to encounter a woman in good society who might help them enter it. They attempt clumsily, each for himself, and fail to a greater or lesser degree, everlastingly, but vainly, echoing the criticisms of the social order uttered on every hand.

Criticism of the Social Order

The middle classes are almost the only Prussians with the ability to express themselves, and they in fact do express their discontents in print, whereas the grievances of the peasants and craftsmen are enshrined only in the police reports accumulating in the secret archives. The lesser nobility have grounds for complaint too, for they are not always able to find places for a progeny too numerous for all of them to live on the family estates; but they are not well enough educated to express themselves articulately and do not, like the middle classes, form a self-contained public, given to reading and responsive to its own utterances. Almost nothing is known, therefore, about their predicament.

When the middle classes complain, they do not blame the state primarily. The Prussians are not revolutionary: a long tradition of loyalty to the state, a profound incapacity to appreciate economic phenomena, and a complete ignorance of the consequences of a high birth rate stand in the way of drawing up a program of constructive reform. They confine themselves to grumbling and tend to reproach the social rather than the political system. In any case, they have no good reason to reject the political system. The executive is far less arbitrary in its use of power in Prussia than it is in France, and the state is far less bound up with the privileges of the nobility. Were these privileges to disappear, enlightened despotism, freed from these long-standing impediments to the adaptation of its institutions to the growth of the population, would be strengthened rather than weakened. This accounts for the fact that the Prussians almost unanimously approved of the French Declaration of the Rights of Man and the decrees of 4 and 11 August 1789, which simply applied the principles of the Aufklärung to France; and it likewise accounts for the fact that the Prussian government took them in its stride; the Revolution appeared irrelevant in Prussia because there was no tyranny in Prussia.

But criticism, tardy in coming in the political sphere, had been voiced in the social sphere long before the storming of the Bastille. It was not always material difficulties that had so embittered the malcontents; the intellectuals, convinced of the natural equality of all men, were far more sensitive to injuries to their self-esteem. What they held against the nobles was not so much any particular political or economic advantages attached to their privileges, which were in any case far less than those enjoyed by the French aristocracy, as the contempt for the commoner, acknowledged genius though he might be, displayed by the most unlettered, most cloddish, and most useless noble. What the burghers objected to was their exclusion from the drawing rooms of the nobility, the custom of addressing commoners in the third person like servants, and the self-assurance with which a noble had the final word on everything, not because he was omniscient but because he had been "born." Almost every bourgeois had had to experience these slights. The least well situated were naturally the most rancorous; but we should be cautious in accepting the testimony of great writers who no longer had any reason for complaint, since they had contrived to forget their own past. Thus the picture of social life in the eighteenth century painted by Goethe is truly idyllic:

Germany . . . had preserved its constitution intact and was experiencing real tranquillity despite the many wars and disturbances. . . . A multiform subordination, which seemed to unite the most varied orders, from the greatest to the least, from the emperor to the Jew, rather than to divide them, promoted a degree of prosperity. . . . If we look only at the extraordinary advantages enjoyed by the ancient families, with the further benefits procured them in the religious foundations, the knightly orders, the ministries and the brotherhoods, we can see that the great mass of the notables, conscious at the same time of their subordination and their coordination, lived a life of perfect satisfaction and all-embracing and wisely regulated activity. Since they were not without some intellectual culture, they secured without great effort and bequeathed to their successors a like prosperity.
    It had as yet hardly occurred to anyone to envy this great mass of privileges or to begrudge it the favorable positions it everywhere enjoyed. The burgher class had devoted itself to commerce and the sciences without hindrance and had thus . . . reached a level of elevation where it largely counterbalanced the nobility. The towns, wholly or partly free, encouraged these activities, and their inhabitants experienced a tranquil sense of well-being. With growing wealth and increasing intellectual activity, in the law and politics especially, they could happily exercise a considerable influence everywhere. [Goethe, *Dichtung* bk. 7; *Werke* XIII, 248–86.]

The minister of state dictating these lines to a secretary, the author whose fame radiates all over the world, does he remember? The patrician whom poverty has never prevented from going on his travels, publishing a book, or adding to his many collections; the amateur who designs the many gardens depicted in his books and the parks laid out to entertain the friends whose conversation, drawn from every source of culture, nourishes the mind, refines the taste, and disposes it to a tranquil serenity; the aged seer whose thought hovers above the vicissitudes of past and present alike—does he never recall those days when he himself was one of those few who did envy those great privileges? Does he never think now of the day when Werther, kept to dinner by a count, was guilty of failing to vanish the instant the nobles who had been invited to the evening party arrived and was brutally thrown out because it was not seemly that a commoner should mingle with the nobility?

When Goethe, living happy and universally honored at the court of Weimar, publishes the final version of *Wilhelm Meister's Apprenticeship* in 1797, he is still fully aware of the complaints of burghers who do not feel "coordinated with the nobility rather than subordinated to it."

Thrice happy are they to be esteemed, whom their birth of itself exalts above the lower stages of mankind; who do not need to traverse those perplexities, not even to skirt them, in which many worthy men so painfully consume the whole period of life. . . . From their very birth, they are placed as it were in a ship, which, in this voyage we all have to make, enables them to profit by the favorable winds, and to ride out the cross ones; while others, bare of help, must wear their strength away in swimming, can derive little profit from the favorable breeze, and in the storm must soon become exhausted and sink to the bottom. What convenience, what ease of movement does a fortune we are born to confer upon us! How securely does a traffic flourish which is founded on a solid capital, where the failure of one or of many enterprises does not of necessity reduce us to inaction! [*Wilhelm Meister*, bk. 3, chap. 2 (trans. Thomas Carlyle).]

Goethe himself succeeded in living down his low birth, but surely his case is almost the only one of its kind in Germany. After all, he himself admits that in Germany a general cultivation is beyond the reach of anyone except a nobleman, that the nobleman alone has a freedom in his movements, a consciousness of his independence, and a self-assurance impervious to affronts without which no man worthy of the name can cultivate his personality. But if it should so fall out that a burgher and a countess are brought close by love, are their very different ranks also "coordinated rather than subordinated?" Not so. "As two hostile outposts will sometimes peacefully and pleasantly converse together across the river which divides them, not thinking of the war in which both their countries are engaged, so did the countess exchange looks full of meaning with our friend across the vast chasm of birth and rank" (ibid., bk. 3, chap. 7).

Throughout his works Garve, too, whose reputation as a philosopher is as solidly established at Berlin as it is at Breslau, continually empasizes the virtual monopoly of social life held by the nobility.

The lower one descends in the classes of bourgeois society, the more frequently one hears disparagement of the taste for life in high society and commendation of the love of solitude. . . . On the other hand, a wealthy and eminent personality, a minister of state, say, or a general, or the owner of large estates is given no credit for preferring solitude to society or confining himself within the circle of his relatives and intimates. On the contrary, this would lose him in the eyes of all society, more especially in those of his equals, some of the consideration ensured to him by his rank and fortune. Costly receptions and social events, which manifestly imply that he has ample leisure, are to all intents and purposes a duty with which a noble is bound to comply.

[So] in a young man born to maintain the appurtenances of his rank and to enjoy the full benefits of his wealth, a taste for the pleasures of social life is approved of by the older members of his class, but on the express condition that he not seek them outside the circle which they trust to bring him up properly and to hold him in leash. Any inclinations, on the other hand, even a taste for art or science, which separate him from high socity and make him prone to solitude or the exclusive company of a few devotees of science are deprecated as an error or at best an excentricity.

There seems, therefore, to be one morality for the upper classes and another for the lower, one for the rich and idle and another for the poor and industrious. Of the upper classes is demanded sociability, of the lower that they should not be seen. [Garve, *Versuche* III, 192, 194, 195.]

The noble is thus in a particularly advantageous position. In any gathering of nobles in his own district or close to its borders he is pretty certain to meet persons who either themselves or by descent are to some degree acquainted with his family, persons to whom his name is familiar and who know of his circumstances and family affairs. Relations between nobles are closer, therefore, simply because they are nobles. Commoners, on the other hand, "have no one with whom they are to some degree in contact before they have made their personal acquaintance or before they have met each other fairly frequently. This is why they do not find it so easy to found a large and varied social group with a prevailing tone of intimacy" (ibid., I, 353–55).

The new philosophy held out hopes that everyone would have the entrée to this good society if he was willing to adopt its good manners, if not its worst prejudices. But the nobility on the whole resists. Except in the reading clubs, which are mainly burgher, the classes remain separated. The nobles become perhaps even more snobbish at a time when external differences are disappearing, dress is becoming standardized, and the German language is spreading; at a time when, too, those who experience the noblemen's snubs are becoming more sensitive to them. Nicolai cites the case of a Fräulein von Ehrenkolb, who was pleased to treat the Reverend Sebaldus Nothanker's daughter as a chambermaid. Marianne was, however, worthier, more intelligent, and far better educated than she; no matter, the noble fräulein kept dropping her snuffbox and giving her orders: "Pick up my box, child." The colonel who was to pay court to the noble snuff-taker took note of Marianne's charms; but she preferred Säugling, who was so passionately in love with her that he ventured to challenge his rival. But the duel did not come off; for one does not fight with a commoner (*Sebaldus Nothanker* I–II, bk. 5, chap. 4, 176–79).

If even those upon whom fortune smiles, like Goethe in his youth and

Garve in his old age, often cannot conceal their jealousy, what of those to whom it brings nothing? In the year 1778, a blessed year for Germany, according to Goethe's memories, his future friend Karl Philipp Moritz is about to quit Hanover, being too poor to continue his studies, and become a hatter's apprentice at Brunswick. From dawn to dusk he toils, sustained only by the hope of the next meal. He lights the fire, carries the water, and scrapes the wool with his numbed fingers in a room unheated in winter (*Anton Reiser*, bk. 10, 60 ff.). When he later obtains a scholarship which enables him to attend secondary school, he studies in such frightful conditions that his success seems miraculous; obliged to dine one day with one benefactor, another day with another, to sing with the choir of schoolchildren in the streets, to dread the gossip of his neighbors, who know of his situation and set themselves to spy on his conduct, the sensitive lad goes through real moral tortures (bk. 2, 144). His friends are worthy persons, but they do not have the influence they should; Dr. Stauer treats only the poor and does not get paid; a good writer, he is reduced to correcting the proofs of third-rate books (bk. 4, 447). The self-satisfied fail to understand this queer fellow Reiser, who takes quite normal circumstances as insults. "The feeling of a humanity oppressed by its burgher condition obsessed him and made his life a torment. He was obliged to tutor a young noble, who paid him for it and could show him the door whenever he felt like it as soon as the lesson was over. What crime had he committed, then, before his birth that he too could not become one of those people who impose on others? Why had the role of worker rather than paymaster fallen precisely to his lot?" (bk. 3, 356).

Complaints, rancor, sudden bouts of revolt, practically none of these intellectuals failed to give similar expression to them. Schelling, who had in his young days planted trees of liberty with Hegel, becomes tutor to the two sons of Baron Riedessel in 1796: "I have to tell you," he writes to his parents, "that the bread of the nobility is not so tasty as the bread of the burgher; one has to earn one's louis d'or; for at Leipzig 50 louis d'or are not precisely riches" (Plitt, *Leben* I, 117). On a journey from Stuttgart to Leipzig he notes the cleavage between the classes at each posting stage; he, as a middle-class young man, is often taken for an agent of the French Revolution, and people show their mistrust of him. Something of the same sort happens to Fichte, who is treated with contempt by his employers at Warsaw, to Hölderlin, and to most of the writers and journalists who undergo the trials of tutoring.

The "Availability" of the Young Intellectuals

Thus, what we meet everywhere after about 1780, what sounds the retreat of the Aufklärung before the onset of the new modes of thought, and what accounts for the mediocrity of many of the writers is a kind of attitude of expectancy, of "availability" on the young intellectuals' part. Trained for combat, they are ready to take on the post of clergyman, civil servant, judge, diplomat or enlightened officer; but there is no room for them all. So they wait, they dream, they write, a second best that is no substitute for action. These ex-soldiers of the Aufklärung do not yet believe that Prussia is ripe for revolution. But they do believe that, as far as they personally are concerned, they were born to act, like the French. "France has made herself free," Wieland writes in 1789. "The noblest action of the century has stormed Olympus. And what of us? I ask in vain; Germans, will you remain silent?"

They do remain silent; not that they too do not believe in the need for reform, in spite of the vast difference between enlightened despotism and absolute monarchy; not that they too do not wish to attain power and play a worthy part. The similarity between the yearnings and needs of the young on both sides of the frontier is, on the contrary, extremely moving. "The third main cause of our ennui," the *Teutsche Merkur* says in 1785, "seems to be that we lack topics of conversation calculated to captivate every listener at a mixed gathering. In Greece and Rome the state supplied this topic, and this is still so in England, Holland, North America, and other free countries, including the Free Towns of the Empire" (*TM* 1785, II, 143). A few years later, in 1791, Friedrich Schlegel explains to his brother the reasons for the Romans' superiority: "It lies in the fact that they did not seek culture for its own sake; with them it was simply a preparation for practical and political action." Even later, Chateaubriand, who had not been astute enough to profit from the Revolution and to whom Bonaparte refused to pay the high price that he placed upon himself, analyzed the causes of his ills with similar precision. "The ancients," he says in *Génie du Christianisme*, published in 1801, "had little acquaintance with this secret restlessness, this sour disposition which is caused by stifled and fermenting passions. An extensive political life, the games in the Gymnasium and on the Campus Martius, the bustle of the Forum and the public squares filled all their time and left no room for the disquietudes of the heart" (pt. 2, bk. 3, chap. 10).

Schubart's son asserts in his life of his father that Schubart was a man of action rather than a thinker.

If, as seems likely, a revolution breaks out in Germany in the course of the coming century, it is certainly not the speculative thinkers who will have furnished the ideas it will need; it is not the great and famous names, but unknown persons drawn from active life who will take the lead. . . .

Many of those who knew Schubart well observed that he would be the very man for a revolution. . . . I am convinced that he would have thundered in the Convention like Danton (whom he resembled surprisingly, at times, indeed, being almost indistinguishable from him). [Schubart, *Leben* II, 236–37.]

But Schubart is dead, and the revolution tarries.

Dorothea, with her remarkable perspicacity, draws the moral of Romanticism and regards its literary expression as a second-best alternative to what it might have become in other political and social circumstances. She writes to Schleiermacher at the time when the new school has just been founded and she can still hope for its success:

Schelling I do not yet know very well; he talks very little. But his demeanor is what one would expect—vigorous, lofty, forthright and noble. In short, rather like a French general. He is not suited to a professorship, and even less, in my opinion, to the literary world. Here is my general view: *all you revolutionary people ought first to risk your life and property in combat, and only after that you might write by way of relaxation, as Götz von Berlichingen wrote the story of his life, for your being, your will is about as fitted to literature, criticism, and all that sort of thing as a giant is fitted to a cradle.* I can see plainly enough that those who are now managing affairs are polite, chilly, tame, and insipid persons, that they cannot employ you on the feeble machines they have built for their own miserable use. Bending low, they pass through the wicket, and you want to pass through it erect; obviously, you are going to bang your head. [Meisner and Schmidt, *Briefe*, 17 and 18.]

Along similar lines Theresa Huber, in her life of her husband, Forster, explains: "As he did not have enough strength of character to make sacrifices without ill humor, as he was not capable of rising above the anxieties he shared with his parents in their straitened circumstances, he grasped at the otherworldly consolation and the hope of miraculous aid held out to him by the Rosicrucians" (Forster, *Briefwechsel* I, 16).

Madame de Staël, lastly, notes in 1803 the isolation and impotence of the young intellectuals:

In no country are there so many means of acquiring an education and perfecting one's faculties. Why, then, does the nation lack energy and in general seem sluggish and narrow, though it contains a very few men who have perhaps the best minds in Europe? The contrast must be attributed to the nature of their governments rather than to their education. Intellectual education is perfect in Germany, but everything ends in theory; practical education depends entirely on affairs. . . . Public education, however good, can produce men of letters but not citizens, warriors and statesmen.

In Germany the philosophical mentality is carried further than it is anywhere else; nothing stands in its way, and the very lack of a political career, fatal though it is to the nation as a whole, gives the thinkers greater freedom. But there is a vast gap between the first-class and the second-class minds, for those who do not rise to the height of concepts on the very broadest level have no interest or purpose in life. Anyone in

Germany who does not concern himself with the universe at large has nothing at all to concern himself with. [*De l'Allemagne*, pt. 1, chap. 18.]

These ideologues relegated to ideology by the political and social structure of their country are to all intents and purposes seeking the same thing as the beggar hopes from the lottery or the vagabond from a lucky ambuscade. Since there is "no country to defend nor freedom to fight for, there is nothing left save the pursuit of happiness." Young Friedrich Schlegel replies to his brother in 1791:

You ask me whether writing would not give me pleasure; certainly, I have a great many plans, and I believe I shall bring most of them to a successful conclusion. Not so much for love of the work as under the pressure of this instinct which has long possessed me, this devouring need for action or, rather, as I should prefer to call it, this ardent need for the infinite. [Walzel, *Schlegel*, 68.]

The closing words admirably sum up the history of the earlier Romantics. Excluded from active life much against their will, they take refuge in literature. But this cannot come about without a psychological transformation, which carries them away from the Aufklärung's "positivism" into the "need for the infinite" and the pursuit of happiness. As they themselves are not conscious of this transformation, they fuse the two successive stages in their development; and so when they speak of the instinct by which they have long been possessed, they believe they mean both their need for action and their need for the infinite.

10

The Political Crisis

The Onslaught on the Aufklärung by the King and His Ministers

Social crisis normally has political repercussions. Indeed, if we contrast the people's profound loyalty to the state around 1775 with its profound apathy towards the military defeat and the collapse of the Prussian state in 1807, we find that it amounted to a real revolution.

At the time, however, people never felt that they were in the midst of a serious political "crisis." The whole process occurred at a deeper level. It was only by imperceptible degrees that the social criticism endorsed by the Aufklärung and intensified by the young writers of the Sturm und Drang turned into political criticism inspired by the French Revolution and was at length expressed in an outburst of sentiments which were unmistakably revolutionary.

It was not the masses alone which were permeated by this disaffection; their total failure to react was due solely to their lack of sufficient guidance. It was the young men, many of whom were to earn fame or notoriety from their collaboration with the earlier Romantics, who, at the very end of the century, openly displayed their indifference or even hostility to the state. Pupils of the Aufklärung though they were, they refused to carry on its tradition. The really important fact is undoubtedly the revolt of the intellectual elite; for once that had happened, the Prussian nation was leaderless.

The tragi-comic interlude of Frederick William II's conversion accounts both for this disaffection, due to the disillusionment of those who deemed themselves victimized by it, and for the way in which it was masked by the success of the enlightened party, which, by very reason of this success, imagined that it was still all-powerful at the very moment when it was beginning to rock on its pedestal.

Frederick William II is hostile to the Aufklärung. Frederick the Great's nephew, ascending the throne at the age of forty-two, tall, stout, affable and stupid, has no personal reason to hate the existing regime. All he asks is that he shall not be overburdened with work and that there shall be no interference with his sensual pleasures. He marries off his mistress to Ritz, the court musician, and creates her Countess von Lichtenau, but she manages to retain his affections despite his remorse at living in sin.

His closest advisers, however, are two men who detest Frederick II and all his works. Johann Christian Wöllner, a former clergyman who rose to the post of *Intendant* and then became son-in-law to Countess Iztenpetz, the patroness of his living, has considerable talent. The treatises on economics which he published in Nicolai's *Allgemeine Deutsche Bibliothek* were commended by his contemporaries; Prince Heinrich chose him in 1770 as one of his advisers. His main characteristic, however, is unscrupulous ambition. He accordingly joined the rationalist Lodge of the Three Universal Globes in Berlin, and rose in it. Frederick II, who heartily disliked misalliances, refused to enoble this "rascally intriguing priestling [*Pfaffe*]."

At this juncture, Wöllner meets Colonel J. R. von Bischofswerder, a Rosicrucian who had served with the crown prince in the War of the Bavarian Succession. One night in his tent at the camp at Schatlzar in Bohemia, the prince feels the touch of an invisible hand, and an unknown voice murmurs "Jesus Christ." From that day forth apparitions appear to him frequently, and he confides in Bischofswerder, who is never very far away. (Schwartz, *Kulturkampf*, 34–38.)

Wöllner realizes how he can exploit the prince's religiosity to his own advantage; but he will not, like Bischofswerder, ask the spirits simply for a place as favorite; it is power that he desires in order to revenge himself upon the late king. He speedily becomes a convert, founds the Rosicrucian Lodge of Frederick the Golden Lion at Berlin, and brings in Bischofswerder, who cunningly induces the crown prince to hope for admission, but keeps him in suspense. On 8 August 1781 the two confederates solemnly induct him under the name of Ormesus. They hold out hopes of rapid promotion to the higher degrees and the knowledge of the secrets of the order. On 20 October 1786, barely two months after Frederick William's accession to the throne, Wöllner is ennobled.

He now mounts a major offensive against the Aufklärung. The king's favor does not slacken for one moment; shoulder to shoulder with the rationalist and freemason ex-clergyman, he fights the good fight in defense of orthodoxy; and his credulity is such that the most barefaced impostures can be acted out before his eyes.

In 1790 he pays a visit to Silesia to conclude the Treaty of Reichenbach with Austria. About this time, von Czeiszek, a lieutenant in the Hohenlohe regiment, is living at Breslau with a poor hunchbacked girl whom he is hypnotizing and who, when in trance, reveals effectual remedies to the sick. Oswald, a former merchant who has been made a bankrupt, is healed by the hunchback, realizes how he can turn her to good account, and shelters her when von Czeiszek is recalled to the colors. He hypnotizes her more deeply, and the somnambulist medium becomes a clairvoyante. Oswald is the son-in-law of Hermes, an orthodox minister and a friend of Wöllner's. He is introduced to the king and tells him of his experiments with the hunchback, whose spirit (*Geist*) parts from her soul and body (*Seele und Leib*) and converses with God during her trances. Through her mouth while she is unconscious the Eternal speaks. The king is most enthusiastic, appoints the bankrupt to the post of *Hofrat* at a salary of 800 thalers a year, and asks to see the hunchback. On the afternoon of 26 August, at the Villa Zimpel and in the presence of von Hoym, the governor of Silesia, Count Brühl, well-known hypnotist, Bischofswerder, Hermes, and Oswald, the king converses with God. God assures him through the hunchback, assiduously coached beforehand, that he pardons him all his sins. God then requests Frederick William to bestow due recognition on the services of all those present. After which the sleeper's body shudders under a violent shock; it is the spirit reentering it, the clairvoyante reverting to a mere somnambulist. The king is most impressed, and on 10 September assembles the same persons again, together with Haugwitz and the Prince of Württemberg and his adviser Hillmer. God bestows his approval on the Treaty of Reichenbach and advises the king to beware of his enemies and to follow the advice of Bischofswerder and all those present, for they love him sincerely. Frederick William requests audience of God on two further occasions, and then instructs Hermes, who has meanwhile been appointed a member of the Central Lutheran Consistory at a salary of 400 thalers a year, to prepare the draft of a reform of the clergy. Wöllner thus obtains control of the church and education.

From Breslau the clairvoyante continues to send the king the commands of Providence through Oswald in 1791. She succeeds in obtaining a pension, the promise of a dowry of 5,000 thalers, and a captaincy for Lieutenant von Czeiszek; whereupon he marries her. Oswald is summoned to Berlin with the title of Privy Councillor and the post of *Lektor* at a salary of 3,000 thalers. Countess von Lichtenau at length takes alarm, for the spirits seem likely to take her royal lover away from her. Cleverly she listens to his confidences and then expresses her surprise at the self-seeking piety of his new friends. Oswald, repulsed in all his attempts to win her over, now decides to pass to the offensive. He transmits to the king the divine command to reconcile himself with the queen in order to beget a prince endowed with extraordinary gifts. Frederick William's flesh, however, is weak. He dismisses Oswald, though allowing him to retain his title and emoluments, and consents to forget the hunchback in the countess's arms. The only loser in the whole affair is the innocent Captain von Czeiszek, who has married the cripple but gets no dowry.

Wöllner is well informed about all these intrigues and encourages them without becoming involved in them; throughout the reign he is able to manipulate the king's religious scruples, and the king allows him to become the chief personage in the realm.

Wöllner desires power; but he does not attack the political constitution of the kingdom in order to dismiss his rivals in office, for enlightened despotism can accomodate itself to any religion. Flattering the king's inclinations, he aims at substituting orthodoxy for liberalism. The reform does not appear revolutionary, and its sponsor himself never ceases to invoke the principle of toleration. "A tolerant governor," he had written in 1785 in his treatise on religion dedicated to the crown prince, "looks upon all his subjects from a single point of view, namely that they should be citizens of the state. He willingly accords them full freedom of thought and freedom of action, provided only that these two freedoms are not prejudicial to the public peace and security, morals, social harmony, or the interests of the state in general" (Schwartz, *Kulturkampf*, 77).

He begins by slandering von der Hagen and Zedlitz, whose places he covets. "The public," he hypocritically declares, "allege that they use pretty girls among the orphans to indulge their desires; when the girls become pregnant, they have them delivered at the Charité, and the children are brought up at the Orphanage at the king's expense. For as these two gentlemen are also heads of the Berlin Poor Board, they control the Charité and the Orphanage" (ibid., 85-86).

It takes Wöllner more than a year, however, to gain his ends. On 3 July 1788 he is appointed minister of the Budget and of Justice and head of the Religious Department of the Lutheran Church. A cabinet order expressly confers upon him full powers over the Central Consistory and over the Higher Board of Education. On July 9 there appears the famous Religious Edict. Prohibiting all proselytism in the name of toleration, affirming respect for every individual's personal convictions, paragraphs 7 and 8 of the edict order Protestants to teach the Christian religion as it is found in the Bible and in the symbolic books and threatens with dismissal every "enlightened" minister who ventures to modify these sacred texts (text in Schrader, *Geschichte* I, 532).

This violates two principles of the Aufklärung, that of the interpretation of the sacred texts by human reason and that of the inferiority of the symbolic books. Protests are so vehement that the government dares not prosecute pastors who ignore the edict.

To put an end to the campaign against him, Wöllner issues his Censorship Edict on 17 December 1789. A commission of seven censors is set up to examine all books treating of God, the state, and morals. The *Berlinische Monatsschrift* promptly transfers its place of publication to Jena, and later to Dessau, and Nicolai moves his *Deutsche Allgemeine Bibliothek* to Kiel.

Few prosecutions are instituted, but the edict may have been effective in a negative way, hard to assess, by deterring authors from writing what they thought.

These measures have little practical effect. They threaten those who do not accept the new principles, but they lack executive force. This Hermes supplies on his return from the visit to Silesia. His draft for the reform of the clergy proposes a Summary Commission of Inquiry, which is set up forthwith by the cabinet order of 14 May 1791. Composed of Hermes, Hillmer, and his friend Woltersdorf, it is attached to the Central Consistory with the special task of investigating officials. Investigating commissions composed of three clergymen responsible to the summary commission itself are attached to each provincial consistory; they are to interrogate every candidate for the post of pastor or schoolmaster to find out "whether he has not been contaminated by the damnable errors of contemporary neologists and the so-called *Aufklärer.*" At its first session the summary commission decides to enforce the Religious Edict and to draw up a list awarding marks to all officials in accordance, first, with their piety and, second, with their private conduct.

The Religious Edict, therefore, lays down the principles, the Censorship Edict prohibits criticism, and the summary commission establishes a surveillance which threatens the recalcitrant, drives them to concealment and ensures recruitment in conformity with Wöllner's own ideas. Since it is precisely for the posts of minister and schoolmaster that candidates are most numerous, many fall into line. The investigating commissions, however, do not begin their work till 1793; and only three years later the king dies.

Wöllner cannot bring it off. His first edict runs into opposition from the greater part of the clergy. The aged Teller gives his advanced age as a pretext for requesting exemption from the obligation to preach, and publishes a defense of the Aufklärung. Sack, a pastor of the Reformed church highly esteemed by the king, calls to mind the fact that on his appointment in 1769 he had undertaken to teach the symbolic books only insofar as they were consistent with the Bible, and offers his resignation; but Frederick William refuses it. Spalding stops preaching. Zöllner requests the king's permission to accept a post at Hamburg, but the king refuses and raises his stipend. Then, on 10 September 1789, all the clerical members of the Central Consistory except Silberschlag address a protest to the king against the obligation to accept the symbolic books as an article of faith. Wöllner waxes indignant at this failure to go through channels, but does not dare to prosecute any clergymen under the edict.

The censorship runs into opposition from the town councillors. There are few trials, and those that are held are followed with passionate interest by a hostile public. The censors themselves show no great zeal. Wöllner fails in his efforts to overcome the passive resistance of the officials.

He places great hopes in his summary commission. But its work is hampered by lack of funds, and the subordinate provincial commissions are slow to constitute themselves. In 1794, however, Hermes and Hillmer are sent on a tour of inspection of the area between the Elbe and the Saale. Their principal objective is the University of Halle, which has consistently displayed hostility to Wöllner. At the Faculty of Theology the aged Semler, who had approved of the Religious Edict and had devoted his last years to alchemy, had died in 1791 and had been replaced by Nösselt, a bustling rector and a champion of the Aufklärung. Instructed to prepare a manual on dogma, which Wöllner wishes to make compulsory in all universities, Nösselt manages to put it off time after time and finally disclaims competence when the summary commission condemns his colleague Niemeyer's *Popular and Practical Theology*. No professor in the faculty is willing to take over the work. Wöllner manifests his displeasure with those whom he regards as the leaders of the resistance by refusing to receive them when they visit Berlin.

The two inspectors reach Halle at nine in the evening of 29 May 1794. They put up at the Golden Lion, the best hotel in town, directly opposite Nösselt's house. Students, learning of their arrival, gather, masked and disguised, beneath their windows, shouting, insulting the visitors and whistling horribly, till Niemeyer intervenes to protect the inspectors, pacifies the students, and sends them home after they have paraded in good order before the inn with the shouts of "*pereat!*" traditionally hurled at unpopular professors.

Next morning Niemeyer makes his apologies to the delegates from Berlin: the demonstration was genuinely spontaneous and he had no troops at his disposal to suppress it. The infuriated inspectors accuse him of fomenting the riot, and then visit the town secondary school, where they are horrified to discover many evidences of Aufklärung. That evening students again gather, in greater numbers than on the previous night, in front of the inn, utter loud threats, and bombard the inspectors' windows with tiles. Hermes and Hillmer are terrified and slip away secretly at seven the next morning. Niemeyer is compelled to chase after their carriage and, far in the countryside, express his regrets, promising that the guilty will be punished.

On the unfortunate inspectors' return to Berlin, Wöllner does not spare them his fury; the whole town is laughing at their discomfiture and their cowardice. Ridicule is lethal in eighteenth-century Prussia. A prosecution is, however, brought before the Council of State, but the report by Hermes and Hillmer is padded out with so many false accusations, Nösselt and Niemeyer defend themselves so resolutely, and the judges are so skeptical of their guilt, which is in any case unprovable, that the case is finally dismissed. The University of Halle has beaten Wöllner.

If, however, we consult the enrollment registers of the faculties of theology after the publication of the Religious Edict, we can see how much damage the authoritarian policy of orthodoxy did to them.

At Halle the number of students falls from 105 to 96 between the summer of 1790 and the summer of 1795; at Frankfort it falls from 15 to 3 between 1788 and 1796, though with large fluctuations between; at Königsberg from 12 to 3 between the summer of 1791 and the summer of 1799, though in the interval it rose as high as 24. The faculties of law pick up many of the young men discouraged from theology. The trend continues, however, after Wöllner's disgrace; in 1804 of 1,873 students enrolled in the five Prussian universities and the upper secondary schools at Breslau and Erfurt, 868 are taking law, 623 theology, 164 medicine, 82 political economy (*Kameralwissenschaft*) in preparation for careers in the administrative service, 130 arts and mathematics, 4 economics, and 2 military science.

After the king's death on 6 November 1797, an all-out attack is launched against the orthodox. Assailed first by Professor Steinbart, headmaster of the Züllichau seminary, whose funds he has cut off, Wöllner yields, but clings to power until Frederick William III grows weary of him and abruptly dismisses him on 11 March 1798.

Wöllner never had a hope of success. In trying to impose a dogma he was attacking the Aufklärung head on and on its own ground. He could not hope to rally the people behind him, for they took very little interest in the symbolic books and simply followed the lead of their pastors and masters. The governing elite when required to change their faith were too self-assured and too solidly organized for Wöllner to have a chance of getting his way.

To overthrow the Aufklärung he should have struck in others quarters; instead of a frontal attack he should have employed a flanking maneuver. There were many signs of discontent among the masses, and if he had investigated its causes and drawn up a program calculated to gain him popularity, he could have transferred the debate to a new terrain and one with which the Aufklärung was unfamiliar. But however good an economist he may have been, he was not able to perceive and interpret the signs. Even in the act of violating the principles, he continued nonetheless to invoke liberalism and toleration. One of the most cogent testimonies to the strength of the Aufklärung and the hold it had acquired on all minds is the fact that even its enemies were totally unable to conceive of any different system.

Criticism of the Political System

At the time when the French are making their Revolution, the Germans are beginning to realize that governments will not carry out social reforms except under compulsion. Contrary to what Kant and others believed and taught, they perceive that freedom of opinion is not enough to ensure that a state is well governed. Even when universal reason has handed down its judgment and has convinced the enlightened prince of the need for a reform, the reform does not come about eo ipso facto. Reason also needs an executive force, which it does not possess. The middle classes now direct their criticism to politics, not with the aim of destroying the existing system, but in order to obtain the right to participate in it and thereby make it more efficient by an injection of fresh vigor. Here they are still obeying the same promptings of self-interest as they do when they urge the abolition the the privileges that go with noble birth. What mortifies their self-regard is the fact that they are not asked to contribute their lights in the same way as the nobility; and the example of the French Revolution incites them to list their grievances specifically. "How incongruous it is to try to inhibit the most enlightened citizens from concerning themselves with affairs of state on the sole pretext that they are intellectuals!" (*PAD* 1786, IV, 363). Is the mere fact that a man is capable of discernment and is recognized to be so a good reason for excluding him from public affairs? And this precisely at the moment when their brothers in France are coming to power? There is nothing at all surprising, therefore; in the outburst of enthusiasm caused by the French Revolution. Almost everyone in the middle classes approves of it in its early days, and most hymn its praises in prose and verse. The most eminent poets express their desire to collaborate in establishing freedom. Klopstock and Schiller are delighted with the Legislative Assembly's decree conferring French citizenship upon them. The war of 1792 is unpopular. "For whom are they calling upon you to fight, my good German people?" Boie writes. "For whom are you consenting to be reft from your wives, your children, and your homes? For the vile breed of princes and nobles and for the priestling vermin!" Voss composes a hymn to liberty to the tune of the *Marseillaise*.

Schiller's friend Schulz returns in 1789 from a brief visit to France with pamphlets recounting the great events of the Revolution in lively, though not always accurate, terms and in a truly partisan spirit. Campe, convinced that the unity of the people has been achieved by the tricolor cocade, "symbol of the liberty carried with a high hand," which everyone, "bourgeois and peasant, old men and boys, priest and beggar," wears in his hat, says that he wants to "embrace everyone he meets." His friend Wilhelm von Humboldt, though of a more sedate temper, displays his sympathy for a people freed. In January 1791 Merck sends Goethe news from Paris.

Several of these German visitors settle in France and remain there until the declaration of war; Oelsner, a Silesian, even stays on from 1787 to 1794, approving of the Constitution of 1791, deploring the intervention by the Prussian armies in 1792, condemning the Terror, and fleeing it, though he nonetheless refuses to jettison the ideal he sees embodied in the France of 1789–93. Archenholz leaves Paris as soon as war is declared, but this former captain in Frederick the Great's armies deplores the coming campaign. He settles at Hamburg and continues publishing his journal *Minerva* there, the first issue appearing in Berlin in January 1792. Though he too is hostile to the Terror, he makes an effort to remain objective and right up to 1812 confutes the flood of misrepresentation spread by the émigrés.

All these Germans take basically the same course; most of them approve of the beginnings of the Revolution but sooner or later grow discouraged by the illegality of the popular insurrections. Few of them accept the regime of the revolutionary government. One of the most equable is Wieland, whose attitude is very typical; though more moderate than his fellow countrymen, he well expresses their sentiments in many articles in the *Teutsche Merkur*; satisfaction at first, uneasiness after the 20th of June, disillusionment during the Terror, but unwavering gratitude to those who have proclaimed the great principles, even if they have not been able to remain true to them. Wieland foretells the dictatorship well before the advent of Bonaparte.

The only one among these thinkers who does not simply sit and dream is J. G. Forster. Born in 1754, he has had an adventurous youth. His father, a clergyman near Königsberg and a well-known naturalist, took him with him to Russia and England; his knowledge of modern languages enabled him when quite young to do translations, with which he supported his family. From 1772 to 1775 he accompanied his father on Cook's voyage round the world. He brought back a large portfolio of sketches, and by publishing them and lecturing on them acquired a reputation as a scientist in his own right. After staying in Paris for several weeks in 1777, he parted from his father, and in 1780 obtained a professorship at the Carolinum at Cassel. He then fell into the hands of the Rosicrucians, along with his friend, the anatomist Soemmerring. But he repented of it, unmasked the fraud, and, fearing the intrigues of the powerful organization, in 1785 accepted a chair at the University of Vilna, taking with him his young wife, Theresa, the daughter of Heyne, the librarian at Göttingen. His exile in Poland came to an end in 1785, and, having been appointed librarian at Mainz, he at length has leisure to write. He is constrained to do so, indeed, because he needs a second source of income. He makes his reputation as a major writer in German with his *Travels in the Rhineland and Holland* (*Ansichten vom Niederrhein*) and his essays (*Kleine Schriften*); his main traits are an exact judgment, self-possession, moderation in criticism, and enlightened humanitarian ideals.

The Revolution fills him with enthusiasm but does not blind him to realities; he is well aware that Germany is not ripe for it. He does not grow indignant at the popular excesses because he is well acquainted with the faults of the aristocrats. More objective than most of his fellow countrymen, he never ceases advocating tolerance and emphasizing the great conquests of the Revolution: liberty, equality, and the real liberation of the peasants, as distinct from the intrigues and disorders from which they issued. After the capture of Mainz by the French in October 1792, Forster decides on action. He enters the local club in November and stays on after the moderates have left, accepts the vice-presidency of the provisional administration set up by Custine, and on 1 January 1793 launches a new journal, which the people of Mainz dub *L'Ami du Peuple*. He collaborates in the destruction of the feudal

system and, fearing the reaction, sees no alternative to annexation to France
in order to safeguard the social reforms. He becomes the leading spirit in
promoting this project in articles and speeches and in his activity in the
National Convention of the Rhine, which meets from 17 to 24 March 1793.
He renders great services to his fellow citizens by intervening between them
and the French, ensuring that property is respected and preventing violence.
Yet all his friends abandon him in the first quarter of 1793; the people of
Mainz claim that he is responsible for the coming siege and others denounce
him as a Jacobin and Terrorist. Soemmerring and his colleagues deprecate
his annexation projects. Huber pays court to his wife and goes off with her
and the children to Strasbourg on the pretext of taking them to a place of
safety. Reviled, jeered at, and mocked, Forster begins his apprenticeship to
solitude. Only Caroline Böhmer, a friend of Theresa's invited to stay for a
few weeks, understands and approves of him. To the accusations he replies
calmly: "I have decided in favor of a cause to which I must sacrifice my
personal tranquillity, my studies, my happiness, maybe my health, my whole
fortune, and perhaps my life. I calmly let all that happens pass over me,
because it is the inevitable consequence of principles when accepted and
found true. One thing only is my own, I know, and out of harm's reach,
because only I can harm it, that is my conscience" (Forster, *Briefwechsel* II,
271).

When he is sent to Paris on 25 March 1793 to convey the Rhineland's
desire for union with France, Forster is compelled to break with most of his
German correspondents. Huber, his self-styled friend, fears lest he be
compromised by receiving letters from him. Lonely, sick, barely subsisting on
the scanty pension awarded him by the Convention, he writes to his wife on
13 April 1793: "Is it true, then, that disinterestedness and the love of
freedom are merely infants' baubles today, meaningless sounds? . . . Is it true,
then, that egotism prevails where I had hoped to find a pure spirit of
self-sacrifice?" Later, he recovers his spirits and notes on July 7:

I have cast up my accounts. . . . My misfortune is the result of my
principles, not my passions. I could not have acted otherwise, and if I had
to start afresh. . . . I know well enough that I am only a ball in the hands
of fate at this moment; but I little care whither I am flung. I have no
home now, no country, no friends; all that was attached to me has
abandoned me. It depends solely on my own choice, on my view of life,
not on the hazard of circumstance, whether I establish new relationships
or, thinking of the past, consider myself bound for ever. A happy reversal
of my fortunes may bring me much; their further decline can take
nothing from me save the pleasure of writing these letters when I can no
longer pay the postage. [Ibid., 494.]

In November he goes to Switzerland. He has asked to see his children once
more, and Theresa brings them to him there. He spends three days with them

and stays on at Pontarlier for several weeks, while his wife goes back to Germany with Huber. He returns to Paris, to die there on 10 January 1794, mourned only by his father-in-law.

Nevertheless, Caroline has made a cult of the late Forster. She goes through a very bad time after he leaves Mainz. Arrested as a supporter of the French, abandoned, like Forster, by her former friends, she retains all her admiration for the writer, the hero, and the martyr, and talks much of him to Wilhelm and Friedrich Schlegel, with whom she takes refuge; with her the spirit of Forster penetrates the company of the Romantics, though they, the young, will express revolutionary sentiments only at the very end of the century, when Bonaparte's dictatorship is already about to be installed in France (see below, chap. 12, in the section "The Romantic Party").

Thus, the immediate influence of the French Revolution is not very great in Prussia, first because most of the intellectuals draw a distinction between absolute monarchy, which makes revolution necessary, and enlightened despotism, which absorbs every sort of reform without trouble; and second because its influence remains wholly in the realm of the ideological. The Prussian middle class is neither experienced in the practices of large-scale trade, like the English, nor spirited in action, like the French. And third, even within the realm of ideas, the proponents of revolution have proved incapable of agreeing among themselves, of mustering their forces, and of making a united stand. They have failed to make use of the machinery and personnel of the establishment of the Aufklärung to propagate the idea that social reforms are indispensable. Only at the very end of the century, with the emergence of early Romanticism, do they display genuinely revolutionary sentiments, that is to say a determination to destroy the existing system and at the same time a consciousness that the poetry, the traditions, and the lessons of the past have become irrelevant.

Revolutionary Sentiments

These lonely and desperate young men detest the society to which they belong; they look forward to its destruction and its replacement by a genuinely enlightened community which would not palter with principles and from which hypocrisy would be banished. Hence there begins to grow up in them a passion for politics which the Aufklärung has never known. To the Aufklärung, enlightened despotism is an unexceptionable idea, and there is no need to go beyond it. Content with the freedoms and safeguards it ensures to the individual, it wishes for nothing further. Its universalism can no more conflict with Prussian patriotism, which indeed it fosters, than the free trade of the English can injure their economy; for the Prussian political system is organized precisely in such a way that it can absorb any and every criticism and assimilate any and every reform; but it deprecates acts of violence and cruelty which distort reform and brutalize the masses. Yet it is precisely such acts of violence which attract the early Romantics because they break down the barriers which they have been unable to traverse. They lack political education, and, Dorothea to the contrary, they are not men of action. But they believe that they would become men of action if some great catastrophe drove them to it. This is why as soon as Schelling becomes a tutor, he urges Hegel to rally publicly to the good cause. "The important thing," he says, "is that young men resolved to dare all and to do all should come together from every quarter and unite on a single task . . . for then victory would be assured. . . . I feel shut in here in a country of priests and hacks" (Plitt, *Leben* I, 92–93). "A country forced to sacrifice itself to a prince's whims, . . . a country which has to buy at no matter what price what other people have wished to rid themselves of at all costs" (ibid., II, 101). When Napoleon crushes Prussia in 1806, "for the first time," Schelling says, displaying no more distress than Goethe does in the letter to which this is a reply,

I observe that I would feel a thousand times more at my ease wielding the sword than the pen. We must wait and see what our age will bring forth. ...If Germany goes down, all that is great and beautiful will be able to emerge into the full light of day, and all that has been hidden before will become public and popular....

We have been quite unable to conceive of the idiocy of the governing circles, the utter baseness of the governments of which we are now watching the downfall. Now it is plain to all, and what I should like to do is not to complain, but to contribute so far as in me lies to the eradication of the past. [ibid., 103, 108–9.]

Wackenroder's and Tieck's experience precisely parallels Schelling's. At first they seem quite indifferent to their country because they are isolated in society. "Vulgar schoolmasters really seem to think that they have made some sort of educational progress," Wackenroder writes, "when they teach eight-year-old boys the history of Brandenburg in all its details as the history of their fatherland. Nowadays, a citizen, or indeed anyone who is not going to become a scholar, really needs the history of our country no more than that of any other. In my opinion, it would be far better to teach any history, no matter whose, in our schools, provided that it is interesting, without troubling about what people, ancient or modern, it relates to. I believe . . . one could advance any number of reasons against a patriotism which is irrelevant to our age" (Wackenroder, *Werke* II, 14). Tieck replies: "Our constitution no longer tolerates a Codrus, a Curtius, or a Scaevola; our bourgeois constitution has stifled all patriotism and every grand virtue; the gentle and humane virtues alone survive to raise man above the beasts; and even they are threatened by our miserable frivolity" (ibid., 64). Then, on the outbreak of the French Revolution, they are lifted on a wave of enthusiasm engendered by its revolutionary deeds rather than its ideas, which are nothing new. "Ah!" Tieck exclaims, "if I was in France now, I would not be sitting calmly by; I would . . . but, alas, I was born in a monarchy which is antagonistic to freedom, among people who are still barbarians enough to despise the French. I have changed greatly . . . I cannot be happy now when I do not see a newspaper. Oh, to be in France now, that would be really exciting, to fight under Dumouriez, to drive out these slaves and put them to rout, and even to fall. What is life without liberty? . . . Were France to fail, I should despise the whole world . . . for then Europe would be doomed to become a dungeon" (ibid., 161). Wackenroder answers: "I have long been surprised that you did not ask me what I think of the French; I think the same as you. I wholeheartedly share your enthusiasm, I assure you. But I really must tell you that I talk to no one at all about the French, simply because whenever anyone here, no matter who it is, speaks of their exploits, he invariably does so with a pitying smile, as if to say: 'What will these lunatics be doing next!' And I always want to hit people who speak of them with that smile" (ibid., 169).

Schleiermacher too, though of a calmer temperament, comes to approve the deeds rather than the ideas of the Revolution. Tutor in the Dohna family, he is irritated at hearing the execution of Louis XVI condemned not because he is innocent but because he is king. "God damn their despotic schemes!" he exclaims of the princes (Dilthey, *Leben* III, 41).

Friedrich Schlegel at first displays only the literary patriotism of the Sturm und Drang, but later, prompted by Caroline's experience of Forster's tragedy, he begins to cherish the Revolution because it opens up so many prospects to youth. So long as he has some hope of a career as a professor, however, his admiration is expressed cautiously. We can chart his growing interest in the events in France by the growing number of foreign words he Germanizes in his letters. His brother is wrong to worry about his reading (*Lektüre*); he knows that what is essential for him is to "have a good political reputation." When he feels a great urge to work, he hopes that it will last till he has finished, in the fashion of the Convention's sublime decree in which it declared that "the Revolution will continue until peace is signed" (Walzel, *Schlegel*, 210; 20 Jan. 1795). He becomes slightly braver after the publication of Fichte's *Contributions to a Correction of the Public's Opinions on the French Revolution* and settles down to prepare a political book. He reassures his brother, however, that "because of the rigor of the scientific approach I shall refrain from any allusion to facts." One cannot say that he does not display a truly philosophic attitude. "I shall shun rather than seek popularity in this. The obscurity of abstract metaphysics will protect me. When one writes solely for philosophers, one can be incredibly daring without anyone in the police perceiving it, or even realizing how daring it is" (ibid., 278; 26 May 1796). He has long wished to publish "something popular on republicanism." He is completely converted. "I am going to work," he says, "at revolutions with incredible enthusiasm. . . . I do not wish to conceal from you that I have

republicanism even more at heart than divine criticism or yet diviner poetry"
(ibid.).

The essay on the idea of the republic appeared in Reichardt's *Deutschland*
in 1796. Taking Kant's categoric imperative as his starting point, Friedrich
establishes that the state is necessarily based upon liberty, equality, and
totality, or rather upon continuity and generality. It follows that only the
general will can be the basis for political action and that the state must be
republican, with universal suffrage by majority vote and a representative
system. A dictatorship may, however, be accepted provisionally and the right
of suffrage limited by individual merit.

The true republic can only be universal, and consequently ensures perpetual peace. Such, broadly, is the political ideal of Friedrich Schlegel at Jena.
He asserts the right of insurrection and would like nothing better than to
plunge into action. But no opportunity arises to replace the society which
rejects him with another society founded on civic equality, the abolition of
prejudice, the emancipation of women, and compulsory education in German. After his setback at the university he becomes more revolutionary, but,
worthy son of the Aufklärung that he is, he is revolutionary only in his
thinking. He writes his *Characteristics of Modern Authors*. He slaughters the
conservative J. G. Schlosser, condemns the hollow elucubrations of Jacobi's
hero, the erratic Woldemar, so like what he himself was as a student, and
makes Lessing out to be a great revolutionary, thereby cutting out this foe of
prejudice and coteries from the pseudoclassical party. Last, he rehabilitates
for posterity Forster, whose works are "truly grandiose and almost sublime."
After which he moves to Berlin, just as Bonaparte's star is about to rise in the
West. Napoleon! All these young men admire him and admire themselves in
him. For is he not one of their own kind? Like them of humble origins, he
displays revolutionary sentiments, as they do, and, like them, believes in the
miraculous destiny of his star. Like all gamblers, he delights in risk. His
career is one long succession of dramatic surprises. His genius has become
patent to all in a great flash of illumination, as theirs will; for they are
slightly younger than he. They greatly hope to follow in his footsteps. Even
those who, like Steffens, detest France cannot help being carried away by
admiration for a man who has been at the very hub of the Revolution and has
risen above it. Friedrich Schlegel thinks that the first consul might make a
subject for a literary success in case of need.

All contemplate him and await their turn. In 1799, "Bonaparte is back in
Paris," Caroline writes to her daughter. "All goes well again. The Russians
are driven from Switzerland, the Russians and the English are forced to a
dishonorable surrender in Holland. The French are advancing in Swabia.
And now Bonaparte is here! Rejoice with me, or I shall have to think that you
are no good for anything save romping and haven't a serious thought in your
head" (Schmidt, *Caroline* I, 671–75). In 1806, after the French conquest of

Prussia, Schelling concludes: "The Revolution has only just begun in Germany. I mean that only now will there be place for a new world" (Plitt, *Leben* II, 310). How they worship Napoleon, their great exemplar! His bust is sold in Berlin. Tieck has one; the Schlegels carry it off to Jena; Jean-Paul asks Tieck for it so that he can present it to one of his friends.

Part 3   The Moral Crisis:
          The New Mentality

11

The Interpretation of
Life as Miracle

The Psychology of the Miraculous

In the moral sphere the crisis took the shape of the slow formation of a new mentality exactly the reverse of that of the Aufklärung, its gradual permeation of the masses, and, finally, its capture of the elite itself.

Once again the mystical trend gains the upper hand; an outlook at the opposite pole from rationalism is adopted by influential forces at all times and at all places—in the churches, in health and hygiene, and in fashions and manners alike. What might be called an explosion of faith and emotion encourages people to avow practices which would have made them ridiculous twenty years earlier. At all levels those dissatisfied with their life and the prospects before them seek highly individual and unconventional outlets. The mass of country dwellers comes increasingly into contact with the recruiting sergeant and the vagabond. Vicissitude is the property of the adventurous life of the soldier and the cutpurse; destitute one day, wealthy and spendthrift the next, they owe their success neither to patient application nor to methodical scruple. It is pure chance that brings victory to the soldier, brings the wealthy traveler as a prey to the vagabond, fame to the actor, and notoriety to the quack. In the towns a poor man may win the lottery; all he needs is luck in order to acquire wealth and power. Some risk their head, others their purse. All acquire a taste for strong emotions that wrack their nerves; and they apply to religion or to sorcery for the means to master the luck they worship. The most cunning and least scrupulous among them exploit this general appetite for the miraculous and thereby spread it further. They sell extraordinary nostrums, which are snapped up eagerly by popular credulity. It is in the midst of such follies that the middle-class youth are taught to combat prejudice and superstition. They are too intelligent and too thoroughly imbued with the critical spirit to believe in ghosts or the elixir of life themselves, but they do not combat such excesses, because they have little interest in the future of society. The name that they give to their ideal may vary; "happiness," "the infinite," "the sublime" are some of the vague terms they use (*Eumonia* 1801, I, 101–2), but all of them denote the same indefinable state, the miracle that will release each of them from mediocrity. Dorothea, whose ideas remain clear and whose feelings are consistent owing to the education she received from her father, Moses Mendelssohn, and to the relatively satisfying position of Jews in an enlightened society, harbors no illusions: "They often mock me," she notes in her diary, "about the early Romantics, and they feel superior to me when I seem to avoid the conventional terms and fashionable adjectives they use to qualify every kind of thing, such as great, sublime, modern, antique, gothic, amiable, marvelous, celestial, divine, and so on. I am quite familiar with the words, but hesitate to use them, for tomorrow they may well mean something quite different from what they meant before, even the opposite, and that would not surprise anyone. The pleasantest, the best thing is, after all, what one thinks; so why talk so much?" (Wienecke, *Caroline und Dorothea*, 351.)

Why? Because each of them, despairing of the reforms inherent in the principle of the Aufklärung, is beginning to dream of a way out for himself, to hope for the unique and unshared solution which will enable him to outstrip the rest and will ensure him personal happiness until such time as the triumph of reason achieves the general happiness of mankind; and, wrapped in the swaddling of his own desires, he moves further and further away from real life, which is no more than a temporary sojourning, a desolate shore, from which some imminent miraculous happening is suddenly to rescue him.

The senior civil servants in Prussia, who had in the past stood rigidly inflexible against the temporary onslaught of the Sturm und Drang, now give way, for they no longer receive orders and guidance from above.

The young, though trained by the Aufklärung to combat the irrational, no longer perform their critical function and find no insuperable difficulty in yielding to the influence of the crowd. The birth of Romanticism can to all intents and purposes be dated from the time when they thus betrayed their vocation. When the very people who represent the values of the intellect cease to be convinced of its superiority, they rapidly descend from the heights they once occupied. Reason was still in the ascendant when the Rosicrucians made their assault on the Aufklärung under Frederick William II, for it was defended by the established officials, all of them over thirty. The next generation, instead of carrying their victory further, betrays them. It was the generation which was under thirty between 1790 and 1800 that made Romanticism.

This new atmosphere, a climate propitious to the efflorescence of Romantic art, is of greater interest to the historian than the art itself. It supplies him with a definition of the phenomemon which is both more general and more specific than any that can be deduced from the works themselves. Romanticism is thus seen to be a mode of thought and the art and literature simply its expression, a type of psychology which is able at all times and at all places to account for the characteristics of its individual manifestations, irrespective of any style of painting, sculpture, or music.

This applies to politics too. When young intellectuals give expression to revolutionary sentiments and long for some catastrophic solution, they are expressing in different terms their taste for the extraordinary quite as much as the wish for practical achievement. Their younger brothers can find a use for their talents, win places and honors and champion ancient Germany against the foreign conqueror; and in their time the second generation of Romantics assume a reactionary cast very different from that of the Schlegels in their youth, the Tiecks, and the Wackenroders. In France, with the coming of the Restoration in 1815 and its regime of political reaction, the young, checked in their forward impetus, revert naturally to revolutionary ideas and methods. In Prussia, as in France and indeed everywhere else, Romanticism is neither of the Right nor of the Left. To associate it with any particular ideology is grossly to misunderstand its very essence; it is unnecessarily to complicate a problem posed in the wrong terms. Social circumstances impel the individual to favor one or the other of the conflicting ideologies; in many cases he may well espouse both of them successively. It is not by doctrine, then, that the distinction between the classical and the romantic in politics is drawn. Here again, the criterion is more general, and, indeed, psychological. The characteristic of Romantic politics is that it is a politics of the miraculous; the new mentality generates political methods into which the Romantics plunge haphazard in every country—the revolutionary rising to bring a new order suddenly into being, political assassination, the secret society with its mysterious rituals, and the conspiracy in which none of the leaders is in the least concerned with the problems that will surely arise on the morrow of success.

The definition of the Romantic, then, comes down essentially to a faith in the miraculous. All his other traits are merely consequential. The primacy accorded to feeling over intellect, to inspiration over hard work, to revolution over reform are only differing expressions of this faith. There is, of course, nothing novel about this mentality; it is to be found at all times in certain individuals and in certain spheres; but in Prussia at the end of the eighteenth century it is characteristic of all the young in every sphere.

It is this universality that confers upon the phenomenon its historical importance. For here we have to deal not with a number of special cases which can be explained by analysis by experts, literary critics, or psychiatrists, but with a mode of thinking shared by a very large number of contemporaries—and hence a social fact. The fact is determinant for the life of every individual in every sphere; it is the level on which he moves, the atmosphere he breathes; it is in existence before anyone is conscious of it, for nothing is harder than to realize the precise significance of a cast of mind. It would be just as important even if the Romantics had failed to perceive that they differed from their forerunners.

This universality was not a feature of the Sturm und Drang, whose leaders, after a spell of Romanticism, "fled it to attain to a loftier culture," a movement which never overwhelmed Prussia as a whole. Like the lottery in its early days, the Sturm und Drang did not take root in Prussia. Why, then, did Romanticism do so later? To invoke the normal psychological reaction of a generation against its elders is not an adequate explanation, for a reaction of this sort would have been more likely to be successful at an earlier period than at a time when classicism had taken over from a rather too arid rationalism and Goethe was universally venerated. The situation becomes quite clear and intelligible, however, if the facts of the economic and social crisis, as analyzed earlier, are borne in mind. The mentality of the miraculous gained the day because of the threat of unemployment hanging over youth at all levels of society, the unemployment which turned the farm laborer into a vagabond, the craftsman into a beggar, and the diplomat into a writer.

The Miraculous and Religion: Illuminati and Prophets

The first to exploit the new situation were the mystics who had infiltrated the religious sects.

Pietism had been an organized church, its miracles duly verified, and its forms of worship known to all. It is now thrust into the background by groups working in greater secrecy, many of them borrowing their form and ritual from the Masonic lodges. The lodges developed in a very characteristic way, showing clearly that the need for the miraculous was growing. Prophets and quacks have always existed; examples can readily be found in every age. The reason why they flourished at the beginning of the eighteenth century is largely the masses' lack of education and, to some extent, their failure to practice their religion; but at the end of the century the elite in the lodges are moving in the same direction. The Grand Lodge of England was founded in London in 1717 by the fusion of four provincial Masonic associations; before that date, the semioccupational, semipolitical associations, most of them English and lower-middle class, had not been of any great importance. Reorganized by Jean Desaguliers, a disciple of Newton, they now admitted the aristocracy and rapidly spread all over the world. The statutes of 1723, which were translated into French and German, contain nothing that conflicts with reason. Deist in tendency, they are notable mainly for their utilitarian conception of morality and their faith in the progress of the crafts and trades, and they trace their history from the earliest ages. The aim is to stand above the religions based on divine revelation and to work for "the intellectual and social unity of man." Since they were indifferent in politics and also secret, they escaped governmental scrutiny.

The first German lodge was founded at Hamburg in 1729 under the supremacy of the Grand Lodge of England. Others came into being a little later, at Hanover, Brunswick, Leipzig, and practically every other town. In Prussia, Frederick II himself encouraged the Masonic movement after 1738, when the Berlin Lodge named "At the Sign of the Three Globes" was founded; he became its Grand Master in 1740.

Everywhere in the second half of the century the character of the lodges changes; in France the Scottish Rite, with its complex hierarchy, grows strong, since the aristocrats deprecate the social equality of Freemasonry and the bourgeois are delighted to attain to the higher degrees. Even in England a third degree additional to those of Brother and Master is created, and the mysterious initiation ceremonies assume greater significance. In Germany the lodges develop even faster, apparently, despite the efforts of rationalist reformers like Fessler, who tried in 1788 to revert to enlightened principles and to get rid of the paraphernalia of mysterious symbols. Almost from the start, the lodges associated themselves with the reading clubs. They formed cultural associations of a sort, but these nurseries of the Aufklärung, in which the elite of the future were nurtured in the chilly light of reason, were very soon overrun by weeds. Among the Freemasons, form became more important than substance. In his last dialogue (1788) Lessing deplores this trend; attracted by Falk's liberal ideal, Ernst becomes a Freemason; the adepts have never been more numerous, but, alas! the passions of the vulgar overwhelm the ardors of the intellect. All that he finds are increasingly mysterious and complicated rituals, increasingly obstinate prejudices, and increasingly vain and murky hopes of irrelevant revelations (*Ernst und Falk*, 4th dialogue).

There is no clear distinction now between the old and the new lodges which spring up everywhere, their founders no longer intent on educating their brother Masons, but rather on initiating them into the secrets in their possession. Hund, in the course of reforming Freemasonry and founding the rite of Strict Observance in 1764, imbues it with mystery and gives it a complex hierarchy. Each adept knows only his immediate superior. He lives in hope that he will eventually learn the secrets to which the Grand Masters hold the key, and his zeal is rewarded by promotion from time to time to higher degrees, with the revelations attached to them. They prove to be merely explanations of meaningless symbols, but who can doubt there are many surprising revelations to come?

The lodges thus become groups of people with a common curiosity about nonexistent secrets. The Templar Lodges, for example, bestow sonorous titles upon their members, and the middle class glories in them and is proud to bear them. At the Convent of all the lodges convened in Wilhelmsbad, near Hanau, in 1782, the Roscrucians succeed in recruiting all those who have been disappointed by the other movements. They expound the *Fama Fraternitatis* and the *Confessio*, narrating the history of a mythical hero, Christian Rosenkreutzer.

Though the Order claims to date from the Flood, it was in fact founded neither in 1620 by the author of those two treatises nor even somewhat later by Frankenberg, the last of the great "pansophists." The mystical strain engendered by the wars of religion had died with him in 1652. It was not until a century later, around 1760, that the first organized group of Rosicrucians makes its appearance in southern Germany. The Order envelopes itself in legends, counters the critical spirit with the secrecy of its rites, offers each adept the aspect of its doctrine that appeals to him in particular, and takes over and combines all the promises of the fashionable quacks of the time. It endows its initiates with the power to transmute base metals into gold and to cure all illnesses, but only when they have traversed the degrees of a lengthy hierarchy and after they have proved their zeal by devoting their income to the association's prosperity.

This prosperity was secured in Prussia after Bischofswerder converted the crown prince in 1781.

Cedrinus, alias Albrecht, passes at this time from the Strict Observance to the Rosicrucians. He learns nothing, however, from his initiation; he dons the apron of the Brothers of Solomon, his wrists are bound with a red cord, he is blindfolded and is led up to a door on which he knocks nine times. A voice cries: "Who is there?" He replies: "An earthly body (*Leib*) asking to be transformed into a spiritual body." He enters, listens to some resonant and hollow speeches; then his hands are loosed and the blindfold is removed. He is standing on a square carpet adorned with a terrestrial globe. There is another globe half full of water on a table covered with a green cloth. Seated behind him, the Brothers swear him to fulfill the seven duties of the Rosicrucian Order: to fear God, love his neighbor, keep the secrets, remain faithful to the Order, and live in harmony with the Creator and with Wisdom.

He is taught the recognition sign: fold the arms across the breast; and then the handclasp: spread the fingers and intertwine them with the Brother's fingers until the two thumbs meet; the password, *dalet das ist Urun*. Nothing more. He receives no explanations, and the meals of which he is henceforth invited to partake are merely infantile question-and-answer sessions.

For instance, the director of the circle asks: "What is fraternization?" The reply must be: "The combination of 1, 3, 4, 5, 7 and 9." "What do these figures mean?" "One means the Beginning, 3 the Holy Trinity, from which the 4 active attributes are derived, which engender the 5th Being, by whom Wisdom is revealed in 7. And 9 is the end of all things created." (Albrecht, *Geschichte*, 256–69.)

Such are the mysteries revealed by the Rosicrucians to their many adepts in return for their contributions. Albrecht concludes that he has been cheated.

Forster becomes a Rosicrucian at Cassel in 1780 together with his friend Soemmering, but is glad to be able to break away from the society when he has to leave for Vilna, for he is disturbed by its power. He has seen through the vanity of its mysticism and alchemy. But many others believe that even if the lodges do not possess the secrets, that is no proof that the mystery does not exist. So they set to work in isolation. They read Jakob Böhme or Franz von Baader; they listen to Baron Eckartshausen and Jung-Stilling in his old age, high priests who wrangle over each other's followers.

They canvass such recent scientific discoveries as electricity, magnetism, and oxygen and combine experiments with them with the ideas of the ancient mystics in new systems based on a popularization of theosophy. Lavater, the "Protestant pope," liberal and mystical in the manner of the Pietists, has a profound knowledge of all the systems and all the experiments. This universal learning and his "physiognomy," by which he can divine a man's character and destiny from his facial traits, procure him an extraordinary ascendancy over all thinking persons in Europe. Pilgrims flock to him at Zürich, whence he keeps up a lively correspondence with many writers and with the princes who sit at his feet. He paves the way for—and does not repudiate—a crowd of quacks like Cagliostro, Count Saint-Germain, and Count Thun.

Less widely known, but appealing more strongly to the young Romantics, Hitter divulges the idea of the "Animal Universe," in which the world is a huge organism, every part of which is integrated in it, all bodies and all beings performing a function of their own; and its essence is expressed in magnetism.

The geologist Werner, Novalis's teacher, opposes the Plutonists; he believes that water is the mother and creator of nature.

Electricity, water, nerve impulses, divine revelation all concur to diminish the role of reason as the creative force. The deep truths are felt intuitively before they are understood intellectually. The main concern of the generation following the Aufklärung is to foster a climate propitious to their manifestation, and this concern supplies the key to much of their literature and art.

Such metaphysical speculations, however, make little headway among the masses, who want less inner illumination and more tangible miracles. The small craftsman and poor peasants—often halfway to becoming vagabonds —who make up the masses elude the influence of the clergy, who try, depending on their temperament and conviction, to guide them either toward reason or toward faith. The masses are credulous and, like all groups with a primitive mentality, are always inclined to dread the sorcerer or to venerate the prophet.

Of the prophets the most remarkable in Prussia is Johann Paul Philipp

Rosenfeld. Son of a respectable family of officials in Thuringia, from his youth up he displayed a notable distaste for work. Born in 1733, he was dismissed from his job as gamekeeper in 1765 for forging documents in connection with a sale of timber and entered upon the career that was to immortalize him. He first travels through the New Mark, begging and prophesying. His long beard, his eloquence, and his acquaintance with Holy Writ impress the local peasants, to whom he explains that Jesus was not the true Messiah. The true Messiah is Rosenfeld, who will save the world, for he possesses the Book of Life which holds the secret of Eternity. The seven seals will have to be broken by seven virgins. The peasants hearken to him, are converted, and are preparing to collect the girls he needs when the prophet is arrested in 1786 after a brawl between his followers and his opponents. He is committed to a lunatic asylum in Berlin, where he behaves submissively and reasonably. His disciple Gumto visits him. "Go," Rosenfeld enjoins him, "fetch your daughter and command her to obey my every order." The peasant complies and returns with his daughter, another daughter's betrothed, and a neighbor woman. Rosenfeld asks the girl: "Do you wish to become the Bride of Christ?" She answers: "Yes indeed!" He lays her down on his bed and has intercourse with her before them all.

He is released in 1771 for his exemplary behavior, but is not permitted to return to the countryside. He settles in Berlin and writes to his disciples that he needs seven virgins to open the Book of Life. The peasants send him their daughters. The prophet takes them into his home and works them unmercifully, barely feeding them and beating them frequently. He is gentler only with his favorite, who becomes a mother of three. He also practices onanism. Denounced by Gumto, he is arrested again in 1784, after two of his wives have died. Sentenced to public flogging and life imprisonment, he dies in the fortress of Spandau in 1788. But his disciples send petition after petition to the king, in 1785, 1787, 1790, 1793, 1794, 1795, and 1797, with ill-spelled pleas not to condemn the world to eternal damnation by preventing the Messiah from fulfilling his mission. It is no use trying to convince them that the prophet is dead. They refuse to believe it, for "that would mean that there would no longer be any hope of the world's salvation." Despite his inexhaustible indulgence toward mystics, Wöllner finally loses patience. He resorts to threats; but even in 1802 the peasants are still begging foreign ambassadors to intercede with the king for Rosenfeld.

This was no exceptional case. Philipp Jakob Bekker, born in Berlin about 1743, the son of a soldier, learned the gilder's trade too inefficiently to make a living at it and led the vagrant life of a street-corner idler, eking out an existence with casual commissions. He spends a good deal of time at Georg's grogshop, where the serving wench involuntarily captivates him with a glance that pierces his heart. Madly impassioned, he vows he will marry the girl but she will have none of him, for he is one-eyed and ill-favored. He resorts to religion to persuade her; he asserts that immediately after he was fired by that glance, he heard the voice of God prophesying that their marriage would save the whole world and all men from Satan's grasp. From that time on he insults Christ "the imposter" and all the prophets, sparing only "his brother Moses." He is jailed in 1784 for kicking up a shindy in the grogshop.

Prussia has no monopoly of these prophets. Every part of Germany can produce its holy man in the last third of the century. Franck, a Polish Jew converted to Catholicism, a former guard in the Uhlans, founds a sect at Offenbach. He is to be seen bathing in the Main several times a day in summer with those of his disciples who follow him everywhere. He goes to the forest daily in all weathers to pray for several hours on end, kneeling on a rug. Sometimes he has more than six hundred persons thronging around him; they give him a great deal of money. He drinks plenty of Hoffmann's Elixir to make himself immortal, but finally gives up the ghost, to his disciples' consternation. Unable to bear such a misfortune, they find that his soul has passed into the body of one of his nephews, who becomes the head of the sect.

An atmosphere so propitious to prophets cannot but attract spirits of every sort; apparitions, those possessed by devils and fortune tellers prophesy on every hand. Some of them cynically take advantage of the public's credulity; others sincerely believe in occult powers. Exorcists swarm all over southern Germany.

The Aufklärung does its utmost to counter the specters which appear more and more often. One man is haunted by his late wife, another by his dog. To unmask frauds is of no avail. The Berlin Natural History Society appoints a commission in 1797 to investigate a ghost which has been haunting the house of the Master of Waters and Forests at Tegel. Professors Bode and Meierotto, Klaproth the chemist, the Reverend Zöllner, and other high dignitaries set a watch on the spot. They discover the cord used by the imposter to strike a metal plate, thus making the noise which had terrifed the neighborhood. The culprit, however, makes his escape.

Fraud is found whenever anyone troubles to check the assertions of people who have seen ghosts or those who believe they are consorting with devils. One result is that even the miracles which have been accepted by the churches become suspect, for it is doubtful whether they could have stood up to contemporary criticism of the evidence or whether the facts could have been verified at the period when they were supposed to have happened.

But the rigorous reasoning of the philosophers, the adroitness with which the chroniclers wield their irony, the perspicacity of the enlightened in criticizing seemingly extraordinary happenings are all in vain. Wekhrlin revels in them: "The prophet's art is a simple one," he says; "it is simply the art of throwing dice. However they fall, it always means something. Can you think of any sort of farrago of nonsense or a single dream of any sort whatever so devoid of taste as to fail to lend itself to interpretation?" (*HB* 1788, II, 294-300). People will insist on seeking for miracles, as if the universe were not "a necessary effect of an absolutely necessary cause" (ibid., 1789, 148-51). They worship things fallen from heaven. A Chinese legend has it that ten thousand stars plunged into the sea all at the same time; but Fontenelle proved that no star is smaller than the earth. A nothing cannot come from something, nor a something from nothing.

Wekhrlin's readers keep his journal carefully on file, but nonetheless seek out Paul Erdmann, who reads the future in the planets and in playing cards. He makes so much money that he is able to buy a large house in the Zimmerstrasse in the best quarter of town. His waiting room is always crowded, the best society throngs to his door. And why not? The craze overtakes the elite, and philosophers virtually give up the struggle; they can understand their contemporaries only too well. They excuse them even as they accuse them: "We are too much philosophers in this age of universal Aufklärung to believe in apparitions," Wieland concludes, "and for all our Aufklärung, we are too little philosophers not to believe in them....Hesitating between belief and skepticism, we usually reason and mock as if we did not believe; yet whenever we hear a new ghost story, we listen just as receptively and our spine crawls just as much as if we did believe it" (*TM* 1781, II, 238-39).

Religion is no less liable to this transformation than any other branch of society. The God of the Aufklärung, the intelligent creator of a universe governed by perceptible and immutable rules, no longer suffices. He is too abstract, and, above all, he is not sufficiently present in his works. Men increasingly demand this presence; but it can be revealed only by miracles. Regardless whether it is a sudden transformation of the inner life of the cultured or a change in the external circumstances of the masses, it is always by some transgression of the laws of reason that the divinity manifests itself.

The Miraculous and Health: Romantic Medicine and Fashionable Maladies

The way in which every moral inclination tends toward the miraculous can be seen even more clearly and typically in physical matters. The Aufklärung opened an era of scientific achievement, for generalized theories by no means exclude the observation of nature. Dr. Hoffmann holds that life is always expressed in movement, and accordingly tries to cure his patients by speeding up or slowing down their organic reactions, though even as he does so, he keeps them under observation and adapts his treatment to their reactions. Such empiricism makes for progress in research; the eighteenth-century physicians are far more effectual than their predecessors. Among their masters is Boerhaave, who trains clinical students at Leyden in the accurate description of diseases; they examine their patients carefully, with the aid of a magnifying glass and a thermometer. Van Swieten and de Haën succeed in introducing similar principles at Vienna, and the best doctors in Germany refer to them for recommendation. Research improves. Cadavers are made available at the celebrated Theatrum Anatomicum at Berlin; and medical students begin to be given access to the patients, not simply instruction in Latin.

Progress is slow, however. The state physicians, pensioners of the princes or the Free Cities, find it extremely hard to enforce reasonable standards of hygiene. In many hospitals several patients are huddled up in one bed when space is short during an epidemic. Even in Berlin, the press in 1796 reveals the scandalous mismanagement of the Charité. This ancient hospital, a former pest house, is isolated in the dark and muddy streets of a northern quarter of the city. The ground floor is used as a hostel for the aged. The two upper floors should normally hold 250 patients, but there are 3,325 when Schleiermacher becomes chaplain there. The doctors, appointed by the Poor Guardians (*Armendirektion*) and supervised by an inspector, cannot get a hearing when they demand the enforcement of hygienic standards and proper food for their patients. The meals are inefficiently prepared by convalescent patients paying off the cost of their treatment. A witticism attributed to foreigners taken to visit the model veterinary college near the hospital gains wide currency: "The college is a place where dogs are treated like people and the Charité a place where people are treated like dogs" (Dilthey, *Leben*, 231).

In medicine, as in every other sphere, traditional prejudice has to be combated and public opinion "enlightened." A man who devoted his life to this task and whose importance cannot be overrated is Christoph Wilhelm Hufeland, professor at Jena and later at Berlin, physician-in-ordinary to the King of Prussia. He spent most of his life demonstrating that doctors must not condone practices repugnant to good sense. In 1795 he founded the *Journal of Practical Medicine*, which published his own observations and those of his colleagues for the general benefit. His intention was "to augment the body of experience (which constitutes the sole true source of medicine) and make the experience of each the property of all" (*JPA* 1795, I, v).

In the name of universal reason, Hufeland declares war on the ever-increasing crowd of quacks who are taking advantage of the credulous public. A remarkable popularizer, he writes for most of the leading periodicals. His articles are written in such an incisive style, are so clearly expounded, with such perfect rigor in the sequence of ideas, that every reader is impressed with the cogency of his conclusions. As a result, the shopkeeper, the craftsman, and the schoolmaster know why they must use plenty of fresh water and why they should revive the custom of taking baths like the ancient Germans, those blue-eyed, golden-haired heroes who earned the admiration even of the Romans for their extraordinary stature, their physical strength, and their bravery. "A people that bathes is healthier and stronger than peoples who do not." They know why children should take physical exercise in summer and should not wrap up too warmly in flannel in winter, why cosmetics are harmful and to what extent hot or alcoholic beverages are good or bad. Most of his articles were collected in a masterly work, which has survived in reprint to this day. *Macrobiotics, or the Art of Prolonging Life* is indeed a masterpiece of medical popularization. It is a truly remarkable contribution to the campaign against superstition. Its theoretical section explains in simple terms why universal healers are quacks, and its practical section expounds what is most likely either to shorten or to lengthen the span of human life. A child's sturdiness and quickness of apprehension depend on his earliest upbringing, which calls for the utmost care; he must be given an abundance of the air and light which are essential to the growth of every organism. A child finds no difficulty in acquiring sober habits. Moderation should be observed in all things. Idleness and excessive labor should therefore be shunned, as well as overindulgence and abstinence alike, and overmuch or too little clothing. The teeth should be cleaned after each meal, the skin kept fresh, and drugs should be treated with caution, for they often do more harm than good. Speedy and miraculous cures are a snare and a delusion. Illness must be treated reasonably. An examination of the means of ensuring long life which are touted so loudly proves that those who publicize them are quacks and that resort to them in most cases results in shortening life.

Hufeland's disciples follow their master's example; they study women's fashions from the medical standpoint and discuss whether dancing is good for children. Dr. Herz of Berlin compiles for his colleagues the observations he has made in the course of a long practice. He comments on them in the light of his great learning; a good empiricist, he always starts by describing his cases, no matter whether he is speaking of the action of cold water, the use of musk, or the nervous system. The enlightened man takes an interest in hygiene. In his book-lined study, Professor Baumgarten chops wood every day. He grows fatter nonetheless. His disciple attributes this setback to indoor work. So, too, the sober Semler devotes at least an hour a day, usually early in the afternoon, to physical exercises in the open air. He hopes thereby to "protect the abdomen against harmful disorders." He is to be seen in the moat of his native town of Halle hurling balls specially made for him; sometimes, too, he aims at a point high up on the ancient rampart; his projectile often falls on the far side, and the theologian has to climb over to get it. Or he goes for long walks, digs his flower beds, or picks his fruit. When the weather is really too bad to go out, he plays with a ball in his room, throwing and catching it 500 to 900 times.

The young, too, follow the advice of the fashionable physicians. They make long excursions on foot, and when they come to a river or lake, they cannot resist the pleasure of flinging off their clothes and plunging into the water. It is true that they are stoned by peasants scandalized at this lack of modesty or are fined by inadequately "enlightened" officials; but what does that matter if they are in the right?

But it is precisely these young people who begin to lend an ear to strange rumors; there is talk of astonishing cures. A new school scorns reasonable diagnoses; its adepts are aware of the great scientific discoveries, but interpret them in their own way. They postualte the existence of an essential vital principle; if they can discover it, they will have the universal therapy. The nervous system, through which all morbid effects are conveyed and in which all internal disorders are expressed, becomes at once their best justification and their most pliable instrument. They pay scant heed to clinical experience in constructing their theories.

Dr. Reichl believes he has found the vital principle in the oxygen recently discovered by Lavoisier. If he is to be believed, fever is caused by lack of oxygen and can best be treated by a liberal absorption of mineral water.

Others rally to the standard of Brown, an English physician, who publicizes the ideas of his master, Cullen, a Scot, in a simplified and distorted form. His posits the principle of irritation; life consists in keeping up the need for it; when stimuli to satisfy this need are lacking or when it weakens, the patient suffers from "direct or indirect asthenia"; the temperature falls, the pulse slows. When on the other hand, the stimulus is too strong, the less common "sthenia" causes a rise in temperature and irritation. All illnesses, therefore, can be overcome by either strengthening or weakening the nervous system, the regulator of the organic functions. Asthenia, contrary to what might be expected, is by far the commonest malady. After vainly trying excessive purges and cuppings, Brown had cured himself of the gout by taking stimulants. He doses all his patients generously with them till a fresh attack carries him off himself.

The Brunonians are far more numerous in Germany than in England and France, where the principle of irritation is subjected to close criticism. The best known is that by Professor Roeschlaub, who holds that sthenia and asthenia are due to oxidation and deoxidation. He is opposed by the partisans of electricity. Galvani, professor of anatomy at the University of Bologna, holds that every malady is due to an excess or insufficiency of electric current, that is to say, of nerve impulse. A crowd of adventurers discourse thereafter on "animal magnetism" and plume themselves on sudden cures of incurables. Mesmer magnetizes them by hypnosis. His principal disciple in Switzerland and Germany is the Zürich clergyman Lavater. But they are surpassed by the famous Cagliostro. This Italian, born Giuseppe Balsamo at Palermo in 1743, is an international figure. Having had to leave Naples after swindling a jeweler, he travels under various aliases. In Rome in 1769 he meets a fifteen-year-old beauty, Lorenza Feliciani, and marries her, despite the objections of her father, an honest ironsmith, who maintains that she is too young. By dint of drawing lessons, forgery, and even blackmail—willingly abetted, when things go badly, by his young wife, who has, for example, to suffer the addresses of a Quaker—and calling himself the Marchese di Pellegrino and, in 1776, Count Cagliostro, he travels all over Europe and gains a vast notoriety. Having looked after the sick as a Brother of the Misericordia at the age of fifteen, he has some experience of the psychology of the sick, if not of medicine. He manufactures an elixir of life, practices hypnotism, and is able to relieve members of the nobility. His success with Cardinal de Rohan (curing him of asthma) at Strasbourg in 1780 and with the Prince de Soubise and the Parisian elite in 1785 raise him to the peak of fame. Short, fat, and nearly bald, this "divine" being, with his olive complexion and extraordinarily deep eyes, founds a novel lodge of the Egyptian rite, of which he becomes Worshipful Master with the title of the Grand Cophta. The initiates acknowledge that he is several centuries old; and from every corner of Europe money rolls in, which he transmutes into the diamonds with which his dress is liberally bespangled. Only Countess von der Recke has seen through him, at Mitau in Kurland, where she met him in 1779. But she remains silent and refrains from dashing his followers' hopes that they will one day come to know the art of transmuting base metals, summoning up spirits, and prolonging human life. This they will achieve when they have been initiated into all the mysteries of the rite and have passed through all thirty degrees of the hierarchy. The Lodge of Isis enables women to aspire to similar privileges. But before they can do so, the count is involved in the Affair of the Necklace and is expelled from France in 1786. The Aufklärung, represented typically by the champions of the Sturm und Drang, attacks him violently. Goethe publishes his *Grand Cophta*, Klinger his *Dervish*, and Schiller his *Clairvoyant* (*Geisterseher*) in 1789. Countess von der Recke publishes her reminiscences. Everyone abandons him. The unfortunate man wanders through Switzerland and Italy, is sentenced by the Inquisition to life imprisonment in 1791, and dies in prison in 1795.

Such extravagances, enabling as they do the meanest adept to confute a physician, make medicine unnecessary. It is replaced by philosophy. What is the used of anatomy and physiology? The universe is a whole, nature develops in accordance with an order which is the same in all its parts. Man's mind, as a part of this vast organism, can know its laws, for it reflects them and is itself subject to them. The causes of disease and the remedies capable of surmounting the obstacles to the free play of natural laws can be inferred from it. Thus the nature philosophers found a novel medicine, owing nothing to clinical experience and wholly deducible from an a priori system. The mystics, however, look to a quasi-religious intuition for the solution of the medical problem.

Miracle workers now multiply at an astonishing rate. Quacks spring up everywhere, their reputation made by eager followers drawn from all classes of society. How, indeed, can they fail when their patients' faith would move mountains? Autosuggestion, say the rationalists; and they prove it. A certain Count Thun has discovered, purely by chance, that his right hand can heal the rheumatics and the gout simply by touch. At the Leipzig Easter Fair in 1794 he daily heals the sufferers besieging him in his hotel and bolstering his reputation. Even Dr. Langermann, a skeptical physician, is unable to deny his success. But he plots with a friend of his, a professor at Halle University, who disguises himself as Count Thun and likewise cures the sick they bring him by touch. So it is not the count's hand, but the patients' faith, that causes the miraculous cures.

May this not also be the explanation for the Moon Doctor, who draws all Berlin in 1783. He has no difficulty in curing sores, wounds, and hernias; all he has to do is to wait until the moon is in its first quarter; the diseased part is then bared and exposed to the moon's rays, and he touches it, murmuring a prayer. Clients, especially from high society, flock to the little room at the inn in the Tiergarten from which he operates. Consultations are free, but tickets of admission are required, which cost at least two groschen.

The next year the renown of Johann Gottfried Mathias spreads from the suburbs and the Linienstrasse, where he lives, through the whole town. He is a former shepherd and farm hand turned weaver, forty-four years of age. He claims to have been born fully clothed. At the age of twenty-five he discovered his powers to heal all sicknesses. He can make a diagnosis only at noon; the person consulting him must remain silent until the twelfth stroke has sounded. He sells an extraordinary remedy, a liquid which he can obtain only during one hour each year. Once, when a patient obstinately failed to be cured, he cut off her hair, placed it crosswise on the table, burned it, and administered a teaspoonful of the ashes mixed in milk; but she still was not healed. He threatens people who fail to pay him with further illnesses, for the Evil One is his partner. He ends up in prison, but those he has healed still aver that he is no quack.

In 1785 a miracle-working doctor and dentist venture to send to Berlin prospectuses embellished with the king's arms, claiming to have obtained a royal patent. In 1794 Doctor della Lana sells a universal remedy, which is so successful that the government commissions Professor Klaproth, the eminent chemist, to analyze it. He finds a little lime, a little sandstone, and some iron. Dr. Franchi, arriving in Berlin from Breslau shortly after to sell his nostrums, is expelled.

The provinces are exploited as thoroughly as the capital. Gottfried Neise, son of a peasant of Goebelsdorf in Pomerania, a mill hand at Hohenbrücke, is deeply troubled on Christmas night, 1801. The Holy Ghost knocks three times inside his head. A year later, the Holy Ghost comes into his bed and sleeps beside him, calling him by name. At Christmas, 1803, the Holy

Ghost, who, though invisible, resembles a fifteen-year-old lad, places his hand on his body and gives him the power to cure every sort of sickness. At thirty-one, Gottfried is illiterate; he is later to sign the records of his interrogations with a cross. He exploits his powers for two years, placing his hands on the patient's back, then on his belly, and then on his heart, murmuring the following invocation:

> Halt, sun
> Until this evil passes
> Halt, moon
> Until this evil passes
> Halt, star
> Until this evil passes
> In the name of God the Father, God the Son and God the Holy Ghost.

He demands no payment and takes what he is given. The Lord Jesus has permitted him to accept 5 thalers 8 groschen from his patients, and the Holy Ghost has permitted him to take 6 thalers (*NBM* Feb. 1804, 146 ff.).

Veterinary surgeons use similar methods. One of them in the Mark, puts his whole faith in animal magnetism. When cows suddenly refuse to give any milk except the blue, which no one wants, our vet, after trying patiently for six months, at last manages to hypnotize one. This is no easy matter, for a cow, unlike a human being, cannot assist the doctor by using its imagination. The success is all the more remarkable. The cow goes into a trance, lifts its head, shuts its eyes, assumes an incredibly noble and intelligent expression, and names the weeds which cause the sickness.

No matter whether true or untrue, the story has its interest, for it is an echo of the talk during the long winter evenings. The peasants listen and nod and exchange the names of remedies discovered by the alchemists. Baron Hirschen, a Silesian, has made up a "potion of salts of air"; Semler, Meier, and Karsten publicize the "philosophic salts of gold," to which all southern Germany takes with vast enthusiasm. Analyses by a pharmacist at Stettin, however, disclose only a little tartar and vitriol in the former; Professor Klaproth reveals that the fine color of the "living gold, the embryonic gold, the *aurum potabile*" which confers upon the latter its value is due to an admixture of urine with the sulphate of magnesia in it.

It is not only Prussia, of course, that enjoys the benefits of these philanthropists. A quack operating at Hanover meets the blacksmith's wife at Osterode market; she bears in her arms her latest child, her seventh. The quack gazes at the babe, congratulates the mother, and tells her that she has born a miraculous child, gifted with the power of curing all diseases by touch. The news spreads, the sick flock round; for two years they jostle to touch the child; they drink its urine, they spread its excrement on sores and wounds. The parents grow rich, until the Hanover consistory intervenes and puts an end to the farce.

The more rudimentary the administration and the police, the more healers travel the countryside, disregarding the regulations on practicing medicine, for the people welcome them everywhere as saviors.

The Aufklärung makes every effort to restore reason to repute. The value of the new discoveries must be established by experiment. Dr. Reichl, summoned to Berlin from Erlangen, reduces the fever of several patients at the Charité. A royal commission investigates his method and comes out in favor of his efficacious and relatively inexpensive cures. He consequently merits the pension of 500 thalers granted him by the king.

Magnetism is a novel phenomenon which may perhaps be of benefit to medicine. But why become infatuated with it? *A consultatione medicorum confarreatorum libera nos, Domine*, as Harvey himself remarked. If there ever was a field in which caution was called for, surely it is this.

Though not denying the truth of some cures, Wieland maintains that it is stupid simply to ascribe them to miraculous remedies. Are not maladies often imaginary, and witnesses, though no doubt in good faith, deceived by their senses? And are not relapses frequent, though not known to the public at large?

People should surely not get these remedies from quacks, of whom Hufeland furnishes a long list.

Unfortunately, "people really want to purchase healthy looks and buy good health. . . . *People like to be deceived*" (*JLM* 1789, IV, 417-30). Everyone takes an interest in medicine; it is the talk of the drawing rooms and the journals alike; people describe their symptoms and confide the secrets of treatments. One talks of elemental fire, another of oxygen, a third of magnetism or electricity. No one consults a doctor any more. People treat themselves and criticize the doctor. "Illnesses come into fashion and pass out of it, drugs and treatments come and go, like Palais-Royal fashions. Instead of seeking the real causes of a disorder, new names are invented for it, and people comfort themselves with the idea that if they are ill, they can at least suffer under the auspices of a fashionable druggist." "The ladies have the vapors, migraines, and spasms; men have spells of weakness and nervous ailments. No one knows what the vapors are." Patients have them, doctors treat them, but neither of them can have any precise notion of what they are.

There was once a happy time when no human being knew that he had nerves. . . . How things have changed! Forty years ago an English doctor (named Whytt) was seized with the unfortunate idea of writing a book on the nerves and their disorders. A chemist who had long been puzzled by the case of one lady—for in England chemists practice medicine—reads the book and cuts the Gordian knot: it's the nerves, Madam. The term gave entire satisfaction and became fashionable; hypochondria, vapors and the like had to yield pride of place. The doctors themselves, compelled to bow to the exigences of fashion, soon found the term so convenient that nothing on earth could induce them to give it up.

Now the entire universe must have nerves. People pique themselves on having strong nerves, irritable nerves, or delicate nerves, as good form requires. A man of nerve was formerly a sturdy and hale son of Adam. Nowadays he is a being whose nerves respond to every impression to the thousandth degree, who swoons at the buzz of a fly, and is thrown into convulsions by the scent of a rose. [*Eumonia* 1801, 481–505.]

Most contemporary chroniclers stress the prevalence of nervous disorders. They may or may not usually be imaginary: the fact to be borne in mind is their overriding importance in contemporary society and thought.

The reason why the Aufklärung ultimately failed to defend medicine against this caricature of it was that the public to which it appealed could no longer grasp what it meant. Reading the *Macrobiotics* requires some little application and a great deal of good sense. Toward the end of the eighteenth century the public mentality is changing so rapidly that most readers are no longer able to understand the author. It is not hard to see what caused this breakdown in communication: reason has no nerves, and the nervous do not exercise their reason. There is no longer any contact between the philosophers and their public. Goekingk sees this quite clearly, and concludes:

Why are people more excitable nowadays than they used to be, why are people everywhere still talking about Aufklärung when human reason seems to be breaking down? . . .

What it all comes down to is nothing but moral hysteria or nervous debility. There are vapors of the spirit . . . and they are due to the way we live and bring up our children. The sight, smell, the mere presence of something repugnant, a piece of disagreeable news, a mere caprice brings on fearful vapors or a nervous swoon in hysterical females, whereas a hardened and hale constitution would not be liable to them. Mysteries, miracles, enthusiasms overheat the self-styled enlightened mind, when a person who harbors clear-headed doubts or uses his powers of reflection would remain unmoved. . . .

This is what happens to enlightened persons if they indulge in mawkish sentimentality and cheap literature and are weak in character. [*JD* 1787, I, 371–74.]

This extreme nervous sensibility is characteristic of nearly all the younger writers; the Romantics are prone to it and complain of it. Partly it is due to genuine ill health; many of them are anemic. Their state of health may well reflect that of the masses in general, though there is not much factual evidence concerning them. It is very possible that tuberculosis ravaged Prussian society in the eighteenth century. There was a surplus of males and a lack of organized hygiene; living standards were very low. The young intellectuals' letters are filled with references to spitting blood, as casual as talk of a cold in the head nowadays. The whole Hardenberg family is consumptive, and all of them die young. Erasmus, the brother of Friedrich, better known by his pseudonym Novalis, died of it; both brothers suffered frequent attacks of "hypochrondria." Friedrich vainly tries to reassure his brother: "Poor old chap," he writes to him in March 1793,

I am terribly sorry about how much you are missing me. If we were together, your consumption [*Schwindsucht*] would very soon disappear, be assured of that, my dear fellow. If your work does not cure you, you will have to attack the trouble from another quarter; and that is easily done. You really must not be so afraid of illness and death, and especially you must not brood so much on both of them. Try to imagine during these bouts of neurasthenia [*Grillen*], *experto crede*, that you are really a merry sort of fellow, even a buffoon, seeing everything in caricature and in a peculiar light. Your mind will at once be cleared of this affected pathos, and you will very soon feel as calm and collected as you do when you are in good health. The first thing to do during your fits of depression is convince yourself that it is weakness and nerve strain; repeat this to yourself incessantly; that is the first step. The second is some occupation to distract you. I admit that that's fairly hard to find. Everything is really a matter of habit; you may even find it possible to acquire the habit of laughing at your weaknesses. . . . Do convince yourself that you must inevitably gain from an incessant struggle with your own self. . . . I beg of you to overlook the defects of the pot and try to savor what is inside it. [Novalis, *Schriften* IV, 64.]

Lesions of the lungs cannot, alas, be cured by moral suasion. A few weeks before his death in April 1797, Erasmus describes his symptoms:

The cough which still persists fairly obstinately [he writes on 2 February] raises my temperature and exhausts me a great deal, and constant shortness of breath, night sweats, and an extraordinary lowering of vitality reduce my enjoyment of the sensual pleasures simply to a good appetite and a fairly decent refreshing sleep; and even that is now broken by a bout of coughing every night, lasting for at least half an hour. Even so, I should not really have any doubts about recovering my youthful vigor if my doctor himself did not say that the lung has been severely affected and if he recommended anything but lung and chest tonics whenever there is any question of going for a spring cure or convalescence. [Ibid., 169.]

Schleiermacher, too, suffered a great deal from a chest ailment. He was afflicted with frequent headaches and stomach pains. Cupping made him severely ill.

Caroline in her youth looked after her mother, who suffered "spells" of nervous debility. She herself complains of the delicacy of her own constitution. After the death of her first child in December 1789, she writes:

I spent the rest of the day in a stupor; I had not been fully aware of what I was doing to save her; my exhaustion brought it home to me. I was so tired by evening that I was unable to walk; when I got to bed, I felt ill and coughed and spat blood; this continued all night and a heavy languor ensued. My strength soon revived. I was able at least to move about. My health since then has been what you might suppose, knowing my constitution. But I suffered from such constriction of the chest that I could not sit up straight, and I still have slight hemorrhages from time to time from the blood which had probably accumulated in the lower belly [Schmidt, *Caroline* I, 199.]

Ten years later, in 1800, her daughter Augusta, who also died young, describes a fresh bout of illness in these terms:

My mother has been really very ill and is still not wholly recovered. She first had a nervous fever, which was very serious for a week; the doctor ordered a mustard plaster on her leg; she kept it on too long, and then they administered the wrong ointment, and that had very serious effects and caused my mother much pain. A relapse ensued, the nervous fever returned, and once it was over, very severe spasms took its place. . . . She was cured by the Brunonian method, but accesses of nervous fever recur from time to time. [Ibid., II, 17.]

The handsome Schelling himself is not spared the common affliction; he has a chest ailment. Kleist often speaks of his disordered nervous system.

Other disorders are doubtless due to neurosis. The information supplied by the sufferers is unfortunately too imprecise for us to be sure. Almost all of them suffer from stomach troubles, colics, and migraines. Friedrich Schlegel, suffers from all of them at once. Forster's digestion has been impaired since his voyage round the world, which, in addition, if he is to be believed, gave him the gout. He died at forty of congestion of the lungs.

As for Jung-Stilling,

his many and arduous engagements and especially an extremely painful stomach cramp, which tormented him daily, particularly toward evening, greatly depressed his spirits that winter at Marburg. He lost his gusto, grew gloomy and so sensitive that he could not refrain from tears at the slightest affecting circumstance. The intermittent pains never left him; they became so fierce that he had to give up the idea of going to Schaffhausen to visit the Rhine Falls with his friends. While he operated on hundreds of patients for cataract, his "horribly painful stomach cramps" made life a misery to him. [*Lebensgeschichte* II, 76–77, 159, 161.]

Kleist has to keep to his bed with the bellyache for two days in three in 1805.

This "nervous fever," of which they all speak, is very hard to identify. It does not seem to worry Caroline unduly; but Wackenroder dies of it at twenty-five.

The word "hypochondria" appears fairly often in the Romantics' correspondence. Novalis mentions it to his brother. Tieck's father-in-law, Bernhardi, suffers from it. The illness does not seem to be a very serious one, for Dr. Herz claims that Karl Philipp Moritz's tormenting fear of death is entirely due to his imagination; he contracts a bout of fever, and the good doctor cures him by telling him that he is of course going to die. Moritz is moved to tears and calmly prepares himself for death; his temperature falls and he recovers. But he has the scrofula, remains manic-depressive, and ends up tubercular.

Their nervous disorders may, therefore, have psychological causes too. In the absence of more precise documentation it is not possible to disentangle the organic from the moral causes of ill health in each individual case. It is, however, possible to note the effects of the new mentality upon constitutions which are in many cases weak to start with. Happiness is an ecstatic state, an exaltation of the spirit, from which there inevitably has to be a return to earth. So they await, long for, and anticipate the next miraculous experience; the alternation of the phases of excitability and depression torments the nerves. Karl Philipp Moritz, who was to die of tuberculosis, experiences and describes these phases.

All the Romantics are manic-depressives. "I can find no words to express what I have most to reproach myself with," Freidrich Schlegel tells his brother. "The reason is that my feelings have a habit of plunging from the heights to the lowest depths" (Walzel, *Schlegel*, 8 Nov. 1791). The phase of depression is bound to be one of neurasthenia or hypochondria if it lasts at all long; and it is a period passed in expectation of the miraculous. Some remain perpetually in expectation and never attain their desire. They are in the grip of the *mal du siècle*, the never-appeased desire for a never-defined object. Everyone knows how hard waiting for a known event can be when the wait is too prolonged. One has only to imagine waiting for no known object and no known period, and one can see that the Romantic disorder is not merely a literary pose, but that its sufferings can be agonizing. "But why," Lovell cries,

Oh, that you could explain it to me! Why can no enjoyment fully satisfy our heart? What is this inexpressible desire, this melancholy that impels me toward new and unknown pleasures? At the very moment that I fully realize my happiness, when I rise to the very peak of enthusiasm, a species of indifference suddenly seizes me, a somber foreboding—how describe it to you? like the cold dawn breeze that sweeps the mountain peak after a sleepless night. . . . I used to think that this sensation of anguish was a desire for love . . . but it is not that. Even beside Amelia this despotic feeling tormented me. If it were to overmaster me, it would drive me, forever empty-hearted, from pole to pole. [Tieck, *William Lovell*, bk. 2, Letter 7.]

The nervous crisis is sometimes artificially induced. The desired exaltation is aroused by deliberate excitation. Thus, Tieck, when a student at Halle, decides to read aloud the two volumes of Grosse's novel *The Genius* with two fellow students at a single sitting. He begins at four in the afternoon and ends at two in the morning, his two friends having fallen asleep. At length he flings himself on his bed, exhausted; but cannot sleep. Under the spell of the characters in the novel, he raves, tosses, feels he is going mad, and swoons. He is quite used to such crises, for he needs to live in an uncommon frame of mind. He has visions, too. His friend Spillner lives in a narrow closet with a glass door between it and Tieck's room. One evening Spillner has a friend in to visit; Tieck sees their shadows outlined on the door. "I shuddered so strongly," he says, "that I fell into a species of raging madness, for they suddenly became strangers to me . . . and they too seemed to me to be madmen. That madness is contagious I find more and more evident, and I believe that Hamlet's words are to be understood in this sense, that these fellows will end by making me really mad, for I believe that a man (if he has weak nerves) becomes mad if he passes himself off as mad for any length of time" (Wackenroder, *Werke* II, 60–61).

There is nothing surprising, at any rate, in the fact that Tieck's stories are "fantastic." Is his Romanticism caused by his nerves or his nerves by his Romanticism? The two interpretations are undoubtedly both true and false. But one thing is certain: if the Romantics had experienced the well-being characteristic of the healthy animal's organic stability, their physical equilibrium would have stood up to the excesses of their imagination, and they would never have thought of putting their nerves to the torture, unwittingly placing such burdens on them that they provoked the crises which put such a strain on their constitution. Jung-Stilling furnishes good illustrations of how this happens.

The Tuesday after Whitsun was the day appointed for the visit to Stilling's birthplace, but he was seized with an inexplicable anguish, which increased as the day drew nearer and finally made it impossible to execute the project. Much as he had rejoiced in the prospect of revisiting the scenes of his youth, so much the more terrified he now became; he felt that great perils awaited him there; . . . so the journey was never made; his friends respected his fears and yielded. [Jung-Stilling, *Lebensgeschichte* II, 201; cf. I, 233.]

All the young writers who gather round the *Athenaeum*, the Romantics' literary organ, have some physical defect which aggravates the hypertrophy of their sensibility. Far from enjoying the optimism which comes from a sound inner balance, they suffer from the instability due to the lack of it. They are despondent, and the basic pessimism of which they perpetually complain sunders them decisively from the society of the Aufklärung.

I could have spent long years in the same occupations and amid the same pleasures [Florentin says], but a secret unease in the depths of my

being, the longing [*Treiben*] for some unknown place seldom allowed me
to feel that I was indeed happy and at liberty wholly to enjoy myself. . . .
Everywhere I found the same habits, the same stupidities, precisely those
from which I desired to escape. One prejudice was heaped on another,
oppressing and governing the world. Everywhere I found slaves and
despots; and above all, I saw intelligence and courage feared and
suppressed, while stupidity and cowardice were protected among those
who derived their power from them. [Dorothea, *Florentin*, 175, 184.]

[Woldemar] pursued with his soul what attracted him, and time after
time he lost himself in it, dreaming and molding it into sympathetic and
poetic form that would render it imperishable and transform it into
something calculated to elevate the heart; everything that is beautiful
encountered within him an image corresponding to this sympathy and, in
dread and delight, delight and dread, augmented his longing. Daily he
sought and explored farther afield, and daily he arrived at a better
understanding of what he sought and what he wished to find. And so he
constantly drew nearer his goal, and yet his goal drew away from him
constantly at the same rate. The secret of this contradiction, which
gradually revealed itself to his delicate sensibility and his critical
intelligence, induced in him a melancholy which every well-bred mind will
appreciate. [Jacobi, *Woldemar*, 14.]

This pessimism and this lack of balance become chronic. The patient
analyzes every facet of it, with a touch of vanity which in fact impedes his
recovery. He is so different from others, from the "enlightened persons" who
are at home in life and always up to the mark! So different that he
exaggerates his inability to make his home among them; and the economic
crisis seems to demand even more pertinacity and perseverance than would
have been called for in the past. The Romantic prefers the line of least
resistance. Why try to resemble these people when one is not only different
from them, but far more interesting? Solitude is the only situation appropriate to genius, and he who finds the daily striving for petty ends repugnant
to him feels his greatness swell within him. "Why," asks William Lovell,

is man destined to find no repose within himself? I would think it so
refreshing now to live in a little hut on the verge of a solitary wood,
forgetting the whole world and by the world forgot, to all eternity. To
know nothing but the land, to descry no man as far as the eye can reach,
to be greeted only by the morning breeze and the whisper of leaves. A
little flock, a little field, what more does man need for his happiness?
And yet, if some divinity suddenly carried me there, would I not renew my
longing for other scenes? Would not my gaze attach itself again, as it once
did, to the clouds golden with twilight, growing dusk with them and
passing on to visit marvelous lands I have never yet known? Would I not
be crushed by the weight of a dreary solitude and would I not long for the
sympathy, the love, the handclasp of some friend? Life stretches before
me like a long tangled thread which a malign destiny compels me to

unravel. A hundred times I refuse the arduous task and a hundred times I take it up again, but make no progress; ah, if only a beneficent slumber would overtake me. . . . I feel like some wretched phantom wandering, somber and nameless, calm and taciturn, among men; to me they are an alien race. [Tieck, *Werke* XVI, 182.]

Gambling and Lotteries

Early in the century, gambling had been the panacea for the boredom of the drawing room; the Aufklärung had tended to substitute conversation. But gambling is also the almost classic method of introducing the extraordinary into ordinary life. By the end of the century everyone indulges in it freely, the young Romantics even more than the rest. "To play faro with an appearance of the most violent passion, and yet be distrait and absent; to risk all in a fit of fury and to turn away indifferently as soon as it is lost" was Friedrich Schlegel's custom in his youth (*Lucinde*, Reclam. ed., 43; cf. ibid., 51). Tieck spends whole nights at cards, despite Wackenroder's disapproval. Tieck's heroes, too, are desperate gamblers. "Do not upbraid me," William Lovell writes,

for does not everything that is called intellectual enjoyment come from play? Whether I play with words or with cards, with definitions, with dice or with verses, surely it all comes to the same thing?

With the cards and their prodigious vicissitudes one can experience every sensation. Fortune rises and falls just as the tides ebb and flow. A new destiny begins with each turn of the cards, and our inmost being moves in perfect harmony with the alternation of the colored pasteboard. Every man has need of emotions. One man seeks them at the theater, others have other distractions. . . . To me gaming takes the place of them all, it carries me far from my own sensations, plunges me into somber emotions and marvelous reveries. [Tieck, *William Lovell*, bk. 6, letter 3.]

Steffens is equally fascinated at Carlsbad and never quits the faro table.

The tardy but general success of lotteries, against which the Aufklärung protests in vain, is no less significant. Frederick II, short of money after the Seven Years' War, introduces a novel form of lottery, the "lottery by numbers" (*Zahlenlotterie*), into Prussia. An Italian, Calzabigi, demonstrates to him the advantages of the system used in Italy; the player chooses one or more of the ninety numbers to be drawn; the smaller the stake, the less the chance of winning and the greater the winnings of the player favored by fortune. The concessionary's share is usually one half of the stakes.

Everyone can try his luck, since there is no minimum stake. That is the great novelty. The "lottery by series" (*Klassenlotterie*), something like the lotteries operating today in some countries, had been known since the beginning of the century; it reduced the part played by luck, as the quantity and value of the winning numbers were fixed beforehand and only a limited number of fairly expensive tickets were put on sale; the profits went to charity or to army pensioners, widows, the schools, or the poor.

The new lottery is open to rich and poor alike. Owing to their shortage of cash, the princes can no longer trouble about the moral objections; though they do prevent the growth of the tontine as an institution, a scheme which enriched the Duke of Saxe-Weimar as late as 1757. Frederick II disregards scruple and signs the license introducing the new type of lottery into Prussia on 8 February 1763. The first drawing takes place in Berlin on 31 August of that year.

The concessionary company farming the lottery is so badly managed, however, that it has to be wound up in July 1765. The enterprise seems hopeless for lack of players. The king refuses to give up, however. He realizes that Calzabigi's company has not been able to adapt itself to local conditions. A new company is formed by Count Reuss, Count Eichstadt, and Baron Geuder; it puts out its publicity in German instead of French, chooses its agents better, and succeeds in gradually persuading the masses to take tickets. The lottery begins to show signs of success in 1770. The company signs a contract for six years, renews it, and extends it to the "lottery by series" as well in 1776. The states's annual revenue from the lottery at that time is 40,000 thalers, plus 6,000 thalers' worth of porcelain, which the company undertakes to accept from the Royal Manufacture and not to resell on Prussian territory, so that it can only get rid of it at a loss. The state's profit rises each time the contract is renewed, reaching 467,000 thalers in 1796.

The lottery takes its place among the local customs. Every three weeks the Berliners throng to the Town Hall; the great wheel revolves five times; with beating hearts the ticket holders watch for the number to come up; the lucky win at least fifteen times their stake and at most—but this never happens—60,000 times.

How many dreams are woven around this astronomical figure! Those who have had no luck soon recover hope; for in three weeks the wheel of fortune will turn again. The provinces follow suit. At first, the agents of the Berlin company travel the towns and countryside to collect the payments for the tickets. Later, when they mount up, new drawing centers are established. The lottery becomes a tool of mercantile policy in that it drains off the neighboring states' gold into Prussia. The Danzigers gamble at Langenfurt; and after the conquest of Danzig, the Poles go there to try their luck. The Prussian lottery is established at Warsaw and then at Anspach (1797). Jewish hawkers place its tickets at Saint Petersburg, Moscow, Vienna, and Amsterdam. The South Germans spend their savings in Berlin. Passions grow heated and are kept alight by the publicity for the drawings. The moral earnestness of Frederick William II and the scruples of Frederick William

III are powerless against the ravages of the gambling crazes, for the state cannot renounce resources allocated to the upkeep of the army.

The lotteries' speedy conquest not only of Prussia but of the whole of Germany cannot be accounted for solely by the concessionary's good business sense. The general mentality is changing, and the new instiution comes at just the right moment to profit from it. All the chroniclers are struck by the frenzy with which all classes of society take to games of chance. At Berlin, at Magdeburg, in all the towns of the kingdom and the empire, a game of cards is the pretext for every reception. Lesser folk play billiards in the taverns. The marauder, the unemployed, and the beggar stand around before the booths which disfigure the bridges and squares in the towns; they hazard at dice all they have, even the rags that clothe them.

Thereafter the desire to get rich quick without working conflicts with the bourgeois virtues practiced by earlier generations and recommended by Ben Franklin. "The number of lotteries and the approval which they everywhere encounter is an indication of the extreme corruption of our manners," Schubart writes.

Men . . . wish to become rich all at once. . . . The taste for frivolous gain has spread all over Germany . . . Formerly, when a company of young adventurers were determined to pursue their luck to the final throw, they thought of digging mines, building canals, fitting out ships and opening up new sources of wealth and trade. But nowadays everyone wants to get rich all at once and in a frivolous way . . . The peasant drinks up the pfennigs he gets for his butter and eggs and no longer believes that many a mickle makes a muckle; he prefers the lottery. Thus, a universal spirit of quackery seems to be becoming prevalent in all classes of society. [DC 1774, I, 534–36.]

But it is in vain that the philosophers contrast stable and well-earned happiness with the thrill of pleasure experienced by those who abandon themselves to fate by confiding their lot to dice and cards; in vain that they discuss the harmful effects of cards, on which, in fact, the whole vitality of social life depends. Indifferent to the moralists' complaints and firmly entrenched owing to the connivance of the princes (for it balances their budgets), the lottery pursues its way and spreads its corruption. It drives nobles to breach of trust, merchants to ruin, and gallant soldiers to suicide. Because of it servants become untrustworthy, married couples separate; the clergy, the very clergy who denounce gambling, have their pockets full of lottery tickets. Honest journeymen lose their week's wage in an hour. In vain the learned make complicated calculations to discover the laws of chance; portent is the key. They meet to interpret their dreams and premonitions. They discover that the results of the drawings are bound up with the movement of the planets.

The passions thus aroused are transferred to other objects; people speculate on their neighbor's death by associating in tontines, which, instead of wisely capitalizing their members' contributions, make promises to everyone so lavish that they cannot be kept and continually attract new participants. Resounding crashes ensue when the average age of the insured rises and deaths become more frequent. In 1781 the Prussian government places a limit on the number of members in each life assurance association; supervision becomes easier and speculation impossible. Eleven funds of this sort operate in Berlin. They cannot engage in such profitable, but dishonest, operations as are denounced at Bremen, where burghers pay the premiums for aged and sickly beggars, domestics, or peasants. Venal physicians certify the health of these unfortunates, and they are handed a few scraps by the "benefactors" for whose profit the insurance policy is taken out. They do not understand what the speculation is about and heedlessly allow themselves to be insured. Some speculators earn their living by searching out aged peasants in the requisite ill health and drive a trade in them.

The Aufklärung calls for the suppression of lotteries, for not only are they profoundly immoral, but the mentality they engender saps the very foundations of rationalism. If belief in luck is to become a substitute for methodical and deliberate effort, the advancement of enlightenment is at an end. The press turns all its resources, therefore, to railing against gambling of every sort. "Nature," a wit writes, "chastises the Turk with the plague and the Christian with lotteries" (*VC* 1776, 471–72). Another versifies:

> In his cavern Satan says to Vizlipuli:
> Go, my friend, go, clad all in black,
> And seduce the humans with some new snare.
> The demon flew off, laboriously devising
> A plot to bring his thousands to the inferno;
> He succeeds . . . thanks to lotteries. [ibid.1787, 77–78.]

The prohibition of games of chance is one of those ancient laws which are everywhere still in force and are nowhere enforced. To strengthen it and suppress lotteries, as the journals loudly demand, is not so easy, for what is to replace lost revenue? When Frederick William II asks the General Directory to abolish lotteries, he is reminded that their yield goes to the upkeep of the army. They are therefore maintained, but are placed under supervision and made responsible to a special branch of the administration.

Frederick William III, a very scrupulous monarch, again tackles the problem and concludes only that the further spread of lotteries must be curbed.

Austria and most of the German princes install lotteries in their own states shortly thereafter to prevent their subjects from buying the tickets of foreign lotteries. They are, however, more receptive to the objurgations of the journalists than are the Hohenzollerns. The Duke of Württemberg renounces lotteries in return for the compensation offered him by his loyal subjects. In the smaller principalities the sovereigns can make a parade of sacrifices, which cause them no great pain, for by making lotteries illegal they prevent their subjects from playing them abroad and thus can put a stop to the export of capital, which they could not have halted otherwise.

Collectors for foreign lotteries are threatened with imprisonment, fines, or expulsion. The abolition of lotteries is decreed in the Palatinate in 1780, in Saxony and Hesse-Cassel in 1785, at Frankfort-on-Main, Hamburg, Hildesheim, and Fulda in 1786. Most of the German states yield to the protests of the press, but the prohibitions are not enforced. The sovereign himself sometimes fails to observe his own edicts and plays the lottery abroad; the Prince of Hesse-Darmstadt is detected doing so by the *Patriotic Archive*. The number of times that the edicts prohibiting lotteries are reissued shows that they have had little effect. A circular sent by the princes of Thurn und Taxis to the staff of the mails in 1788 gives an idea of how seriously intended the prevention of fraud was and of the limits within which it had to be confined; it prohibits the carrying of letters or parcels marked with any indication that they contain stakes or winnings.

The antilottery campaign benefits clandestine gambling "in cafés, taverns, and private homes" (*JD* 1787, II, 145–46). Morals cannot be reformed by law; laws can at best merely retard their degeneration. The taste for gambling is simply one more indication of the profound change that came over the public mentality at the end of the eighteenth century.

The Miraculous and Love: Romantic Friendship

Love too is affected by the new trend. Like religion and medicine, it too partakes of the miraculous. What, however, could be more natural than the attraction of two young people to one another? What could be simpler and more reasonable to anyone who can envisage the consequences of his acts? But what could be more marvelous, and more imperious too, and of more intimate concern to the Romantic, who does not, if he can help it, envisage the consequences of his acts, for to do so would strip the future, pregnant as it is with the miraculous, of its uncertainty? Jung-Stilling experienced both of these conceptions of love and marriage. He describes them perfectly. Christine was the somewhat sickly daughter of a friend of his, of whom he had never taken much notice. As he was sitting by her bedside one evening, she said to him, after a long silence: "Listen, Stilling, I have had a very vivid impression of something which I shall not be able to tell you until later." At these words Stilling went absolutely rigid; from the soles of his feet to the top of his head he felt a disquieting sensation he had never before experienced, and all of a sudden a ray pierced his soul like lightning. He understood in his heart what God's will was and what the young invalid's words meant. He rose with tears in his eyes, bent over the bed, and said: "I know, dear girl, what impression you had and what is God's will." She sat up, and, stretching out her hand to him, repeated: "You know!" Stilling clasped her right hand, saying: "God in His heaven bless you, we are linked together to all eternity" (Jung-Stilling, *Lebensgeschichte*, I, 213–15).

After the death of his hysterical spouse the scales fell from his eyes. He grasped the luminous truth. His father-in-law, his sainted Christine, and he himself had acted in accordance with neither the prescriptions of religion nor those of sound reason. For the Christian's highest duty is to examine, in accordance with the rules of sound reason and the conventions and under the direction of Providence, each of his acts, the choice of a spouse in particular, and then await God's blessing. But all this had been neglected. Christine had been a young, inexperienced girl; she had loved Stilling in secret, had yielded to her love, and had prayed God to fulfill her wishes. Religion and love had thus been mingled together in her fits of hysteria. Neither her parents nor Stilling had had the least idea of this; they had perceived nothing but divine inspiration and the action of God, and they had yielded to it. The unseemly and improvident side of the affair only became clear later from its unfortunate sequel.

Romantic love strikes its victims like a bolt from the blue. It is in clear contrast to the reasoned love of the Aufklärung: "You write," Erasmus says to his brother Novalis, "that a quarter of an hour was enough to make up your mind. How can you get to know a girl in a quarter of an hour? . . . If you had said a quarter of a year, I should still have admired your talent in the knowledge of the feminine heart, but a quarter of an hour, just think of it yourself, a quarter of an hour seems really too miraculous, and I am driven to the conclusion that it was simply passion, that eternal timeserver, that was at the bottom of it" (Novalis, *Schriften* IV, 86).

But "extraordinary people must have an extraordinary destiny." Friedrich Schlegel, too, is of this opinion, recalling his meeting with Caroline: "The first glance was decisive. At the second, he knew and told himself that what he had long foreseen had come to pass" (*Lucinde*, 60).

Later he writes to Dorothea, with whom he fell in love the moment he set eyes on her: "In one second, love is there, total and eternal, or else it is not love. . . . Or do you think one amasses pleasure like money or any other commodity by behaving conventionally? The great happiness takes us by surprise, appears and vanishes, like a strain of music" (*Lucinde*, 39).

As for Caroline in her younger days, she tells us that at their first meeting Link "trembled and could hardly speak" and "poor Caroline was in hardly better plight." Twenty years later, in 1800, after a checkered career in which she had shown herself a hard-headed woman on many occasions, she can still describe receiving a letter from Schelling as "a blinding flash of happiness" (Spenlé, *Novalis*, 63).

This poetic conception of love dominates the literature of the period. The

Aufklärung does not condemn it. It is affected by the influence of the Sturm und Drang writers, who rehabilitated feeling and mocked at the arid rationalism of those who imitated foreign models. The Goethean ideal requires that every individual shall undergo personal experience of everything that life offers in order to achieve maturity; but such experience can only be fruitful and the passions themselves can only be felt intensely if they are experienced and felt consciously. Only control by reason can achieve the harmony between thought and feeling which characterizes the complete man. It is reason that scrutinizes, that analyzes, that torments; it is reason that confers on the passions their form and their lasting effect. Love is the passion par excellence, as the writers describe it. Whether they were motivated by their youth or whether they needed a pure sensation to bring out fully the argument they were putting forward, the Sturm und Drang authors delighted in endowing it with this miraculous character. They did not realize that they were thereby raising a storm of revolt in many a middle-class family. When in 1771 Werther catches sight of Charlotte slicing bread for the children around her, he at once falls in love with her and is "so lost in dreams" that he forgets the rest of the world (Goethe, *Werther*, bk. 1, letter of 16 June). And Schiller's girl in love cries in 1784: "When I saw him for the first time, a blush spread over my brow and my pulse beat joyously. Every motion said, every breath sighed: 'it is he'; and my heart, the eternal longing heart, recognized and confirmed: 'it is he.' And the echo resounded through all the universe, which rejoiced with me" (Schiller, *Kabale und Liebe*, act 1, sc. 1).

Kleist's plays are full of romantic lovers and pensive heroes. Käthchen von Heilbronn, for example, is fifteen, her beauty and innocence the pride of the town. One day Count vom Strahl asks the girl's father, Theobald the blacksmith, to repair his armor. The blacksmith invites him to sit down and share their meal.

The girl [the father relates], bearing a great silver dish on her head,
loaded with bottles, glasses, and the simple meal, slowly opens the door;
she enters; and, look you, if God the Father had appeared to me out of
the clouds, I would have behaved much as she did. The dish, the goblets,
the meal, as soon as she sets eyes upon the knight, she drops them all,
and, pale as death, hands folded as if in prayer, pressing her breast and
her spreading hair to the ground in a kiss, she drops down before him as
if struck by a thunderbolt. And as I cry, "Lord of my life, what ails the
child?" and raise her up, she throws her arms round me and falls back,
folding up like a jackknife, her burning countenance turned to him as if
she were seeing an apparition. . . . Then, as she comes to herself, casting
timid glances at the count, it seems to me that the fit is over, and I set to
work again with my needles and awls. After which I say, "There we are,
Sir Knight. . . . " The count rises, gazes meditatively at the girl, who
comes up to his breastbone, bends down to her, and says: "The Lord bless

you and keep you and give you his peace, amen." And as we go to the
window, at the very moment he mounts his charger, the girl raises her
hands above her head and plunges thirty feet to the pavement, like a
lost girl taken leave of her five senses. . . . And as soon as she has
recovered a little, she essays to walk, straps up her little bundle, and
passes through the door in the rays of the morning sun. "Where are you
going?" the servant asks her. She replies: "To Count Wetter vom Strahl,"
and vanishes. [Kleist, *Käthchen von Heilbronn*, act 1, sc. 1.]

It is often some time before the young Romantic is struck by this
miraculous love, the existence of which he has learned from his reading. The
less he goes into society, the less chance he has of encountering it. His
slender, even precarious, means, his inexperience of worldly manners, and
his shyness keep him apart. He dreams of the woman he will love, as
Chateaubriand dreams of his Sylph, but instead of falling in love with an
image all by himself, he seeks among his fellows a confidant to understand
him and to share his melancholy. Seldom has friendship between young men
been so much cultivated and so widespread. It is virtually a social institution
in Germany. Some critics have tried to account for it by tracing it back to its
origins. Ever since the beginning of the century young intellectuals had
bound themselves in friendships which lasted all their lives. Lessing and
Mendelssohn, Goethe and Schiller, Forster and Soemmerring are cases in
point. The Romantics are simply imitating their elders. But this does not take
us very far. Even if the fathers had not had any friends, the sons would surely
nonetheless have formed the relationships they needed. Adolescents are
naturally prone to confidences and sentimental effusions. It does not,
therefore, seem essential "to account for this tendency," especially since too
close a scrutiny of its origin may lead us to overlook its most striking aspect.

In the age of the Aufklärung, friendship had much the same characteristics as it has today; it involved both the intellect and the feelings. The esteem
felt by two friends for one another, the intimate acquaintance with each
other's qualities they acquired, and the mutual confidence they displayed
ensured them the tranquility, the equality, and the enduring relationship
which distinguish friendship from love. The Romantics' propensity to bind
themselves utterly is something very different. It might be said that those
who are not favored by love seek to endow their attachments with the same
characteristics as union with a woman, though the fact is that they break
with their friend as soon as they meet a woman and address her in the same
style as they had once addressed him. Relationships between young men,
then, are essentially different in the age of the Aufklärung from what they
are in the age of Romanticism; Romantic friendship is a passionate
friendship. It devastates their youthful hearts. Friedrich Schlegel at first
finds the necessary confidant in his brother Wilhelm.

I want to see whether the love of men cannot obliterate the love for
women, and I ask you too to appreciate its primacy for a few years. In the

depths of my soul there slumbers a sublime image of friendship. It will become a reality if we live together again. . . . A bond with you, a long-lasting bond, should be founded, too, on a reciprocal moral impulsion, for it will become ever closer and closer, eternally.

Above all, he whom I must love must be capable of living for one person only and of forgetting all save him. Above all, the strength of love must be equal on either side; it may issue from the desire for the infinite, the heart believing that it will find in the beloved that infinite good for which it longs. Reflecting on all this coolly and calmly, I find all this in you, and that is why I shall not fear satiety, however frequently I enjoy it. True, love must necessarily have its ebb and flow; the heart for a moment believes it possesses the infinite good, and then is engulfed in disappointment once more; but the return of the tide may assuredly be expected. I have never found in woman anything of this aspiration for the infinite, and I have never yet met a woman whom it seemed possible to love. [Walzel, *Schlegel*, 30, 46–47.]

It is not very likely that Wilhelm responded to this passion as heartily as his brother believed. Dealing with this friendship in *Lucinde*, Friedrich writes: "Each of them burned with a noble love. . . . Often they expressed in crude, but appropriate, terms sublime thoughts on the miracles of art, on the value of life . . . on the divine nature of masculine love, which Julius was resolved to make the principal occupation of his life" (*Lucinde*, 57). But Friedrich finds other friends, a Count Schweinitz first, of whom all other traces have been lost, and then Novalis and Schleiermacher, with whom he sets up house in Berlin in 1797.

Tieck and Wackenroder first meet in the classroom at Friedrichswerder grammar school. The son of the ropemaker and the son of the Chief of the Municipal Police make friends. What grief when they have to part! Tieck goes off alone to study at Halle. The mails carry lengthy declarations from one friend to the other. On 5 May 1792, Wackenroder writes:

Your letter gave me inexpressible pleasure. Yes, it really moved me to tears . . . See, I am utterly delighted that you love me so much . . . If I have any value in your eyes, to what do I owe it save to yourself? To you! To you I owe all that I am, everything. What would have become of me had I never known you? O Tieck, be proud of making a man happy forever by your friendship, so proud am I to be esteemed sufficiently by you for you to be my friend . . . It will soon be midnight . . . I am going to bed. Believe that it is an utter delight to me to write to you. Happy the day that I end with thoughts of you! A thought that will not leave me even while I sleep. Dream of me too . . . It has just struck midnight. Good night. Tieck, hasten to me, and let me press the most ardent kiss upon your lips. Good night, heaven be with you. Good night . . . See, is it not a fine thing that I have gone to bed thinking of you and that it is thinking of you that I rose this morning . . . Yes, dear Tieck, we must see each other again at Michaelmas . . . Oh! the memory of our walks in the Tiergarten is for me too the holiest of all things. You may readily imagine my state of mind when I go there now. Every path, every tree reminds me of you. At each step I think of you, I long to take your arm, and I feel that there is something which is always lacking. [Wackenroder, *Werke* II, 10–17; cf. ibid., 39–48.]

What despair when the distant friend is sad or sick! And what joy at the idea of reunion and a visit to Reichardt, the composer, at Gielbichenstein!

I am beside myself with joy . . . who would have thought that I was born to be so happy? I already see us in spirit walking in the romantic garden and contemplating from the cliff at Gielbichenstein the landscape spread at our feet. And then, my arm in yours, my mouth on yours, I know of nothing more sublime. [Ibid.]

This friendship for each other felt by very young men and described in their books is perhaps not solely intellectual. The fact that a great freedom of morals prevails in Berlin, where even "the Italian taste" is tolerated, whereas at Nuremberg, for instance, a journeyman confectioner is sentenced to six months' solitary confinement for indulging in it, and these young men's propensity to shock the bourgeois and to defy the ordinary conventions of society inevitably raise the question. Friedrich Schlegel defends "unnatural" love in the *Athenaeum* in a piece which his enemies use against him. There is nothing in his friends' correspondence or memoirs to suggest that they thought any the worse of him for it.

Thus, love becomes miraculous and friendship becomes love. A similar transformation fantasticates far less significant incidents of daily life.

The Miraculous and Careers

The cult of the miraculous leads young men to expect destiny to point out their careers to them, for this is one way of satisfying their appetite for the miraculous. Yet for all that, they show themselves remarkably assiduous in the conduct of their affairs and far more realistic than one would expect. These two seemingly contradictory traits are due to the comparative lack of outlets for the talents of the young, and they combine perfectly well in the case of any single individual, who will in after life complacently attribute to chance what actually was due to merit.

The ideal is that one should be so extraordinary that one is hailed on every hand as a genius; and the ease with which public opinion, increasingly imbued as it is with Romanticism, recognizes genius makes this less unlikely than might be expected.

Germany [Moser writes in 1786] is suffering from an epidemic which is causing a great deal of harm. It differs from the many diseases which are shunned like the plague inasmuch as it is a very agreeable one; it has even become fashionable and is the more pernicious in that neither age nor morals stand in the way of the pursuit of it. This is the mania for genius. . . . Etiquette has come to such a pass that every court has to have at least one *génie en titre*. At one court he enjoys the monopoly of conversation, at another he plays the part of minister; at yet others he is employed on embassies. The natural result is that in the smaller states, with their interlocking enclaves, you have a different sovereignty, a different currency, and a different genius at each posting stage. [*PAD* 1786, IV, 397–408.]

The property of genius is to overturn all the conventions. Goethe remarks on it in *Dichtung und Wahrheit*:

A new world seemed suddenly to come into being. The physician, the general, the statesman, and soon enough anyone who had any pretension to eminence in theory or practice was required to be a genius. . . . The term "genius" became the key to everything, and as it was so frequently employed, people came to believe that what it ought to denote was tolerably common. Since everyone was entitled to demand that his neighbor should be a genius, he came to think that he was one too. It was a far cry from the time when it was believed as a matter of course that "genius is the power with which man is endowed by the laws and regulations as a consequence of what he does" (Kant). Quite to the contrary: it was displayed only by transgressing the existing laws and overturning the regulations, for it openly claimed that there were no limits to its powers. So it was very easy to be a genius. . . . If someone trotted around the globe with no great notion why he was doing it or where he was going, it was called a voyage of genius. To embark on a thing which had neither sense nor utility was a stroke of genius. Enthusiastic young men, some of them truly gifted, lost themselves in the infinite. [Goethe, *Werke* XIII, 334–35.]

Genius is not acquired; it is revealed. Thus, around Christmas 1792, "for the first time, like a flash of light, the desire to be a soldier" entered Novalis' mind (*Schriften* IV, 36).

Jung-Stilling began by learning the tailor's trade. He then became a schoolmaster. Tutor to the children of Hochberg, a merchant, and harshly treated by him, he was deeply unhappy and could see no way out. But he has made a pact with God, who never abandons him. On 12 April 1792 he awoke

with the same afflictions as when he had gone to bed the night before. He went down as usual, drank his coffee, and went off to school. At nine o'clock, while seated at his desk in his dungeon, wrapped in thought and enduring the torment of his afflictions, he was suddenly conscious of a total transformation of his condition; his melancholy and his griefs had totally vanished; he experienced such a ravishment of the spirit and so deep a peace of soul that he could barely contain himself for very pleasure and happiness. On reflection, he realized that he must go. He had resolved on it without knowing it. In a trice, he rose, went up to his room, and set to pondering. Only those who have found themselves in similar circumstances can understand what tears of joy and gratitude were shed on that occasion. [*Athenaeum* I, 180–81.]

So off he went. After a long tramp and after traversing the small town of Waldstätt, he came to a wood and only then did he realize that he had not a penny and nothing to eat. He decided to put his trust in God, who furnishes food to the fledgling birds. As he thus debated within himself, he suddenly felt refreshed, and it was as if someone spoke to him and said: "Go into the town and seek a master." He at once retraced his steps and, fumbling in his pockets, discovered that, without having been aware of it, he had his scissors and thimble with him. . . . He found a master tailor, who took him on; he lived happily in his house, and then took employment as a tutor again. The wealthy Spanier treated him well and said to him one day, "Listen, tutor, I have suddenly had an idea about what you ought to do. You should study medicine." I cannot express how deeply struck Stilling was by this proposal; he could hardly keep his feet. Herr Spanier took alarm and supported him, asking: "What is wrong?" "Oh, Herr Spanier, what am I to say or think? This is my destiny. Yes, I feel it in my soul, this is the great thing which has always been hidden from me, which I have sought so long in vain." [Jung-Stilling, *Lebensgeschichte* I, 180, 182.]

This is an unusually clear-cut case of the distortion of reality into the miraculous. A rationalist ill treated by his employer would undoubtedly have decided, after due reflection, to leave him. A rationalist tailor, if starving, would have resolved to find work immediately. Jung-Stilling does not act counter to his interests in entrusting himself to inspiration. Indeed, he actually makes a rather good career for himself by moving from one occupation to another, and his fame and fortune continually increase. For after a spell as doctor, failing to make a really good living at it, he discovers a vocation as professor. Then, at the age of fifty-four, he confesses his error for the last time and perceives that God has predestined him for His own service. His material situation continually improves from job to job. He offers thanks to the Providence which has directed him, for he himself absolutely refuses to take any responsibility for his own actions.

There is a similar mixture of application and casualness in Friedrich Schlegel. A bank clerk at Leipzig, he perceives somewhat tardily that he was really destined for study. Making up for lost time by assiduous labor, he accomplishes several years' work in a few months and joins his brother Wilhelm at Göttingen University. He applies for the few posts vacant, but proves an unfortunate and clumsy applicant, and so he too ends by chafing at restraints and watching for a sign from destiny.

There is really nothing new about this appeal to destiny. The Sturm und Drang too had made it. Herder constantly repeated it in his youth: "A large part of the events of our life," he wrote in 1763 on the boat carrying him from Riga to France, "depends in reality on a throw of the dice. It was thus that I went to Riga, and thus that I entered the church; and thus that I left it. It was thus that I set out on this journey, and my journey is something of an adventure" (Bossert, *Herder*, 37).

And from Strasbourg he writes first one thing, then another: "I do not know what is to become of me, but have I ever known? Has not every resolution I have ever taken in my life been a sudden impulse which has never taken me where I meant to go?" and: "I hope that circumstances will decide. At the turning points in my life I have always entrusted myself directly to these children of Providence, as an honest augur trusts to the flight of birds" (ibid., 37, 56).

Heinse's hero Ardinghello likewise feels driven by destiny, which impels him to commit completely unreasonable acts. But, on the other hand, he has faith in his star. Premonitions and indefinable forebodings invariably fore-warn him of danger and enable him to avoid it.

When the writers of the Sturm und Drang abandon themselves to destiny, it rewards them. It is deafer to the pleas of the Romantics and leaves them too much leisure to dream of what they would do if it were to favor them. These dreams are so heady that they become an ever more insatiable need. Instead of remaining patient and beginning afresh, the Romantics abandon themselves to these dreams at the first setback and have daily recourse to them as if to a drug.

The Miraculous in Daily Life: Dramatic Surprises, Debt, Suicide

Some adventures are of too rare occurrence for anyone to be their hero very often. The schoolboy plays truant; the student enlivens the road from his parents' home to the university with a thousand detours; the merchant neglects his affairs. When tramping the countryside, Anton Reiser, Steffens, Tieck, and Wackenroder harbor secret hopes of happening upon intriguing encounters, whereas the enlightened burgher on his travels harbors the simpler fear of being held up and robbed. But these young men have nothing to lose. Nor do they encounter any very extraordinary adventures. They therefore invent their own. Their way of interpreting encounters illustrates their psychology very typically. These meetings are quite distinct from their usual life, are presented in isolation, and are described at length. Sometimes, indeed, they are so well prepared in the hero's mind and so long matured in his imagination that it is hard to decide whether they are the product of dream or reality. "This evening," Friedrich Schlegel writes on 29 December 1792, "exhausted by philosophic study, I went out to the café to play chess, and all of a sudden there was Schweinitz standing before me, frank, open, full of the most profound feelings: I love and am loved! Why would I so gladly shed my blood for him?" (Walzel, *Schlegel*, 73). Likewise, after meeting Novalis, "Destiny," he says, "has placed in my keeping a very young man with boundless possibilities" (ibid., 34). When Tieck goes to meet his betrothed, he suddenly sees on the Hamburg road the inn where their reunion is to take place. He is not unduly surprised to find that he has arrived so much sooner than he expected; he resolves to enter, and, as he cannot find a bridge, decides to leap the ditch. He falls hard enough to dispel his hallucination. When at last he meets Goethe in 1799, after "foreseeing this moment dimly as a small boy and hoping for it with an ardent longing as an adolescent . . . a violent gush of emotion overpowers him at first glance" (Koepke, *Tieck* I, 234). And in *The Travels of Franz Sternbald* Ludwig appears unexpectedly at the very moment when his friend Rodrigo has despaired of ever seeing him again (bk. 2, chap. 1).

Everyone Jung-Stilling meets on his way has virtually been placed there by Providence.

These encounters have a theatrical aspect which is also very typical. The theater has in fact become one of the most important elements in life. The young men are envious of the actors traveling in companies all over the country. Everyone, poor and rich, Anton Reiser and Wilhelm Meister, longs to tread the boards, to impersonate the heroes they admire, and to play the parts denied them in real life. The burgher at last becomes a noble, the pauper strews gold in profusion, everyone drains from the cup of true poesy the intoxicating illusions which take him into a world of faery, where all is extraordinary but eminently human, the realm of Shakespeare—Shakespeare, this generation's grand discovery, Shakespeare whose most desperately unhappy heroes are yet to be envied because their misfortune is unique.

The passion for dramatic turns which we find so hard to appreciate today is accounted for just as much by this familiarity with the stage itself as by a life of wanderings that may well lead to unexpected happenings. Contemporaries were not troubled, therefore, by the self-indulgence with which coincidence was piled upon coincidence in every novel. In *William Lovell*, for instance, characters appear, disappear, and reappear, and turn out to be identical with others who did not in the least resemble them. Ferdinand, the young page who saves Lovell's life defending him against brigands while crossing the Alps in book 1, turns out to be an old woman in book 7. The mysterious Andreas, who holds all the threads of the plot in his hands, is only unmasked at the very end of the book by a posthumous diary. We then learn, to our surprise, that he has been actuated by an undying hatred of the whole Lovell family and that it is he who has caused the father's ruin and the son's destruction.

The only tragedy Friedrich Schlegel wrote, *Alarcos*, has no less than three dramatic surprises in its second and last act. The whole plot is typical. The Infanta Solisa loves Count Alarcos, who, after plighting his troth with her, marries the gentle Clara. The traitor Alvaro, who hopes to seize the throne through her, persuades her to complain to the king, who commands his vassal to keep his sworn word. Alarcos is noble and chivalrous; he acknowledges the facts, but he loves his innocent spouse. The king advises him to have her murdered, for he is a villain at heart; he it is who has done away with Garcia, the brother of Clara, for her virtue had given him umbrage. In the very depths of the night, in his ancient castle perched on a lofty mountain, Alarcos tells all to his tender spouse. She is prepared to die to save him, heroically plunges the knife into her breast, and takes an unconscionable time dying; so he finishes her off. He is busy mourning her and listening to her mother's plaints, when Alvaro enters and announces that the infanta is dead. Later, we learn of the death of the king her father, summoned to the other world by the ghost of the pallid Clara. There is nothing for Alarcos save to follow suit, which he does with all despatch.

Most of the novels and plays of the period are full of dramatic surprises of a similar sort. Enemies suddenly discover that they are brothers; betrothed couples are prevented from marrying by a close kinship of which they were totally unaware; lovers learn to their horror that they are committing incest. The poor man awakes to find himself wealthy, the rich man is suddenly ruined, the burgher becomes a minister of state, and the princess turns out to be a whore.

The Romantics were not alone in employing what many regarded as a useful literary convention. Nicolai drops his marionettes down their trap and hauls them up again as needed. The novels are, of course, of greater importance for the themes they illustrate than for the psychology of their heroes; but if dramatic surprises had not seemed natural at the period, the enemies of the Romantics, at any rate, would not have used them.

Scores of them are to be found even in a work of the order of *Wilhelm Meister's Apprenticeship*. The book is a true portrait of the age. All the trends of the period are reflected in it. The diverse attitudes of mind, that of the rationalist and that of the man of feeling, are expressed in it, as they are in the generation of 1790, which thinks in the manner of the Aufklärung and feels in the manner of Romanticism. They are contrasted in discussions on art, which may be appreciated subjectively or objectively, on the role of chance and freewill in the destiny of man (bk. 1, chap. 16; bk. 2, chap. 2; bk. 7, chap. 7) and on the best system of education (bk. 6, *in fine*; bk. 7, chap. 9; bk. 8, chap. 3). Strolling players act *Hamlet*, a mystic writes up her diary, a group of enlightened people found a secret society. The social conflicts of the time are depicted. Nothing is omitted, and the novel preserves to the end a humane character and an equable tone which fleshes out the precision and elegance of the form with a content worthy of it. Why, then, are irrelevant intrigues mixed up with it? The critics' answer is that Goethe was in a hurry to get his book finished. But surely he could have finished it just as well without these meaningless theatrical effects? His subject is an apprenticeship to life; whether or no the harp player is Mignon's father and the Italian marquis's brother matters not in the slightest; the apprenticeship is served just as fully. The reader feels no compulsion to discover that most of the characters he has encountered during this long journey are related to one another; and since the story ends with the announcement of a second volume, Goethe's hurry to finish it cannot be the true reason. No, these very improbabilities, accumulated at the close of a study which can hardly be faulted for the least error in psychology, are additional and conclusive testimony to the spirit of the age. The miraculous appeared true at the time, for it was a matter of common observation. Reading Friedrich Schlegel's review of the book, we are struck by his care to bring out precisely those mysteries and coincidences whose artifice irritates the twentieth-century reader.

None of these traits are new. There had always been prophets and love at first sight, quack healers and dramatic surprises, gamblers, adventurers, and astrologers. But the public for them had lain mainly among the masses, or at any rate the uneducated. Even while these were rampant, the scientists were creating experimental medicine. Toward the end of the century, however, the enlightened public is no longer combating superstition, but is being seduced by it. The physicians turn away from patient observation to study the philosophy of nature, the lodges abandon universal reason and cultivate the mysteries of initiations and symbols. Formerly when good writers resorted to such theatrical devices, they were using them as an easy way of ending a play once they had said in it everything that they had had to say. Now they make the device an essential element in their work, just as the miraculous has become an essential element in living.

The cult of the unforeseen is not a good training for life, for it engenders a certain indifference to everyday realities. But everyday life does become familiar to these young men and is expressed in the form of frequent appeals for funds. All the future Romantics are short of cash. Schleiermacher is forever waiting for his father to send him the small sums essential for his living expenses, a journey, or an examination. He is perhaps the most truly penurious among them; not that the others are wealthy, but being in debt seems to be virtually a trait of character. Novalis dresses on credit at Leipzig and sometimes calls on his friends for a loan. Friedrich Schlegel perpetually complains of his poverty, yet if we scrutinize his accounts, we find that as a student he could live quite well on his means. He is short of cash and will be all his life, however much he earns. He suffers in fact from a total incapacity to regulate his expenditure in terms of his income. He cannot budget; and this is a trait common to many of the Romantics. They allege their necessities as an excuse for publishing fragments and unfinished works. But the one defect is not a direct consequence of the other; both of them are due to the mentality of the miraculous, which unconsciously drives them to count upon manna from heaven when they are destitute and upon inspiration when they feel inclined to assert their genius. Jung-Stilling, one of the neediest of them, periodically begs God, who is apparently always ready to listen to him, to send him an advance, for he himself cannot bring himself to demand payment of his salary, cannot resist buying medicines on credit for the poor, is not willing to learn the value of money. All this time he is in fact earning more and more; but he always lacks money. Yet, at critical moments there is always a client who suddenly pays his bills, a feminine admirer who sends him a draft or a friend who comes to the rescue. After his first crisis of despair, Kleist returns to literature to assuage his need for cash.

Financial embarassment sometimes leads to bouts of neurasthenia. It leads to musings on death. The fact is that, since the Sturm und Drang, death is no longer felt to be annihilation but man's liberation. By its means these dreamers aspire to find the solution of the problem of knowledge, to discover what lies behind the external world perceived by their senses. But this philosophy of death, brought into fashion by *Werther*, will not alone account for suicide; there must be other circumstances to incite these young men to resort to it as a remedy; for, after all, despite *Werther*, not one of the Sturm und Drang writers committed suicide; they had no time for it! On the other hand, many of the young Romantics dream of putting an end to themselves. Novalis desires closer spiritual reunion with Sophie by this means. Though Friedrich Schlegel does not have Werther's reasons, he wishes to quit a world in which he does not feel at home. "Why live?" he asks his brother. "You can neither reply nor can you advise me to live by trying to find any other reasons to persuade me than your own sympathy. For three years suicide has been in my daily thoughts. If I had continued on the course I was pursuing at Göttingen, it would certainly have soon brought me to suicide" (Walzel, *Schlegel*, letters of 28 July, 11 Feb. 1792). The members of the *Athenaeum* group resist the temptation, but the isolated, those who are not members of the new school, are not so resolute. Caroline von Günderode, for example, kills herself for love. Kleist, disappointed in all his hopes, puts his pistol in his mouth and fires.

Contemporaries had the impression that on the whole the number of suicides was on the increase. One chronicler, after questioning officials on the causes of fatal accidents to persons buried at the public expense, found that 239 Berliners committed suicide between 1781 and 1786, accounting for 8 percent of all deaths. More than half of these were soldiers, most of whom committed suicide during the spring maneuvers. Of these 239 deaths 136 were by drowning, 53 by hanging, 42 by shooting, and 8 cut their throat. These figures are probably not entirely reliable. For instance, the number of drownings increased because of the new fashion for bathing. There is nothing to prove that suicide was intended in every case. That there was an aggregate increase does, however, seem to be a fact. It was noted at Frankfort-on-Main and in quite small places such as Künzelsan-am-Kocherfluss, where four persons committed suicide in three years. The main cause seems to have been debt, itself due to the spread of luxury. The available contemporary statistics were too crudely recorded to enable us to come to any final conclusion either on the increase in the number of suicides or on the reasons for them. It may well be that after *Werther* more attention was given to recording them, or that many accidents were interpreted as suicides. Recent studies based on reliable statistics have sought to determine the causes of suicide. It is a striking fact that all the circumstances liable to promote suicides, as disclosed by these modern studies, were present together in Prussia at the end of the eighteenth century: a rapid growth of the population and the beginnings of the expansion of large towns; the evolution of society and the slackening of the traditional ties of family and religion which bind the discontented to it; economic crisis; and, lastly, the manic-depressive temperament resulting from the combination of social factors and some degree of pathological debility. The reasons which, conversely, habitually reduce the number of suicides appeared only after 1806: a relative equilibrium between town and country, wars, and acute political crisis.

Portrait of the Romantic as a Young Man

If we were to combine all the typical traits of the young intellectual, we could compose something like a portrait of the Romantic in isolation, a miniature on which the preceding sections would simply be a lengthy commentary. Friedrich Schlegel himself outlined a portrait of this sort in his short novel *Lucinde*. Most of his young readers recognized themselves in Friedrich as he saw himself on the eve of his arrival at Berlin and his meeting with Dorothea:

A love without object burned in him and convulsed his inner being. At the slightest provocation the flames of passion flared up; but soon—was it pride or caprice?—this passion seemed to despise its object, recoiled on itself with redoubled fury and turned against him, gnawing at the very marrow of his heart. His mind was in a continual ferment; at every instant he expected some extraordinary event to befall him. Nothing would have surprised him, his own destruction least of all. Idle and aimless, he prowled among things and men like one anxiously seeking for an object upon which his whole happiness depends. Everything attracted him, nothing held him. . . . He could not grow used to dissipation of any kind, for his disdain was equaled only by his fickleness. . . . But neither in excesses nor in fantasy nor in the wide-ranging studies into which he plunged with the voracious appetite for knowledge of a youthful enthusiasm could he discover the great happiness that his heart so impetuously demanded. Intimations of happiness were all around him; they beguiled his obstinacy and filled him with bitterness. Sociability of every kind drew him especially, and though he was often repelled by it, it was to society's distractions that he invariably returned. Women he knew not, absolutely not at all. . . . They appeared to him astonishingly alien, often incomprehensible and scarcely beings of his own species. But to the young men who in some degree resembled him he devoted an ardent love and a veritable frenzy of friendship. This, however, was still not all that he needed. It was as if he wished to embrace a whole world and could hold nothing in his grasp. And so his frustrated longing made him increasingly unsociable; he became sensual in despair of the spiritual and began to engage in the most absurd actions in defiance of his destiny. He saw the abyss opening before him plainly enough, but he decided that it was not worth his while to hold back. . . .

With a nature of this kind he was bound often to be lonely even amid the gayest and most affable society, and indeed it was precisely when no one was with him that he felt least alone. At such times he intoxicated himself with hopes and memories and deliberately let himself be led astray by his imagination. His every desire moved with measureless rapidity and without transition from the first and slightest impulsion to unfettered passion. . . . Far from trying firmly to hold the reins of self-control, he deliberately flung them aside to plunge joyfully and arrogantly into the chaos of the inner life. . . . All that he loved. . . . lay in pieces. In his imaginings his whole existence was made up of a mass of incoherent fragments. [*Lucinde*, 44–45.]

12   The Revolt
of the Intellectuals

The Romantic Generation

Between 1740 and 1780 two generations grew up under the aegis of the Aufklärung. They followed on without a break. Modes of thought changed, of course; the Aufklärung campaigned for new objectives; and there had been advances in science and technology; Kant, who assumed the leadership of the philosophical movement after 1780, differed so greatly from Lessing and Mendelssohn that the latter was unable to understand him. But they esteemed each other highly nonetheless and did not feel that they belonged to different worlds. Kant assured Mendelssohn that he could understand if he would only apply himself, and Mendelssohn excused himself on the ground of his advanced age. There is no trace here of that hostility to the Aufklärung displayed by Hamann and Tieck, for instance, who *refused* to understand.

The young men who are coming of age at the end of the century have grown up during the crisis. Without realizing it, they deviate from the paths traced out by their elders. As we have seen, they are troubled, nerve-ridden, a prey to a yearning for the "sublime," the "infinite," the "miraculous," abruptly summoned to some vocation, stricken by love at first sight as if by lightning, astounded by the most commonplace encounters. Highly educated though they are, the moral climate to which they have adjusted is not that of rationalism. They have remained too close to the people not to be infected by its passions, and the economic crisis affects them too nearly for them to listen with any patience to the wisdom of the Establishment. So that, when their turn comes to assert themselves, they no longer speak the language they were taught. The need for the miraculous seasons their discourse as it spices the masses' existence.

It makes little difference, therefore, whether they group themselves round a literary review and form a school or whether they spend their life in isolation. The best Romantic writers are precisely those who never joined the Romantic group. Neither Hölderlin, Kleist, nor Jean-Paul contributed to the *Athenaeum*. But in their biographies, letters, and works we find exactly the same tone of voice as in Friedrich Schlegel, Tieck, and Novalis.

The story of the foundation of the earlier Romantic group, first at Berlin and later at Jena, the course of the *Athenaeum* from 1799 to 1801 and the break-up of the group after its failure are too well known to need recounting in detail here. Besides, the purpose of this study is not so much to describe the characteristics of a literary movement as to detect its genesis in a general change in modes of living, feeling, and thinking. Our aim is to depict the background against which the Romantic drama was played out.

We may, however, venture to make a few comments on the ideas peculiar to the *Athenaeum*; the historian does not have the same perspectives as the literary critic, for he looks behind manifestoes of doctrines to discover the postures, passions and resentments of men. His interest lies not so much in the theoretical expositions of the earlier Romantics as in their actions, their thirst for novelty, their taste for the outrageous and their revolutionary utterances. For it is by these rather than by their ideas that they confront the Aufklärung, tolerant as it is, and oppose it, contemn it, and finally betray it.

The Romantic Ideas

The two classic works on which all modern Romantic studies have been based appeared in 1870. In his *Life of Schleiermacher*, Dilthey patiently reconstructed his hero's intellectual history. He studied and published his complete correspondence; he was familiar with all the doctrines and religious beliefs with which Schleiermacher concerned himself; the intellectual portrait is definitive. He also took the trouble to investigate all Schleiermacher's friends and acquaintances and thus to establish the similarity of the cast of mind shared by all these young men. At the same period, Haym in his *Romantic School* collected together the writers of the same generation and drew a definitive distinction between the older Romantic group (*ältere Romantik*) and the nineteenth-century school (*jüngere Romantik*). But he did not assert that all the authors he dealt with held the same ideas.

It was their successors who constructed the general theory of Romanticism and studied the artists' ideas and inspiration in depth. They concentrated on their ideas. Walzel noted the kinship between the ideas of the Romantics and those of the enlightened rationalists and distinguished them from the Sturm und Drang writers (*Deutsche Romantik*, 1923). Strich contrasted classical perfection, based on tranquil acceptance of the present, with the Romantic infinite, involving fluidity and longing (*Deutsche Klassik und Romantik*, 1928). Poetzsch rightly saw that the Romantics' politics must be related to their literature, but he studied this in the realm of ideas rather than fact (*Studien . . .*, 1926). Borries posited the principle of a connection between the ideas, the period and the people concerned, but he still thought of people only in terms of ideas, since he defined these ideas only by the way in which the Romantics held them (*Die Romantik und die Geschichte*, 1925). Carl Schmitt had a better grasp of the social problem, but did not go into it adequately; he was attracted by Malebranche and borrowed new ideological elements from him (*Politische Romantik*, 2d ed., 1925). Nadler asserted that he had established the fact that Romanticism is the contribution of the peoples of northeastern Europe to German literature; the history of German literature, according to him, is nothing but a struggle for influence between the various regions of Germany; each of them produces a literary form peculiar to itself, which is accounted for by its inhabitants' ethnic stock; intellectual currents ultimately mingle and blend, like the bloods of the Germanic tribes. This highly poetic demonstration neglects, with an insouciance which the author justifies solely by his faith in his own genius, every fact, every name, and every date at all calculated to invalidate it. A hemophilic conception of literature is thus imposed on contemporary Germany (*Literaturgeschichte* and *Berliner Romantik*, 1921).

A much longer list of theories of Romanticism could be given. Many of them are of interest, but the reason why they fail to find a central focus that provides a key to the understanding of Romanticism everywhere—not only in Germany—is that they pay too little regard to people and their daily lives. By and large, critics select the ideas exclusively from the abundant correspondence and the published intimate journals and ignore everything else. This unduly narrow approach undoubtedly accounts for the fact that no really scholarly and complete study of German society in the age of Romanticism exists as yet. This gap, really astonishing in view of the importance of this period in the history of Germany, is due to the predominance of the history of ideas. Fathered by Dilthey, it brought new life into historical studies at a time when they were concerned mainly with politics and was therefore welcome in that it helped to bring these studies closer to human history. But what the new school ought to have done was to continue to enrich the synthesis begun by Dilthey with all the elements likely to contribute to the understanding of people in their own time. Only too often, however, even in such masterly works as those of Meinecke, historians have striven to pursue an idea down the ages or to trace it through all the works of a single writer, dissect it in order to discover its source and then to trace its growth. A review of the theoreticians of the *raison d'état* from the Middle Ages onward does not adequately account for its success at certain periods and in certain countries and its failure in others. To discover that the idea of the "sublime," to which Friedrich Schlegel attached so much importance, comes from Longinus and to demonstrate the channels through which it reached the young Romantic hardly makes a contribution of the first importance to an explanation of the way in which the idea took shape.

Many of these ideas originated with contributors to the *Athenaeum*. These writers certainly formed a group and claimed that they shared a common mode of thought. Samuel and Kluckhohn, following Spenlé, have examined the religion practiced chiefly by Novalis, and Schlagdenhauffen has given us a good conspectus in French of the recent state of studies on the *Athenaeum* circle (*Frédéric Schlegel*, 1934). But to explicate these ideas as those of a group is not enough. What should first have been established was whether each of the contributors to the *Athenaeum* adopted all the ideas expressed in the review until they became a unity in his personal thinking. Reading these young men's letters, however, we come to wonder whether, despite their enthusiasm for certain concepts such as "totality," any single one of them really held the whole system of thought as we now see it. The castaways of Jena did try to think together for some weeks. They talked a great deal about the "symphilosophizing" of which Friedrich dreamed. "I have become great friends with Schelling," Novalis wrote to Wilhelm on 25 December 1797. "We 'symphilosophized' for some precious hours" (Novalis, *Schriften* IV, 217–18). But did he not mean merely that he had enjoyed a pleasant conversation; and is he thinking of the same thing as his correspondent when he speaks to Friedrich of their "symphysique" (ibid., 237–39, 240–42)? "A completely new era might perhaps begin in science and the arts," Friedrich wrote, "if symphilosophy and sympoetics became so general that it would no longer be uncommon for complementary natures to compose joint works. Often one cannot help thinking that two spirits should belong to each other like two separated halves; and that only when reunited would they be what they should"; but of course "one must not try to symphilosophize with just anyone, only with those who are equal to it" (*Jugendschriften* II, 264, 267).

Schleiermacher pricks the bladder of this "totality" when he notes on 10 June 1810 that in actual fact nothing is done in common: "Our common philophoumenoi should, I think, not merely exist side by side, but as it were be part of a single whole; otherwise there is no real symphilosophy" (Dilthey, *Leben* III, 194). If we keep only to what can be derived strictly from texts which can be dated and collated, we can find only two instances of this much-discussed community (and there is nothing new about them), namely collaboration on a single article, such as the *Dialogues on Art* and the *Fragments*, in which everyone adds his brick to a "synconstruction" (ibid., 77–78, 81), which looks singularly like a pile of rubble; and a collection of personal views which tend to be regarded as a system simply because they are expressed in the same journal, whereas each contributor in fact holds only his own view. Novalis, though growing increasingly mystical, concerns himself with chemistry and the new physics; Tieck contributes his conception of art as emotion directly felt and understood intuitively; Schleiermacher tries to create a new morality; and Wilhelm devotes himself to the sonnet but at the same time translates foreign masterpieces. But which of them is really and truly thinking of a total system compounded from the pet theory of each? Friedrich is the only one of them who espouses all these ideas in succession and engorges his vocabulary with all these technical terms. We should, then, really speak of Friedrich's philosophy, not the philosophy of the Romantics. And, even so, will this do? Friedrich in his early days really had no system. He was to acquire one—but only after he had been converted to Catholicism. In the meantime, it is barely possible by exercising some subtlety to construct an entire system with the self-contradictory fragments he puffs out in every direction like a child playing with soap bubbles. But it would be easier and fairer to place the emphasis on the contradictions rather than try doggedly to reconcile them. There is no Romantic system, in the sense that there is a philosophy of the Aufklärung, for a Romantic system could only be negative. It would set the seal on the consensus of those unwilling to continue to submit to the laws of reason. Once universal principles are repudiated, nothing is left except the special, the individual, case, which the Schlegels claim to respect. "We have many views in common," they write in the manifesto introducing the *Athenaeum*, "but we do not assume that everyone will adopt the opinions of everyone else. Everyone, therefore, is responsible for his own statements. And, above all, there is no question of sacrificing to some petty agreement the slightest spark of independence of mind, by which alone the work of a thinking writer can prosper" (*Athenaeum* I). Why stress the symphilosopy of the *Fragments* rather than the individualism of the manifesto?

In the absence of a Romantic system, there are, however, certain ideas held by one particular writer, and sometimes taken up by another as well, which can be accounted for not by simply discovering their precise source, but more truly by looking into their psychology and effect; for they are in fact these young men's common property. If they are viewed in the abstract apart from the writer who holds them, they are simply an expression of individual traits rather than universal truths, and so are valueless. "An idea," Friedrich declares, "is a concept perfected to the point of irony, an absolute synthesis of absolute antitheses, the alternation of two contradictory notions incessantly reproducing itself spontaneously" (*Jugendschriften* II, 222).

Looking at the two most important ideas sponsored chiefly by Friedrich, or, at any rate, in the system of aesthetics adopted by him, the ideas of totality and irony, we are at once struck by the way in which the Romantics' mode of thinking seems to be dominated by their conception of time. This of course differs from generation to generation. The notorious German dynamism comes to the fore at the time of the Reformation and at the beginning of the nineteenth century. It is hardly apparent in the eighteenth; time is of no interest to the generality in the age of enlightenment. Reason is ageless, and the men of the Aufklärung are not conscious of the flight of time; their universe is immutable and complete. To them progress simply means that an event falls into the place appointed to it beforehand within a rigid pattern. The Romantics, on the other hand, are very conscious of the flight of time. They feel that every moment is pregnant with possibilities, and they despair of their inability to choose among them, that is to say, to exclude whatever they would not themselves have elected. But to abstain from choosing means that the passage of time itself makes the choice for them, and this embitters their soul with a melancholy engendered by their impotence to affect the flight of time. This feeling is at the root of their philosophy. What would really suit them would be to live several lives at once. Hence their feeling for totality, which Hemsterhuys had developed into the travesty of an idea. This thirst forever unquenched, this jealously cherished feeling that body and soul must at all times be free to break off any attachment, this abhorrence of the finite—all lead to the perpetual flight toward an ever more distant and ever more exalted ideal uniting contraries in an impossible, a nonhuman and miraculous perfection and so removing the necessity for choice. "To have or not to have a system is equally fatal to the spirit," Friedrich writes, for instance. "The only solution is a decision to combine the two" (ibid., 211).

In point of time this escape looks either toward the future, with its promise of the miraculous, or toward the past, with its achievement of a golden age. So they study history in order to find in the past the happiness which so obstinately eludes them in the present. Unlike that of the Aufklärung, their history is not a moral picture of human progress or a satirical demolition of old legends; it replaces events in their period, concluding, with Herder, that "prejudice is good at its own time; it makes people happy. For it is alive, a flowing river, a growing tree, the image of time's continuity and flux" (Herder, *Werke* I, 447-513).

Perfection may possibly be attained through literature. "Romantic poetry," Friedrich writes,

is a progressive, universal poetry. Its destiny is not merely to reunite the
distinct styles of poetry and to bring together poetry, philosophy,
and rhetoric. It can and must at times commingle and at times blend
poetry with prose, inspiration with criticism, formal poetry with folk
poetry; it must make poetry vital and sociable, and life and society poetic,
it must poeticize wit and inform and saturate the modes of art with every
sort of element of pure culture. . . . It embraces everything provided only
that it is poetic, from the greatest systems of art, which themselves contain
other systems, to the sigh, the kiss breathed out by the infant as it
composes its artless lay. . . . Other literary styles are completed and can
therefore be completely analyzed. The Romantic style is still in process of
evolving; indeed, it is its essential nature that it can forever only be in
process of becoming, can never be completed. . . . No theory can exhaust
it and only "divinatory" criticism can venture to try to define its ideal. It
alone is infinite, as it alone is free; and the first law it acknowledges is
that the poet acknowledges no law other than his own arbitrary will.
[*Jugendschriften* II, 220.]

Romantic poetry, therefore, *is* not, but is *becoming*, yet is all-containing. It is a general synthesis which is perpetually in the process of formation. An idea can be defined; but how do you describe the characteristics of something that does not exist? By intuition or "divinatory" criticism it is just possible to gain some inkling of the future shape of what is in process of becoming. But since something which is becoming is constantly evolving, we distort the definition if we try "to completely analyze" its content at any given moment; for by doing so, we interrupt the movement arbitrarily and thereby disregard the second factor, which is essential. Besides, it is highly likely that we shall not concur with the next man, who may interrupt the process in a similar way at some other moment. All definitions of Romanticism and all studies of it which view it solely as a body of ideas suffer from the same basic flaw: they transpose to the realm of ideas something which is primarily a matter of feeling; they wrench the fruit from the tree and therefore dissect something dead, deprived as it is of the vital sap.

This deliberate fusion of feeling and thought is one of the most noteworthy characteristics of Romanticism and a trait peculiar to Germany at those periods of its history in which Romanticism gains the upper hand. The German does not recognize the dichotomy of thought and feeling, where one of them always ends by dominating the other and expresses its chagrin at its defeat in the form of remorse. He wants to be totally possessed and demands a total satisfaction unprocurable by critical thinking. Instead of *thinking* an idea and *feeling* an emotion, he maintains that he can simultaneously *understand* and *feel* an idea. Hence the famous distinction between reason and understanding, *Vernunft* and *Verstand*, which Friedrich borrows from Kant and takes further. He expounded it to Wilhelm in his youth and constantly reverted to it till the day of his death in the lectures he gave after his conversion to Catholicism. Reason is spirit, and God has given it to us to combine and distinguish our concepts, but it cannot enable us to know God. Understanding alone is all-penetrating and each of the soul's faculties needs its help. We "understand" an apparition, an intuition, an object when we have found its inner meaning, its special characteristic, the significance peculiar to itself. There is something very moving about the sight of Schlegel trying vainly to express *everything* in his mania for definition and still more definition, to blurt out something that will not be a mere farrago of portentous nonsense. One can see how rationalism would seem jejune to such a one-man band. But what on earth are we to say of such definitions as: "The beautiful is something which is at once charming and sublime"; "Understanding is the chemical word, the organizing genius of the mechanic spirit"; "The flash of wit is logical sensitivity" (*Jugendschriften* II, 215, 268).

Irony, for which Friedrich devises a theory, is yet another method of remaining in expectation of the miraculous. It is expressed in the *Witz*, an "explosion of wit." The imagination, "charged with electricity" by the friction of social intercourse, gives off lightning sparks (ibid., 195, 187; cf.

197, 198, 203). The flash of wit therefore enables the writer to preserve the perfect objectivity of Goethe in *Wilhelm Meister* and to keep himself independent of the external world. The faith in the miraculous can thus accommodate itself to a certain skepticism toward everything that is not of it; and it is not surprising that the early Romantics delighted in Montaigne. The idealist deals with the external world by means of irony; in other words, irony deracinates; it enables the Romantic to preserve toward a given object or possibility the basic indifference necessary to the ideal of totality. It prevents him from identifying himself with an object, from devoting himself body and soul to a single task; it universalizes him, enables him to interest himself at all times in all things, to believe that he can change direction at any moment. "A truly free and cultured man," Friedrich declares, "should be able to attune himself at will to philosophy or philology, criticism or poetry, history or rhetoric, the ancients or the moderns, wholly arbitrarily, as one tunes an instrument at any time to any note" (ibid., 191). In France, where the young still find political life absorbing, feelings of this sort make a fugitive appearance, in a flash of wit at the tail end of a letter. Chateaubriand was forever asserting that what he did was all one to him; politics, travel, literature—the Romantic is always prepared for the evangel which will summon him from his temporary occupations and thrust him on the path to glory. In Germany, where writers are unable to engage in political action, they everlastingly theorize about their souls. It is psychology again which enables us to account for Romantic irony. Hence the obscurity of some of Friedrich's alleged definitions: "The *Witz*," says he, "is logical sociability. Irony is the form of paradox, paradox is everything which is both good and great. Philosophy is the true home of irony, which might be defined as logical beauty. The *Witz* most assuredly partakes of the spirit of sociability or of fragmentary inspiration" (ibid., 184). One could amuse oneself by reconciling all these sallies to make up a theory. But what for? Friedrich harbors no illusions. He amuses himself mightily at the expense of the dismayed reader who understands not a word of his irony. In a witty article on obscurity in literature he classifies and defines for the layman coarse irony and fine or delicate irony; extrafine and dramatic irony; double irony, which is made up of two parallel lines of irony, one intended for the pit, the other for the boxes; the irony of irony; and the whole brood of little ironies engendered by it.

The third idea shared by the *Athenaeum* writers is the aesthetic theory of Tieck and Wackenroder.

The group is passionately interested in the art of the Middle Ages and the Renaissance. In the spring of 1798 all the young Romantics of Jena, except Schleiermacher who could not leave his duties at Berlin, went on a visit to Dresden. Together they discovered the Sistine Madonna, which Friedrich had failed to notice during his two years stay at Dresden with his sister, Charlotte Ernst. Wilhelm, Caroline, Friedrich, Novalis, and his friend

Steffens were celebrating the birth of the review, the first number of which was about to appear. Steffens, born at Stavanger, Norway, on 2 May 1773, was a typical example of the generation of liberals who were unable to find a place in ordinary society. An enthusiast for revolutionary ideas, self-taught, a great walker, a talented student and competent naturalist, he had met Novalis at Werner's lectures at Freiberg. Practically as soon as they arrive at Dresden, he and his companions rush to the picture gallery, and he is struck with love at first sight; the Madonna captures him heart and soul, he bursts into sobs, forgets about everything but her, and later talks of her "appearance" to him; he goes off to Jena to work on the philosophy of nature.

Is this a new aesthetic? Perhaps; but it will not do to make too much of it. It is in fact an emotion which Wackenroder expresses in the outpouring of religious sentiment in his naive and spontaneous sketches, which Tieck exaggerates a good deal less sincerely, and which Friedrich seizes on with his usual enthusiasm as raw material for theorizing. Wilhelm displays little such enthusiasm, and Schleiermacher takes no interest at all in art. The group finally adopts the position taken by Wilhelm and Caroline in their essay on painting. In the course of conversation Luise asserts the primacy of painting over the other arts. The theme of the *Dialogue* is furnished by the visit to Dresden; Gothic architecture has not yet been discovered. Luise wants to experience the emotion which springs straight from contemplation; she does not want to understand the work of art through the intelligence, but to become one with it through intuition: "I wish," she says, "to delight in beautiful appearances, to surfeit myself with them, to draw them wholly into myself. . . . Effortless enjoyment is the artist's aim. . . . I gather impressions in contemplation and silence and within me they must later be translated into words." Reinhard urges against this that a picture cannot be understood if nothing is known of its technique, its painter, and the period at which it was painted. It is not for the layman to judge it. But Luise absolutely rejects any knowledge of the history of the works with which she holds communion. Walter reconciles them by drawing a distinction between the critical judgment, which is the connoisseur's preserve, and the impression anyone is entitled to express, which may often be translated into other media, poetry or music. (*Athenaeum*, I, pt. 1, 39–51, 44–50, 86, 94–95, 143–44). In this discussion we can still trace the earlier Romantics' tendency to rehabilitate pure emotion and to abandon themselves to feeling, without, however, repudiating reason. They are farther than they think from the young man who revealed the beauty of old pictures to them. They do not follow him into the extremes of ecstatic appreciation. The Aufklärung still has a hold on them; they are as liberal as the Romantics of 1815 were to be illiberal. They do not renounce judgment, they welcome their differences from each other, and they acknowledge that Catholicism furnishes the artist with deeper sources of inspiration than the Reformation does.

The Romantic "Party"

These ideas themselves are certainly not calculated to bring down on the Romantics the hostility of their fellow writers. The most distinguished of them are sympathetic to the new review or at worst indifferent. Goethe, whom it lauds to the skies, deigns to take some interest in those who proclaim him the greatest novelist in the world and declare that "his purely poetic poetry is the completest poetry of poetry, the quintessence of poetry" (Schlegel, *Jugendschriften* II, 244). Schiller forgets his resentment of Schlegel, and Schlegel, together with all the best society of Jena, goes to Weimar to attend the opening night of *Die Piccolomini*, the first part of *Wallenstein*. Wieland preserves his customary serenity toward the newcomers; and the major literary review of the period, the *Jenaische allgemeine Literatur-Zeitung*, remains silent, much as its editors dislike innovators. When the literary quarrel breaks out, the great writers avoid taking part in it. But the substance of the debate does not lie there. Its contemporaries did not regard the earlier Romanticism as a literary school, as they did the second Romantic generation and the Sturm und Drang; and the contributors to the *Athenaeum* themselves were not regarded solely as such. It took Wilhelm's lectures, given at the very moment when the group was breaking up, the attacks by some of the Aufklärung writers, the illustration of the term Romantic by the leaders of the "Christian-Romantic populist (*Volksthümlisch*) school and religious-patriotic-neo-German art" (Heine, *Schule*) after 1815 and, lastly, the works of scholars concerned solely with the criticism of ideas to turn into an exclusively literary movement what was equally a psychological and social revolution.

Berlin society [Varnhagen wrote] was something quite different from what may be supposed from the way it developed later. . . . The tide of the French Revolution rose and swelled, and while it occupied the state externally, it had a potent influence on its internal life. Modes of thought, education, the movement of mind, trends in taste had become completely free. . . . Estate, rank, and wealth certainly kept their value in society, as they always will, but they in no way laid down the rules to which life in society conformed, for it was shaped rather by intelligence, talent, and the actions of individuals. [Varnhagen von Ense, *Denkwürdigkeiten* VIII, 342–43.]

This atmosphere gave the last disciples of the Aufklärung the impression that the time had come at length for the overthrow of an order based upon received ideas. Since the old rules no longer governed the assessment of values, why not, amid this growing anarchy, propose new rules? They have already provided for them in every sphere, but, worthy sons of the Aufklärung as they are, these inveterate intellectuals cannot conceive of a revolution without a philosophy. Recalling his major intellectual influences, Friedrich proclaims in a famous *Fragment*: "The French Revolution, Fichte's *Theory of Knowledge*, and Goethe's *Wilhelm Meister* are the greatest tendencies of the age." And Steffens, reading the first issue of the *Athenaeum*, discovers the vital current which unites science, poetry, and art; he perceives that "a new age is born" and that he belongs to it (*Was ich erlebte* IV, 80). He follows the experiments of Galvani and Ritter, reads Novalis's essays, places his hopes in the philosophy of nature, and many years later still writes with emotion: "I sometimes felt that I had suddenly been transported straight into the midst of the full ferment of a new age and that its leaders counted on me to work with them. . . . Yes, it was a time of warm and rich enthusiasm, and though I was not the only one to be stirred in those days, their sudden illumination was calculated to move more profoundly and stir more deeply a foreigner from distant lands" (ibid., 83, 87).

In their endeavor to create this new world, Schlegel's friends did not think of literature first. This world must be endowed with all it needs. It must be given a religion to replace that of a world in dissolution, a morality to take the place of the conventions on which society was based, a new political constitution. Within this paradise literary masterpieces would later come into being as a matter of course.

"A religion must be created," Friedrich wrote to Wilhelm on 7 May 1799. "The time has come to found one. This is the aim of aims and the central point. Yes, I already see the grandest birth of the new age emerging, modest as early Christianity, which no one realized would shortly tear apart the Roman Empire" (Walzel, *Schlegel*, 423).

Friedrich deals with this religion only in "fragments." But his maxims are calculated to disturb those who do not have intuition enough to divine their author's purity of heart: "There are no fully cultured men as yet, there is as yet no religion." "Religion is in most cases only a supplement to culture (*Bildung*) or even a substitute for it, and nothing is religious in the strict sense which is not a product of freedom. One can say, therefore, the freer, the more religious and the more cultured things are, the less religion."

Christianity has had its day.

It has been said of many a monarch that he would have been a very honest fellow in private life, but as a king he was no good. Might the same not be true of the Bible? Is it not a very good book, only it ought not to be a Bible?

A: You maintain that you are a Christian, what do you mean by Christianity? B: What Christians have been doing or trying to do as Christians for eighteen centuries. I hold Christianity to be a fact—but a fact hardly begun, which cannot therefore be expounded historically in a system, but can only be defined by divinatory criticism.

Every good man is unceasingly becoming more and more God. To become God, to be Man, to cultivate oneself are all expressions which have the same meaning. [*Jugendschriften* II, 300, 205, 238-39, 247; Dilthey, *Leben*, 473.]

Schleiermacher, luckily, is more intelligible and less revolutionary. He publishes his *Discourses on Religion* in 1799.

Religion originates neither in the fear of death nor in the fear of God, but corresponds to a profound need in man. It is neither a metaphysic nor a morality, but first and foremost an intuition and a feeling, the intuition whereby we can grasp the universe which eludes the grosser senses, the feeling which comes from individual experience; for in each of us the intuition of the infinite engenders humility, love toward other men, gratitude, and pity. Dogmas are not strictly part of religion; they derive from it. Religion is the miracle of the immediate rapport with the infinite and dogmas are meditations on this miracle. Nor is belief in God and personal survival necessarily part of religion; it is possible to conceive of a religion without God which would be pure contemplation of the universe; and the desire for immortality seems indeed to be irreligious, for religion assumes the existence of a desire to lose oneself in the infinite rather than to preserve one's finite being. We need to look more closely into the spirit of religion if we are to remove the burden weighing on the sense of the infinite. Like the Moravian brethren, every believer should conduct himself as a priest within communities of the devout united by the same faith.

As Novalis too elaborates a form of mysticism which can interest no one but his friends, no consensus on religion is to be found among the Romantics other than the common determination to create something new. With morality, however, it is otherwise. Here the young men try to act on their ideas—or idealize their acts. Their past drives them not merely to disdain the current morality—for this they would have been readily forgiven in that age of toleration—but to outrage it. For Friedrich, adultery is not enough; he must publish *Lucinde*. And this is something upon which the whole of the *Athenaeum* group certainly appears to agree.

The Aufklärung itself has done a great deal for women's liberation. It gives girls of good family, both noble and middle-class, the same education as boys. They are allowed to display their knowledge and express their views in public. Their literary works and their quarrels resound all through the last years of the century. Whether they amuse themselves by publishing gossip, like the wife of Unger, the publisher, or in solitude wrap themselves in meditation and study, hothouse plants, some of the most perfect incarnations of the humane idea, like the "Beautiful Soul" depicted by Goethe in book 6 of *Wilhelm Meister*, they are quite content. It is hard to see what more they could want. They would be the first to scorn the suggestion that they should demand access to public office on an equality with men. They wish for no liberation beyond freedom to think and freedom in daily living. They simply want men to cease regarding them as domestic servants devoted solely to household tasks, and they wish no longer to be segregated in their homes and their social life no longer to be confined to intercourse only with other women, but to be treated as men's companions, capable of sharing their lives with them; and this is all that the philosophers campaigning on their behalf demand for them. One of the best known of these campaigners is the *Kriegsgeheimrat* and president of the city of Königsberg in charge of organizing the administration of recently conquered Danzig, the copious and superficial publicist Theodor Gottlieb von Hippel. He writes one book on marriage and another on the civic improvement of women, urging that they should be able to lead active and intelligent lives. His opponents object that the women of the North differ from those of the South. In the South, where "the despotism of the council chamber" prevails, women "insinuate themselves through salon after salon leading from the boudoir to the council chamber; their aim is not simply to display their charms but to gain entry into politics"—much to the detriment of politics. In the North, contrary to the customs of the Greeks and Romans, women are excluded from politics. The chivalry of the Middle Ages rightly assigned them to the home. Nature has appointed strength and arduous labor to men, love and motherhood to women. (*BAZ* 1799, I, 403-12, 501-12; II, 56-66.)

Hippel's supporters reply, "in order to preserve the honor of the sex," that "women do not possess feelings and taste alone; they, like men, also have reason and the right to use it. Berlin society is an example that proves that they can conduct themselves like men" (ibid., Oct. 1799, 299-307; March/ Aug. 1800). The dispute often resolves itself basically into a debate about sexual equality. Women want to live for other things besides men's pleasure. Even the sober Krug asks in his *Philosophy of Marriage* why they should not choose their husbands. He concludes, however, rather subtly, that while it is a man's business to seek out a wife, she ought to be able to find her husband by letting him find her.

Educated women do not wait for the philosophers' permission before they liberate themselves. They emancipate themselves in the large cities such as Berlin and in the university towns, the most brilliant perhaps being Göttingen, where the English influence ensures that liberalism has a firm hold. These women are not Romantics; but they play a leading part in the foundation of the new school. They it is who welcome the young solitaries, discover their talent, and put them in touch with each other. They draw them out of their solitude. In intellectual circles they provide the transition between the Aufklärung and Romanticism. It is precisely because they are not Romantics that they enable their husbands to remain Romantics. They do not feel the need to transform everything that happens to them into something miraculous. Their emotional reactions spring from their sex, not from their mode of thought. Loving, but capable of judging everyone objectively, including their husbands and themselves, they know what they want to do, and they do it. While their husbands wait in expectation, despair or wax enthusiastic,they finish their articles for them and darn their socks. There is something at once fanatical and maternal in their devotion to the man they choose and are able to win and keep despite the social conventions. Their total self-sacrifice when they love blinds them to such a degree that they do not realize that they are worth far more than their lovers; they bear every disappointment bravely and prevent those fortunate enough to encounter them from foundering in madness, suicide, or mediocrity.

Caroline and Dorothea are of this temper.

Caroline, daughter of Michaelis, professor of oriental languages at Göttingen, had been in Mainz during the siege. A confidant of Forster, compromised by a young French officer, Dubois-Crancé, who abandoned her when pregnant, she was rescued by Wilhelm Schlegel, whom she had previously rebuffed. He married her in 1794. Energetic, intelligent, and passionate, Caroline had been of great help to Friedrich in overcoming his difficulties in sloughing off his adolescence. It was not for some time, however, that Friedrich met Dorothea Mendelssohn, his lifelong companion, in Henrietta Herz's drawing room. The philosopher's daughter was married and mother of two boys. She did not shrink from the scandal, and in 1798 went off with the man with whom she was to remain in love to the end. Whereas Caroline, disappointed in a husband as courteous as he was inadequate, left Wilhelm for the handsome Schelling, Dorothea never ceased admiring, encouraging, and finding excuses for Friedrich.

It may readily be seen, therefore, that free union appears to be the basis of the new world in Romantic thinking, as marriage had been of the old. The sober Schleiermacher himself did not hesitate to express his approval of the conduct of Caroline and Schelling, and of Dorothea, in his *Intimate Letters on Lucinde*, published in 1801. Marriage, he says, should be a complete union, physical and moral, and it should also be final. Trials and experiments may be advisable before marriage. Friedrich echoes this in his *Fragments*:

Almost all marriages are merely concubinage, irregular unions, or rather
tentative trials and distant approaches to true marriage, whose essence
. . . lies in the notion that a number of people should become one. A
sound idea; but putting it into practice seems to raise many serious
difficulties. And for that very reason, as few restraints as possible should
be placed in such matters on the arbitrary will, which certainly has some
say in the question whether one wishes to be an individual for one's own
sake or merely an integral part of a shared personality. It is hard to see
what serious objection could be raised to a *mariage à quatre*. The state,
however, by trying forcibly to maintain even failed marriages prevents the
achievement of that union which might have been promoted by further
and perhaps more successful experiments. [*Jugendschriften* II, 208–9.]

Friedrich might surely have left it at that, but there are no limits to his need to flout convention. Hardly has the sensation aroused by his adultery died down, hardly have the pamphlets launched against Dorothea by evil-minded scribblers been forgotten, when the bombshell of *Lucinde* bursts on Berlin. In order to attract attention to the new school, the leadership of which he has assumed, Friedrich surely does not have to prostitute his wife, proclaim from the housetops what no one wants to know and display such exceedingly bad taste in carrying to extremes a freedom which no one disputes.

What a feast for the scandalmongers!

If they are interested in discovering which of the new lovers has more ardor, this dialogue between Julius and Lucinde will enlighten them:

"Surely you are at least going to draw the blind first?" [Lucinde protests, stretching out in the garden pavilion.]

"Yes, it makes a much more seductive light. How beautifully this white thigh glimmers in this rosy glow. . . . Why so cold, Lucinde?"

"Dear, please move the hyacinths further away, their scent is making me drowsy."

"How firm and erect, how smooth and delicate!"

"Oh no, Julius, please leave me alone, I don't want to."

"May I not feel whether you're not eager as I am? Let me hearken to your heartbeats, let me cool my lips on the snow of your bosom! . . . Can you repulse me? I shall have my revenge. Hold me tighter, kiss for kiss! No, not kisses upon kisses, but one kiss only, one everlasting kiss. Take my whole soul and give me yours. . . . Ah, what a wonderful, admirable embrace! Are we not children? But, speak! How was it that you were at first so cool and indifferent and then, as you at length drew me to you, your expression, as you clapsed me, seemed as if it pained you, as if it hurt you to respond to my ardor? What is amiss? Do you weep? Don't hide your face! Look at me, dearest!" [*Lucinde*, 36–37.]

If the reader is curious about which of them is better made:

Julius found his youth again in Lucinde's arms. Her ample forms, her buxom charms aroused the fury of his love and his senses more fiercely than would the more charming freshness and the image of a maidenly breast. Her clasp and the warmth of her embrace were more to his taste than a young girl's; her enthusiasm and the depth of her feeling were those that a mother alone can experience.

As she leaned toward him in the enchanting dusk of a mild twilight, endlessly he caressed and flattered her swelling forms and enjoyed the sensation of the warm stream of delicate being pulsing beneath the smooth skin's soft surface. Meantime, his gaze was ravished by the hues which seemed ever to change as the shadows shifted, yet ever to remain the same, a combination of pure color in which neither the white nor the brown nor the rose ever stood alone or emerged unmingled. . . . Julius too had a male beauty, but the virility of his limbs was not expressed in swelling muscles. The forms were sleek, rather, and the limbs full and rounded, and nowhere was there any excess. In full light all the surfaces formed broad masses and the smooth shape appeared as solid and dense as marble; and in the combats of love the entire richness of his powerful body proclaimed itself all at once. [ibid., 70–71.]

If the reader is curious about their little philosophical games, he should watch them seeking "the finest situation."

It is, says Julius,

when we exchange roles, and with childish glee see which of us can imitate the other most deceptively, whether the considerate violence of the male suits you better or the attractive surrender of the female suits me. . . . But do you know that for me this sweet game has attractions quite beyond its own, beyond the pleasant fatigue of satiety or the foretaste of revenge? I see in it a wonderfully rich and significant allegory of the male and female developing and combining into the total, the unique human being. There are depths in this, and what lies deep in these depths most certainly does not erect itself as promptly as I do when I am lying beneath you. [ibid., 13.]

When Caroline received this strange and outrageous book at Jena (having herself edited the manuscript), she writes to Novalis: "If I had been his lover, it could not have been printed. But I am not condemning it. There are things which one can neither condemn nor blame nor wish they did not exist nor alter, and what Friedrich does is usually something of that sort" (Wienecke, *Caroline und Dorothea*, 132–33). Most of Friedrich's other friends are dismayed and annoyed. Poor Dorothea! "As to *Lucinde*," she writes to Schleiermacher on 8 April 1799,

yes, as to *Lucinde*, I often turn hot and cold at heart at the idea that the most intimate things have to be brought out into the open like this. Everything I held so sacred, so secret, prostituted henceforth to the gaze of all the curious, all those who hate us. He vainly tries to recover his spirits by telling himself that they are all even more audacious than he. But it is not this audacity that terrifies me. . . . And, then again, I think: all these evil things will pass away with my life, and life with them, and one should not prize things that pass away to the point of preventing the publication of a work which will last eternally. Yes, it will only be later, when all these accessory details have vanished, that the world will judge the book aright. . . . Already the Cat (Frau Unger) cannot forbear to gossip about this affair with all those whom her envenomed breath can reach. People are already talking about the impropriety of *Lucinde*, and she is behind it; she has complained that no young man could set the type of such a text. [Meisner and Schmidt, *Briefe*, 8–9.]

To indignant ladies Friedrich replies: "Prudery is a pretension to innocence without innocence. Women will be compelled to remain prudes so long as men are sentimental, stupid and malicious enough to demand of them eternal innocence and lack of culture. For only innocence can ennoble the lack of culture" (*Jugendschriften* II, 208-9).

He protests against the tyranny of morals in social life: "Why should there not be immoral people, just as there are people who are neither poets nor philosophers? Only anti-poets and the unjust (*Unrechtliche*) should not be tolerated" (ibid., 248).

As for morals, mostly they are based on nothing but the fear of what people will say: "In the fashionable lists of all the possible principles of morality, why is ridicule never included? Can it be because this principle is of universal validity only in practice?" (ibid., 257). Moreover, "morality without the sense of paradox is vulgar" (ibid., 297).

Friedrich, who so often contemplated killing himself in his youth, defends suicide:

It is usually only a fact, seldom an act. In the former case, the suicide is always in the wrong, like a child trying to emancipate himself. But if it is an act, what is at issue cannot be justice, but only the occasion. For the arbitrary will depends on that alone, and the arbitrary will must decide everything which cannot be determined by regular laws, such as the time and place of death; one is entitled to make his own decision on everything which does not prevent other men from exercising their arbitrary will, for to eliminate that would entail eliminating his own will. It is never wrong to die deliberately, but it is often unseemly to live long. [Ibid., 205.]

Lastly, in politics Friedrich seems to be disappointed by the Revolution, but he does not become so skeptical that he does not retain his former predilection for the Republic. "Perhaps no nation deserves freedom," he says, "but that is a matter for the *forum dei*." In any event, "only a state in which the minority despotically governing the majority has at any rate a republican constitution merits the name of an aristocracy" (ibid., 212, 213). It was only later, with the second Romantic generation, that a theory of the state appeared, based on the ideas of Novalis and Adam Müller.

The taste for flouting convention and the hatred of convention are sometimes expressed so naïvely as to become ridiculous. Are the bombastic terms which Friedrich employs in his *Portrait of Little Wilhelmine, the Model Baby* really necessary?

And see, it is not strange that little Wilhelmine finds an inexpressible pleasure in gesticulating, lying on her back, legs in air, with not a care for clothes or the world's censure. If Wilhelmine behaves like this, what should I not dare, I who am, by God, a man and need no more be delicate than the most delicate of feminine beings? Oh, enviable freedom from convention! And you, too, dear friend, cast far from you all the remnants of false shame, as I have often torn off your hampering clothes and flung them in splendid disarray all around you! [*Lucinde*, 14-16.]

Thus, to a soured middle-class woman like Frau Unger the new group's morality would seem to recommend a yielding to every instinct as well as indecency, adultery and suicide; and its politics are the defence of Revolution. All the Romantics have proclaimed themselves republicans and have expressed their admiration for the French Revolution. No one is aware that Novalis is writing an essay on Europe from which the conservative politics of the second Romantic generation can be deduced. The new world, therefore, has a religion opposed to the Christian churches, is a rebel society opposed to the existing society, with a system of ethics which is at the very least amoral, and a revolutionary politics.

This is why their contemporaries used a term to designate the earlier Romantics which is not normally used except in literary quarrels. They spoke of a "party," and they quite correctly saw that the Romantics represented something other than merely a literary style. In its first number the review *Eumonia* observed that a distinction must be drawn between the principles and the works of the Romantics. The latter do not correspond to the former, which had given grounds for hopes of something quite different. Similarly, Tieck in his memoirs deplores the fact that the Romantics were not understood; he defends them against the accusation of founding a party, a conspiracy. "But," he says, "people waxed indignant at the spirit of the *Athenaeum* and *Lucinde* because they did not understand them. Everyone at that time concurred in repudiating all authority. But when novelists claim to put these ideas into practice, they are accused of praising each other and despising everyone else" (Tieck, *Nachgelassene Schriften* II, 40).

This plea is not altogether convincing because it does not allow for the revolutionaries' provocative tone. "They believe that they alone are in possession of everything that is true and beautiful," *Eumonia* notes. "They call anyone who does not adopt their opinions weak and incapable, and they ingenuously pass themselves off as the lawgivers of the nation. Their party wishes to dominate the spirit of the age, but if we look at their works, we are obliged to assign to them a mainly negative role in the solution of literary problems" (I, 5-6).

Their arrogance was bound to provoke a reaction. But they could only be attacked by pamphlet. Their work as revolutionaries remained theoretical, and their morality, insofar as they put it into practice, could only be discredited by satire. So the quarrel had necessarily to take a literary turn; it had to take the form of a polemic. In this strange dispute the greatest writers, "the nation's best minds," as *Eumonia* put it, stand between the two parties and refuse to take a position because they are well aware that literature is not really the fundamental issue in dispute. But it is all too evident that at the literary level, the only level at which combat is possible, the Romantics are defeated in advance. Their best writers are second-rate and dissipate their energies in their preoccupation with revolution in general and their scientific, metaphysical, and synthetic research. If they had not enjoyed the protection of Goethe, they would have foundered in ridicule. The esteem shown them by the most popular and most revered writer in the Germanies hampered their enemies.

The attack is launched from Berlin, and it is a personal attack. It is the private life of the philo-Semite Romantics that Frau Unger mocks in her witty and malicious letters published in the *Jahrbücher* for 1798. The most biting criticisms thereafter are always concerned with morals or the new social life; for instance, the "Diogenes Lantern" with which Dorothea is shown seeking a husband, or the witty paraphrase of the *Fragments* reproduced in the *Archiv der Zeit* are very typical of the way the battle was waged:

The Schlegel brothers' *Athenaeum* is a sign of the times. These gentlemen possess the gift of thinking the unthinkable, feeling what is only thinkable, having an intuition of what is only tangible and seizing tangibly what can only be grasped by intuition. The Fragment stating that "the French Revolution, Fichte's *Theory of Knowledge*, and Goethe's *Wilhelm Meister* are the greatest tendencies of the age" is the gospel which these gentlemen proclaim to their contemporaries, holding a knife to their throat.... You should read the *Fragments* after dinner or in bed before you go to sleep. As I did so, my imagination brought to mind another fragment I had read in the *Golden Book of Mount Kynast* in Silesia. It was written by Heinrich Adlo Gesaner, alias Meltzer, doctor of universal wisdom. I am drawing up a comparative table of the two fragments to show how close to each other "fine wits who smile only on each other, what a splendid thing" often come.

Athenaeum	*Golden Book of Mount Kynast*
The French Revolution	The highest mountains:
Fichte's Theory of Knowledge	the Schneekoppe
Goethe's *Meister*	the Kynast
are the greatest tendencies	are destroyed by the all-
of the age	devouring tooth of time

Some Fragments are even more remarkable. For instance, that on page iii of the first issue: "The love of gods and heroes for the celebrated boys and youths of antiquity and the direction of this love toward the male sex may be regarded as merely poetic by people who do not acknowledge that beauty is the sole law and the true morality of the feelings, that a free man has the right to be unnatural, and that certain things erroneous in themselves may be necessary, and therefore also good, at a particular period and at a particular stage of development! [*BAZ* 1799, I, 44–47.]

This article is very typical in that it sums up all the issues in the polemic. The Romantics are vulnerable by the obscurity of their philosophy, the audacity of their morality, and their intolerable pretentiousness.

Similar criticisms appear repeatedly in other pamphlets; "enlightened" publicists like Kotzebue and Merkel weigh in gleefully. In the *Hyperboreal Ass* the former depicts a student returning home and expressing himself solely in maxims borrowed from the *Fragments*. To his mother he declares that he no longer believes in Christ and that he himself is God; to his uncle the baron he expounds his philosophy, which boils down to the assertion of his own genius; to his betrothed he speaks of love, *mariage à quatre*, and the right to be immoral; and when the local prince turns up, he is greeted with praise for the the French Revolution. The prince sends him to a lunatic asylum, and bestows the hand of his betrothed, together with a good post as head forester, on the philosopher's brother, the solid Hans. In the *Cameleon*, produced by Heck at Berlin in 1800, a famished writer (Tieck) is shown insinuating himself into society and passing round a pornographic novel; Lorraine (Lucinde) expresses herself in maxims as mystical as they are incomprehensible; the writer ruins an honest publisher (Nicolai) and founds a clique of friends who praise each other in an outrageously arrogant review.

In his Voltairean *Letters to a Lady* on the most recent literary publications, Merkel, an "enlightened" critic who came from Lithuania to Berlin, where he was taken up by the circle around the young Nicolai, attacks first Tieck, "the licensed humorist of the Schlegel clique" (*Briefe* I, 17–32), and then *Lucinde*. In one of his letters he draws up a sort of general bill of indictment of the Romantics. It is here that the dispute emerges at its most literary. Of what does he accuse them? In the first place, of self-complacency; he borrows the title of a play by Falk produced at Jena, *The Gigantomachia*, and shows the Romantic Titans mounting to the assault of Olympus under the protection of Goethe; Goethe cannot prevent their defeat, but is welcomed by the Gods after the Titans have been put to flight. Two very gifted young men entered the world of letters, Merkel says. Good work might have been expected of them, and people praised them by way of encouraging them. The incense went to their head.

One of them began a translation of Shakespeare, which is rightly considered something of a success; but he was the only person who forgot that it was not he, but the English poet, who had written the admirable things which he printed. He himself would hardly have understood them if Wieland and Eschenberg had not translated them before him.

He assumed an exceedingly lofty tone, which raised a smile here and there. The other wrote a sort of combination of aesthetics and adventure story on Hellenism. People now laughed aloud, but still never failed to do justice to the two brothers' talents.

Instead of working patiently, they were all for quick success. As they could not acquire enthusiastic panegyrists, they tried at least to make enemies who would cause a stir. They therefore used their contributions to various reviews to pronounce in haughty tones severe criticism of the best writers in Germany. They humbly revered only one poet, but he was a minister of state as well.

The inspired clique of *Lucinde* manufacturers does not merely scold; it spits on men who would not be honored even if it paid them the most respectful homage. Conscious of their mediocrity, these people raise a clamor against everything superior to them, in the hopes of thereby bringing them down to their own level.... They hope to earn immortality of a sort by their attacks on immortal names, just as the rags with which precious metals are wiped finally acquire a species of patina; this is not because any of the metal has rubbed off on them, only the dirt. [*Briefe* I, 113–26.]

These gentlemen are guilty of "forming a party and playing at dictators of letters," of insolently disparaging authors superior to them in order to give themselves an appearance of superiority; *item*, of pronouncing platitudes "in sonorous, contorted, and incomprehensible sentences" in order to win over women and half-wits; *item*, of holding that genius consists in preaching obscenities; *item*, of announcing, in order to give themselves importance, a new poetic era that will last a thousand years (Dilthey, *Leben*, iii, iv, 85–88).

All this puerile nonsense was reproduced in the *Muses' Almanac for 1802*, published by Wilhelm Schlegel and Tieck.

At this period the group had dispersed; Friedrich and Dorothea were living in Paris, and Wilhelm no longer had a platform in the *Allgemeine Literatur-Zeitung*, in which he had published most of his reviews; he had had to resign in November 1799 because Schütz, the editor, and most of his Kantian and enlightened contributors had refused to continue to support the *Athenaeum* against its enemies.

This dispute, arbitrated by Goethe, was the most serious in which the Romantic group was involved, since the Jena review had the largest circulation and carried the most authority in literary circles. It became envenomed, however, mainly by personal quarrels, often aroused by the clumsy and starchy behavior of Wilhelm Schlegel and Schelling. (For a useful summary of the incident, see Schlagdenhauffen, *Schlegel*, 314–27.)

The Romantics reply to the attacks, but they have only their own review and the *Archiv der Zeit*, which is sympathetic to them. They are more vulnerable than their enemies and they have no means of staging plays against them. Tieck, however, publishes his *Last Judgment* in 1801. He depicts Nicolai sentenced, despite his culture, to listen for two thousand years to the devils' jests without uttering a word.

But soon after, loud cries were heard, and the devils came back again; they demanded that the cultured Nicolai should be received in heaven or elsewhere, for he was really too crashing a bore; he was absolutely incapable of keeping silent, so that no devil could bear to stay near him, and even the fire of hell threatened to go out. Infinite Mercy was moved by these complaints, and Nicolai was sentenced to go to Nowhere, a valley lying between life and death, which, as a matter of fact, does not exist at all. He went off with pleasure, saying that he would be very comfortable there, for it was his former home; leaving it had been what had most grieved him at the resurrection. [*Poetisches Journal* 1800, 236–37.]

It is mainly a personal battle that Tieck wages in his attacks, however, and his main target is invariably Nicolai. The Romantics hardly defend themselves as a body; they only form a party when viewed from outside. Basically they are divided and have nothing in common except their negations; and this does not make for a victorious offensive. Other things being equal, they are rather like the French Girondins, who also formed a group to which it would be wrong to attribute any very well-defined doctrine. A certain shared background, a similar experience of life and society, a revolutionary social ideal, and a large personal ambition are what give them the family likeness which misleads strangers.

The silence of major writers like Goethe, Wieland, Herder, Kant, and Fichte save the Romantics from irremediable defeat, but what these great minds respect them for cannot be their talent or their literary worth.

Rereading all the evidence in the case, we seek in vain for any real ideological ground in this quarrel, for all its violence. The issues are neither that of the Ancients versus the Moderns nor the crusade against French influences nor a campaign for spontaneous feeling, as they had been in the Sturm und Drang. Any new positions that can be identified in the group's writings are really an anticipation of what their authors were to be saying much later or of the tenets of the second Romantic generation. The return to the Middle Ages, Gothic art, Catholicism, and national patriotism are not topical issues between 1797 and 1800; they are not the substance of the dispute between the Romantics and their enemies. The movement's importance does not lie in the theories formulated by it, for, depending on who is saying what at what moment, all of them were asserted at one moment and repudiated at the next. No, the interest of the first Romantic generation lies in the fact that it brings together the typical representatives of a transitional generation hesitating between two different modes of thought.

This hesitation originates in the social crisis, which casts doubt on the validity of the promises of the Aufklärung. The young dissidents, assembled by chance in the most tolerant and most liberal capital in Europe, believe that the time has come to transform a society which has proved incapable of absorbing them.

They proclaim a new era; they are to be its founders, and, worthy ideologues and disciples of the Aufklärung that they are, they harness themselves to a gigantic task which they try to perform simultaneously in thought and action. But just because they have to create something new, they are unable to think rationally and are constrained to adumbrate doctrines so vague as hardly to be likely to commend themselves to men of action.

Their own past exercises so great an influence upon them that their own action cannot amount to more than a refusal to accommodate themselves to the conventions of a society which would in fact be only too pleased to overlook their indiscretions. Instead of settling down and enjoying a modest, but probably stable, position in the second rank of literature and in journalism, they set themselves up for imitation and urge their contemporaries, "holding the knife to their throat," to espouse their idiosyncracies and share their errors.

As they are no geniuses, however much they assert that they are, they cover themselves with ridicule, and their new era, which was to last a thousand years, closes with the collapse of the *Athenaeum* after little more than two years. They would not deserve the attention of posterity had they not been representative of a whole generation and if the new modes of thinking and feeling expressed in their writings were not everywhere to be found. More than a literary movement, the first generation of Romantics in Germany is a moral and psychological phenomenon largely caused by the social crisis.

In Prussia the young are consciously revolutionaries, however, and not from the political standpoint alone, on ground where opposition to the existing regime is common, but even more so in the realm of morals; their aim is to destroy the old world in order to create a new. They form a party of the revolution, which they envisage in the broadest sense. All the institutions of the society into which they were born—religion, morals, politics, and art—must disappear. Those who brandish the threat and brave the scandal are few; their union is fragile; it was formed by chance and is shattered by fate. There would be no good reason to trouble about their bombast if it did not express what most young people of their age were confusedly thinking and feeling. The universality of this revolutionary urge rightly alarms the Establishment, the friends of the Aufklärung, as they too now become conscious of the spread of this new mode of thinking; for, if it spreads further, it means the destruction of everything they revere. Thus, behind the literary quarrel, in which the great writers, many of them attracted by some aspects of the new program, refuse to take part, we can trace the lineaments of the struggle between the Aufklärung and those who wish to free it from its conventions and the hypocrisy it practices of necessity, like any organized group.

The fact that this mode of thinking is shared by almost everyone also provides some justification for the argument that Romanticism was one of the most profound movements ever to affect Germany. It can be likened to some extent to the Reformation, but only if it is realized that, as between the two cultures, the Aufklärung is just as important; for its modes of thought, too, prevailed almost universally for nearly a century. Romanticism itselt would have remained only a superficial movement had it not had to tackle a deeply rooted system and to transform the mentality of a whole people. The Aufklärung is to Romanticism what the Catholic Church is to Protestantism. Aufklärung and Catholicism each represent an almost perfect culture, eroded and finally brought down by a progressive transformation of modes of living, modes of thinking, and political systems.

13   The Aufklarung: Conclusions

Ever since Vidal de Lablache posited the notion of modes of living, geographers have ceased merely to "describe the earth." To define modes of living they establish the relation between man and his environment and compare men with environments. The terms of these relations are always variable. Geography has become a fluid science. It adapts itself to the areas it studies and evolves with them.

Modes of thought in history are somewhat similar to modes of living. They evolve unceasingly, and to grasp them entails being willing to accompany them for the stretch of time between joining them on their way and leaving them as they proceed further. They vary like modes of living. If we were to try to classify them, we would first investigate what might be termed a natural mentality, which is found in children and primitive peoples. It is characterized by a confused sense of mystery, a vague awareness of the limits of knowledge and a marked tendency to let things slide. It introduces the supernatural into every aspect of life and prefers the miraculous to other less convenient explanations.

Other types of mentality are the result of a more conscious conformation of the personality; where they are rational, they assume the existence of a proper education, by which children are taught to think. The Aufklärung in Prussia is of this sort. Rationalism continues to subsist there only by dint of constant effort; the whole system reposes on teaching and constant indoctrination. The intense interest in teaching methods always displayed by elites had never been stronger. It scarcely declined thereafter, and it can be said that from the eighteenth century onward every succeeding regime in Germany maintained itself to the extent that its educational performance assured it the support of youth.

When youth emancipated itself, when the Aufklärung crumbled, the "natural" mentality latent in the popular masses reappeared and reasserted itself.

Economic conditions undoubtedly helped to weaken the Aufklärung. If the Aufklärung had adapted itself to overpopulation and the technological revolution, both agricultural and industrial, it is unlikely that Romanticism would have gained the upper hand. But in order to discover the precise extent to which the effect of economic and moral factors ensured its success, we would need many more and much fuller studies than we have. The ways in which the Romantic mentality manifested itself in daily life are not those of the Romanticism of the philosophers and poets. It is expressed in manners and customs, in everyday incidents, in the collective reactions of social groups and in forms which necessarily differ from those reflected in slowly matured literary works and works of art. To define it in far more general terms than those in which it is defined by individuals among the cultured elite means reducing the members of a society at a given moment to their common psychological denominator.

The Romantic mentality is the mentality of the miraculous. During its domination it tinges everything, people and things alike, with its patina of the miraculous. We must be careful, therefore, not to select any object haphazard and call it typically Romantic simply because it wears this patina. It is, for instance, just as simple-minded to call the French Revolution Romantic as it is to describe the Restoration as Romantic. Each of them appears Romantic or Rationalist depending on the viewer's position in time. The earlier Romanticism assumed a revolutionary guise in Prussia, the later can be classified farther to the Right. In reality, Romanticism is a mode of thinking based on the mentality of the miraculous; it is reflected in politics by a preference for revolution over evolution, by the practice of conspiracy, the coup d'état and political assassination. But in the party struggle with the Right, just as much as with the Left, these methods are out of date. Nor does the growth of nationalism seem to be closely tied to any particular mode of thinking. The Napoleonic oppression provoked national reactions in Romantic Germany, but the Aufklärung would have put up a similar resistance. Looking at individuals, we find in Germany leading Romantics, like Schelling, among those who ignored nationalist passion to the end.

The question how far Romanticism is specifically German is, however, legitimate. A people's character changes in the course of the centuries; there is no such thing as an eternal Germany, any more than there is an eternal France. But it does seem as though some nations do display a certain predilection for one mode of thought rather than another throughout their history. France certainly seems to incline more to rationalism; Germany seems on the whole to be prone to Romanticism. It is true, though, that political and economic crises occur more frequently in Germany than elsewhere. The Wars of Religion, the Napoleonic conquest, National Socialism—it is striking that such crises are invariably accompanied by a recrudescence of Romanticism.

Appendix: The Struggle for the Emancipation of the Jews in Prussia

The Status of the Jews

It is toward the end of the eighteenth century that the Jewish question begins to come to the fore in Prussia. Until then the Jews lived isolated from the rest of the population, dressing in a costume peculiar to themselves, wearing beards, speaking a dialect of their own, and practicing mysterious customs, about which sinister tales were current.

This state of affairs changed under Frederick the Great. The Seven Years War, in particular, though very onerous to the mass of the Jews, over-burdened as they were with taxes and imposts, brought considerable wealth to a few Jewish families. The Ephraims of Berlin founded their fortune on the minting of the royal currency; the Itzigs, the Gumpertzes, and the Meyers were army contractors. The king compelled their sons to establish factories on pain of forfeiting their inheritance of their fathers' "privileges." All Berlin Jews who were doing at all well abandoned the traditional petty retail trade to set up as manufacturers or wholesalers. They soon rose above the verminous masses of the ghetto to form an aristocracy of Jews who adopted a middle-class style of life. Similar groups prospered in other towns, especially in the recently conquered provinces of Silesia and Poland.

Since the prevailing philosophy was that of the Enlightenment, the Jews found friends, too, among the educated Christians. They encouraged their sons to study, they spread Kant's doctrines, brought to Berlin by many immigrants from Königsberg, and some of them became outstanding personalities in medicine, philosophy, and literature.

In the philosophers' opinion, there could be no justification for a system involving discrimination. The "enlightened" Jews did not feel that they differed in any way from their Christian brothers—or competitors—and sought to abolish this system. We shall not here narrate the full history of their emancipation, but, without adding any new factual material, we shall comb the periodicals and newspapers for the reflection of the debates which

249

exercised public opinion. This will lead us to pose questions which have been barely examined by historians as yet. Was the Jews' condition as harsh and the government's hostility to them as inveterate as the philosophers claimed? Were not the Jews themselves partly responsible for their own plight, and did the enlightened minority which tried to relieve them from it deserve the contempt with which the orthodox, both Jewish and Christian, often heaped upon them?

The Constitution of 1750 established several different classes of Jews. The most favored were the "holders of general privileges," who might live with their families in any town in the kingdom in which Jews were permitted to settle, travel freely without paying the humiliating poll tax, and engage, "like Christians," in wholesale trade, banking, and the liberal professions. The class of "Jews entitled to ordinary protection" held a royal warrant specifying the place at which they must reside, the trade in which they might engage, and the number of their relatives entitled to similar advantages. Only one son, as a rule, inherited his father's "privileges," for the intention was to prevent the Jews from multiplying; but after 1763, owing to the state's penury, wealthy Jews might also have a second son privileged. The class of "Jews entitled to extraordinary protection" enjoyed the personal right for life to live in a specified place and engage in a specified trade there, but they might not set up on their own and mostly lived on work put out by the holder of a "general" or an "ordinary" privilege. The class of "tolerated Jews"—the children of "protected" Jews who had not inherited their privileges, and immigrants accepted by the Jewish community—formed a mass of poverty-stricken Jews who might neither marry nor engage in any trade. Peddlers, junk merchants, or usurers, most of them spoke no German and were dependent on the Jewish community, which was solely responsible for them to the authorities.

All Jewish affairs were centralized in a General Directorate, staffed by officials from the Ministries of the Interior and Finance, which negotiated with the communities. The largest community was that at Berlin, represented by its Council of Elders (*Älteste* and *Oberälteste*), from which the two *Oberlandesälteste* were drawn, selected by the king and responsible for representing all the communities in the kingdom to the government. The communities were jointly and severally liable for the payment of taxes and for all offences committed by their members; the elders were responsible for supervising their fellow Jews, for denouncing in due time any of them who was going bankrupt or was planning a robbery or receiving stolen goods, for giving their opinion on any Jew applying for a "privilege," and for authorizing the residence of foreign Jews waiting outside the one gate by which they might enter a town.

The Jews were excluded from all posts in the civil service, from teaching, surgery, and the guild trades. They might not open a barber's shop nor sell alcoholic beverages or fish, bread, meat, or dairy produce. They had access only to the petty trades not grouped in corporations, such as lens grinding, diamond cutting, seal engraving, gold and silver embroidery, painting, and the like, and to manufacturing, encouraged by the government and very often linked with wholesale trade and banking. Most of them were in fact confined to petty trading in secondhand articles and to peddling.

The Jews were liable to special taxes, varying from place to place; a complete list would be tedious. The main tax was the *Schutzgeld*, paid in acknowledgment of the protection afforded them by the state. The Berlin community, some 3,500 strong, paid 25,000 thalers (about 95,000 gold francs); besides the *Rekrutengeld* (4,800 thalers), since Jews were not liable to military service, the tax for the "confirmation of elders," elected every three months (150 thalers), and part of the *Silberlieferung*, a compulsory yearly delivery of 12,000 silver marks to the Royal Mint by the Jews in the hereditary provinces and Silesia, calculated at 12 thalers to the mark, though the real rate varied from 13.22 to 14 thalers. Except for the *Silberlieferung*, these taxes were not levied on the recently conquered provinces of Silesia, East Prussia, and East Friesland. Jews were also taxed individually on every sort of occasion; if they married, 14 thalers (in Berlin); if their bride was under twenty-five, 15 thalers; if a fire broke out in a town, the community paid 15 thalers, because the Jews were not permitted to help extinguish it. Most of the complaints related to the tax on porcelains and the poll tax. One of Frederick II's most original ideas was to use his Jews to promote the export of the Royal Factory porcelain. To obtain the recognition of their children's entitlement to inherit their fathers' privileges they had to buy 300 thalers' worth of porcelain for each child. For an application to acquire a house—an exceptional favor, since the number of houses owned by Jews was supposed to be limited to forty at Berlin and to five in each provincial town in which Jews could freely reside—and for any advantage of any sort, the price was invariably 300 thalers' worth of porcelain. It would not have been so bad if any choice had been allowed; but the factory automatically delivered one-third of the order in porcelain of the best quality, one-third of medium quality, and one-third in current articles. It was not easy to get rid of the goods afterwards. The average loss was 50 percent, even if a purchaser could be found, for they were liable to be landed with rejects, such as the twenty lifesize monkeys dumped on the illustrious Mendelssohn.

The poll tax (*Leibzoll, Geleitzoll*) was humiliating rather than onerous. Levied at the town gate, it was akin to the excise duty on cattle. The "privileged" were exempt from it only in their own province and had always to present their "privilege" to foul-mouthed petty officials amid the jeers of the bystanders. The tax was levied throughout the empire, to the great indignation of the philosophers, who carried on an incessant campaign against it. They invoked the Rights of Man and commended Joseph II's abolition of it by his great edict of 1782; and they frequently referred to French condemnation of it. Thus, in 1785, Wieland published in his *Merkur* the "Letters of a Traveler in Germany"; one letter described how a diligence is caught in a storm; a passenger who had only been able to find a seat on the box was shivering, when a passenger called to him and offered him a cloak.

I turn round and, think of it, the voice and cloak belong to a Jew! I must confess, my dear K, that this incident surprised me. One is not ordinarily accustomed to such politeness from Jews. But he was from Paris, as I afterwards learned, traveling on business to Frankfort-on-Oder. He was a reasonable and enlightened person, and engaged in most agreeable converse with all his fellow travelers!

I was therefore particularly embarrassed when the postmaster at the next station addressed him peremptorily in the coarsest terms. In Prussian territory the poor Jews still customarily pay duty like cattle. Wherever there is a customs shield they have to pay for a certificate, to be presented at the next customs post, so that they cannot pass any post. As soon as we arrived at the posting stage, the postmaster fell on the Jew, shouting, "Where's your certificate, Jew?" This impolite apostrophe shocked us, but the Jew smiled and produced his papers. "You scoundrel," the postmaster suddenly roared out, "you have passed a customs post!" It turned out in the end that it was a place we had not yet reached, but the Jew, who would have been soundly thrashed if the other passengers had not intervened, nevertheless paid the fine. And this happened a few leagues from Berlin, where the Rights of Man are on every tongue. In France less is written in favor of the Jews, but they are better treated. In France the levying of any tax on the movement of Jews, whether French or foreign travelers, is prohibited by royal edict, for the days when people were treated like cattle are over. [*TM* 1785, I, 235.]

Frederick William II abolished the tax on Prussian Jews traveling from one province to another and on foreign Jews going to the Frankfort Fair (31 December 1787 and 4 July 1788). But most of the German princes failed to follow suit, and foreign Jews in Prussia itself continued to pay the poll tax. Disputes arose in consequence. In 1801 some French Jews were arrested at Mainz and the tax was levied on them. "But," the *National-Zeitung der Teutschen* explained, "since under the present constitution no distinction is made any longer in France between Jews and Christians, Jollivet, the prefect of Mainz, ordered that both should be treated on an equal footing in all respects and wrote to all the French ministers at the German courts to urge them to take up this matter" (30 July 1801). It was undoubtedly representations by the minister Beurnonville that prompted the king of Prussia to summon the meeting of the censorship commission which put an end to the joint and several liability of the communities, and thereafter issued passports to foreign Jews.

The exertions of two enlightened Jews, Israel Jacobson of Brunswick and Wolff Breidenbach, finally won over most of the German princes. Wealthy and highly placed at court—the former as *Hofagent* managed the duke's properties—they negotiated with the princes successively, and in many cases redeemed the poll taxes with funds collected for the purpose.

Since they were subject to special laws, the Jews were of course strictly ostracized by society; they were rather feared in the countryside and much despised in the towns, and people only resorted to them in secret. They were extremely useful, however, in petty trade. The history of the peddler has not yet been studied thoroughly; but it was the itinerant merchants, whose circumstances progressively deteriorated over the years, who were the most constant culture bearers in the countryside. The almanacs distributed by them ensured the success first of the Reformation and then of the Aufklärung. The stories they told, the groceries, laces, watches, and other novelties they distributed, gradually changed styles of life and modes of thought. The Jews seem to have sold chiefly secondhand clothes, cattle, and luxury articles bought cheap or smuggled. They sold Prussian or Saxon porcelains all over Germany and thus introduced the rococo style. For six thousand crowns Salomon Liebmann brought in, on 31 January 1771, the costly clocks of the Royal Hungarian Factory which Huguenin, the royal inspector, had had to get rid of for lack of a market. But the real reason why he could not find buyers was the vast quantity of cheaper foreign clocks smuggled in by other Jews.

Usury was the chief reproach leveled against the Jews. They were accused of pushing their way into students' lodgings and selling them all sorts of things on credit. Or else they lent money to landowners, who sank further and further into debt, until the day came when their creditor forced them to redeem the pledge. But this they could do only with the connivance of Christian capitalists. Forster learned at Göttingen that "people of whom you would hardly believe it are said to have become implicated in the shameful practices of the Jews, and the Hanover police is accused of reprehensible connivance in these affairs." (Forster, *Briefwechsel* II, 75). In Silesia, where everyone quoted cases of landowners ruined by Jewish usurers who had lent them quite small sums, "undeniable facts could also be cited" to the opposite effect: "Jews have lost large sums in the bankruptcies of landowners; in certain flagrant cases of usury the Jew is simply a tool in the hands of a rich landowner, who remains behind the scenes, advances him the capital and fraternally shares the loot with his tool" (*Zeitung für die elegante Welt*, 2 Apr. 1803, col. 316).

Enriched by petty trade, the Jews were able to become bankers or manufacturers, for the king of Prussia was trying to develop banking and industry, nonexistent as yet in his states. Good society, however, continued to look askance at them. They were not received anywhere at the beginning of the century, and the middle class of burghers still regarded them with distrust and hostility at the time of the French Revolution. But by then, just as the authorities turned a blind eye to the enforcement of the laws, so the cream of society was quite prepared to forget the origins of the few Jews who had become Germanized. Enlightened persons would not accept anti-Semitic any more than aristocratic prejudice. At Brückenau spa, near Fulda, for example, burghers and nobles consorted in the prince's gardens. "There was even a Jew," a visitor noted in 1782, "who actually gave himself out as a Christian; he had taken another name, but everyone knew he was a Jew. No one, however, gave any indication of knowing, and they addressed him politely, even amicably, for the Jew was an amiable and well-bred person" (*DM* 1782, I, 337). More and more Jews took Christian surnames. "Circumcised themselves and, indeed, accustomed to circumcise ducats of a Christian stamp and halo, this people has long circumcised its tribal names as well. They turn and twist them till they come to bear some resemblance to the name of Christians. Thus, the Jew Brendel calls himself Brenna, Judith becomes Jettchen, and so on" (*Jahrb.* 1800, II, 17).

Reading the laws on the Jews and the comments by the authorities on the margins of their petitions, listening to their complaints and their friends' pleas on their behalf, we often get the impression that there was real persecution. But the whole question lies in the extent to which the laws were applied. Were they not mitigated by the liberal spirit of the age? The documents are silent on the whole, but individual instances culled from the press make it necessary to raise the question.

By law, any Christian who was converted to Judaism was liable to the death penalty. But when Councillor Josef Steblitzki, of Nikolai in Upper Silesia, was circumcised in 1786 and took the name Josef Abraham, the government failed to prosecute him.

By law, Jews were not permitted to become citizens, but the government itself granted the Itzig family a decree of Prussian naturalization on 2 May 1791. It is a single exception, admittedly, but one from which it may be inferred that the authorities were not on the face of it hostile to Judaism.

By law, the Jews were not permitted to own more than forty houses in Berlin. How many did they actually own? Frederick II was certainly the sovereign who was most ill-disposed toward the Jews, as is attested by every document and every historian. We rather begin to wonder, therefore, when we learn that, despite all restrictions, the number of Jews residing in Breslau rose between 1744 and 1786 from 300 to 3,000. When we think of the society that thronged the salons of Henrietta Herz and Rahel Levin in Berlin, where the cream of the aristocracy mingled with Jewish intellectuals and financiers, we are forced to the conclusion that the authorities were inclined to turn a blind eye to breaches of the law.

In 1790 the Royal War and Domains Chamber prepared a new reglement for the Jews of Silesia and took a drastic step that caused a sensation. It expelled all the nonprivileged Jews from Breslau and authorized only 160 families to reside there. A harsh enough decree; but all contemporary documents stress what large families the Jews had; the 160 families authorized therefore represented a figure far higher than the 300 persons legally admitted in 1740. May not the Royal Domains Chamber, then, have made a selection and perhaps have in fact acted with moderation? Did it in fact enforce its decree to the full? Its harshness appears in a rather singular light when we read in a newspaper of 1806: "Some 3,000 Jews (the families have a great many children) live here" (*NZT*, 12 June 1808, 496–97). Had the 160 families left in the town proliferated so greatly in thirteen years as to produce the same number of persons as those originally expelled? Or had those expelled returned? But what evidence is there that they ever left or that the Chamber had not simply meant to take powers to expel without further formalities only the undesirable?

The fact is that the Chamber was always notoriously liberal. Under von Hoym, an official who may have been vain, shifty, and mediocre, but claimed to be enlightened and sought to prove it, it invariably defended the Jews against their detractors. The reglement of 1790 embodied some remarkable innovations; it authorized the Jews to engage in all forms of commerce, to practice any and all trades and to found schools in which their children were to be taught German.

The reglement for the new Polish provinces issued in 1797 was equally liberal. Von Hoym, the governor of Silesia, had been ordered to organize these provinces. It is true that many of the restrictions were maintained, but Jews might henceforth engage in all trades, acquire and farm land and those who did their military service were exempted from the *Schutzgeld*. Schools were founded with Jewish teachers able to teach German and Polish, who were paid by the state. In these regions the Jews were definitely more advanced intellectually than the peasant masses. There may possibly have been some plan to make them agents for Germanizing the region. The Prussian administration apparently sought to secure their loyalty wherever possible; the reglements concerning them were undoubtedly based on the Austrian grand edict of 1782. The Silesian Jews had probably to be induced to forget that they once had been Austrians and might well become Austrian again.

In considering the opposition to Jewish emancipation their own responsibility for it should not be overlooked. While the people were on the whole hostile to the reforms, the authorities were consistently favorable to them. But the apathy of most of the Jews and their repugnance to the slightest change certainly seemed to show that their enemies were in the right. In many cases it was the Jews themselves who refused to renounce their traditional customs and assimilate with their "fellow citizens." We shall see below how vehemently they fought against change clearly designed to be humanitarian in such matters as burial rites. The mass of the Jews differed profoundly from the "enlightened" minority; the major problem was the education of this obstinately conservative mass, which found progress of any sort repugnant. The anti-Semites did not believe that "improvement" was possible; but if they had encountered Jews as advanced as they were to become a century later, almost all of them would have yielded, for these enemies of the Aufklärung thought and debated after the manner of the Aufklärung. They accepted the philosophers' principles, but doubted whether they could possibly be applied.

The Aufklärung and the Jews: Moses Mendelssohn

The philosophy of the Aufklärung was engendered by theology. On the morrow of the wars of religion and the Thirty Years' War it teaches reason and tolerance; first Leibniz, then Wolff and Baumgarten, and thirdly the English philosopher Locke, who had a considerable influence in Prussia, lay more stress on basic principles than on rites. These principles—the existence of God, the immortality of the soul, the judgment of man—are common to all religions. The human personality, moreover, is increasingly respected. Faith, if it is to be sincere, must spring from the believer's inmost experience; to impose it would be to profane religion, for a man can be compelled only to engage in external practices, and these, in the absence of true faith, are nothing but blasphemy.

The enlightened religion resulting from the meditation of a reasonable being therefore leads to tolerance toward those who have not yet arrived at similar conclusions. This tolerance readily prevails in Prussia because the government desires it. The Hohenzollerns enriched their states by granting asylum to those expelled by their neighbors by reason of the principle *cujus regio ejus religio*. They can enjoy and increase this prosperity only if they maintain strict religious neutrality, and so they encourage a clergy which preaches the somewhat abstract religion of the Aufklärung.

From religion, reason proceeds to morals. Usage and custom are often a form of intolerance. Just as people will not permit their neighbors to practice a religion different from their own, so they claim the right to impose their own mode of living upon them. This form of social imposition is equally repugnant to individual reason, which therefore sets to criticizing each and every custom, reforming styles of living and challenging political constitutions, creating the notion of "prejudice," with which it ruthlessly undermines age-old traditions. Prejudice is the equivalent in the temporal sphere of superstition in the religious—practicing rites which have no ground in reason. Absurd fashions, the alleged superiority conferred by a title of nobility, the claim to absolute power—all these are prejudices.

This is the intellectual climate in which the Jews begin to emerge from their age-old isolation. After stagnating in their oriental traditions for centuries, they now encounter true friends among Christians who pride themselves on their lack of anti-Semitic prejudice. But the Jews themselves have to make a tremendous effort to free themselves from the even greater mass of prejudices which confine and stifle them in their ghettoes.

There can be no doubt that here they were helped by economic circumstances, of which, however, little is yet known. Prussia is not an isolated instance. Throughout Europe in the eighteenth century the Jews entered the social and political life of nations from which they had been virtually excluded. May not the moment when the ghettoes opened up in all countries have been one of the neglected milestones of history, and is it not possible that the ensuing technological progress could not have been so rapid and so widespread without the Jews? In the absence of sufficient and sufficiently reliable studies the question is arguable rather than historical. What precisely was it that stimulated Jewish mobility? The Enlightenment, that is to say, an intellectual current flowing in from outside, appealed to them in the eighteenth century, whereas in the past they had always been practically impervious to Western ideas. Yet there is little difference in essence between the Humanism of the sixteenth century, in its early days and in its highest expression, and the Enlightenment. In the countries into which the Enlightenment barely penetrates, in eastern Europe, the ghettoes continue to exist. But this philosophy is inseparable from the economic, social, and even demographic, changes accompanying it. Isolation becomes increasingly difficult in an overpopulated and urbanized Europe. To some extent the Christians went out to meet the Jews and invite them in, though they were not wholly aware of what they were doing. As soon as they became less despised and less rigorously segregated, Jewish peddlers, manufacturers, and doctors set themselves to learn German. Their natural curiosity and their love of gain led them to draw closer to the Christians as soon as they realized that they could do so. One of the first to embark upon this escape from the Hebraic world was Moses Mendelssohn. He was not the only one; but, owing to his place in the intellectual history of Germany, his example is the one most frequently cited and the one about whom most is known. The part he played in the tragicomedy of Jewish emancipation calls for a brief account of his life.

Besides teaching school, Mendel copied the scriptures and kept the registers of births, marriages, and deaths for the Jewish community at Dessau. He taught children to read. The most gifted then went on to the classes given by Rabbi Hirschel Fraenkel, who took them as far as disputations on the Talmud. These German Jews, who lived self-centered lives, spoke Yiddish at home and learned Hebrew at school, were almost always taught by Polish rabbis. The fact that their religious leaders came from countries in which the assimilation of Jews with Christians was to be the slowest—in which, indeed, it was not yet completed even in the twentieth century—undoubtedly accounts for the resistance to it long displayed by the mass of the Jews. The enlightened minority which later coalesced round Mendelssohn was to come into continual conflict with the rabbis. The rabbis do not understand what this group is trying to do; they condemn social secularization because they refuse to make any distinction between religion and the political and administrative organization of the Jewish communities; they reject an emancipation which seems to them to spell the death of Jewry.

The child Moses, born on 6 September 1729, has nothing to complain of in his early teachers. He attends his father's classes from the age of three; at five he knows the whole Bible by heart, and Fraenkel is loud in praise of his assiduity. Introduced, with some of his schoolfellows, to the philosophy of Maimonides, he dreams of devoting his life to study. He has a serious illness at the age of ten, which leaves him humpbacked, with a stammer which he was never able to master, and with his whole character hampered by an almost morbid shyness. After his confirmation at the age of thirteen he has to earn his living, and his parents wish him to take up peddling. Fraenkel has become Chief Rabbi of Berlin and is no longer there to give advice. The formidably ugly and formidably intelligent lad perseveres. He wishes to return to his master and continue his studies. His parents give way in the end, and he goes off to Berlin. At the age of fourteen he arrives at the Rosenthal Gate, the only one open to Jews, alone and penniless. He finds Fraenkel, who takes him in but cannot afford to feed him. He invites him to dinner on holidays and gets him lodged in an attic in the house of the devout Bamberger. For seven years Moses lives in utter poverty. He earns little as a copy clerk; often he has only a slice of bread to last him all day.

He endures bodily hunger by feasting his mind. Soon Fraenkel has nothing more to teach him. Zamosc, a Pole, teaches him mathematics from a Hebrew translation of Euclid. Kisch, a doctor, teaches him Latin and introduces him to the works of Locke, the master of the enlightened. Gumpertz encourages him to learn German. Nothing could be more fraught with difficulty at that time; the rabbis expelled Bleichroder, Moses's accomplice, from Berlin for appearing in public with a German book under his arm. The young Abraham Posner causes a scandal at about the same time by shaving his beard, and his father compels him to grow it again. Moses, however, manages to learn to read and write the Christians' language. He plunges into the works of Leibniz and Wolff and translations of Shaftesbury. In 1750 a nouveau riche silk manufacturer, Bernhard, employs him as tutor to his children. In 1754 he takes him on to keep his books and to see to his correspondence, and later takes him into partnership. Secure henceforth against need, even wealthy enough to have a house and garden, to marry the daughter of Abraham Gugenheim of Hamburg in 1762 and to bring up six children, Moses is able to afford Greek lessons and to write his first essays.

In 1754, too, when he at last achieves security, he makes the acquaintance of his best and most faithful friend. Lessing, just graduated from the university, is exactly the same age as Mendelssohn. They meet over a game of chess. Lessing guides Moses's reading, puts him in touch with Nicolai, and gets his earliest work published, the *Philosophical Dialogues*. Had it not been for the Aufklärung, Lessing might well have been unwilling to play chess with a Jew. Or, at any rate—for there are free spirits in every age—he would not have been able to introduce him into the circle of enlightened Germans received by Nicolai in his garden; meetings between individuals would have been possible, but not an introduction into society.

Mendelssohn's philosophical work, though noteworthy for its impeccable style, shows little originality. The book which makes him famous is a translation of the *Phaidon* (1767) with a commentary which is a digest of all the principles of enlightened religion. Moses is totally unable to understand the *Critique of Pure Reason* when it is published in 1782. He apologizes to Kant on the grounds that he is too old to be able to take in a new philosophy. Nor is he interested in the beginnings of Romanticism. He is not one of the great solitaries like Spinoza and he produces nothing new. This is at once his limitation and his merit, for he could not otherwise have played the part he did in the struggle for Jewish emancipation. He is and remains essentially a perfect representative of the Aufklärung. His most intelligent contemporaries are compelled to approve of him. Whatever he does and whatever he says, they are forced to admit that he could not have done or said anything else. His reasoning is correct, his tolerance surpasses that of the Christians, his private life is a model of virtue, his honesty is wholly above suspicion. His mere existence, even though he does nothing in particular, refutes all the arguments against the Jews. If it is contended that the Jews will never speak German correctly, you have only to read Moses Mendelssohn. If it is contended that they will never give up cheating, usury, and smuggling, you have only to look at Mendelssohn and Bernhard. If it is contended that they will forever refuse to abandon rites and customs incompatible with modern life, you have only to visit the Mendelssohns in the Jewish quarter, and you will find that they live exactly like any German middle-class family.

Mendelssohn does not, in fact, serve only as an example. He is also drawn to set out his ideas on religion on several occasions. Actually, he does not like to talk about it, for his position at Berlin as a merely "tolerated" Jew dictates a certain degree of reserve. In 1769, however, Lavater, a clergyman at Zürich, translates into German a book published in France entitled *The Evidences of Christianity*. Its author, Bonnet, defends religion against the deists and atheists. Lavater, an acquaintance and good friend of Mendelssohn's, dedicates his translation to him and challenges him either to refute the work or be converted.

Moses is extremely embarrassed at a public challenge like this, but he is bound to reply. He can do this only with very great caution, for a polemic against Christianity is likely to get him into trouble. He has obtained the "general privilege" only in 1763, through a Frenchman, the marquis d'Argens, a friend of Frederick II, who framed a rather elegant petition on his behalf: "A Philosopher who is not much of a Catholic begs a Philosopher who is not much of a Protestant to award the Privilege to a Philosopher who is not much of a Jew. There is too much Philosophy in all this for Reason not to be on the side of the request" (Kayserling, *Mendelssohn* I, 51). The nobility with which Mendelssohn reproaches Lavater for not writing to him privately, as was fitting between friends, the simplicity with which he asserts his conviction of the truth of his religion, and the skill of his argumentation bring everyone over to his side.

As a true disciple of the Aufklärung, he acknowledges in the first place that the Jewish religion is no more devoid of prejudices, abuses, and human accretions to the divine principles than any other. But that is no reason to condemn its basic precepts. Instead of expounding these precepts and engaging in a comparison or controversy with Christianity, he points out that his religion has always deprecated conversions. It allows its devotees to esteem and love persons of other creeds. Persons professing another religon should not be accused of prejudice. True, in the eyes of the believer they are in error, but they are not harming anyone else. Their prejudice is distinguished from other prejudices which have an immediate practical impact and which should be combated by the Aufklärung. And, in any event, when it comes down to first principles, are the revealed religions so very different? Bonnet's arguments for Christianity could equally well be invoked by any other creed.

This reply earns Mendelssohn apologies from Lavater and a letter from Bonnet, also disapproving of Lavater's dedication. In the ensuing correspondence Mendelssohn notes that Bonnet passes over in silence everything that other religions or reason alone must censure in Catholicism. He is not, therefore, wholly convincing. These comments are expanded in a letter to the Heir Apparent of Brunswick, who asks him "why he accepts historical evidence for the Old Testament but not for the New." Moses replies that the Old Testament does not offend his reason; if it did, he would reject it as he rejects the New. He cannot accept the mystery of the Trinity, or that God became man, or, above all, that the suffering, death, and humiliation of the Second Person of the Divinity are necessary for the satisfaction of the First. He does not believe, either, in eternal damnation, the inheritance of sin, the responsibility of the innocent for the fault of others, or in Satan. He blames Christians for their intolerance of Jews.

His attitude toward his fellow Jews is equally clear-cut. He asserts his attachment to their religion and even to its rites. Though he personally makes a distinction between rites and dogma and though, for example, he refrains from fasting because of his ill health and does not compel his children to fast, he is on the whole in favor of the Jewish rites. Not that they are wholly consonant with reason, but, as he explains to Homburg, an enlightened Jew from Prague and tutor to his children,

even if they have lost their meaning as written formulas or symbolic language, they are still needed as a bond of union. And it seems to me that, in accordance with the plan of Providence, this union should last so long as polytheism, anthropomorphism, and religious usurpation dominate the terrestrial sphere. So long as these frames of mind which are harmful to reason are united, true deists should accept a sort of bond between them. And what should this bond be? Principles and opinions? That would give us articles of faith, symbols, formulas—in short, reason in fetters. Rites, therefore, are preferable, significant rites, or in other words, ceremonies. Our efforts should be directed in one direction only, toward eliminating inveterate abuses and giving the ceremonies an authentic and genuine meaning and to making the Scriptures, which have become incomprehensible owing to the hypocrisy and cunning of priests, once again legible and intelligible. [Kayserling, *Mendelssohn* V, 669.]

This passage, written in 1782 when Mendelssohn was fighting on two fronts, against the anti-Semites on the one hand and the orthodox Jews on the other, in the struggle for Jewish emancipation, goes very far. The philosopher demonstrates the danger of the rationalist, necessarily isolated and individualistic as he must be, being crushed by the organized churches. He therefore justifies the creation of the species of "rationalist churches" which were coming together spontaneously in the form of the reading clubs and Freemasonry, and he agrees with the Lessing of the *Dialogues between Ernst and Falk*. While he is prepared to dilute his religion so far as to reduce it to no more than a form of deism, Moses fears the isolation of those who seem to have reached a similar degree of abstraction and moral elevation. He makes his meaning clearer in March 1784 in expressing his concern at a certain type of Christian tolerance which barely conceals the hope of converting the enlightened Jews: the prerequisite for "saving the small group which wishes neither to convert nor to be converted," he says, "is ceremonies" (ibid., 677).

He has no interest in the mass of orthodox Jews. He feels that they will never understand him; apprehensive of the struggle, he hesitates for a long time before embarking upon it. In 1764 he writes to his friend Abbt, who has been discussing the future of the nonenlightened Jews: "I wash my hands of them" (ibid., 525), and to a noble submitting a project for political reform to him in 1770, he replies:

The great difficulty in the way of your project seems to me the character of my nation. It is not prepared for any great enterprise.
    The pressure under which we have been living for so many centuries has

deprived our spirits of all "vigor." It is not our fault; but we cannot deny that the natural aspiration toward freedom has lost all its impetus among us. We have acquired a monkish virtue, which expresses itself not in action but in prayer and resignation.

I do not even expect from my nation, scattered as it is, the urge toward unity without which the best-conceived project is doomed to failure.

It seems to me, too, that the enterprise requires inordinate sums of money. I do not believe, knowing as I do that my nation's wealth consists in credit rather than in real capital, that it would be capable of collecting such sums; and this would be true even if the aspiration toward freedom exercised a great influence on it and the love of shining metal a very slight one. [Ibid., 493-94.]

Thus, Mendelssohn is attached to his religion because its monotheism is more abstract than that of the Christian creeds and closer than they to philosophical deism. He adheres to its rites—which he purges—because a bond between the faithful is still needed. He feels that this bond is useful because the faithful are likely to be unable to continue to follow the light of reason. Reason means granting civic equality to the Jews. Enlightened Christians recognize this, but the masses, whether Jewish or Christian, are equally hard to convince. The former regard it simply as profanation and blasphemy, the latter as a trick whereby the Jews can become assimilated with the Christians without being converted and can exploit them by insinuating themselves into their special preserves.

This mistrust is explicable, for the "small group" is expanding rapidly. Initially, it comprised hardly more than Mendelssohn himself and the disciples to whom he himself was teaching German at his house on Saturday afternoons, like the Friedländers and the Ben Davids, genuine intellectuals. Later, they are joined by the nouveaux riches of the Thirty Years' War, the Cohens, the Ephraims and the Meyers, persons not as self-effacing as their rather shady financial background should have warranted. Toward the end of his life, Moses, who is still sometimes jeered at and stoned by children on the streets, sees the sons of these nouveaux riches lording it in Berlin. Though he admires their success, he feels that they have outstripped him. These emancipated Jews do not wish to form a group bound together by non-Jewish ceremonies. They do not consider a liberalized Judaism the highest form of the Aufklärung, and they definitely prefer something less rarefied. Their ideal ideal is to merge their identity with everyone who is prepared to accept them. The "small group" dissolves in the enlightened society.

Moses in his old age is not alone in observing this change. "The present generation of Berlin Jews constitutes a real turning point in contemporary history," the author of *Letters on Berlin* writes in the *Berliner Monatsschrift* in 1784, wondering how "a people oppressed for thousands of years both by its unfortunate situation and by our fault, their millions fallen almost below the human condition, has yet found the endurance, strength, and skill to recover" (*BM,* Dec. 1784, 561).

Thirteen years later, Böttiger observes in his travel notes:

The high level of culture of the Berlin Jews is indisputably attested by the existence of the two families mentioned above [the Hertzes and Itzigs]; it has made such progress in the past twenty years that, in the circles in Berlin in which one seeks some converse more elevated than the mere pleasures of gaming or the table, there is practically none in which the Jews do not play a considerable part. So much so, indeed, that so far as good taste and the prevailing philosophy (of Kant) are concerned, the Christians feed their meager little lamp with the oil supplied by the Jewish brokers of enlightenment. The Jewish beauties were once capable only of giving the cue for finery and fashion at Berlin, but in the past few years they have also taken upon themselves to act as arbiters of the most intricate points of logic, the wittiest play, the most versatile actor, and the best poetry. [Böttiger, *Zustände* II, 102.]

This state of affairs dates from the Seven Years' War. The nouveaux riches Jews have acquired an education; their children have become free-thinkers. This necessarily entails some dangers. All too many of these spoiled young people display an unpleasing arrogance and are cocksure in and out of season about matters of which they know nothing. Too many pseudo-intellectuals have only a veneer of education, which is mocked by the satirists Ienisch and Rekker in the *Archiv der Zeit*:

Just look at those two little Jewesses! Do listen to them chattering Kantian philosophy in one another's ear! Dear sister, isn't it marvelous to be a philosopher! . . . Look how the Christian folk throng to church, little knowing that God is only an Idea. . . . Since I have begun teaching my little Rachel the Cacagoric Amberatif, you've no idea how charming and obedient she has become! And how she loves it! She's sure to grow up a great Kantian too, for it is weaning her from sensuality so well that she's becoming positively transcendental! [1796, I, 516–34.]

The real anti-Semites too will be able to exploit this vein of mockery; but every thinking person pays a tribute to the Jews. We cannot leaf through any periodical, travel journal, or correspondence without finding some mention of them. It is the Jews who frequent the reading clubs, in which innovations are judged; they it is who fill the theaters, and it is Jews whom nobles, bored stiff by etiquette, meet in the only drawing-rooms in which people are never bored. In their salons you do not have to sit in solemn silence playing cards until the tea is brought in; you do not have to take your appointed place in the circle of chairs where well-bred ladies pay their tribute to good manners and boredom. At Henrietta Herz's or in Rahel's small coterie the gentlemen are not segregated from the ladies, as they are in middle-class drawing rooms; the guests are not invariably the same; people stroll about chatting;

you can listen to Ben David, the Kantian philosopher and president of the "Tuesday Society" pontificate; you can congratulate Dr. Herz on his illuminating lectures on physiology at the "Wednesday Society," with which Fessler hopes to compete with his "Friday Society"; you can enjoy the pleasure of talking French with Mirabeau or English or Italian with other notable foreigners; they laud Goethe to the skies, but they also encourage the young Romantics; they smile on suitors without giving them to hope and without casting a stone at anyone who does otherwise. They commend the graces of the poet discovered by the *Deutsches Museum*, Ephraim Moses Kuh, yet another Jew, who can turn a madrigal as elegantly as any French fop. His poems, it is true, have not worn well, but their German is as stylistically correct as their wit is heavily Teutonic.

> *Der Säufer*
> Dass man nicht mehr trinken müsse
> Wenn man voll ist, welch' ein Wahn!
> Brüder, seht den Ozean
> Der ist voll bis eben an,
> Und doch trinkt er tausend Flüsse! [*DM* 1784, I, 43.]

[The drinker: That one should not go one drinking when one is full, what nonsense! Brothers, regard the ocean; it is full to the brim, yet drinks a thousand rivers.]

> *To Lisette*
> Lisette, sei nicht allzuwild,
> Geh nicht so rasch zum Wald hinein;
> Kupido fliegt, als Bienelein,
> In diesem schönen Lindenheim
> Und was der Lose stickt, das schwillt. [*DM* 1784, II, 203.]

[Lisette, don't be too rash, don't rush to the wood so fast; Cupid flies like a little bee in this pretty lime copse, and where this rogue stings, it swells.]

In these salons, in which Prince Ludwig-Ferdinand demonstratively flirts with the delicate Rahel, how could the company have failed to be shocked by the legal disabilities imposed upon their hosts? How could it fail to have wished that these Jews at least, whom they could not but admire and esteem, should no longer be constantly humiliated? And even if it is held that the condition of the majority of Jews was still inconsistent with total assimilation, surely they were bound to think that a distinction should be drawn between enlightened Jews, so close to Christians, and other Jews?

Too little attention has been paid hitherto to these minority groups formed by cultivated Jews in the midst of hostile communities. It is true that the documentation is scanty in many cases and that the statutes of any legal associations which may have been formed by enlightened Jews have not come to light to any great extent. In Berlin the salons are a sufficient form of association. Reading clubs, or more private associations, such as the League of Virtue, of which Henrietta Herz, Mendelssohn's two daughters, the

Humboldt brothers, and Charles de Laroche are members, flourish. Elsewhere the publication of an enlightened review, some of it written in Hebrew, provides a link among the educated Jews, such as the *Sammler* (*Ha Meassef*) at Königsberg and the *Sulamith* at Dessau, a review for the promotion of culture and humanism among the Jewish nation. Conflict with the orthodox Jews is also often a bond between the enlightened Jews; we shall find this the case at Breslau and at a number of towns in Silesia. Usually it was the need for education that prompted individuals to come together.

The sole means of acquiring citizenship was obviously to become assimilated as speedily as possible. Jews who had encountered innumerable difficulties in acquiring an education by themselves and in secret, learning German in despite of their fellow Jews, wished to spare their children the troubles they themselves had suffered. There could be no hope, however, of reforming the Jewish schools. They had, therefore, inevitably to establish new ones. Bankers and wealthy merchants supplied the funds; and pedagogy was in any case the order of the day. The earliest and most successful experiment was tried in Berlin itself. Taking up an original project suggested by his father-in-law, Daniel Itzig, David Friedländer in 1778 founded the Free Jewish School together with Isaac Daniel Itzig, his brother-in-law. Both Jewish and Christian teachers taught German, French, Hebrew, arithmetic and bookkeeping, calligraphy, and drawing. Most of the pupils held scholarships; they paid what they could when they could. Five or six hundred pupils were taught in ten years and spread the new spirit. A similar experiment was conducted at Dessau. The struggle against the orthodox Jews, who did their utmost to prevent the Free School from flourishing or to take it over, was often very violent; and here too we find the authorities backing the enlightened groups. The school at Breslau, after long struggles, finally fell into the hands of the orthodox Jews. At Frankfort-on-Main twelve families founded a school:

When it became clear that they wished not only to bring up their children for Jerusalem, but also to ensure that they would be able to associate on decent terms with their fellow citizens and contemporaries, when they then sought teachers of German, French, writing, and arithmetic and applied to a Christian clergyman, Dr. Hufnagel, the worthy dean of the Frankfort ministry, to put them in touch with a competent person for that purpose, the ancient orthodoxy could not remain silent in face of this spirit of religious indifference and innovation; and the Chief Rabbi laid a "school repugnant to religion" under his interdict. The worthy Hufnagel had to alert the town council, which finally ordered the "Jewish Pope" to withdraw his decree. [*BM* 1795, I, 520–35.]

The governments intervene almost everywhere in Germany to compel the Jews to acquire an education. They make it a condition for the relief of their disabilities and their acquisition of further privileges that they should be able to read and write German. They require the accounts to be kept henceforth in German. Under an edict of 20 December 1784, the Jews at Fulda are compelled to open a school at which their children are to learn German. The Rabbi for State Schools holds public examinations; those failing to attend are fined, and private tutors are prohibited. On 18 October 1786 the Jews at Darmstadt are given one year to learn German; all their contracts must thereafter be drawn in that language. At Mainz the Jews are treated better, and in 1784 they obtain permission to attend classes at Christian schools, where they set up special divinity classes for their children, for they are too scattered through the Elector's states to open private schools of their own.

Most of these schools are too poor to use the new teaching methods, but a wealthy Jew, Jacobson, is able to afford an experiment; he buys a parcel of land at Seesen in 1801 and on it builds an institution for ten poor Jewish children. The school owns fields, a coach house, a stable, and a barn. The boarders are dressed in light blue uniforms; they have their dormitory, dining hall, and synagogue, attend classes for four hours daily, two in Hebrew and two in German, and are also taught farming or a trade. The institute flourishes, adds further outbuildings in 1805, and is opened to foreigners, who pay 100 to 150 thalers a year. The number of Jewish pupils rises from ten to thirty-five and, later, to sixty.

The enlightened Jews thus come into conflict with their fellow Jews, and the conflict intensifies day by day. When newspapers and periodicals begin publicly to air the question of assimilation, attitudes cannot but harden. The change has been so rapid that even the most intelligent of the older generation find it hard to follow. Those who opened the way, with Mendelssohn, to the new ideas, while affirming the sincerity of their belief and remaining faithful to the ancient rites, are appalled at the spectacle of their children renouncing religion altogether. Families are divided: "Practically no father of a family in our colony," a tolerant Jew writes in 1798, "shares the ideas of his sons and daughters and sons-in-law and daughters-in-law about religion. . . . Where will this lead us? . . . Children are already taking care to avoid all dealings with their parents, they are already moving away from the circle of their friends of the same religious persuasion. . . . Parents no longer trust their children, and children, for fear of betrayal, slink stealthily around, as if they were guilty criminals" (*Gespräch*, 122).

Civil Rights

The Alsatian Jews, discontented with their lot, asked Mendelssohn to intervene on their behalf. He referred them to his friend Christian-Wilhelm von Dohm, Military Adviser and Royal Archivist, who published his well-known apologia in 1781. The general tone is struck in the introduction: "After I have demonstrated historically that the Jews as men and citizens have appeared corrupted only because they have been refused the rights of man and the citizen, I shall probably be more successful in venturing to encourage governments to augment the number of good citizens by ceasing to compel the Jews to be bad citizens" (Dohm, *Verbesserung*, ix).

He goes on to demonstrate that the reason for the present inferiority of the Jews cannot be their religion, which is good and moral; those who assert the contrary are merely tediously repeating the unfounded accusations, the distorted quotations and the tales collected long ago by Eisenmenger in his well-known treatise.

The state should be tolerant and should recognize none but citizens: "The Jew is even more a man than a Jew, and how could he fail to be loyal to a state in which he was permitted to acquire property of his own and to enjoy it freely, in which his taxes were no heavier than those of other citizens, and in which there was nothing to prevent him from aspiring to esteem and consideration?" (Dohm, *Verbesserung*, 33.)

History confirms these contentions. The Jews in Holland, England, and even southern France are well treated and well behaved. All Jews should be granted civil rights and access to agriculture, the trades, the civil service, and the liberal professions. In order to speed up this access, a special tax might even be levied temporarily on commerce, for this would deter them from it and the temptations to corruption inherent in it. Lastly, a large number of schools should be set up to instruct and educate the Jews without restricting their religious freedom.

Dohm's line of argument was repeated virtually in so many words by all those who wrote in favor of the reforms, from David Friedländer, who addressed a *Memorandum* to Frederick William II in 1786, following which a commission on reforms was set up, to the anonymous contributor to the *Jahrbücher* in 1801. The entire Aufklärung campaigned on behalf of the Jews. When we read these pamphlets and articles, we must take care not to misconstrue them; many of them deprecate assimilation and do not believe that the Jews can be improved; but this does not make their authors anti-Semites, savage persecutors of innocent victims. Their views are not unreasonable.

Every Jew perfectly understands [an enlightened Jew writes in 1801] that it must be extremely difficult to turn the bulk of the Jewish nation from its ancient customs and usages, some of them harmful to the state, some of them absurd, and all of them unsuited to the spirit and circumstances of our age, by means of rational arguments and well-meant exhortations and to push it to a much needed and most salutary reform of its religion, distorted as it has been by man-made rules.

To which the Christian commentator footnotes:

It is precisely the misfortune of this people that the individuals among them have not progressed at an equal rate. Some of them give the impression that they have just returned from the Babylonian captivity. . . . The spirit of the Aufklärung has fully enlightened others; they make claims and are able to argue them effectually. . . . The misfortune of this unhappy people is that all its components are not coherent; a cultivated person claiming rights . . . must recognize forthwith that the state, obliged as it is to consider the class as a whole, must be extremely cautious about granting these rights to an entire religious tribe. [*Jahrb.* 1801, III, 101–2.]

These are facts which must not be overlooked in examining the polemics raised by Dohm's works and by the many pamphlets which, for more than twenty years, harp on the same themes. The question was the more pressing inasmuch as Joseph II at about that time promulgated the Reglement of 19 July 1782, whereby the Jews, compelled to speak the national language and to attend Jewish or Christian schools, could lease land for farming and engage in any trade, while "all humiliating and discouraging laws, such as those distinguishing Jews by dress and other outward signs" were "totally abolished."

The basic idea of the Aufklärung is that assimilation should come about inevitably by a species of tacit evolution. "We all know that men forget their mother tongue when they live far away in foreign countries for a long time with no contact with their compatriots; we know that European dogs at length learn not to bark in South America because the dogs there perhaps prefer to meditate rather than to bay for no particular reason. Why, then, should men not be able completely to discard certain proclivities if they have no chance to exercise them daily?" (*Jahrb.* 1801, III, 116.)

And why should not assimilated Jews become taller and stronger as well?

The anti-Semites were passionately to maintain that the Jews were fundamentally evil and unadaptable. The champions of the Aufklärung, too, however, acknowledge that Jews are more "prone to vice" than Christians, but maintain that this corruption is due solely to persecution and exists only among poor Jews engaged in petty trade. Once a Jew is in easy circumstances, he becomes perfectly honest in Germany, just as he does in Holland and England. But, it is said, the Jews, who account for about one twenty-fifth part of the population of Germany, alone account for as many thieves and robbers as the whole of the rest of the population; even supposing they slowly improve, is the Christian population, until future generations of Jews become more honest, to be handed over defenseless to those whom the very rights they are granted will make even more dangerous? But how valid are such estimates of Jewish criminality? If murders, treasons, arson and prostitution are taken into account as well as frauds and thefts, their proportionate share is far less. There are many Jewish receivers, but few Jewish thieves. The files of the Prussian courts confirm this. In 1789 they heard 1,703 criminal cases; 22 Jews were involved; but not a single one in a case of murder. One Jewess was convicted of abortion, but 83 Christians were convicted. Of 1,014 convictions for theft only 3 concerned Jews—and they were foreigners. Of

264 cases of forgery, usury, fraudulent bankruptcy, purchase of stolen goods, and receiving stolen goods, only 15 involved Jews.

Race is practically never adduced as the reason for the Jews' inferiority. Eighteenth-century scholars were too intelligent to construct sweeping ethnic theories. Only a few venture an explanation of this sort, but very hesitantly and without seeming any too convinced themselves. Meiners, the copious professor at Göttingen, for example, believes in proclivities. He suggests that physical dexterity, strength, wit, perspicacity, and judgment are characteristics essentially of the descendants of the Celts, to a far lesser extent of those of the Scythians and Slavs, and even less again of those of the "Indostasians, to whom the Jews and Gypsies belong" (*Moses und Christus*). Since the last-named do not possess "the moral character which makes a man a man," they can acquire it only by interbreeding with noble Celts.

According to another philosopher, in order to account for the special characteristics of the Jews "it must be accepted that their physical strength has been paralyzed or enfeebled by a hereditary mixture of humors, that their higher mental faculties have been distorted by a system of education and training to which they have been subjected from ancestral times, that they have been led astray and that their dispositions and feelings have been corrupted, especially as regards living in society; they have become outlandish and very harmful as a result of inherited modes of thinking, maxims sucked with their mothers' milk, and dubious company." "This explanation is doubtful," the author adds, "but there is no other"! (*BAZ* 1799, 230–31.)

Corrupted or not, are not the Jews prevented by their religion itself from mingling with other peoples? Did not Moses do everything possible to isolate them? "All the Jews observe the law of Moses," writes the famous Orientalist, Michaelis, an impartial observer.

So long as a Jew cannot, for instance, eat with us and seal an intimate friendship over dinner—or, among the lower classes, over a glass of beer—he will never merge with us like the Catholic and the Lutheran, the German, the Wend, and the Frenchman who live in one and the same state. A people of this sort may perhaps become more useful to us in agriculture or industry . . . but our burghers will never be able to esteem them as equals, for they will never . . . become patriotic, they will never take a heartfelt pride in the state, and they will never be wholly to be trusted in times of crisis. [*JD* 1700, I, 290–97.]

Besides, according to the Bible itself, the Jews must consider the state as a temporary place of sojourn, "which they will quit one day for their heart's desire"; for they must "return to Palestine." One learned author, of the sort to be found at every period, claims that the Jews cannot become assimilated because their religion forbids them to work on 282 holy days every year! (Hartmann, *Freiheit*; Geiger, *Geschichte* II, 155–58; cf. the virulent *Treue Relation*.)

All this is of little moment, according to Dohm; the history of Christianity shows that even dogmas gradually change under the pressure of the needs of the state if the faithful form a fairly large group and are not oppressed.

Eisenmenger asserts that any oath given to a Christian by a Jew is invalid. This view was widely held. It was asserted that at the first evening service (Kol Nidre) on the Day of Atonement (Yom Kippur) three Jews dressed in white shirts recited before the Ark the solemn declaration that all pledges given during the coming year would be invalid, and the congregation, standing, replied Amen (Grattenauer, *Wider die Juden*, 18–54). Let us look at a Prayer Book; at the beginning of the Kol Nidre we read: "All personal vows we are likely to make, all personal oaths and pledges we are likely to take between this Yom Kippur and next Yom Kippur, we publicly renounce. Let them all be relinquished and abandoned, null and void, neither firm nor established. Let our personal vows, pledges and oaths be considered neither vows nor pledges nor oaths." The Hebrew text, however, is to be interpreted in the sense indicated by a translator's note: "By vows or oaths . . . should be understood only those which are pronounced in error, in rash or unreflecting exaltation, but by no means those which are the fruit of reflection or those which justice imposes upon us; these can neither be dissolved nor annulled" (Durlacher, *Rituel*).

Many glosses of a similar sort are quoted as early as the eighteenth century. The rabbis had long insisted on the sacrosanct nature of oaths, irrespective of the parties to them. Read literally, the Kol Nidre in fact made no distinction between Jews and non-Jews. Even the anti-Semites paid a tribute to the rabbis' efforts, "but," they said, "Yom Kippur, by pardoning all sins, encourages the Jews to commit fresh ones, the more so because perjury to the Jews is merely a sin, not a crime nor a blasphemy; and, furthermore, all the rabbis' admonitions are vain, for it is an inveterate habit among the Jews to swear purely at random" (Grattenauer, *Wider die Juden*, 18–64).

The main objection to permitting the Jews to engage in trade is the danger of their competition with Christians, for Jews are more avid of gain than Christians. But is it a fact that Jews do better than Christians solely because they are more dishonest? They have acquired a complete monopoly of the silk trade at Berlin by selling cheaper than their competitors; but might not this success be due mainly to the fact that they live more simply? They do not indulge in sumptuous dinners or debauches, nor do they keep carriages or lose their gold at gaming; they work hard, they are polite to their customers; a Christian who imitates them will find that trickery is not necessarily the prerequisite for success.

Access to the trades or agriculture is the best way to cure even the most corrupted, as has been abundantly proved in Denmark and in large cities like Amsterdam, London, and Hamburg; "What poor Jewish lad would not rather learn a trade ensuring him a steady pittance or become a peasant than wander about all day with no notion whether he will have earned a morsel of bread by nightfall?" (*Jahrb.* 1801, III, 113–16.) Von Hoym tries the experiment in Silesia. Too little attention has been paid to his efforts to secure the admission of Jews to the corporations. The entire enlightened press, however, echoes the Breslau *Provinzialblätter.* The quotation by the *National-Zeitung der Teutschen* of the poster placarded by the Royal Domains Chamber on 18 January 1798 shows how widely the ideas of the Aufklärung have spread; a workman is of more value to the state than a merchant. The Jews have hitherto been confined to commerce because they were prevented by prejudice from learning any of the trades taught by the guilds and from engaging in any trade outside them as well. The way to progress has, however, already been cleared in Upper Silesia, where it has been recognized that a Jew is just as much a man as a Christian and that he may be equally useful to the state. Jewish apprentices have been taken on. (The *Provinzialblätter* cites one example at Loslau in 1792 and sixteen for the whole of Silesia between 1798 and 1804.) Graetz, a jeweler at Breslau, follows suit in Lower Silesia and is awarded a bounty of 50 thalers; "The Royal Domains Chamber hereby officially notifies him of this award and expresses the hope that a sense of humanity and of the public interest will once and for all overcome ingrained prejudice and that a great many of our craftsmen will imitate this shining example."

The policy of awarding bounties is continued in 1799. A stocking knitter is awarded 25 thalers for taking on his Jewish apprentice as a journeyman; the tailors' guild at Landsberg receives 15 thalers for admitting two Jewish masters and a Jewish journeyman in 1804; and steps are taken to enable the newly admitted journeymen to make the traditional tour.

Similar principles are decided on at Mainz and in Hesse-Darmstadt, but these premature experiments are unsuccessful. (For farming permitted at Mainz, *JD* 1788, II, 846.) Very few Jewish apprentices are taken on, most probably because of local hostility. At Brieg in 1801, for example, the master weavers try to compel a guild member to dismiss his Jewish apprentice, and when he refuses, they threaten to strike. The affair is taken as far as the Royal Domains Chamber at Breslau, and the guild declares to it that it will never admit Jews. The Chamber replies that it will appoint the apprentice a "free master" on its own authority and will permit him to sell his wares without belonging to a guild. "A wise decision," the *National-Zeitung* comments, proposing that a Sunday school should be established to wean the Brieg craftsmen from their prejudices (9 Apr. 1801). Similar objections were frequent, and the local authorities often found themselves at loggerheads with the Royal Domains Chamber. The Jews themselves, however, were far from eager to force their way into the trades.

Competition is less to be feared in agriculture; labor is scarcer than land for farming. But, some people insinuate, can a Jew be a farmer? Is not the agricultural system based on hog raising? How will a Jew be able to feed his farmhands without pork? His costs would be too high for the farm to pay its way. How, too, will he be able to live on his own meat so far from a kosher slaughterhouse? If the experiment is nonetheless to be tried, Christians should not have forced upon them as neighbors the generation of Jews which is still corrupt. Let them clear the waste lands and do some useful work instead of drying up a source of revenue to the state by acquiring the lands of solid Prussian peasants.

The main objection invoked by all the opponents of Jewish emancipation is their unfitness for military service. Does not Moses command them not to fight on the Sabbath unless they are attacked? Supposing the Jews are free, they will multiply fast, for they marry early; they shun prostitution and relations with Christian women, for they may cost them much of the money which they cherish above all things; and they fear "the disease, a single dose of which is enough to hamper procreation later." They will take the jobs vacant in agriculture and the trades while the Christian population, less prolific to start with, will be decimated by wars and will gradually die out. The law of Moses can, however, be interpreted in such a way that Jews would certainly not hesitate to fight on a Saturday. They still would not be fit for the army, for how could they observe their complicated dietary laws in it? Or would special regiments be formed for them? What good would that be? The army needs good soldiers, tall and strong; it has no use for stunted Jews.

Mendelssohn has an answer, however: does the Christian religion permit war? The Quakers and Mennonites refuse military service. If the laws command the Jews to defend their country, they will submit to them, for at all times and at all places individuals develop and adjust their opinions to necessity; would the Christians otherwise have become the masters of the world, the oppressors and the slave traders that they are? The best proof can be found in the newspapers, which detect in Strasbourg and Berlin, and indeed almost everywhere, excellent soldiers whom nobody realized were Jews. In the Austrian army there are even Jews who have earned their commissions on the battlefield.

For more than twenty years the debate continues, forever going over the same ground. Hardly anyone is in favor of the status quo, repugnant as it is to the Aufklärung. Some original thinkers suggest that the Jews should be granted full freedom, but should be isolated in towns of their own, or else that they should all be banished. But nobody takes such drastic solutions too seriously. At bottom, people are perfectly well aware that Jews are human beings and Christians are no saints. "I have seldom found a shady transaction by a Jew which did not conceal a Christian rogue behind it," one of Dohm's correspondents declares (Dohm, *Verbesserung* II, 118–23); and throughout the Germanies the enlightened press cites examples of good behavior by Jews; such as the devout Daniel Itzig distributing alms outside his door to the poor, both Jewish and Christian, on the first day of each month, in accordance with the calendars of the two creeds; a money changer at Breslau reimbursing a sum paid him in error, even though there is no means of compelling him to do so; a girl at Danzig volunteering to go to prison in place of her paralytic seventy-year-old father convicted of receiving stolen goods; the merchants of Schwerin sending their bills marked "paid with thanks" to a debtor suddenly ruined by a fire; and merchants at Schwarzbach refusing to utter a forgery for an ecclesiastical dignitary. Christians, too, provide fine examples of tolerance, such as saving a Jewish child from drowning at Frankfort-on-Main or amicably welcoming a Jewish fellow pupil at the secondary school in Wurzburg in 1787, and so on.

Emancipation was, however, slow in coming. The Commission appointed by the king in December 1787 proposed a new constitution, but the Jewish deputies rejected it in February 1790. They demand "not lighter chains, but their total removal." The affair dragged on. The General Directorate took action only after the king intervened in person in January 1792. A further project came to nothing in 1798, this time owing to the Directorate's reluctance. As the solution was continually deferred (the emancipation laws were finally enacted only in 1805-12), both Jewish and Christian philosophers settled for advocating a compromise, which was merely to widen the gulf created by Reason between the enlightened and the orthodox Jews.

The Conflict with the Orthodox Jews: Premature Burials

In every Jewish community there is a "brotherhood of benefactors and tenders of the sick," the senior member of which must attend his fellow believer's deathbed; flanked by nine witnesses of the male sex, he watches over the dying man, taking care not to touch him for fear of hastening his end. When it comes, a feather of down is placed under the corpse's nose; if it has not moved a quarter of an hour later, the body is lifted off the bed and placed on the ground, and they keep vigil over it for three hours. It is then turned over to the brethren responsible for laying it out and for the burial. This speedy interment disturbs Christians; they cannot but think that a lengthy fainting spell very often closely resembles death and they express the greatest anxiety about unfortunates who may have been buried alive. This accounts for such legends as that in order to spare the deceased these posthumous throes, the Jews have them strangled with a cord by a man known as the Angel of Death!

This is not, however, something that concerns the Jews alone. When the removal of all prejudices is at issue, it is always social conventions that first come under attack. The early Romantics champion free love at the precise moment when philosophers throughout Germany are launching a campaign against ruinously expensive ceremonies.

So many people feel obliged to spend all their savings on a baptism, a marriage, or a funeral. So many feel duty bound to wrap their dead in silken shrouds, bury them in coffins of precious wood with chased silver handles, swathe their house and dress their servants in black, hire mutes and offer sumptuous funeral banquets.

Such excesses are therefore prohibited by a number of sumptuary decrees, whereby an armband or a ribbon in the women's hair replaces mourning for all but the closest relations and hired mutes and funeral banquets are abolished.

The orthodox Jews look askance at this humanitarian enthusiasm. In 1772 the Duke of Mecklenburg-Schwerin expressly forbids them to bury the dead until three days have elapsed. The elders of the community beg Mendelssohn to use his influence to have the decree rescinded. But he, to their great surprise, supports the duke and tries hard to demonstrate that the traditional usage is not based on any sacred text. The enraged elders then apply to Rabbi Jakob Hirschel of Hamburg; he does his best to confute Mendelssohn with a mass of texts. Heartily abused as he had been by the celebrated Rabbi Jakob Emden of Altona, who had had to abandon the idea of remonstrating with the duke because he did not know German well enough, Mendelssohn, as is his habit, shuns publicity. After the formidable rabbi's death, however, *Der Sammler*, the Jewish journal at Königsberg, publishes the correspondence between them and so places the question in the public domain.

At this very moment the authorities at Prague prohibit all burials until forty-eight hours have elapsed and issue detailed regulations for them in response to the rabbi's plea that his support for the tradition rests on cramped conditions in the Jewish quarter and the danger of an epidemic.

Ten years of campaigning are needed before a similar reform is obtained in Prussia. In 1787 *Der Sammler* consults Marcus Herz, the eminent physician, whose reply is later published as a pamphlet (Herz, *Frühe Beerdigung*); it is reprinted in 1788, augmented with replies to increasingly furious criticisms by the orthodox Jews. (Good summary in *Königlichprivilegierte Berlinische Zeitung*, 28 Dec. 1787.)

"Are there any irrefutable signs," Herz asks at the outset, "by which apparent death can be distinguished from real death within four hours?" No, reply all the medical authorities, quoting several cases of apparent death. The Talmud itself prescribes, in case of doubt, that "vigil shall be kept over the dead until the third day, for in former days one of them arose and lived on for twenty-five years; and another afterwards begat five children." The recent instance of a woman whom Dr. Hirschberg of Königsberg resuscitated after three days also recommends caution.

To the slight extent that such signs do exist, the visitors of the Jewish burial societies are not sufficiently acquainted with them; as soon as the pulse ceases, the eyes glaze and the breath cannot be discerned, the man is declared dead. But breathing and circulation may slow down to a point at which they become imperceptible. Are there really imperative religious reasons for immediate burial? The only texts on which the devout rely are, in the first place, Deuteronomy XXI, 22, 23: "And if a man have committed a sin worthy of death, and he be put to death, and thou hang him on a tree; his body shall not remain all night upon the tree, but thou shalt in any wise bury him that day; (for he that is hanged is accursed of God); that the land be not defiled, which the Lord thy God giveth thee for an inheritance." This is a special case in which death is quite evidently real; the Talmudists are not justified, therefore, in relying on this text to order immediate burial as a general prescription. They do so, nevertheless, to lend more authority to medieval prescriptions. There were probably political or hygienic reasons for the rules at the time, which no longer exist in the eighteenth century. They knew nothing of the frequency of apparent deaths and believed their standards of judgment to be adequate. For they were not so narrow-minded as people like Jakob Emden or Ezechiel of Prague. The latter actually contends that every sick person "who does not breathe through the nose" is dead, relying on Genesis VII, 22: "All in whose nostrils was the breath of life, of all that was in the dry land, died." And that immediate burial is necessary because Solomon said: "Then shall the dust return to the earth as it was: and the spirit shall return unto God who gave it" (Ecclesiastes XII, 7). It is indeed most painful for the soul to separate from the body in which it had its habitation; it prowls round the corpse until it is buried and cannot return to God until then, for Solomon mentioned the body first; it is therefore a pious duty to spare the soul a painful span of waiting.

The Talmud itself recognizes that it is possible to make a mistake and advises waiting when there is no certainty. Religion, which is Life and Truth, cannot possibly order a murder. And, Herz adds rather subtly, even if the Talmudist rule had sacred validity (in any case, it orders burial before nightfall, not within the traditional four hours), would not burying someone alive be a breach of that rule? Between the two sins of burying a corpse too late or killing a brother, should one not choose the lesser? Think of the torments of being buried alive. Imagine "the mortal anguish; the choking constriction of the chest; the rush of blood to the head; the convulsive shuddering of the whole body; the muscles' vain struggle to throw off the crushing weight; the stench of the neighboring corpses. . . ." Put yourself in the place of a patient who has gone to sleep the night before among his kin, waking up, thinking he is in bed, groping and finding bones, growing more and more terrified and struggling madly . . . in vain!

Such cases cannot be very common. Marx, the Rabbi of Hanover, who is also a physician, certifies that the volunteer, and therefore disinterested, visitors are throughly conscientious. He reminds his readers that the Talmud itself prescribes delay when death is consequent upon nervous diseases, effusions of blood, or fainting spells, or when it is sudden; that a doctor is usually consulted, and that the first signs of putrefaction are awaited whenever there is any possibility of doubt. The argument from Solomon is not so absurd after all, since it is quite definitely confirmed by Psalm 49, 12: "Man being in honour abideth not [the night]" (*JD* 1784, II, 227-34).

Herz certainly appears to admit that cases are not very frequent; but even if there were only one case, would not that suffice to make reform necessary? Two rabbis were even rash enough to write to Mendelssohn that apparent death is something exceptional, and religion need not take account of the exceptional.

Herz's pamphlet in German fires public opinion, and the whole of the Aufklärung joins in; but to no avail. All parties stick to their guns till 1797. Toward the end of that year, Baruch Wesel's child nearly dies at Breslau. The group of enlightened Jews there have taken a stand against immediate burial since 1793, and the Brotherhood of Visitors had exceptionally granted Dr. Zadig a respite of twenty-four hours when his father died. Such compromises could not, however, be lasting. The Wesel child dies, according to the brother, at eight o'clock in the evening. It is too late to bury him, so they carry out the ritual. The child is laid on the floor in the room in which his baby brother is sleeping. In the middle of the night the watcher is awakened by moans; he rushes over to the cradle; the baby is sleeping peacefully; shortly afterwards, the moaning begins again; the fact has to be faced: it is the dead child who is giving utterance.

The incident at once creates a sensation; if the child had lost consciousness a few hours earlier, he would have been buried alive; so the enlightened Jews' campaign is something more than a doctrinal dispute. Von Hoym, judging the time auspicious, orders the committee of the brotherhood to wait in future till there really is no hope of resuscitation before burying a body. Bodies are to be deposited in the mortuary in the Jewish cemetary, where they will be examined by a Jewish doctor and the brothers will keep vigil. The regulation is not enforced; von Hoym himself is hesitant; controversy rages at Breslau; the enlightened Jews rally round Joel Löwe, the author of a pamphlet published in 1793, while the orthodox Jews find an unexpected champion in Salomon Seligmann Pappenheim, who had been reputed a liberal; the *Provinzialblätter* thunders against people blinded by their prejudices; von Hoym, minister of state in Prussia and tolerant at bottom, decides to investigate before he issues an order with force of law. He circularizes all the Jewish notabilities and scholars asking whether the Bible and the Talmud absolutely prohibit a longer period before burial; is it a point of conscience or a matter of public policy, which the state is entitled to settle? Without awaiting the results of the inquiry, thirty heads of households decide to found an association for burying the dead after the Christian fashion; they will wait three days; they will lay out the corpse at home instead of handing it over to the brotherhood or to the "old woman" paid by it, for corpses often were not undressed in the presence of a stranger lest some blemish be exposed; the respect due to the dead forbids handing them over to outsiders. Burials will be more ceremonious than they were in the past; a hearse will be provided.

Dr. Zadig, the author of *Considerations on the Treatment of the Dead among the Christians and the Jews*, countered by Seligmann's *Necessity for Speedy Burial among the Jews*, is a member of the new association. Before it is finally formed, however, and before it has registered its articles with the Royal Chamber, it loses a male infant thirteen days old. The body is treated in accordance with the new principles, and Zadig notifies Jakob Gottheiner, the president of the brotherhood, that he will bury his son in three days. Gottheiner forbids the burial. Zadig, a contributing member of the brotherhood, challenges the brothers' self-assumed entitlement to the ownership of the cemetery, refuses to submit "to prejudices imported from Poland," and brings an action against them. Fairly late on the third day, the Royal Chamber sends Gottheiner a message that though it has not resorted to force to apply its December decree, it cannot, nevertheless, allow Jews to be prevented from complying with it voluntarily. It therefore authorizes Zadig to require the assistance of the police to compel Gottheiner to bury his child (8 April). In December 1799, as a result of the campaign carried on by all the supporters of the Aufklärung around the Breslau incident, a general law having effect for the whole of Prussia is finally promulgated. It applies to Jews and Christians alike. No burial may take place until three days after death nor before the first signs of putrefaction have appeared. Jewish grave diggers and all other persons concerned in burials shall swear an oath in the synagogue to obey the law. The police will supervise its enforcement and must be represented at every Jewish burial. Recalcitrant "bigots" will be liable to penalties ranging from simple imprisonment to imprisonment with hard labor. "That this humane decree fell on the orthodox Jews of Breslau like a thunderbolt can readily be imagined." They become frenziedly busy, send deputations to protest, and seek support from other communities. To no avail, however; reason carries the day. Similar conflicts break out almost everywhere in Germany. The Berlin Friendly Society decides to build a mortuary in 1797. Fifty heads of households form an association at Hamburg in 1804 to bury their dead in accordance with the Aufklärung; and to bring the brotherhood to heel, they obtain a royal rescript from Copenhagen.

The Religious Question

Twenty-seven years—1772 to 1799—were needed for the victory of a reform dictated by reason and not repugnant to religion. If we imagine the difficulties amid which the enlightened Jews lived, harassed by the orthodox, shunned by the masses of the mistrustful common people, and encouraged only in the abstract by their Christian friends, we can well appreciate their weariness and their desire to have done with it all.

Early in 1799 some Jewish heads of households addressed an open letter to

Dean (*Probst*) Teller, senior councillor of the Evangelical consistory, the most eminent of the enlightened clergy.

We are Jews, David Friedländer, the author of the letter, says in substance, and we remain attached to the religion of our fathers, but we contemn its obsolete rites. In this age of enlightenment everyone acknowledges that the essence of any religion lies in the knowledge of God and his infinite attributes, of the immortal and incorporeal soul, of duties toward one's neighbor, and of human destiny, which is to strive toward perfection. These are the foundations of virtue and happiness.

Moses held much the same view. The rites he imposed on a rude people in order to wean them from their idols were designed to spread these principles gradually; they were designed, too, as regulations at a time when there was no distinction between church and state. Moses' intention in forbidding these customs to be written down was that they should develop as they were transmitted orally and adapt themselves to the people's civilization as it developed. Putting them in writing prevented this development and halted progress; a long decadence set in, which was to last into our own time.

The Aufklärung has enabled us, like the Christians, to return to the true principles. We are becoming assimilated; admittedly, we lag behind the Christians in education, but not in moral dignity. We are neither more vicious nor more evil than others, and we do not deserve our disabilities. At odds with our orthodox fellow Jews, prepared to renounce the religion of our fathers, how shall we be able to live in a society which recognizes only Jews and Christians? We may be granted citizenship if we become converts. But if we renounce Judaism because we can only recognize truths of reason very different from those of history, we cannot become Christians. "What profession of faith would you and the venerable persons who sit beside you in the venerable consistory require of us if we decided to choose the great Protestant Christian society as a place of refuge?" (*Sendschreiben.*)

Teller's reply well reflects the mentality of a clergy imbued with the spirit of the age and itself almost prepared to accept, above rites suitable enough for the common people, a rationalized religion within which all cultivated minds would be able to partake of the same sacrament. Commending the Jews for renouncing their practices, he declares that this gesture in itself suffices to fit them for citizenship. It is not for him, however, to amend the existing law. In any case, why not become converts? To the physician thinking in accordance with reason Christ said: "Thou art not far from the Kingdom of God." This, therefore, is the essence of Christianity. Teller, for his part, is prepared to hold out his hand to anyone who thinks reasonably. Jewish converts would not need to practice any rite. Let them only acknowledge that Christ is the founder of the best moral religion, and no more is asked of them. They will be baptized with a simplified form of words: "In the name of Christ, Savior of man." They will participate in Holy Communion, for "at least some positive action" is necessary, and no one will worry about what they think of dogmas, miracles, or the Holy Ghost.

Public opinion is divided. Some Christians are indignant that religion should be divested to such an extent of all sentiment and all faith. The mystical reaction against rationalism is growing stronger under the influence of Rosicrucianism on the one hand and the young Romantics on the other. But when Schleiermacher protests against a purely rationalist conception of religion, he is not prompted by any hatred of the Jews. He is Henrietta Herz's best friend and often defends the Jews, advocating their emancipation.

Some Jews regretted that the enlightened Jews should separate off from their brothers instead of devoting themselves to the thankless task of educating them. On the whole, however, the letter—though modern Jewish historians freely condemn its tone (Graetz goes so far as to call Friedländer an ape)—was fairly well received. It reflected ideas that accorded with those of the educated public, which was observing the development of theophilanthropy in France with interest. The press discussed several projects which, if carried out, would have made citizens of the Jews. One philosopher eager to bring the two religions closer begs the Jews to give up their Purim. The rites are absurd; what is the sense of little boys going about the streets hammering on a plate bearing the name of Haman? The story of Esther is not very creditable to the Jews, since all they do in it is to weep and fast, go into mourning and knock defenseless people on the head. Mordecai is simply being pig-headed in refusing to render to the first minister of Persia honors which his ancestors had often rendered to far less distinguished persons without being asked.

Another sends to the *Jahrbücher* (1790, I, 425–31) from Breslau in 1798 a splendid plan for reform. It is essential that the two creeds be brought closer. A baby is born; he is brought up in one faith or the other without being consulted on the matter; and there he is, a Jew or a Christian without any idea why! This is absurd. The reasonable Jews should found a new religion in accordance with the Aufklärung, and the state should recognize the sect. All that is needed is that they should give up Hebrew, substitute teachers of morality for rabbis and Talmud and replace circumcision with a festival identical for both sexes, adopt the Christian calendar and move the Sabbath to Sunday and concord the Jewish holidays with the Christian, abolish dietary restrictions, and permit mixed marriages; and such citizens, who would have nothing Jewish left but the name, should call themselves "Purists"—they would be able to celebrate their religious holidays in "a wholly theophilanthropic" fashion. And let no "rabbi zealot" claim that this reform will lead to Christianity! There is no question of that. It simply establishes a deist and reasonable sect which the state could recognize.

A similar hope is expressed in the brief essay *Moses and Christ* and in many articles, in which the increasingly frequent mixed marriages and conversions are heartily welcomed.

In these circumstances it is easy to see why Teller's proposal comes to the fore. Since the clergy, after all, turn out to be so enlightened and so little exigent, since a modicum of good sense and reason suffice for acceptance by the Protestants and to obtain civic equality, why so much hesitation? The orthodox Jews are thrusting all those with any education into the arms of the Christians. It is true that many among the lower classes become converts with ulterior motives. Solid citizens are concerned by this, and propose that political rights shall only be granted to the newly converted after six years, a period requisite for their assimilation. Many Jews, however, under the influence of the sentimental reaction against the sway of reason at the end of the century, throw themselves passionately on the bosom of Mother Church. Henrietta Herz becomes a Catholic, as does Mendelssohn's own daughter, Dorothea. Dr. Zadig goes over to Protestantism with his young son late in 1802. This conversion creates a sensation among the orthodox, Christians and Jews alike: among the Christians because they consider that Zadig, as a physician, cannot expect any material advantage from his gesture and that he is therefore the first person baptized in the new age to quit the faith of his fathers out of sincere conviction; among the Jews because they consider the baptism of a six-year-old child an infringement of their rights, since Prussian law prohibits baptism—except for infants—before the age of fourteen.

Many of his fellow Jews imitate Zadig's example. Liberal Christians do not despair of a general conversion. "You are surprised that so many Jews are getting baptized at Breslau? You would be less surprised if you knew these people's situation and frame of mind as well as I do. The only reason why all of them do not get baptized is that many of them fear lest both parties may accuse them of self-interest, or that they think that this step may be inconsistent with their conscience and honor, or simply that they are accustomed to being Jews like their fathers before them; but very few of them are convinced." The trend everywhere is marked enough to disturb both Jews and Christians. It continues in Berlin till around 1810. Measures such as the requirement to produce a certificate from the police testifying to the would-be convert's respectability and good faith are less important than the emancipating decrees of 1812 in putting an end to this development.

There are no statistics of conversions. Friedländer states that fifty Jewish families were converted at Berlin between 1806 and 1811 (Freund, *Geschichte* I, 214–19). He also states that there were 453 Jewish families there in 1806. The proportion of baptisms must have been equally high in the larger towns, but lower in the smaller ones. If we add in the conversions before 1806, an estimate that 10 percent of the Jews renounced their religion to acquire citizenship is certainly on the conservative side. The proportion is high enough to attract Christians' attention and to account for the growth of a certain amount of anti-Semitism among the nonenlightened masses. Probably this anti-Semitism is not more widespread simply because there were not a great many Jews. According to a contemporary statistician, there were 224,380 in all the Prussian states, including Silesia, in 1806, that is, one person in every forty-three was a Jew (Küster, *Beitrage*, 237–39).

Anti-Semitism

Any remark hostile to the Jews is commonly regarded as a display of anti-Semitism. It has even been contended that thinkers like Kant or Goethe were anti-Semitic, though their writings are liberal to the core. It would be easy enough, however, to pick out of their copious output plenty of contrasting passages or to cite Kant's reception of Mendelssohn at Königsberg amid jeering students, though they were soon called to order, and the battles which Fichte, as a supporter of the French Revolution, had to wage against accusations of atheism. Fichte had no belief in Jewish assimilation, and when he says that in order to turn a Jew into a Prussian citizen one would have to cut off his head and screw a different one on his shoulders, he is merely expressing a view which the orthodox Jews' vehement rejection of even the most essential reforms put into many people's minds. This does not make him an anti-Semite, however, for he would not refuse equality to enlightened Jews. He is not against the Jews as such, but against the orthodox Jews. The true criterion for anti-Semitism is the virulence of an emotional reaction which rejects discussion and is incapable of listening to reason. This is a feeling which is not even always openly expressed, but traces of it are everywhere apparent.

At a period when the whole press is in the hands of the Aufklärung and when the younger writers of the new Romantic school take pride in their political liberalism, this kind of reaction has little opportunity for expression. It is latent, however, in both town and country. The very fact that the philosophers combat it as a prejudice reveals its existence.

In Berlin the Jews take Christian surnames; they set the fashion in manners and dress and entertain notabilities, but they are not received in middle-class homes: "The Berlin dandies and young scholars," Frau Unger says, chagrined to find her salon deserted by the young Romantics,

who do not have, and do not want, the entree to the houses of persons of distinction, resort to those of the wealthy Jews. The educated Jews form a special class and in fact now exercise more influence than their baptized fellow citizens would wish to concede to them. Though some good speculative brains have issued from this seed of Abraham, which has always been as innumerable as the sands on the shore, they are only a very small group amid a vast crowd, and from this they derive an inexpressible vanity. They will never forget until the end of all things created that they once had a Moses Mendelssohn! The Jews and the friends of Jews incessantly adore this luminary, while hundreds of perfectly worthy scholars, who, however, have not been ranked among these "curiosities," are neglected. [*Berlin* 1799, I, 126–28.]

The Jewesses are especially attracted by culture, but let them beware; in aspiring to the heights of culture without acquiring an ordinary education they make themselves ridiculous; they have no taste, carry everything to extremes, and are far too arrogant.

This is true at Breslau, too, where the "enlightened" Jews have a hard time of it. A Jewish doctor and his wife have only to be introduced into a group which meets at the fashionable cafe every Sunday for the Christians to boycott it until the interlopers cease to frequent it.

"Prejudice" is sometimes taken to inordinate lengths. In Berlin itself, in 1785, a Jew collapses on the street in an apoplectic fit. A doctor says that his life could be saved if he were given a room to rest in; but the owner of the house on whose threshold the scene takes place flatly refuses to let a Jew into his house; and the Jew dies on his doorstep.

Hostility to the Jews is even more widespread in the country. In East Prussia there are complaints of increased competition by Jews after the liberal Reglement of 1797; "The prisons are crammed with Jews, and the roads are thronged with vagrants and beggars of that nation." Trading is the Jews' sole occupation, but they will soon throw farming out of gear too. The only way to rid the country of them is to muster them all into the army. (*Jahrb.* 1801, I, 268 ff.; II, 73.)

In August 1796 several inhabitants of Kranzien in the New Mark find they have been robbed. They suspect a band of Jewish vagrants which has passed through the village. Instead of preferring charges, they make the village authorities take it upon themselves to prosecute. The Jews are arrested not far from the village and are brought back there. Erdmann Sauer, the blacksmith, plays the prosecutor. He suspects the wife of Salomon Moses and tries to make her confess. He succeeds in convincing the majority of the village council, despite the opposition of the mayor (*Schulze*), who points out that the proceedings are wholly illegal. Sauer plaits a switch of rope and soaks it in water to harden it. As soon as the Jews are brought back to the village, he strips Moses' wife, pregnant though she is, and calls on her to confess; she protests her innocence and he flogs her savagely until he is exhausted and is relieved by someone else. The woman falls, is picked up, and falls again, but does not confess, and dies after two hours of torment. The judge is informed, but drags out the investigation; and it is only eighteen months later that he sentences Sauer to eight years' hard labor and his accomplices to lesser penalties; but the eleven Jews of the band are expelled, and Moses, together with one of his friends, is convicted of suspected theft and vagrancy and sentenced to six months' hard labor and costs.

The murder of a Jew is not regarded as a crime.

Quite recently a Jew was murdered and stripped of his possessions in the county of Sayn. The perpetrator of the act, a peasant, was quite convinced that he had not committed a crime, and stayed on quietly at home for several weeks, going so far as to wear his victim's clothes. At length he hears from one of his relatives that the authorities will not after all be able to overlook the matter; he then decides to absent himself for a while. The local criminal magistrate (*gerichtliche Centschopf*), whose special function is to report crimes, even accompanies him across the frontier. The peasant is naturally brought to book, but does not believe he was at fault. It was, after all, only a Jew! [*JD* 1785, I, 415–16; 1786, II, 73–89, 523–24.]

Similar cases, equally tragic or only a little less so, are found everywhere. A child disappears at Neustadt-an-der-Aisch; the Jews are at once suspected, for their women in labor must drink the blood of a Christian child. They are persecuted, their homes are attacked, they are stoned throughout the district, until the strayed child's body is found. The post mortem establishes that he died of exposure.

How sad it is that such instances of barbarity, such incredible brutality, must be acknowledged to be widespread through a large part of the Neustadt district, among the people of Beyreuth, among Prussian subjects! How shameful before the world, before our neighbors it is that such a thing should still be possible among us! The laws are of no avail. The authorities, even the clergy, cannot make enough impression on the people. Reason must be inculcated early; what is needed is a good education, good schools. [*NZT*, 30 June 1803; 22 Aug. 1805 (Berlin); 2 Dec. 1802 (Posen); 23 Feb. 1797 (Heidelberg).]

The authorities indeed try to suppress anti-Semitism, and there are hardly any open expressions of it before 1803. Around that date two legal officials launch a campaign of extreme violence. Christian Ludwig von Paalzow, a criminal councillor at the Berlin Court of Appeal (*Kammergericht*), publishes a historical book in Latin, *De civitate judaeorum*, in which he sets out to prove that the Jews are and always have been incapable of assimilation. A colleague of his, an officer of the same court with police functions, takes this as a pretext for a headlong onslaught "against the Jews" in a savage diatribe conducted with such irrepressible verve that it was to carry with him a large proportion of public opinion (Grattenauer, *Wider die Juden*). Arguments based purely on emotion cannot be discussed; if we are to see what Grattenauer did, a better course is to quote him at some length. We must however, deal with one preliminary point. It appears from the catalogue of the Berlin library that Grattenauer is also the author of a pamphlet published anonymously in 1791 which has many points of similarity with that of 1803

(*Über die physische* . . .). This brochure, which is bound up with Grattenauer's other pamphlets, is not mentioned in any of the known biographies of him. We shall assume that it is in fact his and quote from both texts indiscriminately. No matter who the author is, the problem remains, namely that fact that no notice whatever was taken of the 1791 pamphlet, while the one published in 1803 was all the rage throughout Germany. Something similar occurs with Paalzow; in 1798 he published a treatise on the Jews, very similar in substance to the bulkier publication of 1803; indeed, it is a species of first draft of it. In 1798 it attracted no notice at all.

The reason generally given to account for the public outcry in 1803 is the petition by Jews to the Diet of Ratisbon for at least the rights of passive citizenship. All those who believed their interests threatened by Jewish competition no doubt tried to stave off the danger. But the situation was virtually the same in 1791. In that year there was every reason to fear that the commission on reforms might grant far-reaching concessions after the Jewish deputies had rejected the partial improvements offered in 1790. The commission consulted von Hoym, who was known to be favorable to the Jews, and submitted a fresh draft to the king, at his request, in January 1792. Surely the relevant point here is the general trend in thinking after the death of Frederick the Great rather than any specific fact. To the France of the Rights of Man and the right of peoples to self-determination has succeeded the imperialist and all-conquering Republic of the First Consul. Similarly, too, the cult of feeling is coming to replace the dominance of the Aufklärung and Reason; Goethe and Schiller have replaced Lessing and Wieland as the idols of the literary world. The Romantics are cultivating dreams and mysticism. Schelling is at variance with Kant and even Fichte. Religious sentiment has revived, and the mob's bigotry has reawakened its anti-Semitism.

Another point is that the Jews were most certainly freer than they had been. To judge by their progress in all respects in the past ten years, the results of competition by them might well be formidable once they became entirely free. It would be different if they were at least likable; but only too often the children of Mendelssohn's modest circle display an unpleasing arrogance; neither their intelligence nor their culture, more apparent than real, entitles them to display such contempt for the rest of mankind. They are not, on the whole, notable for their tact. It is easy, then, to see that many even of those who still held to the ideas of the Aufklärung were not too ill-pleased by the diffusion of pamphlets calculated to distress these conceited young dandies.

Grattenauer's first work, couched oddly enough in terms of "enlightened" thought, takes a stand in 1791 against the reform of the system of Jewish disabilities (*Über die physische* . . . , iv–v). Toleration has its limits when faced with a false and noxious doctrine which infringes moral principles "respected even by the Savage, the Red Indian, and the Negro." The God of the Jews is not love and trust, like the God of the Christians, but a tyrant and a despot; that is why the Jews "make it an article of faith to deceive and dupe Christians; their scanty moral sense prompts them to pride themselves on being perfidious, dishonest, false, and ruthless toward those who profess themselves Christians." The assimilation of the Jews is a vain hope, for they differ from Christians in every respect. They will not amend a form of morals which makes them prone to vice and cruelty, for they regard themselves as the Chosen People and despise all others. They will not change their mode of life in any way, for they are fit for nothing but trading, which enables them to creep in everywhere, lend money to women and young persons and corrupt servants; they sell trash cheap. If only there were no Jews in Berlin! No one would go bankrupt, there would be no poor, and everyone would be happy. "Christians owe the smallpox to the Jews, too." Those who become converts do so purely for material gain and dupe the clergy. No toleration for Jews!

The Jews dominate the whole of society by usury. In his *Hieroglyphs*, published in 1780, Hartmann depicts Jews refusing to renew a bill of exchange unless a new and much larger bill is signed, or lending to minors who pretend to be of age, so that the creditor can allege that he believed them adults and hence the contract is valid, or offering officials advances on their salary so that they are thenceforth at the Jews' mercy. Despite the Aufklärung, such people cannot be granted rights: "Man . . . is always a man; he is always entitled to expect help from his brother; all national hatred is therefore unjustified, for it springs from poisonous pride . . . unless a nation has attracted to itself by its moral vices the absolute contempt of mankind and unless it itself deliberately opposes all enlightenment of heart and mind. Is this not the case with the Jews?" The Turks and the Hottentots have some virtues; the Iroquois, the Kaffirs, the Mongols, and the Eskimos reform themselves and abandon their idols. Only the Jews remain obstinately themselves.

There are, indeed, exceptions; enlightened Jews, however, are no longer Jews but deists; they may be granted citizenship if they are genuinely and profoundly changed, if they are really no longer subject to the despotism of the rabbis and meaningless rites.

Paalzow's first pamphlet is a reply to an open letter by some Jewish heads of households. Written in German, it has no success whatever; that may be why the author publishes his second edition, considerably augmented, in Latin. He feigns erudition, but borrows all his arguments from Eisenmenger or contemporaries hostile to assimilation. His main contention is that the Jews have no religion of their own, but have simply adopted the theocratic system of the Egyptians. The priests, relying on the laws of Moses, all of them secular, are the leaders of the people, as they were in Egypt. "The god who was formerly named Apis is called Jehovah by the Jews. . . . There is hardly any mention of God in the Ten Commandments." Moses never speaks of a future life. As Kant rightly observed, the laws of the Jews are political, not religious (*Die Juden*).

The reason why the Jews should not be received into the state is that they have always been despised and hated. "They were execrated because they were known to detest all other men, and they have been despised because of their superstitions and strange customs" (ibid.). They massacre the children of other peoples, as ordered in Psalm 137: "O daughter of Babylon, who art to be destroyed; happy shall he be that rewardeth thee as thou hast served us. Happy shall he be that taketh and dasheth thy little ones against the stones."

Moses orders his people to hate other nations: "And when the Lord thy God shall deliver them before thee, thou shalt smite them and utterly destroy them; thou shalt make no covenant with them, nor shew mercy unto them." (Deuteronomy VII, 2). They have never forgotten this throughout their history. As they have not developed for two thousand years, the Romans' objections to them still hold good. A Chosen People, the more they are despised, the prouder of it they are. Christian law they consider invalid. They refuse military service, are dishonest, and cannot possibly become good citizens.

Paalzow's work in Latin serves Grattenauer as a pretext to resume the campaign in 1803. The tone becomes more truculent:

According to evidence by reliable authors, the Jews were expelled from Egypt because the whole nation was infected with scabies and leprosy, and the herdsmen even contaminated the beasts at pasture. This disease was known as elephantiasis, or leprosy, and Lucretius attests that the Egyptian Jews alone were stricken with it. The Jews poisoned wells by means of lepers in France (1321), and in Switzerland and Alsace (1348). (Cf. *Taeglicher Schauplatz* by Ans. Heinr. von Ziegler, Frankfurt, 1695, Fol. p. 5, col. 2, p. 353, col. 1 and 2. To the same effect Sebast. Münster, *Cosmographie*, Basel, 1550, pp. 192, 656, 660). Even though they wash at least ten times a day, filth and stink remain their peculiar national heritage, and their breath, according to medical testimony, is extremely dangerous to the public health. That is why a tenant is quite rightly forbidden to sublet to a Jew (*Beitr. zur Juristichen Litterat.* in *Preuss. Staaten*, vol. I, p. 36), and it is precisely for this reason that Jews should not be allowed to live in the clean wide streets of capitals. Of the outrageous way in which the Jews have stolen and then tortured, violated and crucified Christian children and sucked their blood through a quill we find instances in the most reliable authors (*Bavaria sancta*, Munich, 1626, part 2, p. 315). [*Wider die Juden*, 12-13.]

The work continues in the same vein, repeating the familiar complaints about oaths, and provides an abundant bibliography. In response to objectors Grattenauer publishes, also in 1803, his *Explanation to the Public*

(*Erklärung*) and, later, an appendix (*Erster Nachtrag*) to the first pamphlet. He hates the Jews, he says; he is perfectly entitled to do so; their protests will have no effect upon him.

The Jewesses, the poetic, musical, lovely daughters of Israel! They too will be stirred up against me! . . . The Jewesses' dresses are extremely elegant and often, beholding the indescribable arsenal of scent flasks, packets of perfumes and musk, bottles of lavender water, jugs of vinegar, and sponge cases, I could not but think that some malevolent person might some day take it into his head to affirm that all these pretty girls believe that they really need all these preparations; for their own odor is not of the most pleasing.

It has, indeed, been established chemically that the Jews have a special smell. But let us be clear about this: "I have not said that all Jews smell, but only that this smell is a national heritage and that it has something quite peculiar about it, something characteristic." The question, therefore, is not whether each individual smells or not, but whether there is a distinctive Jewish smell, as there is a distinctive Jewish physiognomy. Does not the smell of a Jewish synagogue (the plague stench) differ from that of a Gothic cathedral (the incense cloud which elevates the soul)?" The chemical analysis of the air reveals the presence of ammonium pyroleosum (*Stinkmild Ammonium*). What is its origin? The uncleanliness of the Jews? An excessive consumption of onions? An unhealthy diet based on herrings and olives? Who knows? (Grattenauer, *Erklärung*, 17; *Erster Nachtrag*, 23.)

Jewish doctors have always been very dangerous; though this does not mean that there are not exceptions, as there are exceptions among their philosophers too; Grattenauer pays a tribute to Jews like Spinoza and Marcus Herz.

The Jews claim that they are indispensable. Perhaps. There is such a thing as necessary evils. But "the evils alleged to be necessary, such as public brothels, . . . are subjected to special police surveillance." The Jews should be given a special constitution.

Grattenauer's diatribes provide interesting information on the society of the period. The author is an officer of the court with police functions; he is able to tell what he has seen and even, without realizing it, to confirm the opinion of those who claim that Jews are no more corrupt than Christians. All Jews are foul usurers; but the rich supply the poor with capital for these transactions. But,

Wherever the Jews have crept in, the character of the Christian merchants, craftsmen and burghers has greatly deteriorated, for they learn the most degraded wiles from them; that is why there are also so many Christian usurers [in Berlin], who lend money on pledges and carry on usury at 50 percent with Christian money; there are Christian merchants who charge very dear for the goods sold to young libertines instead of lending them money; . . . and this is also why there are rascally artists and artisans falsifying gold and silver and producing shoddy work at high prices, . . . who grossly deceive Christians because they too are duped by Jews who advance them money. This is why there are jewelers who engage in the worst kind of deception with rings and jewelry, as happened to an acquaintance of mine who had a gold watch-chain made for him for 22 thalers; but it was only worth 3 thalers, for it was of bad gold, alloyed with even worse metal. . . .

Debauch and prostitution are the Jews' ruling vices. Young Jews keep Christian girls as mistresses [in Berlin]; . . . they are found in the brothels. Jewish wives and daughters, however, make up to Christians; for gold they are for sale to any debauchee and they even open their bedrooms to them, provided that the father knows nothing of it. They thus reduce many Christians to beggary, ruined in estate and fortune. [Über die physische . . . , 34.]

Grattenauer's pamphlet inspires others. Eisenmenger is plundered once again, especially by one writer who proposes that the Jews should be shut up in ghettoes, clothed in a special costume with distinguishing colored patches, forbidden for evermore to bring suits against Christians, and all their sons except the eldest castrated.

The Jews defend themselves clumsily (Können die Juden . . . ?); they have no pamphleteers with Grattenauer's talent. Professor Kosmann (Für die Juden) and the sober Diebitsch (Unpartheyische Gedanken) try to talk reason to a public which devours five editions of Grattenauer in a year. We shall not summarize the whole controversy.

The press, however, never wavers in its stand; in 1803 it remains as favorable to the Jews and their emancipation as it was in the past. Nor does the government's view change; it prohibits all further publications on the subject in order to calm public opinion. Grattenauer at first protests against the prohibition because it prevents him from publishing an anti-Semitic paper at Frankfort-on-Oder. Later he falls silent, though there is nothing to prevent his publishing outside Prussia. His silence may have been bought. This intriguing explanation might be deduced from a letter by a Jew to the Zeitung für die elegante Welt: Grattenauer, dismissed for his insufferable behavior and reduced to poverty, was, according to this source, living on a large sum given him by the Berlin Jewish community.

Emancipation

Emancipation was slow in coming. Giving some show of reason to those who became converts rather than await it indefinitely, it would perhaps not have come about at all had circumstances not to some extent forced the government's hand. It was introduced by Baron von Schroetter, the official in charge of East Prussian affairs in the General Directorate since 1795, who had displayed consistent hostility to the Jews.

It had taken Napoleon's Prussian campaign and the collapse of an entire system, whose military and administrative foundations had seemed proof against every contingency, to change his mind.

The French Revolution had first to overrun Europe, too, and Napoleon to create the Kingdom of Westphalia, in which the Jews were emancipated by the law of 27 January 1808. At the time there seemed to be some danger lest the wealthy and cultivated Jews quit Prussia, and that only the usurers and the poverty-stricken would stay or flock there. Von Worschke, a Silesian official, expressed this fear in a report in February 1808. Von Schroetter received it at Königsberg, whither he had followed the court when driven by the French from Berlin. He probably discussed it with Caspar, a Jewish banker whom he had come to appreciate. In the disaster which had befallen the kingdom the Jews had behaved no worse than the mass of the people, whose lack of dignity and patriotism had surprised and shocked officers and officials. And, lastly, it had required the general reforms undertaken by Stein to regenerate the moribund state. Since, in a general revision of all previous principles, social prejudice was at length under attack and since, under the municipal edict of 19 November 1808, citizenship no longer depended on birth, social rank, or religion, the status of the Jews had also to be revised. Economic stress made it prominent among the government's concerns. So long as the Jews were excluded from the nation, their money—hoarded or invested abroad—was out of circulation in Prussia. Assimilation "unfroze" their capital.

Von Schroetter first contemplated mere improvements in the Jews' status. He consulted one of his subordinates, von Troschel, a Councillor in the War and Domains Chamber, as to whether the Jews in East Prussia should be permitted to "establish" a second son. The reply came in the form of a long report to the effect that "either the Jews are irremediably and absolutely evil, in which case they should all be exterminated, or their defects are due to their legal disabilities, in which case the laws should be repealed. Reforms in minor details are inoperative. We should take a definitive stand and follow a definite policy."

Von Schroetter thereupon decided to break with the past. He drafted the bill of 20 November 1808, with an explanatory memorandum quoting other countries' experience. The Jews should be granted citizenship so that they could fulfill all the duties of the citizen and become liable to military service. Other occupations besides banking and trade would be opened to them; their capital would then come back into circulation, and some of it would go to Christians. The bill, comprising 122 articles, was submitted to the king on 22 December. It would naturalize all Jews permitted to reside in Prussia and abolish all their legal disabilities, in particular the prohibition of mixed marriages, in order to promote a redistribution of Jewish capital, "for unions between wealthy Jews and Christians may be confidently expected."

The Jews would, however, be obliged to shave their beards, dress in the German manner, take surnames, and learn to read and write the Roman or Gothic script.

Transitional measures would impose some restrictions on the present generation which was not yet assimilated. Members of it would not be able to enter the civil service, though they would be liable to military service. They would be permitted to live in the country only if they engaged in farming or a craft. They would have to get permission to acquire land, which would be granted only if for at least six years not less than one quarter of the hands employed by them were Jews or if they released their Christian peasants from feudal dues. In the towns the proportion of Jews was not to exceed between one-tenth and one-quarter of the merchants, according to the size of the place.

The practice of the Jewish religion would be free, but the appointments of the rabbis in charge of religious teaching in the public schools would be subject to approval by the authorities. The denominational schools would be closed.

Approval of the bill was delayed by the administrative reform. Then Stein was dismissed, and his successor, Count Dohna, instructed State Councillor Köhler to go over it. Hardenberg had become state chancellor, on 6 June 1810, before a decision was taken. Prompted by a petition from the Berlin Jewish community, he persuaded the king to accept the principle of full equality between Jews and Christians and instructed State Councillor von Raumer to draft a new bill. Von Raumer met with the same objections during his consultations and was blocked by the hostility of von Kircheisen, the minister of justice, in particular. It required Hardenberg's personal intervention for Pfeiffer, an official in the Ministry of Justice, to get a text based on von Schroetter's original draft approved at last. This text, as amended, became the Edict of 11 March 1812.

Under this emancipating decree the Jews acquire full rights as citizens. They may settle in the towns and in the country, acquire properties, and engage in all trades. The special taxes are abolished, mixed marriages are permitted, and the courts are open to all citizens alike; but Jews may serve as teachers only in secondary schools and universities and as officials only of local authorities. After 1815 this right is even restricted to those who had been decorated with the Iron Cross during the War of Liberation. The final removal of all restrictions on the rights of citizens imposed for social or religious reasons did not come until the 1848 revolution and articles 4 and 11 of the Constitution of 5 December of that year.

The new citizens had to prove their worth immediately. They do not seem to have behaved any less well, from the national standpoint, than their fellow countrymen. National sentiment, Prussian patriotism, is something almost equally novel to both of them in the twilight of the Aufklärung. It grows throughout Germany, however, from the end of the eighteenth century, promoted by the new schools of literature opposed to foreign influences. The word "fatherland" is coming into use, indeed into misuse; "appeals to Germany" against enslavement to French fashions are finding eager readers; the susceptible are encouraged to enter into patriotic marriages; to curb the rise in the price of wheat actually becomes a civic duty.

Nationalists dealing with the Jewish question invariably take a definitely pro-Jewish stand, encouraging assimilation and combating prejudice. This is as true of Becker, the founder of the *National-Zeitung der Teutschen*, as it is of Garlieb Merkel, a writer who engages in fierce polemics against the Romantics in literature and the French in politics. It is therefore quite intelligible that the Prussian Jews were not much concerned when Bonaparte conquered Jerusalem. There were rumors that he would summon the Jews to return there. "But," said the philosopher Baruch, "though I am a devout Jew in the narrowest sense of the term, I have never entertained the hope of living a better life at Jerusalem than I do here, where I was born and brought up. I have too much esteem for the men among whom we live, and I am too indifferent to place to conceive that the Jews would live more happily elsewhere or in a fashion more consonant with their destiny; and several of my brother Jews feel the same (*Gespräch*, 45).

There was no reason to fear, therefore, that the Jews would be seduced by Napoleon. The idea, nevertheless, crossed Merkel's mind in 1805. That year the Abbé Grégoire, now a senator, paid a visit to Germany on the pretext of studying education. Merkel asserts that he there became aware of the power of the Jews. He stayed with Jacobson, the founder of the school at Seesen, the liberator of the Jews subjected to the poll tax and the Duke of Brunswick's agent. It was shortly after the abbé's return to France that Napoleon summoned the Sanhedrin. Jacobson then addressed a petition to the emperor suggesting that he become the Grand Protector of the Jews throughout the world. A Jewish sovereign council would meet in Paris with a patriarch presiding. The Jews throughout the world would be gathered in synods under the supervision of the French government and the sovereign council, which would be empowered to grant all Jews the necessary dispensations to "fulfill the duties of the citizen" in every country.

Published by Jacobson in French and German, the petition was widely distributed. After Jena, however, Napoleon felt himself strong enough to dispense with the Jews.

Both the enlightened Jews and the Christians are equally indignant at the general lack of patriotism after Jena, and their testimony accords with that of the officers. Hardenberg had no reason to regret the edict of 11 March 1812; the Jewish volunteers fought valiantly for the fatherland in 1813. Several of them became officers and were decorated. "The young men of the

Jewish religion," Hardenberg writes to Count Grothe, the Prussian minister at Hamburg, "have been brothers-in-arms to their Christian fellow citizens; among them, too, we can point to examples of truly heroic courage and a glorious contempt for the dangers of war; the rest of the Jewish inhabitants, especially the women, have likewise associated themselves with the Christians in their sacrifices" (Freund, *Geschichte* I, 230).

Conclusion

The passage of time since the disputes revived in this book has demonstrated to those who denied the possibility of the Jews' ever improving that they could resolutely abandon their obsolete rites and collaborate with their fellow citizens in every sphere. The Jews even became, as Dohm had predicted, more robust and less prolific. The zeal of the Jewish volunteers in 1813 confuted those who had doubted their aptitude for arms. In confirmation of the Aufklärung's judgment, those who had so passionately canvassed utterly irrational arguments were reminded that Reason is eternal and universal. But time also confirmed the fears of the orthodox Jews, who wanted no reforms because they felt that their religion thrived on persecution. Their law was not religious merely, but was, as Friedländer observed in his letter to Teller, in fact the civic framework of the former nation. The granting of civil rights to the Jews in Prussia was tantamount to the separation of their church and state; and Judaism would have needed a Luther to survive the operation. In trying to preserve ancient laws for the governance of the people in the form of rites which were purely religious, the synagogue was tending to overlay its major fundamental principles with formalistic and finical practices; and the mass of the faithful still had to shake off this yoke.

Assimilation was never as complete in Prussia, however, as it was elsewhere, not because of the few remaining legal restrictions, but owing to the continuous immigration of Jews from eastern Europe, who revived in the nineteenth century the conflict between the liberal and the orthodox Jews; the problem of the relations between Christian and Jew received no complete solution; and these disputes kept anti-Semitism alive until a new doctrine imbued it with a virulence far more savage than it had ever displayed in the past.

Abbreviations

BAZ	*Berlinisches Archiv der Zeit und ihres Geschmacks*
Berlin	*Berlin, eine Zeitschrift*
BJA	*Berlinisches Journal für Aufklärung*
BM	*Berlinische Monatsschrift*
Briefe	*Briefe an ein Frauenzimmer*
Briefwechsel	*Briefwechsel, meist historischen und politischen Inhalts*
DC	*Deutsche Chronik*
DM	*Deutsches Museum* and *Neues deutsches Museum*
Eumonia	*Eumonia, eine Zeitschrift des neunzehnten Jahrhunderts*
GHM	*Göttingisches historisches Magazin* and *Neues Göttingisches historisches Magazin*
GU	*Das graue Ungeheuer*
HB	*Hyperboreische Briefe*
Jahrb.	*Jahrbücher der preussischen Monarchie unter der Regierung Friedrichs-Wilhelms des Dritten*
JD	*Journal von und für Deutschland*
JLM	*Journal des Luxus und der Moden*
JPA	*Journal der practischen Arzneykunde und Wundearzneykunde*
NBM	*Neue Berlinische Monatschrift*
NTM	*Der neue teutsche Merkur*
NZT	*National-Zeitung der Teutschen*
PAD	*Patriotisches Archiv für Deutschland*
TM	*Der teutsche Merkur*
VC	*Vaterländische Chronik*

Bibliography

A really exhaustive bibliography of works on German Romanticism would fill a volume in itself. This bibliography, therefore, lists only the books that have proved useful for this particular study, and the brief evaluations accompanying some works bear only on their relevance for this subject. Readily accessible standard editions of literary works have been used wherever the texts can be regarded as authoritative.

Manuscripts in the Prussian State Archives at Berlin-Dahlem

1. *On Censorship, the Press, and Reprints*

Rep. IX, B. I, F, 2a: Fasc. 15 (1777–82); 21 (1788–91); 22 (1788–96); 23 (*Journal de Strasbourg*); 24, 25 (1772–94); 27 (1793–95); 33, 35, 36 (1798); 39 (1799); 42 (1800–1802); 44 (1801–3); 46 (Grattenauer, 1803); 47 (1803–10). Fasc. 18 (reprints, 1783–87).

Rep. IX, B. I, F, 2a, 1: Fasc. 3 (privileges, 1736–93); 10 (1787–92); 13 (1793–1803).

Rep. XVI, no. 112 (imperial censorship).

2. *On Domestic Servants and Old Clothes Dealers*

Rep. IX, X, I, B: Fasc. 96 (ordinance on domestic servants in the Mark, 1768).

Gen. Dir., Magdeburg, 1795, Tit. CCVII, no. 9 (old clothes dealers at Halle and at Magdeburg, 1795, 1805, 1806).

3. *On the Military*

Rep. IX, X, I, B: Fascs. 96 (deserters, 1769); 97 (1766–69); 17 (disputes between soldiers and civilians, 1790).

4. *On the Poor and Vagrants*

Gen. Dir., CLXVIII.
Mark, I–X, 3 (poorhouse).

Neumark, Materien III, Polizeiprotocolle 1–2 (Generalvisitationen).

Pommern, Materien III, Vagabondensachen, nos. 3, 5, 10, 11.

Westpreussen und Netzebezirk, Materien, Tit. CXXIX, nos. 3, 8, 10, I–III (vagrancy on the Polish frontier).

Ostpreussen und Litauen, Materien, Tit. CXIV, no. 9, vol. 2 (General-visitationen and actions against apprehended vagabonds, 1804, 1805, 1806).

5. *On the Status and Examinations of Assessoren and Refendarien to the Courts and War and Domains Chambers*

Rep. 125, III *a* (candidates examined by the Ober-Examinations Com-mission).

Rep. 9, J, 7*c* (status of Auskultatoren).

Rep. 52, B. 69, Magdeburg (records of examinations, 1789).

Gen. Dir., Magdeburg, Rep. 39, Tit. VIII, no. 5 (too many candidates, 1802–4).

Rep. 32, B. 9, Minden (records of examinations, 1799–1800).

Gen. Dir., Behörden- und Bestallungssachen, Minden, Tit. VII, Referen-darien, no. 1 (1802–6).

6. *On Legal and Clerical Officials*

Rep. IX, J, 6. Fasc. 3 (Stadtgericht). Fascs. 125, 126.

Rep. IX, J, 7, Fascs. 125, 126 (Stadtgericht). Fascs. 5, 7, 19, 87, 127, 128, 151 (Auskultatoren und Referendarien im Cammergericht).

Rep. IX, J, 7, B and J, 7*c* (Referendarien im Cammergericht, 1775–1808).

Registraturbuch Churmark (1786–96), B. 12, 13, 14.

Pommern, Rep. 30 (1785–1806).

Westpreussen, Rep. 7, B. 28–29 (1786–1806).

Ostpreussen und Litauen, Convolute (1781–1810).

Ostfriesland, Rep. 68, Repertorium, B. 65 (1744–1800); B. 64 (1800–1810).

Cleve-Ravensberg, Rep. 34, Repertorium, B. 50 (1780–1817).

Minden, Rep. 32, B. 40 (1648–1785); B. 41 (1787–1815).

Magdeburg, Rep. 52, B. 60–61 (1786–1815).

Dossiers of Officials

Provinz Brandenburg, Rep. 2, vols. 19–21; Rep. 3, Tit. 3*b*, nos. 36–37.

Pommern, Rep. 30, no. 48.

Westpreussen, Rep. 7*b*, nos. 32*a*, 32*b*.

Ostpreussen, Rep. 7, no. 16*b*.

Ostfriesland, Rep. 68, no. 5*a*.

Cleve, Rep. 34, no. 18*a*.

Minden, Rep. 32, B. 9.

Magdeburg, Rep. 52, B. 69.

7. On Officials of the War and Domains Chambers

Gen. Dir., Behörden- und Bestallungssachen:
Churmark, Tit. V, no. 2 (1783–1806); Tit. VI, no. 19 (Referendarien, 1794–1806).

Pommern, Tit. III, no. 2 (K. u. D. Räte, 1786–1806); Tit. IV, no. 1 (Steuer-räte, 1776–1806); Tit. VI, no. 1 (Assessoren und Referendarien, 1790–1806).

Westpreussen und Netzebezirk: Kammer zu Marienwerder, Tit. IX, no. 1, vols. I*b*, II, III, IV, V (Räte, Assessoren, Referendarien, 1772–1806); Tit. XXIII, vols. I–III (Landräte, 1753–1806); Tit. XXV, vols. I–II (Kriegs- und Steuerräte, 1772–1806); Kammerdeputation Bromberg, Tit. III, no. 1, vols. I–III (Räte, 1775–1806); Tit. IV, no. 1 (Referen-darien, 1776–1804); Tit. V, no. 1 (Auskultatoren, 1787–90).

Ostpreussen, Tit. X, nos. 11, 15, 16 (K. u. D. Räte); Tit. XI, nos. 24, 40, 41, 60 (Referendarien, Assessoren).

Ostfriesland, Tit. VII, nos. 5, 7, 8, 9 (Assessoren, 1786–1804); Tit. IX, nos. 8, 9, 10, 12, 13, 14, 15 (Referendarien, 1791–93, 1803–4).

Cleve, Tit. VIII, nos. 1–2, B. 1 (Assessoren, Räte, 1786–1804).

Minden, Tit. IV, nos. 1–3 (K. u. D. Räte, 1746–87, 1798–1806); Tit. VI, nos. 2–3, and Tit. VII, no. 1 (Referendarien, 1802–6).

Magdeburg, Rep. 39, Tit. V (K. u. D. Räte, 1750–1800); Tit. VI (Landräte); Tit. VIII (Referendarien, 1799–1806).

8. On Other Officials

Gen. Dir., Zoll und Accise Departement, Register XLII, no. 3, vols. I–III.

Rep. 89–91, A–H J. N (Conduitenlisten des Justizdepartements, vol. I, 1800–1802).

Rep. 96, 4, II D (officials of the Gen. Dir.).

Rep. 47, 5 (Landpfarrbesetzungen Churmark, 1796–1806).

Primary Sources

1. Annuals

Adresskalender der königlich-preussischen Haupt und Residentzstadt Berlin besonderes der daselbst befindlichen hohen und niederen Collegien, Instanzien und Expeditionen auf das Jahr 1786. Berlin, 1786.

Adresskalender der königlich-preussischen Haupt und Residentzstadt Berlin, und Potsdam . . . auf das Jahr 1800. Berlin, 1800.

Allerneuester Zustand der königlichen preussischen Armee mit Angang des Jahres 1776.

Rangliste der königlich-preussischen Armee für das Jahr 1805. Berlin, 1806.

Stammliste aller Regimenter und Corps der königlich-preussischen Armee für das Jahr 1806. Berlin, 1806.

Zustand der königlich-preussischen Armee im Jahre 1786. Breslau, 1786.

2. Journals and Newspapers

Allgemeine deutsche Bibliothek. Ed. Nicolai. Berlin and Stettin, 1785–92. (See also *Neue allgemeine deutsche Bibliothek.*)

Allgemeine Literatur-Zeitung. Ed. Moser. Jena and Leipzig, 1785–1803. Cont. as *Jenaische Literatur-Zeitung*, 1804–48.

Allgemeine Zeitung. Ed. Posselt. Tübingen, 1798–1803. Cont. as *Kaiserlich und kurbayrisch privilegierte allgemeine Zeitung* to 1837.

Athenaeum. Ed. A.-W. and F. Schlegel. Berlin, 1799–1801.

Berlin, eine Zeitschrift. Ed. Rhode. Berlin, 1799.

Berlinische Blätter. Ed. Gedicke and Biester. Berlin, 1797–98.

Berlinische Monatsschrift. Ed. Gedicke and Biester. Berlin, 1783–96. (See also *Neue* . . .)

Berlinisches Archiv der Zeit und ihres Geschmacks. Ed. Rambach and Fessler. Berlin, 1798–1801.

Berlinisches Journal für Auklärung. Ed. Fischer and Riem. Berlin, 1788–90.

Braunschweigisches Journal, philosophischen, philologischen und pädagogischen Inhalts. Ed. Trapp, Stuve, Hensinger, and Campe. Brunswick, 1788–91.

Briefe an ein Frauenzimmer. Ed. Merkel. Berlin, 1801–2.

Briefwechsel, meist historischen und politischen Inhalts. Ed. Schloezer. Göttingen, 1776–83.

Chronologen. Ed. Wekhrlin. Frankfurt and Leipzig, 1779–81.

Deutsche Chronik. Ed. Schubart. Augsburg, 1774–77. Ed. Miller, Köhler, Haid, Laib, and Gradmann to 1891.

Deutsches Museum. Ed. Boie and Dohm. Leipzig, 1776–81. (See also *Neues* . . .)

Erholungen. Ed. G. W. Becker. Leipzig, 1796–1805.

Eumonia, eine Zeitschrift des neunzehnten Jahrhunderts. Ed. Fessler and Rhode. Berlin, 1801.

Europa, eine Zeitschrift. Ed. F. Schlegel. Berlin, 1799–1801.

Freimüthige, der. Ed. Kotzebue and Merkel. Berlin, 1792–1808.

Göttingisches historisches Magazin. Ed. Meiners and Spittler. Hanover, 1791–94. (See also *Neues* . . .)

Graue Ungeheuer, das. Ed. Wekhrlin. Nuremberg, 1784–87.

Hyperboreische Briefe. Ed. Wekhrlin. Nuremberg, 1788–90.

Jahrbücher der preussischen Monarchie unter der Regierung Friedrichs-Wilhelms des Dritten. Ed. Unger. Berlin, 1795–1801.

Jenaische Literatur-Zeitung. See *Allgemeine Literatur-Zeitung.*

Journal von und für Deutschland. Ed. Goekingk and Bibra. Ellrich, 1784–92.

Journal des Luxus und der Moden. Ed. Bertuch and Kraus. Weimar, 1787–1837.

Journal der practischen Arzneykunde und Wundearzneykunde. Ed. Hufe-
land. Jena, 1795–1837. Cont. as *Journal der practischen Heilkunde* to
1844.
Kaiserlich und kurbayrisch privilegierte allgemeine Zeitung. See *Allgemeine
Zeitung.*
*Königlich-privilegierte Berlinische Zeitung von Staats- und gelehrten Sachen
(Vossische Zeitung).*
Magazin für die Geographie und Statistik der preussischen Staaten.
Musenalmanach für das Jahr 1802. Ed. A.-W. and F. Schlegel and L. Tieck.
Tübingen, 1802.
National-Zeitung der Teutschen. Ed. Z. Becker. 1796–1805.
Neue allgemeine deutsche Bibliothek. Ed. Nicolai. Kiel, 1793–1800. Berlin
and Stettin, 1801–6.
Neue Berlinische Monatschrift. Ed. Biester. 1799.
Neue teutsche Merkur, der. Ed. Wieland. Weimar, 1798–1810.
Neues deutsches Museum. Ed. Boie. Leipzig, 1782–91.
Neues Göttingisches historisches Magazin. Ed. Meiners and Spittler.
Hanover, 1791–94.
Neues patriotisches Archiv für Deutschland. Ed. Moser. Leipzig, 1792–99.
Neueste Weltkunde. Ed. Posselt. Tübingen, 1798.
Patriotisches Archiv für Deutschland. Ed. Moser. Leipzig, 1784–90. (See also
Neues . . .)
Poetisches Journal. Ed. Tieck. Jena, 1800.
Politisches Journal. Ed. Schirach. Hamburg, 1781–1804.
Statsanzeigen. Ed. Schloezer. Göttingen, 1783–95.
Teutsche Merkur, der. Ed. Wieland. Weimar, 1773–89. (See also *Neue . . .*)
Vaterländische Chronik. Ed. Schubart. Augsburg, 1787–91.
Zeitung für die elegante Welt. Ed. Spazier. Leipzig, 1801–5.

3. Books and Pamphlets

Albrecht, H. C. *Geheime Geschichte eines Rosenkreutzers.* Hamburg, 1792.
*Allgemeines Landrecht für die preussischen Staaten, in Verbindung mit
ergänzenden Verordnungen.* Ed. A. G. Mannkopff. 9 vols. Berlin, 1837.
Augustin, F. L. *Die königlich-preussische Medicinalverfassung, oder voll-
ständige Darstellung aller das Medicinalwesen und die medicinische
Polizei in den königlich-preussischen Staaten betreffenden Gesetze,
Verordnungen, Einrichtungen.* 2 vols. Potsdam, 1818.
Bachmann, T. C. *Kurzer Entwurf einer Statistik der preussischen Staaten.*
Halle, 1790. (With bibliography.)
Bertuch, J. C. *Über Erziehung des künftigen Soldaten, nebst einem
Vorschlag bei einzelnen Regimentern Schulen zu errichten.* Berlin, 1781.
Boettchers, J. F. *Bemerkungen über Medicinalverfassung, Hospitäler und
Kurarten.* 2 vols. Königsberg, 1800.

Böttiger, K. A. *Literarische Zustände und Zeitgenossen aus dem Nachlasse.* 8 vols. Leipzig, 1839.

Brandes, E. *Über die Weiber.* Leipzig, 1787.

Briefe über die Auswanderung der Unterthanen, besonders nach Russland. Gotha, 1770.

Chateaubriand. *Génie du Christianisme.* Paris, 1802.

Die Mainzer Klubbisten zu Königstein, oder die Weiber decken einander die Schanden auf. Ein tragi-komisches Schauspiel in einem Auszuge. 1793. (Facsimile ed., Leipzig, 1906.)

Der brandenburgisch-preussische Staat am Schlusse des achtzehnten Jahrhunderts, oder Reise durch sämtliche königliche preussische Provinzen. Berlin, 1801.

Diebitsch, Freiherr von. *Unpartheyische Gedanken über Juden und Christen.* Berlin, 1804.

Dilthey, W. *Aus Schleiermachers Leben, in Briefen.* 4 vols. Berlin, 1860–69.

Dohm, C. W. *Über die bürgerliche Verbesserung der Juden.* 2 vols. Berlin and Stettin, 1781–82.

(Dorothea.) *Florentin.* Ein Roman. Ed. Schlegel. Lübeck and Leipzig, 1801.

Eberhard, J. A. *Uber die Zeichen der Aufklärung einer Nation. Eine Vorlesung.* Halle, 1783.

Ein Wort an die Herrschaften, die gutes Gesinde haben wollen. Breslau, 1797.

Eisenmenger, J. A. *Das . . . entdeckte Judenthum* . . . Amsterdam, 1761.

Emmermann, F. W. *Geprüfte Einleitung zur Einrichtung und Verwaltung der öffentlichen Armenanstalten überhaupt und besonders auf dem Lande.* 2d. ed. Giessen, 1814.

————. *Über öffentliche Armenanstalten auf dem Lande. Ein Versuch.* Siegen, 1809.

Fincke, H. *Briefe an Friedrich Schlegel.* Cologne, 1917.

Forster, J. G. *Ansichten vom Niederrhein, von Brabant, Flandern, Holland, England, und Frankreich in April, Mai, und Juni 1790.* 2 vols. Leipzig, 1790.

————. *Briefwechsel.* 2 vols. Leipzig, 1829.

Frederick the Great. *Oeuvres de Frédéric le Grand.* Ed. J. D. E. Preuss. 31 vols. Berlin, 1846–57.

Fricke, J. E. *Grundsätze des Rechts der Handwerker.* 2d ed. Göttingen and Kiel, 1778.

Friedländer, D. *Aktenstücke, die Reform der jüdischen Kolonie betreffend.* Berlin, 1793.

————.*Bibliographie méthodique des ouvrages publiés en Allemagne sur les pauvres.* Paris, 1833.

Garve, C. *Versuche über verschiedene Gegenstände aus der Moral, der Literatur und dem gesellschaftlichen Leben.* 5 vols. Breslau, 1802.

Gespräch über das Sendschreiben von einigen jüdischen Hausvätern . . . zwischen einem christlichen Theologen und einem alten Juden. Berlin, 1799.

Goethe, J. W. von. *Werke.* Ed. Heinemann. 30 vols. Leipzig and Vienna, n.d.

(Grattenauer, C. W.) *Erster Nachtrag zu einer Erklärung über seine Schrift: Wider die Juden. Ein Anhang zur fünften Auflage.* Berlin, 1803.

(————.) *Erklärung an das Publikum.* Berlin, 1803.

(————.) *Uber die physische und moralische Verfassung der heutigen Juden. Stimme eines Kosmopoliten.* Germanien, 1791.

(————.) *Wider die Juden.* Berlin, 1803.

Grellmann, N. N. G. *Staatskunde von Teutschland im Grundrisse.* Göttingen, 1780.

Gries, J. D. *Aus dem Leben von Johann Diederich Gries. Nach seinen eigenen und den Briefen seiner Zeitgenossen.* Leipzig, 1855.

Grolman, K. *Versuch einer Entwickelung der rechtlichen Natur der Ausspiel-Geschäfte.* Giessen, 1797.

Hagen, T. P. von der. *Nachricht von den Medicinal-Anstalten und medicinischen Collegiis in den preussischen Staaten.* Berlin, 1786.

Hahnemann, S. *Der Kaffee in seinen Wirkungen, nach eignen Beobachtungen.* Leipzig, 1803.

Hartmann, F. *Ob die bürgerliche Freiheit den Juden zu gestatten sei.* Berlin, 1783.

Herder, J. G. von. *Sämmtliche Werke.* Ed. Suphan. 33 vols. Berlin, 1877–1913.

Hertzberg, E. F. *Huit dissertations lues dans les assemblées publiques de l'Académie royale des Sciences et Lettres de Berlin, tenues pour l'anniversaire du roi Frédéric II dans les années 1780–87.* Berlin, 1787.

————. *Oeuvres politiques.* 3 vols. Berlin and Paris, 1795.

Herz, M. *Briefe an Ärzte.* 2d ed. 2 vols. Berlin, 1784.

————. *Über die frühe Beerdigung der Juden.* Berlin, 1787.

Hess, L. *Gedanken über Prachtgesetze.* Hamburg, 1781.

(————.) *Die Schädlichkeit der Zahlenlotterie. Ein Geschenk an das Publikum.*

Hippel, T. G. von. *Biographie des königlichen preussischen Geheimenkriegraths zu Königsberg . . . zum Theil von ihm selbst verfasst.* Gotha, 1801.

————. *Über die Ehe.* 4th ed. Berlin, 1793.

————. *Versuch über die bürgerliche Verbesserung der Weiber.* Berlin, 1792.

Hoff, A. *Über Gesinde, Gesindeordnung und deren Verbesserungen.* Berlin, 1789.

Holtei, K. *Briefe an Ludwig Tieck.* 4 vols. Breslau, 1864.

Hufeland, C. W. *Makrobiotik oder Kunst das menschliche Leben zu verlängern.* 3d. ed. 2 vols. Berlin, 1805.

Humboldt. W. *Gesammelte Schriften.* Ed. Leitzmann. Berlin, 1903.

————. *Ideen zu einem Versuch die Grenzen der Wirksamkeit des Staats zu bestimmen.* Vol. 1 of *Gesammelte Schriften* (see above).

————. *Tagebücher.* Vols. 14 and 16 of *Gesammelte Schriften* (see above).

Jacobi, F. H. *Woldemar.* 2 vols. Königsberg, 1796.

Jacobi, J. L. *Schleiermachers Briefe an den Graf zu Dohna.* 1887.

Jung-Stilling, J. H. *Lebensgeschichte.* 2 vols. Berlin, n.d.

Kant, I. *Werke.* Ed. Cassirer. 11 vols. Berlin, 1912–22.

(Kerndoerffer, H. A.) *Lotterien und Kunst zu gewinnen.* Frankfurt and Leipzig, 1796.

Kleist, H. von. *Dramen.* Leipzig, n.d.

Knigge, A. von. *Über den Umgang mit Menschen.* Berlin (1788).

Knoblauch, H. *Über die sittliche und wissenschaftliche Bildung der jungen Leute, welche dem Militär sich widmen.* Berlin, 1800.

Koerner, H. *Briefe von und an Friedrich und Dorothea Schlegel.* Berlin, 1926.

————, and Wienecke, H. *August-Wilhelm und Friedrich Schlegel im Briefwechsel mit Schiller und Goethe.* Leipzig, n.d.

Können die Juden ohne Nachtheil für den Staat in ihrer jetzigen Verfassung bleiben? Berlin, 1803.

Kortum, K. A. *Der Kaffee und seine Stellvertreter.* Leipzig, 1809.

Kosmann. *Für die Juden.* Berlin, 1803.

(Kotzebue, A. von.) *Der hyperboreische Esel oder die heutige Bildung.* . . . Leipzig, 1799.

Korff, H. de. *Essai statistique sur la monarchie prussienne.* Berlin, 1791. (Superficial.)

Kruenitz, J. G. *Das Gesindwesen nach Grundsätzen der Oekonomie und Polizeywissenschaft abgehandelt.* Berlin, 1779.

Krug, L. *Philosophie der Ehe.* Leipzig, 1792.

————. "Was ist für die preussische Staatskunde bis jetzt gethan und was ist für dieselbe noch zu thun übrig?" *Jahrbücher* (see sec. 2 above) 1798, II, 422–33, and III, 25–35. (General and regional bibliography, very detailed.)

Kulenkamp, E. J. *Das Recht der Handwerke und Zünfte.* Marburg, 1807.

Kurze Darstellung einiger Handwerks-Missbräuche und Vorschläge wie solche zu verbessern sein können. Von einem Unstudierten. Nebst einer gekrönten Preisschrift über das Wandern der Handwerkgesellen.

Küster, J. E. *Beiträge zur preussischen Staatskunde.* Berlin, 1806.

Leitzmann, A. *Briefe von Wilhelm von Humboldt an Friedrich Heinrich Jacobi.* Halle, 1892.

Lessing, G. E. *Werke.* 6 vols. in 2. Leipzig, n.d.

Liebecke, J. C. G. *Auszüge aus den königlich-preussischen Polizey-Gesetzen in Beziehung auf Gesundheit und Leben der Menschen.* Magdeburg, 1805.

Locke, John. *Essay concerning Human Understanding.* 1690.

(Lorenz, J. G.) *Zuruf an alle Generale, Regimentschefs, Magistrate, Inspectoren, Prediger und Beamte, veranlasst durch das in der kölnische Vorstadtkirche gehaltene Examen mit der Kasernenschule des Infanterieregiments von Pfuhl.* Berlin, 1778.

Luc, J. de. *Lettre aux auteurs juifs d'un mémoire adressé à M. Teller.* Berlin, 1799.

Luedecke, H. *Ludwig Tieck und die Gebrüder Schlegel. Briefe mit Einleitung . . .* Frankfurt, 1930.

Meisner, H. *Briefe August Ludwig Hülsens, J. B. Vermehrens, und Fritz Weicharts an Friedrich Schleiermacher.* Berlin, 1913.

————. *Briefe Friedrich Schleiermachers an Ehrenfried und Henriette von Willich, geb. von Mühlenfels, 1801–1806.* Berlin, 1914.

————, and Schmidt, E. *Briefe von Dorothea Schlegel an Friedrich Schleiermacher.* Berlin, 1913.

————. *Briefe von Karl Gustav von Brinkmann an Friedrich Schleiermacher.* Berlin, 1912.

Mendelssohn, M. *Gesammelte Schriften.* 7 vols. Leipzig, 1843–45.

Meusel, F. *Friedrich August von Marwitz. Ein Märkischer Edelmann im Zeitalter der Befreiungskriege.* 3 vols. Berlin, 1908–13.

Mirabeau, Comte de. *De la monarchie prussienne sous Frédéric le Grand.* London, 1788.

Moritz, K. P. *Anton Reiser. Ein autobiographischer Roman.* Munich, 1912.

Moses und Christus. Berlin, 1799.

Nachricht an das Publikum wie der warme Rokentrank auf eine gute Art zubereitet und mit welchen Nutzen selbiger anstatt des Coffe gebraucht werden kann. Berlin, 1786.

Nicolai, C. F. *Beschreibung der königlichen Residenzstädte Berlin und Potsdam.* 3d ed. 3 vols. Berlin, 1786. (With bibliography.)

————. *Beschreibung einer Reise durch Deutschland und die Schweiz im Jahre 1785.* 12 vols. Berlin and Stettin, 1783–1806.

————. *Das Leben und die Meinungen des Herrn Sebaldus Nothanker.* 2d ed. 3 vols. Berlin, 1774–76.

Novalis. *Schriften.* Ed. Kluckholn. 4 vols. Leipzig (1929).

Paalzow, C. L. von. *Bernhard und Philibert. Gespräche über Glückspiele, in Sonderheit über die Lotterie.* Dessau, 1819.

————. *De civitate Judaeorum.* Berlin, 1803. Trans. as *Über das Bürgerrecht der Juden.* Leipzig, 1804.

————. *Von den Juden.* Berlin, 1799.

Patriotische Gedanken über die Bevölkerung. Frankfurt and Leipzig, 1781.

Pilat, R. J. *Über Arme und Armenpflege.* Berlin, 1804.

Plitt, G. L. *Aus Schellings Leben. In Briefen.* 3 vols. Leipzig, 1869–70.

Rahel. *Ein Buch des Andenkens für ihre Freunde.* 3 vols. Berlin, 1834.

Raich, J. M. *Dorothea von Schlegel und deren Söhne Johannes und Philipp Veit. Briefwechsel.* Mainz, 1881.

————. *Novalis. Briefwechsel mit Friedrich, August-Wilhelm, Charlotte und Caroline Schlegel.* 2 vols. Mainz, 1881.

Reichl, G. C. *Vom Fieber und dessen Behandlung überhaupt.* Berlin, 1800.

Rochow, F. E. *Von Verbesserung des Volksschulkarakters durch Volksschulen.* Dessau and Leipzig, 1781.

Rumpf, J. D. F. *Deutschlands Goldgrube, oder durch welche inländischen Erzeugnisse kann der fremde Kaffee, Thee und Zucker möglichst ersetzt werden? Und was ist insbesonders von der Zubereitung aus Runkelrüben und Ahornbäumen zu erwarten?* Berlin, 1799.

Schiller, J. C. F. von. *Werke.* 6 vols. Leipzig, 1905–6.

Schlegel, F. von. *Lucinde.* Reclam ed.

————. *Sämmtliche Werke.* 15 vols. Vienna, 1846.

————. *Ode an Napoleon.* Leipzig, n.d.

————. *Prosaische Jugendschriften, 1794–1802.* Ed. Minor. 2 vols. Vienna, 1882.

Schleiermacher, F. *Briefe bei Gelegenheit der politisch-theologischen Aufgabe.* Berlin, 1799.

————. *Reden über die Religion.* 1799.

————. *Vertraute Briefe über Lucinde.* 1801.

Schmidt, E. *Caroline. Briefe aus der Frühromantik.* 2 vols. Leipzig, 1913.

Schoen, T. von. *Aus den Papieren des Ministers und Burggrafen von Marienburg, Theodor von Schoen.* 6 vols. Halle and Berlin, 1875–83.

Schubart, C. F. D. *Leben und Gesinnungen von ihm selbst im Kerker aufgesetzt.* 2 vols. Stuttgart, 1839.

Seligmann Pappenheim, S. *Notwendigkeit der früheren Beerdigung der Juden.* Breslau, 1798.

Semler, J. S. *Lebensbeschreibung.* 2 vols. Halle, 1781.

Sendschreiben an Seine Hochwürden Herrn Oberconsistorialrath und Probst Teller zu Berlin, von einigen Hausvätern jüdischer Religion. Berlin, 1799.

Shaftesbury, Earl of. *Characteristicks of Men, Manners, Opinions, Times.* 3 vols. 1711.

Spalding, J. J. *Über die Nutzbarkeit des Predigtamtes und deren Beförderung.* 3d ed. Berlin, 1791.

(Spazier.) *Carl Pilgers Roman seines Lebens.* 2 vols. Berlin, 1792–93.

Staël, Madame de. *De l'Allemagne.* Paris, 1810.

Steffens, F. *Was ich erlebte.* 4 vols. Breslau, 1840–41.

Süssmilch, J. P. *Die göttliche Ordnung in den Veränderung des menschlichen Geschlechts aus der Geburt, dem Tode und der Fortpflanzung derselben erwiesen.* 4th ed. 3 vols. Berlin, 1775.

Tax-Ordnung für die Medicinal-Personen in den königlich-preussischen Staaten. Berlin, 1802.

Teller, W. A. *Beantwortung des Sendschreibens einiger Hausväter jüdischer Religion an mich.* Berlin, 1799.

Tieck, L. *Kritische Schriften.* 4 vols. Leipzig, 1842–52.

———. *Nachgelassene Schriften.* Ed. R. Koepke. 2 vols. Leipzig, 1855.

———. *Schriften.* 28 vols. Berlin, 1828–54.

Treue Relation des Eindrucks den das . . . Sendschreiben . . . machte. Ein Fingerzeig für die Juden. Berlin, 1799.

Über Gesinde, Gesinde-Ordnung und deren Verbesserung. Ein Beitrag zu des Herrn von Hoffs Abhandlung über diesen Gegenstand. Von einem Bedienten. Berlin, 1790.

Unger, R. *Briefe von Dorothea und Friedrich Schlegel an die Familie Paulus.* Berlin, 1913.

Varnhagen von Ense, K. A. *Biographische Denkmale.* 2d ed. 5 vols. 1845–46.

———. *Denkwürdigkeiten und vermischte Schriften.* Mannheim, 1837.

Wackenroder, W. H. *Werke und Briefe.* Ed. Franz von der Leyen. 2 vols. Jena, 1910.

Wahrhold, E. *Die Weinhold'sche Übervölkerung Mittel-Europas.* Halle, 1827.

Walzel, O. *August-Wilhelm und Friedrich Schlegel. In Auswahl.* Stuttgart, 1892.

———. *Friedrich Schlegel. Briefe an seinen Bruder August-Wilhelm Schlegel.* Berlin, 1890.

Weber. F. B. *Staatswirtschaftlicher Versuch über das Armenwesen und die Armenpolicey mit vorzüglicher Hinsicht auf die dahin einschlagende Literatur.* Göttingen, 1807.

Weinhold, C. A. *Von der Übervölkerung in Mittel-Europa und deren Folgen auf die Staaten und ihre Civilisation.* Halle, 1827.

(Wenzel, O. T.) *Politische und statistische Meynungen über die Auswanderungen der Teutschen. Ihre Ursachen und Mittel ihnen vorzubeugen.* Dresden, 1781.

Wieland, C. M. *Gesammelte Schriften.* 16 vols. Berlin, 1916–30.

Wienecke, E. *Caroline und Dorothea Schlegel in Briefen.* Weimar, 1914.

Zadig, Dr. *Betrachtungen über das Verfahren mit verstorbenen Personen bei Christen und Juden.* Breslau, 1798.

Zincke, P., and Leitmann, A. *Forster. Tagebücher.* Berlin, 1914.

Secondary Sources

Allgemeine deutsche Biographie.

Alt, C. *Schiller und die Gebrüder Schlegel.* Weimar, 1904.

Ayrault, R. *Heinrich von Kleist.* Paris, 1932.

Basch, V. *Les doctrines politiques des philosophies classiques de l'Allemagne.* Paris, 1927.

Behre, O. *Geschichte der Statistik in Brandenburg-Preussen bis zur Grün-

dung des königlichen statistischen Bureaus. Berlin, 1905. (Very valuable. Compiles, criticizes, and comments on data before the end of the eighteenth century.)

Biedermann, K. *Deutschlands geistige, sittliche und gesellige Zustände im achtzehnten Jahrhundert.* 2d ed. 2 vols. Leipzig, 1880. (Superficial and out-of-date.)

Blamquis, G. *Caroline de Günderode, 1780–1806.* Paris, 1910.

Boos, N. *Geschichte der Freimauerei.* 2d ed. Aarau, 1906. (Excellent handbook on subject of freemasonry as a whole.)

Borries, K. *Die Romantik und die Geschichte.* Berlin, 1925.

Bossert, A. *Histoire de la littérature allemande.* 8th ed. Paris, 1928.

———. *Un Prussien libéré. Herder, sa vie, son oeuvre.* Paris, 1916.

Braun, A.; Roethe, G.; and Schmidt, E. *Dorothea als Schriftstellerin in Zusammenhang mit der romantischen Schule. Untersuchungen und Texte.* Berlin, 1905.

Bruford, W. H. *Germany in the Eighteenth Century: The Social Background of the Literary Revival.* Cambridge, 1935. (Rather superficial but stimulating, with well-selected quotations from contemporary authors.)

Cavaignac, O. *La formation de la Prusse contemporaine.* 2 vols. Paris, 1891.

Chapuis, A. "Le grand Frédéric et ses horlogers." *Journal suisse d'horlogerie et de bijouterie,* 1938.

Consentius, E. "Friedrich der Grosse und die Zeitungs-Censur. Mit Benutzung der Akten des geheimen Staats-Archivs." *Preussische Jahrbücher* 1904, pp. 222–49.

Das Ideengut der deutschen Romantik. Halle, 1941. (Excellent conspectus of the Romantic eras from 1797 to 1830.)

Das Zeitalter der deutschen Erhebung, 1795–1815. 2d ed. Leipzig, 1913.

Diepgen, P. *Deutsche Medizin vor hundert Jahren. Ein Beitrag zur Geschichte der Romantik.*

———. *Geschichte der Medizin.* Vol. 3. Berlin and Leipzig, 1919.

Dilthey, W. *Das Erlebnis und die Dichtung. Lessing, Goethe, Novalis, Hölderlin.* 7th ed. Leipzig and Berlin, 1921.

———. *Leben Schleiermachers.* 2d ed., rev. H. Mulert. Leipzig, 1922.

———. "Schleiermachers politische Gesinnung und Tätigkeit." *Preussische Jahrbücher* 1862, X, 236 ff.

———. *Studien zur Geschichte des deutschen Geistes. Gesammelte Schriften,* vol. 3. Leipzig and Berlin, 1927. (Basic for the history of ideas.)

Dubnow, S. *Die Geschichte des jüdischen Volkes in der Neuzeit.* Vols. 8 and 9. Berlin, 1928. (Translated from the Russian.)

Durlacher, E. *Rituel de toutes les grandes fêtes à l'usage des Israélites du rite allemand, traduit en français. Veille et matin de Kippour.* 3d ed. Paris, 1891.

Eckardt, J. *Garlieb Merkel über Deutschland zur Schiller-Goethezeit, 1797–1806.* Berlin, 1887.

Enders, C. *Friedrich Schlegel. Die Quellen seines Wesens und Werdens.* Leipzig, 1913. (Basic, with great detail on literary questions.)

Ermatinger, H. *Deutsche Kultur im Zeitalter der Aufklärung.* Potsdam, 1935. (Good popular study, lavishly and intelligently illustrated.)

Etzin, F. "Die Freiheit der öffentlichen Meinung unter der Regierung Friedrichs des Grossen." *Forschungen für brandenburgische und preussische Geschichte* 1921, XXXIII, 89–129, 293–326. (The best study of this topic.)

Fincke, H. *Über Friedrich und Dorothea Schlegel.* Cologne, 1918.

———. "Über Friedrich Schlegel (Schwierigkeiten seiner Beurteilung. Die Arbeitsgebiete seiner zweiten Lebenshälfte)." *Reden, gehalten im Mai 1918, bei der Übergabe des Prorektorats . . . ,* pp. 25–108. Freiburg-in-Bresgau, 1918.

Flitner, W. *August Ludwig Hülsen und der Bund der freien Männer.* Jena, 1913.

Förster, N. *Die Entstehung der preussischen Landkirche unter der Regierung Königs Friedrich-Wilhelms des Dritten.* 2 vols. Tübingen, 1905–7.

Freudenthal, M. "Die ersten Emanzipationsbestrebungen der Juden in Breslau." *Monatsschrift für Geschichte und Wissenschaft des Judenthums,* 1891–92, pp. 570 ff.

Freund, J. *Geschichte der jüdischen Emanzipation.* 2 vols. Berlin, 1912.

Friedländer, E. *Ältere Universitäts-Matrikeln. I. Frankfurt an der Oder.* 3 vols. Leipzig, 1887–91.

Fuchs, A. *Les apports français dans l'oeuvre de Wieland, 1772–1789.* Paris, 1934.

Fürst, J. *Henriette Herz. Ihr Leben und ihre Erinnerungen.* 2d ed. Berlin, 1858.

Gebhart, B. *Handbuch der deutschen Geschichte.* 7th ed. 2 vols. Stuttgart and Berlin, 1930.

Geiger, L. *Geschichte der Juden in Berlin.* 2 vols. Berlin, 1871.

Glawe, W. *Die Religion Friedrich Schlegels. Ein Beitrag zur Geschichte der Romantik.* Berlin, 1906.

Gneisau und die deutsche Freiheitsidee. Tübingen, 1932. (Public lecture bringing out general ideas.)

Graetz, H. *Geschichte der Juden.* 2d ed. Vol. 6. Leipzig, 1900.

Halbwachs, H. *Le Suicide.* Paris, 1930.

Haeser, H. *Lehrbuch der Geschichte der Medizin und der epidemischen Krankheiten.* 3d ed. Vol. 3. Jena, 1881. (Basic.)

Hartung, F. "Die Epochen der absoluten Monarchie in der neueren Geschichte." *Historische Zeitschrift* 1932, CXLV, 46–52.

Haym, R. *Die romantische Schule. Ein Beitrag zur Geschichte des deutschen Geistes.* 5th ed., rev. O. Walzel. Berlin, 1928. (Basic.)

Heilmann, K. *Geschichte der Pädagogik.* 9th ed. Vol. 3 of *Handbuch der Pädagogik.* Leipzig, 1911. (Excellent handbook.)

Heimann, O., et al. *Romantik. Forschungen.* Halle, 1929. (*Deutsche Viertel-jahrsschrift für Literaturwissenschaft und Geistesgeschichte.*)

Heine, H. *Die romantische Schule.* Leipzig, n.d.

Hensel, S. *Die Familie Mendelssohn, 1729-1747.* Rev. Brandès. 2 vols. Leipzig, 1929.

Hettner, H. *Literaturgeschichte des achtzehnten Jahrhunderts.* 3d ed. 6 vols. Brunswick, 1872. (Less concerned with ideas but much more accurate and objective than many later works.)

Hillebrand, K. "La société à Berlin de 1789 à 1815." *Revue des deux mondes* 1870, XXXIV, 448 ff.

Hinrichs, C. *Die Wollindustrie in Preussen unter Friedrich Wilhelm I.* Berlin, 1935.

Hintze, O. *Die preussische Seidenindustrie im 18. Jahrhundert und ihre Begründung durch Friedrich den Grossen.* 3 vols. Berlin, 1892.

———. "Zur Agrarpolitik Friedrichs des Grossen." *Forschungen zur bran-denburgischen und preussischen Geschichte* X, 275-309.

Hirschfeld, E. "Romantische Medizin. Zu einer künftigen Geschichte der naturphilosophischen Aera." *Kykos, Jahrbuch für Geschichte und Philo-sophie der Medizin.* (Institut für Geschichte der Medizin, University of Leipzig) 1930, 1-30.

Holstein, G. *Die Staatsphilosophie Schleiermachers.* Bonn and Leipzig, 1923.

Holtze, F. *Geschichte der königlich-preussischen Armee bis zum Jahre 1807.* 3 vols. Berlin, 1928-29. (Basic.)

Huch, R. *Die Romantik.* 2d ed. Leipzig, 1908. (More an attempt to recon-struct a climate than to give specific facts.)

Imle, F. *Friedrich von Schlegels Entwicklung von Kant zum Katholismus.* Paderborn, 1927.

Kapp, F. "Berliner geschriebene Zeitungen aus dem vorigen Jahrhundert." *Deutsche Rundschau* 1879, XXI, 107-22. (Out-of-date.)

———, and Goldfriedrich, J. *Geschichte des deutschen Buchhandels.* 3 vols. Berlin, 1886. (Basic.)

Kapp, G. F. *Die Bauernbefreiung und der Ursprung der Landarbeiten in den älteren Teilen Preussens.* Leipzig, 1887.

Kayserling, M. *Moses Mendelssohn. Sein Leben und seine Wirkung.* 2d ed. Leipzig, 1888. (Basic.)

Kluckhohn, P. *Die deutsche Romantik.* Bielefeld and Leipzig, 1924.

———. *Weltanschauung der Frühromantik . . .* Leipzig, 1932.

Koepke, R. *Ludwig Tieck. Erinnerungen aus dem Leben des Dichters nach dessen mündlichen und schriftlichen Mitteilungen.* 2 vols. Leipzig, 1855.

Koerner, J. "Mendelssohns Töchter." *Preussische Jahrbücher* 1928, CCXIV, 167-82.

Korff, H. A. *Geist der Goethezeit. Sturm und Drang.* Leipzig, 1923. (Basic.)

Koser, R. "Friedrich der Grosse und die preussischen Universitäten." *Forschungen zur brandenburgischen und preussischen Geschichte* 1900, XVII, 95-155.

————. *Geschichte Friedrichs des Grossen.* 4th ed. 4 vols. Stuttgart and Berlin, 1912-14. (Still the fullest and most important study.)

Kühn, S. *Der Hirschberger Leinwand und Schleierhandel von 1648-1806.* Breslau, 1938. (Basic.)

Lamprecht, K. *Deutsche Geschichte.* 4th ed. Vol. 9. Berlin, 1922.

Lederbogen, L. *Friedrich Schlegels Geschichtsphilosophie.* Leipzig, 1908.

Lefèbvre, G. *Les paysans du nord pendant la Révolution.* Lille, 1924.

Léon, X. *Fichte et son temps.* 3 vols. Paris, 1924-27.

Lerch, P. *Friedrich Schlegels philosophische Anschauungen in ihrer Entwicklung und systematischer Ausgestaltung.* Berlin, 1905.

Leroux, R. *Guillaume de Humboldt. La formation de sa pensée jusqu'en 1794.* Strasbourg, 1932.

————. *La théorie du despotisme éclairé chez Karl Theodor Dalberg.* Strasbourg, 1932.

Lévy-Bruhl, L. *L'Allemagne depuis Leibnitz. Essai sur le développement de la conscience nationale en Allemagne, 1700-1848.* 2d ed. Paris, 1907. (Best study in French.)

Lewalter, E. *Friedrich Schlegel und sein romantischer Witz.* Leipzig, 1917.

Lichtenberger, H. *Novalis.* Paris, 1912.

Lotz, A. *Geschichte des deutschen Beamtentums.* Berlin, 1909. (Superficial.)

Mann. O. *Der junge Friedrich Schlegel. Eine Analyse von Existenz und Werk.* Berlin, 1932.

Marcinowski, F. *Das Lotteriewesen im Königreich Preussen.* Berlin, 1892.

Martiny, F. *Die Adelsfrage in Preussen vor 1806 als politisches und soziales Problem.* Stuttgart and Berlin, 1938. (Very useful.)

Meinecke, F. *Weltbürgertum und Nationalstaat.* 7th ed. Munich, 1928. (Essential for political doctrines.)

Meyer, E. R. *Schleiermachers und Brinckmanns Gang durch die Brüdergemeinde.* Berlin, 1927.

Meyer, M. *Geschichte der preussischen Handwerkerpolitik, 1640-1740.* 2 vols. Minden, 1884-88.

Meyer-Montfort, P. *Dorothea im Ideenkreis ihrer Zeit und in ihrer religiösen, philosophischen und ethischen Entwicklung.*

Milkau, F. *Handbuch der Bibliothekswissenschaft.* 2 vols. Leipzig, 1931. (Basic.)

Minder, R. *Un poète romantique allemand: Ludwig Tieck, 1773-1855.* Paris, 1936.

————. *Die religiöse Entwicklung von Karl Philipp Moritz auf Grund seiner autobiographischen Schriften. Formen der Mystik und des Pietismus in "Reiser" und "Hartknopf."* Berlin, 1936. (Of particular value for Quietism.)

Minor, J. "Wilhelm Schlegel, 1804-1845." *Zeitschrift für österreichische Gymnasien* 1837, pp. 590 ff and 733 ff.

Müsebeck, E. *Schleiermacher in der Geschichte der Staatsidee und des Nationalbewusstseins.* Berlin, 1927.

Müsenbeck, N. "Zur Geschichte der Reformbestrebungen vor dem Zusammenbruch des alten Preussens." *Forschungen zur brandenburgischen und preussischen Geschichte* 1918.

Nadler, J. *Die Berliner Romantik, 1800-1814.* Berlin, 1921. (Superficial and implausible attempt to substantiate author's theories.)

―――. *Literaturgeschichte der deutschen Stämme und Landschaften.* 2d ed. 4 vols. Regensburg, 1923-28.

Obernauer, K. *August Ludwig Hülsen. Seine Schriften und seine Beziehungen zur Romantik.* Erlangen, 1910.

Olléon, H. *La philosophie générale de John Locke.* Paris, 1908.

Pariset, G. *L'état et les eglises en Prusse sous Frédéric Guillaume I, 1713-1740.* Paris, 1896.

Persönlichkeits- und Gemeinschaftsstudien zur Staatsauffassung der deutschen Romantik. Halle, 1925. (*Deutsches Vierteljahrsschrift für Literaturwissenschaft und Geistesgeschichte.*)

Perthes, C. T. *Friedrich Perthes Leben.* 6th ed. 3 vols. Gotha, 1872.

Peuckert, W. H. *Die Rosenkreutzer. Zur Geschichte einer Reformation.* Jena, 1928. (Valuable for origins of Rosicrucian movement in sixteenth and seventeenth centuries.)

Philippson, M. *Geschichte des preussischen Staatswesens unter Friedrich-Wilhelm dem Zweiten.* 2 vols. Berlin, 1886. (The only scholarly work on the period as a whole, very valuable despite its bad organization and omissions.)

Pinloche, A. *La réforme de l'éducation en Allemagne au XVIIIe siècle. Basedow et le philanthropinisme.* Paris, 1889. (Basic.)

Poetzsch, A. *Studien zur frühromantischen Politik und Geschichtsauffassung.* Leipzig, 1926. (Useful summary of the various definitions of Romanticism.)

Rachel, H. *Die Handels-Zoll und Akzisepolitik, 1740-1786.* Berlin, 1931. Preface published separately as "Der Merkantilismus in Brandenburg-Preussen." *Forschungen zur brandenburgischen und preussischen Geschichte* 1927, XL, 221-26. (Admirable general survey of Prussian economic policy in the eighteenth century.)

Ritschl, A. *Geschichte des Pietismus in der reformierten Kirche.* 3 vols. Bonn, 1880-86. (Basic.)

Ritter, G. *Stein. Eine politische Biographie.* 2 vols. Stuttgart and Berlin, 1921.

Rouge, I. *Frédéric Schlegel et la genèse du romantisme allemand, 1791-1797.* Paris and Bordeaux, 1904.

———. *Wackenroder et la genèse de l'esthétique romantique.* Paris, 1934.

Rumler, M. "Die Bestrebungen zur Befreiung der Privatbauern in Preussen, 1797-1806." *Forschungen zur brandenburgischen und preussischen Geschichte* 1921, XXXIII, 179-92, 327-67; 1922, XXXIV, 1-24, 265-96. (The fullest study.)

Salomon, L. *Geschichte des deutschen Zeitungswesens von den ersten Anfängen bis zur Wiederaufrichtung des deutschen Reiches.* Oldenburg and Leipzig, 1906. (Basic.)

Samuel, R. *Die poetische Staats- und Geschichtsauffassung Friedrich von Hardenbergs.* Frankfurt, 1925.

Schauer, M. *Caroline Schlegel-Schelling.* Greifswald, 1922.

Scherer, W. *Geschichte der deutschen Literatur.* Berlin, n.d. (Useful for trends of thought but not for biographies.)

Schlagdenhauffen, A. *Frédéric Schlegel et son groupe. La doctrine de l'Athenaeum, 1798-1800.* Paris, 1934. (The best summary in French of present work in literary history.)

Schmitt, C. *Politische Romantik.* 2d. ed. Munich and Leipzig, 1925. (Often wrong but always stimulating.)

Schnabel, F. *Deutsche Geschichte im 19. Jahrhundert.* Vol. 1. Freiburg, 1934.

Schneider, F. J. *Die Freimauerei und ihr Einfluss auf die geistige Kultur am Ende des XVIII. Jahrhunderts.* Prague, 1909.

Schrader, *Geschichte der Friedrichs-Universität zu Halle.* 2 vols. Berlin, 1894.

Schroetter, F. von. *Das preussische Münzewesen im 18. Jahrhundert.* Berlin, 1913.

Schultze, J. *Die Auseinandersetzung zwischen Adel und Bürgertum in den deutschen Zeitschriften der letzten drei Jahrzehnten des 18. Jahrhunderts, 1773-1806.* Berlin, 1925.

Schwartz, P. *Die Gelehrtenschulen Preussens unter dem Oberschulkollegium, 1786-1806, und das Abiturientenexamen.* Berlin, 1910.

———. *Der erste Kulturkampf in Preussen in Kirche und Schule, 1778-1798.* Berlin, 1925. (Very thorough, scholarly, and accurate.)

Seillière, E. *La religion romantique et ses conquêtes.* Paris, 1930.

———. *Le romantisme et la politique.* Paris, 1932.

Skalweit, A. *Die Getreidehandelspolitik und Kriegsmagazinverwaltung Preussens, 1756-1806.* Berlin, 1931.

Spenle, E. *Novalis. Essai sur l'idéalisme romantique en Allemagne.* Paris, 1904. (Basic.)

———. *Rahel, Madame Varnhagen von Ense. Histoire d'un salon romantique en Allemagne.* Paris, 1910.

Spenle, J. E. *La pensée allemande de Luther à Nietzsche.* Paris, 1934.

Srbik, Freiherr von. *Deutsche Einheit.* 2 vols. Munich, 1935. (Many stimulating insights.)

Stadelmann, R. *Preussens Könige in ihrer Tätigkeit für die Landeskultur.* 2 vols. Leipzig, 1878.

Stern, A. *Der Einfluss der französischen Revolution auf das deutsche Geistesleben.* Stuttgart and Berlin, 1928. (Compilation of eye-witness reports.)

Stoelzel, A. *Brandenburg-Preussens Rechtsverwaltung und Rechtsverfassung dargestellt im Wirken seiner Landesfürsten und obersten Justizbeamten.* 2 vols. Berlin, 1888. (Of more use for persons than for institutions.)

Strich, F. *Deutsche Klassik und Romantik, oder Vollendung und Unendlichkeit. Ein Versuch.* Munich, 1928.

Südhoff, K. *Kurzes Handbuch der Geschichte der Medizin.* 3d ed. Berlin, 1922.

Tschirch, O. *Geschichte der öffentliche Meinung in Preussen vom Baseler Frieden bis zum Zusammenbruch des Staates, 1795-1806.* 2 vols. Weimar, 1933-34. (Scholarly, but restricted to foreign policy.)

Viatte, A. *Les sources occultes du romantisme. Illuminisme—théosophie, 1770-1820.* Paris, 1928.

Walzel, O. *Deutsche Romantik.* 5th ed. 2 vols. Leipzig and Berlin, 1923. (Very intelligent but very abstract and contrived.)

Warschauer, O. *Lotteriestudien.* Berlin, 1912.

Wenck, W. *Deutschland vor hundert Jahren. Politische Meinungen und Stimmungen bei Ausbruch der Revolutionszeit.* 2 vols. Leipzig, 1887-90. (Superficial and out-of-date.)

Windischmann, E. J. H. *Friedrich Schlegels philosophische Vorlesungen aus den Jahren 1804 bis 1806.* 2 vols. Bonn, 1836.

Wienecke, E. *Patriotismus und Religion in Friedrich Schlegels Gedichten.* Dresden, 1913.

Wiese, B. von. *Friedrich Schlegel. Ein Beitrag zur Geschichte der romantischen Konversionen.* Berlin, 1927.

Winkler, R. *Johann Gottfried Frey und die Entstehung der preussischen Selbstverwaltung.* Stuttgart and Berlin, 1936. (Useful on the municipal history of Königsberg.)

Zottmann, A. *Die Wirtschaftspolitik Friedrichs des Grossen. Mit besonderer Berücksichtigung der Kriegswirtschaft.* Leipzig and Vienna, 1937. (Rather academic conspectus, but well documented, full, and concise.)

Zwiedeneck-Südenhorst, H. von. *Deutsche Geschichte von der Auflösung des alten bis zur Errichtung des neuen Kaiserreiches.* Vol. 2. Stuttgart, 1903.

Index